Beyond the Crises in the Church

Other Books of Interest from St. Augustine's Press

George Gänswein, *Who Believes Is Not Alone:*
My Life Beside Benedict XVI

Maurice Ashley Agbaw-Ebai and Kizito Forbi S.J., Editors,
An African Perspective on the Thought of Benedict XVI

John Tanyi Nquah Lebui, *The Cross and the Flag:*
Papal Diplomacy and John Paul II's Struggle Against the Tyranny of the Possible

Peter Kreeft, *Ha!: A Christian Philosopher of Humor*

Peter Kreeft, *A Socratic Introduction to Plato's Republic*

Peter Kreeft, *The Philosophy of Jesus*

Josef Pieper, *In Tune with the World*

Michael Davis, *Electras*

D. C. Schindler, *God and the City*

William Shakespeare (Jan H. Blits, Editor), *Hamlet*

Jeremy Black, *The Importance of Being Poirot*

Jeremy Black, *Smollett's Britain*

Anne Drury Hall, *Where the Muses Still Haunt: The Second Reading*

David K. O'Connor, *Plato's Bedroom: Ancient Wisdom and Modern Love*

Marvin R. O'Connell, *Telling Stories that Matter: Memoirs and Essays*

Francisco Insa, *The Formation Affectivity: A Christian Approach*

John Poch, *God's Poems: The Beauty of Poetry and the Christian Imagination*

Roger Scruton, *The Politics of Culture and Other Essays*

Rainer Maria Rilke, *The Sonnets of Maria Rilke*

Marion Montgomery, *With Walker Percy at the Tupperware Party*

Stanley Rosen, *The Language of Love: An Interpretation of Plato's Phaedrus*

Will Morrisey, *Shakespeare's Politic Comedy*

Will Morrisey, *Herman Melville's Ship of State*

Winston Churchill, *The River War*

Beyond the Crises in the Church

The Pontificate of Benedict XVI

ROBERTO REGOLI

TRANSLATED BY DANIEL B. GALLAGHER

ST. AUGUSTINE'S PRESS

South Bend, Indiana

Manufactured in the United States of America.

1 2 3 4 5 6   29 28 27 26 25 24

Library of Congress Control Number: 2024934935

Paperback ISBN: 978-1-58731-071-3
Ebook ISBN: 978-1-58731-072-0

∞ The paper used in this publication meets the minimum requirements of the American National Standard for Information Sciences – Permanence of Paper for Printed Materials, ANSI Z39.48-1984.

Translation made possible through the attention and generosity of Mr. Francesco Baggi Sisini

St. Augustine's Press
www.staugustine.net

TABLE OF CONTENTS

INTRODUCTION

> Within a few decades, we will probably realize that the
> highly celebrated, triumphant pontificate of John Paul
> II, as well as that of the current pope (Benedict XVI)—
> by now old and grey—were but a phase butting up
> against the dramatic, irrevocable process of genuine *ag-
> giornamento* in the Church as she confronts the true
> challenges of modernity.[1]

So wrote the historian Vincenzo Ferrone in 2013. His interpretation of events is not the story I tell here. A dispassionate account
of recent history requires not only serenity of mind, but also a
viewpoint from a proper distance. I will immediately confess that
I am not impressed by grandiose, apodictic claims.

The present work examines and attempts to deepen our understanding of the general orientation of Benedict XVI's pontificate. I am well aware of the limitations of such a work, both due
to the few sources available to us and the fact that this "history"
is so fresh. Indeed, it is very difficult to trace the general outlines
of a pontificate that ended so recently, simply because we need
time for things to settle and come into sharper focus. This, I trust,
will be evident in the pages that follow, but I must be honest
about it up front. At the same time, I will not shy away from individuating some of the fundamental characteristics that might
already be pinpointed. Where do we find these characteristics?
We identify them in encyclicals, speeches, and other writings (not
necessarily all of them, but in those with a significant impact, for

1   Vincenzo Ferrone, *Lo strano illuminismo di Joseph Ratzinger. Chiesa,
    modernita' e diritti dell'uomo* (Rome: Laterza, 2013), 108.

example the speech given at Regensburg in 2006), certain papal appointments, voyages, and audiences, as well as in the style of governance Benedict XVI showed in moments of crisis.

Ultimately, we will understand any pontificate sufficiently only if we view it in light of the one preceding it. We are then in a position to see how one pontificate is in continuity with what preceded it, how it incorporated innovations, and where it broke from it. In the case of Benedict XVI, there is visceral link with the pontificate of John Paul II, yet he made no pretense to outdo his predecessor.

Unfortunately, we do not have archival material at our disposal to help us evaluate Benedict XVI's pontificate, since those files will remain secret for decades. We must therefore rely on material already made public, such as doctrinal documents (including encyclicals and "condemnations") and speeches (audiences, papal visits, and voyages) that were either written directly by the pope, or at least by someone intimately involved in the pontificate. For Church history (as a theological reality), what is ultimately important is the final "result" rather than the decision-making process that led up to it because the action of any pope will always be more or less conditioned by the work of his collaborators. This corpus, in any case, is what makes a study of the pontificate possible. It is a very difficult task to distinguish the pope's direct action from that of his collaborators,[2] even though in some cases it is abundantly clear that Benedict was the author of a text.

Consequently, the results of the research I present here really do not amount to a history *per se*, but rather, in the words of Giovanni Miccoli, "a contribution for future historians,"[3] as well as an interpretative framework to orient the reader to the thrust of Benedict's pontificate.

2   This was a more serious problem during the pontificate of John Paul II. See Giovanni Miccoli, *In difesa della fede. La Chiesa di Giovanni Paolo II e Benedetto XVI* (Milan: Rizzoli, 2007), 7.

3   Giovanni Miccoli, *La Chiesa dell'anticoncilio. I tradizionalisti alla riconquista di Roma* (Rome: Laterza, 2011), viii. See also Miccoli, *In difesa della fede*, 11.

The present edition in the English language makes use of authentic sources of Pope Benedict himself, and of people close to him, published during his period as Pope Emeritus. These sources are testimonies that illuminate the years of Benedict's pontificate and have value *per se*. Nonetheless, they have been used with caution and prudence because they are not coeval historical sources but instead represent personal interpretations of history. It is important to keep this in mind when considering the critical value of these sources.

A number of books, articles, and doctoral theses on Benedict XVI's thought have already been published, both during his pontificate and after his resignation on 28 February 2013, by journalists, historians, theologians, and doctoral candidates. The quality and results of this body of writing vary considerably depending on the author's explicit or implicit aims. Some of these are of an apologetic tone, while others are attacks. Some are subtle theological analyses, others are political. In any event, all these writings express a general interest in Benedict's pontificate, and furthermore indicate a burning interest in the history of the contemporary papacy.

The present book follows two lines of reasoning simultaneously—namely, "immediate history" and the much longer course of historiography.[4] Nevertheless, immediate history must not be confused with "hot-off-the-press" journalism, even though they both share the following characteristic: the author has lived through that which he recounts and he wants to interpret it or at least understand it. Unlike a journalist, an historian has the privilege of knowing what happened in the wake of past events and what the "conclusion" of the story is, even if after only a brief time.

On the other hand, journalism is food for the historian, especially if he is writing about recent events. In fact, a historian

---

4   See Hervé Yannou, *Éphémère et éternité: médias et historiographie officielle des papes au début du XXIe siècle*, in François Bougard, Michel Sot (ed.), *Liber, gesta, histoire. Écrire l'histoire des évêques et des papes de l'Antiquité au XXIe siècle* (Turnhout: Brepols, 2009), 219–239.

cannot help but utilize news stories, interviews, and other media, viewing them through the lens of historical methodology, always aware of their limitations. For example, one of the important things to keep in mind is that media coverage of the pope and the Vatican is predominately written from a Western point of view. Journalists who specialize in coverage of the Vatican, the papacy, and the Curia are typically 42% Italian, 28% European, 19% North American, with only 1% coming from the rest of the world. Third world countries are virtually absent. Furthermore, in a majority of cases the mass media tends to overlook the spiritual and religious dimensions of papal, curial, and other ecclesial news in favor of politics, and they usually frame it in the overly simplistic, limited couplets of left/right and conservative/progressive.

Benedict XVI's pontificate appears significant not only because of its unexpected conclusion (i.e., a resignation resulting in a new entity of a "pope emeritus"), but also because it opened new questions waiting to be resolved. In fact, Benedict—in virtue of his predominantly magisterial method of governance in the exercise of the Petrine ministry for nearly eight years—gave us new and influential ways of viewing the life of the Church, not by enacting grandiose reforms or impressive interventions, but rather by daily directing the life of the Church with his teaching. We can think of his implementation of Vatican II (giving space to positions that, until then, were largely marginalized), his approach to ecumenical relations (the novelty of personal ordinariates for Anglicans becoming Catholics, and the announcement of that news jointly with Anglican officials), and relations with other religions, particularly Islam (the Regensburg speech and its aftermath), and the ecclesiological consequences of certain actions (i.e., the creation of a "pope emeritus" gave birth to new theological and canonical discussions). The central question of his general focus on was faith in Jesus Christ: something clearly waning in the West. It is no accident that the trips he made as pontiff were predominantly to Western countries. He made no visits to the Far East.

In this book, I consider—and, to a certain degree, evaluate—the documentation that we *do* have so that I can put together a

4

synthesis of how Benedict's pontificate has affected the Church and the world. At the same time, I am aware of the necessity of looking at other evidence that must be considered when trying to understand and evaluate any pontificate.

Despite the paucity of source material, we will still develop a firm grasp on Benedict XVI's pontificate by starting with the conclave that (rather rapidly) elected him in 2005. We then move on to consider the Roman Curia, Benedict's universal governance of the Church, his concern for Christian unity and the relationship of the Church to the world—particularly through the web of Vartican diplomacy—and finally by considering his resignation from the Petrine ministry, an act that resulted in history's first "pope emeritus".

In short, this is not meant to be a comprehensive biography of Benedict XVI. It is rather an attempt to outline the history of his pontificate and shed initial light on how these decisive years affect the present and future of Catholicism.

I also have no intention of presenting an exhaustive bibliography on the subject. The footnotes will accordingly indicate only texts and documents I actually used in my research.

Several people have had a decisive role in helping me clarify the themes presented in this book. I especially wish to thank Antonio Menniti Ippolito, Silvano Giordano, Francesco Castelli, and Paolo Valvo. Monica Mondo, Ruggero Ramella, Gianfranco Ghirlanda, Hans Zollner, Ilaria Morali, and Dimitrios Keramidas have also offered valuable advice. I wish to thank them for their willingness and patience in assisting me, even when we disagreed on how to interpret certain events. I also owe a deep debt of gratitude to my students who have always stimulated me and helped me find new material. In particular, I would like to thank Antonella Piccinin, Riccardo Battiloro, and Jesús Treviño. Others have helped me edit the manuscript, including Salvatore Iaccarino and Piercarlo Donatiello, as well as Luca Bechis. Martin Kammerer deserves my genuine appreciation for locating a mountain retreat in the Tyrolean Alps where I could write in peace. The present English translation has been made possible thanks to Francesco Baggi Sisini and John Paul Kimes. This book would not have been possible without the boundless generosity of many people. I regret that limited space prevents me from mentioning each by name.

CHAPTER ONE
THE CONCLAVE AND THE PROGRAM OF THE PONTIFICATE

Much has been said and written about conclaves and the process of electing a pope. The main question revolves around the role of the cardinals and the ecclesial, social, and political factors that influence them. Simply put, what ultimately "makes" a pope? Is it the electoral jockeying of the cardinals? Political or media pressure? Is it the Holy Spirit? In 1997, Cardinal Joseph Ratzinger somewhat sardonically remarked, "The role of the Holy Spirit must be understood in a very flexible sense. It is not as if the Holy Spirit dictates the candidate everyone is supposed to vote for. Ultimately, the only solid criterion is that the one to be elected will not be someone who ruins everything."[1] Cardinal Giuseppe Siri, on the eve of the penultimate conclave of the twentieth century, made a similar point to his fellow cardinals during the nine days of mourning for Paul VI: "[W]e cannot glibly dismiss the task that lies before us and say, 'the Holy Spirit will take care of everything,' throwing up our hands and putting no effort into the process, sidestepping trouble and giving into our first, sudden impulse. Indeed, the human element is decisive in a conclave."[2]

So what happened in the 2005 conclave that led to the election of the German curial cardinal, Joseph Ratzinger? What kind of game were the cardinals playing that transformed what was

1   Davide Malacaria, "Il conclave del dopo Wojtyla," in *30Giorni*, n.1 (2007).
2   Giuseppe Siri, "Homily during the nine days of mourning for Paul VI, Saint Peter's Basilica (13 August 1978)," in *Rivista Diocesana Genovese*, n. 4 (1978): 158–159.

supposed to be one of the longest expected conclaves in history into one of the shortest?

The archival records are still locked under secrecy, and a reconstruction of those days depends primarily on unverifiable claims offered to the media.[3] More certain are interviews and statements given by the cardinals before they entered the conclave and the rapid developments observable in the public domain.

The rules of the game

Conclaves are governed by rules. The rules governing the conclave of 2005 were promulgated by John Paul II on February 22nd, 1996. Like his immediate predecessors, John Paul II adjusted the rules, which were promulgated through the Apostolic Constitution *Universi Dominici Gregis* that, among other things, changed a secular norm instituted in 1179 requiring a two-thirds majority of the participating cardinals to elect a new pope. This was to ensure a decisive block of support well above an absolute majority (fifty percent plus one), which originally was allowed only after fifteen days, or more precisely, after thirty-four rounds of voting.[4] At that point, the cardinals would choose between the two leading candidates with the highest number of votes. Prior to John Paul II, Paul VI also considered the possibility of allowing an election to take place by an absolute majority, but only with the prior unanimous consent of the cardinal electors present at the conclave.[5]

---

3   On the conclave of 2005, see Roberto Regoli, "Santa Sede: l'elezione della massima carica. Il conclave del 2005," in *Rivista di Studi Politici*, n. 2, a. XXVII (2015): 9–30.

4   Cf. John Paul II, Apostolic Constitution *Universi Dominici Gregis*, 22 February 1996, *Acta Apostolicae Sedis*, n. 88 (1996): 305–343.

5   "The criterion of requiring, for an effective vote, two thirds of the votes plus one must not be abandoned, unless all the Cardinal electors unanimously, that is with no exception, express themselves in favour of a different criterion, which may consist of the *delegation* (cf. no. 64) or of the absolute majority of votes plus one, or of balloting

John Paul II also eliminated the option of election by acclamation or compromise.

There are various possible reasons for these changes. Some say that they were motivated by John Paul II's knowledge and fear of internal divisions within the College of Cardinals. He wanted to avoid the delicate and difficult scenario of stonewalling that could have favored the so-called "progressive" block.[6] Such an explanation, however, is not fully satisfactory in that it seems to be too contingent on immediate circumstances; such a narrow vision would have been uncharacteristic of the broad-minded Wojtyła. It also does not take into account Paul VI's prior sanctioning of this possibility. Viewed through the lens of *aggiornamento* so dear to the pope, it seems more likely that this change was consistent with the Church's increasingly favorable view of democracy (the document, in fact, refers to the "needs of our times"). The logic of a simple majority thus came into play in the most important election within the Catholic Church only after it had already made its way into other ecclesial arenas, such as general chapters of religious orders and monasteries, as well as ecclesial commissions and councils. In the case of a conclave, it was envisioned only as a "last resort" after a protracted and exhausting canvassing of opinions over a period of fifteen days (the last conclave to have reached and exceeded that length was the 1830–1831 election of Gregory XVI).

The cardinal electors were aware of these rules and how they opened the possibility for new scenarios. It was possible, for example, for small groups to initially impede a swift election and only later come together to elect an individual by simple majority. But this is not the way it happened. Indeed, the conclave of 2005 was

between the two who in the session immediately preceding have gained the greatest number of votes." Paul VI, Apostolic Constitution *Romano Pontifici Eligendo*, 1 October 1975, *Acta Apostolicae Sedis*, n. 67 (1975): 609–645.

6   Cf. Marco Politi, *Joseph Ratzinger. Crisi di un papato* (Rome: Laterza, 2013), 19.

one of the shortest in history, consisting of only four rounds of votes. The cardinals, therefore, must have had a rather clear idea of the kind of person they were looking for. And the pre-conclave sessions were an opportunity to voice those opinions to one another.

The pre-conclave

The time preceding a conclave normally helps the cardinals get familiar with one another's opinions and to gain a preliminary idea of the kind of person they would like to vote for. It is usually not a very long period, extending from the death of a pope to the beginning of the ensuing conclave. Some considered the pre-conclave period of 2005 exceptionally long, given the evident ill health and declining physical and mental condition of John Paul II that lasted for months if not years before his passing. Some even date this period back to 1992 when the pope underwent surgery to remove a benign intestinal tumor.[7] In 1993, one cardinal was already saying that John Paul II was entering the final chapter of his life.[8] Such a long period, observers claim, would have been even more conducive to the typical pre-conclave debate, but now it could also be done in places far away from Rome. The cardinals would have had plenty of time prior to the sede vacante to make plans and discuss candidates.

Journalists were not far off the mark, in fact. Sources later spoke of pressure groups[9] of cardinals and bishops, such as one (ironically) referred to as the "mafia" that gathered around a key player,[10] Cardinal Godfried Danneels. This was the so-called

---

7   Cf. Andrea Tornielli, *Benedetto XVI. Il Custode della fede* (Casale Monferrato: Piemme, 2005), 17–18; George Weigel, *God's Choice: Pope Benedict XVI and the Future of the Catholic Church* (New York, Harper Collins, 2005), 5.

8   Tornielli, 19.

9   Cf. Jürgen Mettepenningen and Karim Schelkens, *Godfried Danneels. Biographie* (Antwerpen: Éditions Polis, 2015), 445–458.

10   Cf. Marco Tosatti, "Francesco: elezione preparata da anni," *La Stampa,* 24 September 2015. On the various groups of prelates, see Walter Pauli, *Godfried Danneels a oeuvré pendant des années à l'élection*

"Sankt-Gallen Group," which took its name from the place where they would periodically gather (Sankt-Gallen in Switzerland) at the invitation of the local bishop. The group met from the middle of the 1990s to 2006, and included such figures as Cardinals Carlo Maria Martini (Archbishop of Milan, who remained part of the group until 2003), Danneels (Bruxelles), Walter Kasper (one-time Bishop of Rottenburg-Stuttgart and then head of a Vatican dicastery), Karl Lehmann (from Mainz, who left the group in 2000), Cormac Murphy-O'Connor (Westminster, joining in 2001), Achille Silvestrini (from the Roman Curia, who entered in 2003), Lubomyr Husar (Lviv, from 2003), and José da Cruz Policarpo (Lisbona, joining in 2004). Bishops Ivo Fürer (Sankt-Gallen), Paul Verschuren (Helsinki), Jean Vilnet (Lille), Johann Weber (Graz-Seckau), Adrianus van Luyn (Rotterdam), Joseph Doré (Strasburgo, from 2001), and Alois Kothgasser (Innsbruck, from 2002) were also part of the group. Their unofficial leader was Cardinal Martini, who together with Cardinal Fürerc founded the group. All these prelates considered Ratzinger a promoter of both centralist and restorationist currents in the Catholic Church. During their gatherings they discussed papal primacy, ecclesial centralism, collegiality, the role of episcopal conferences, the development of priestly ministry, deaconesses, sexual morality, the politics of episcopal nominations, and other topics. Their goal was to point the Church in a political-ecclesial direction that was different from the one John Paul II took. The documents of the Congregation for the Doctrine of the Faith were their guide. Between 2003 and 2005, with the encouragement of Cardinal Silvestrini, the group turned its attention to the post-John Paul II Church.

du pape François, 23 September 2015: http://www.levif.be/actualite/belgique/godfried-danneels-a-oeuvre-pendant-des-annees-a-l-election-du-pape-francois/article-normal-420243.html; Edward Pentin, "Cardinal Danneels Admits to Being Part of 'Mafia' Club Opposed to Benedict XVI," in *The National Catholic Register,* 24 September 2015: http://www.ncregister.com/blog/edward-pentin/cardinal-danneels-part-of-mafia-club-opposed-to-benedict-xvi.

The group thus acquired a strategic importance while a conclave was looming on the horizon.

Toward the end of John Paul II's pontificate, journalists lost no time in divvying up cardinals into various parties such as John Allen's "Border Patrol Party," a theologically conservative faction concerned about the impact of relativism and secularism on the Church ("members" included Cardinals Joseph Ratzinger, Giacomo Biffi, Jorge Medina, Jan Schotte, Christoph Schönborn, Bernard Law, Francis George, Johannes Degenhardt, Ivan Dias, Desmond Connell, Aloysius Ambrozic, Marian Jaworski, and Jozef Tomko). There was also the "Salt of the Earth Party" primarily interested in the Church's role in society. This party was divided into rightward and leftward leaning branches. The former included Camillo Ruini, Alfonso López Trujillo, Angelo Sodano, Józef Glemp, Norberto Rivera Carrera, Juan Luis Cipriani Thorne, and Antonio María Rouco Varela. The latter included Theodore Edgar McCarrick, Medardo Joseph Mazombwe, Óscar Rodríguez Maradiaga, and Dionigi Tettamanzi. There was also the "Reform Party" consisting of Franz König, Lehmann, Kasper, Martini, Danneels, Roger Michael Mahony, and Edward Cassidy.[11] The name of Ratzinger, incidentally, did not appear on the lists of those most likely to succeed John Paul II.[12]

During this lengthy pre-conclave period, important remarks were made by members of the sacred college that were apparently intended to influence the voting. There were times when the reigning pope also seemed to indicate a favorite. That was at least one way of interpreting a comment John Paul II made about Cardinal Ratzinger in his book *Rise, Let Us Be On Our Way*, in which the pontiff said that the cardinal was a "trustworthy friend" for whom he was "grateful to God."[13] In that same year, a list—albeit

11   Cf. John L. Jr. Allen, *Conclave: The Politics, Personalities, and Process of the Next Papal Election* (New York: Doubleday, 2002), 138–157.
12   Cf. Ibid.,199–200.
13   John Paul II, *Rise, Let Us Be on Our Way!* (New York: Warner Books, 2004).

with little solid evidence—emerged indicating the cardinals in favor of Ratzinger. They included the Spanish-speaking Cardinals Alfonso López Trujillo, Darío Castrillón Hoyos, Julián Herranz, and Jorge Medina Estévez.[14] These men apparently believed that secularism was the biggest challenge facing Catholicism, and they decided to combat it through Roman centralization, a strengthening of internal discipline within the Church, and a reassertion of doctrine. The problem of the day was at its heart "Western," and therefore the best candidate to fight it would be the only true expert in the Western intellectual and cultural tradition: Joseph Ratzinger. There were other cardinals who would follow this line, including Italians Tarcisio Bertone and Giacomo Biffi, and an Australian, George Pell. The true electoral movements, however, would manifest themselves more clearly only in 2005 at the time of *sede vacante.*

It was at that moment that the true feelings of the cardinals began to emerge in public statements. We still do not know what was being said privately or in secret, but explicit allusions were clear enough.

On the one hand, there were cardinals such as Danneels, who not only wanted a strong pope, but a strong episcopate reflecting authentic collegiality, as well as wider space for women in Church governance.[15] At the same time, other cardinals (about a dozen), convening at the Villa Nazareth (the residence of Cardinal Achille Silvestrini), also began to speak openly. Their leader seemed to be Carlo Maria Martini,[16] Archbishop emeritus of Milan, a Church figure who wanted to come to terms with modern ethics and who highlighted episcopal collegiality over papal centralism. It is significant that Cardinal Kasper was spoken of in these same terms, and who on Saturday, April 16th, in a homily delivered at the church of Santa Maria in Trastevere, offered his profile of the new pontificate. The new pope should not be a "clone of John Paul II"

---

14   Cf. Politi, *Joseph Ratzinger. Crisi di un papato,* 24.
15   Cf. Ibid., 31.
16   Ibid., 35.

(i.e., there should be discontinuity), he should be a "pastor" (and therefore not curial), but above all, "we should look for someone who is not too frightened by doubt and the secularization of the modern world."[17] This reflected the opinion of the Sankt-Gallen Group. Kasper suggested a new approach to secularization different from the one that had characterized the papacy of the previous two centuries, and which was represented by several of his fellow cardinals (such as López Trujillo, Castrillón Hoyos, Herranz, and Medina Estévez). Kasper outlined a new approach to oppose secularism. Moreover, immediately after the death of John Paul II, he gave a clear indication that what was needed was a pope who could "dialogue with the people in the way that Wojtyła did; a pope capable of speaking through documents, speeches, and books, but above all someone who could show the world his authentic face, his suffering, and his humanity."[18] Nevertheless, the German cardinal underlined the challenges facing the new pope—namely, "relativism, indifferentism, and pluralism." The movements most closely associated with this spirit of openness were the Focolari and the Community of Sant'Egidio.[19]

The rest of the cardinals indicated a variety of needs, including carrying on the international presence of the papacy (Cardinal Angelo Sodano), and the importance of being a "great" pope (Cardinal Giovanni Battista Re) capable of facing the superhuman challenges that come with the Petrine office (Cardinal Roger Etchegaray).[20] Curial cardinal Jean-Louis Tauran, one of the Holy See's most adept diplomats in recent decades, described the priorities of the new papacy in these terms: "I am concerned about the transmission of the faith [...] faith cannot be a mere feeling [...] we need to see Christians leading an integral life [...]

---

17 Sante Montanaro, *Dalla breccia di Porta Pia alla nuova immagine profetica del Papato nel mondo globale: la storia della Chiesa attraverso i papi*, vol. II (Alberobello, 2011), 657.

18 Fabrizio Caccia, "La Chiesa ha bisogno di un altro Papa simpatico," in *Corriere della Sera*, 3 April 2005.

19 Cf. Marco Politi, *Joseph Ratzinger. Crisi di un papato*, 25.

20 Cf. Ibid., 33.

structures are secondary; what matters is an integrity of life."[21] The future problem of the Church is not the reform of curial or ecclesial structures, but the integrity of individual Christians who embrace responsibilities within the Church and in the world. Obviously, Tauran cared deeply about diplomatic issues, especially the Middle East. But the question of freedom cannot be restricted to the political sphere; it must begin with human interiority. When it comes to the relationship between the Vatican and bishops and the value of episcopal conferences, the cardinal said he does not believe "it is that important an issue."

Showing similar views were Cardinals López Trujillo and Medina Estévez. According to the trustworthy testimony of an anonymous Brazilian cardinal after the conclave, these cardinals, with the support of Opus Dei, were organizing a strong campaign in favor of Ratzinger.[22] Even Christoph Schönborn joined the movement. Cardinal Julián Herranz became a central figure during meetings of the Ratzinger contingent.[23] In Rome, there were informal meeting points for cardinals of the same language group, such as the Venerable English College on the *Via Monserrato*, where many of the English-speaking cardinals would gather as guests of Cardinal Cormac Murphy-O'Connor.[24]

The areas of importance stressed by the cardinals before the conclave obviously varied. Cardinal Angelo Scola pointed to the central theme of the respect for life from conception to natural death, while Cardinal McCarrick drew attention to dialogue with non-Catholics.[25] Cardinal Cormac Murphy-O'-

---

21 Interview with Jean-Louis Tauran, in *La Repubblica*, 10 April 2005; Marco Politi, *Joseph Ratzinger. Crisi di un papato*, 34.

22 Cf. Gerson Camarotti, *O Globo*, 24 December 2005, cited in Politi, *Joseph Ratzinger. Crisi di un papato*, 37.

23 Cf. Marco Politi, *Joseph Ratzinger. Crisi di un papato*, 30.

24 Cf. John Allen, *The Rise of Benedict XVI: The Inside Story of How the Pope Was Elected and Where He Will Take the Catholic Church* (New York: Doubleday Religion, 2005), 91.

25 Cf. Gian Guido Vecchi, "Dai messaggi dei cardinali le indicazioni sul conclave," in *Corriere della Sera*, 4 April 2005.

Connor highlighted the importance of peace and of dialogue with Islam.[26]

There was also a group more attentive to the theme of globalization, including Cardinals Cláudio Hummes and Oscar Rodríguez Maradiaga. Hummes emphasized Wojtyła's pillars of ecumenical dialogue, evangelization, and the fight against poverty, addressing particularly the Church's need to adapt to the modern world, to respond to progress, and to maintain an open dialogue between faith and science. Maradiaga highlighted the important themes of poverty, the problems associated with globalization, and the dangers of biogenetics.[27]

The theme of collegiality in view of an internal reorganization of the Church won the attention of many cardinals who otherwise held significantly different opinions.[28]

The college seemed generally to be in agreement about the need to choose someone who would accept the legacy of Wojtyła's pontificate and apply it appropriately,[29] and follow the ancient logic of alternating between long and short pontificates. The general expectation was that this should be a short pontificate, and therefore the spotlight turned to older candidates.[30] After the conclave, Cardinal Martini remarked that the final decision was not so much based on "the choice of a transition candidate as much as it was on the desire for a shorter pontificate

26   Cf. John Allen, *The Rise of Benedict XVI*, 79.
27   Cf. George Weigel, *God's Choice*, 133–134; Gian Guido Vecchi, *Dai messaggi dei cardinali le indicazioni sul conclave*, 14.
28   Cf. Giulio Anselmi, "Intra omnes. La Chiesa dentro i media," in *Il Mulino*, n. 54 (2005): 539; Robert Moynihan, "The Last Farewell," in *Inside the Vatican*, n. 5 (2005): 21–22.
29   Cf. Allen, *The Rise of Benedict XVI*, 48–49; Politi, *Joseph Ratzinger. Crisi di un papato*, 33; Vecchi, "Conclave tra 11 giorni. 'Sarà breve,'" in *Corriere della Sera*, 7 April 2005.
30   Cf. Luigi Accattoli, "Le chiese giovani decideranno il successore," in *Corriere della Sera*, 3 April 2005; Politi, *Joseph Ratzinger. Crisi di un papato*, 37; Weigel, *God's Choice*, 135; Giancarlo Zizola, *L'elezione di papa Ratzinger*, *Il Mulino*, n. 54 (2005): 506.

after a lengthy one. This general rule was also observed in the past."[31]

A consistent nucleus of cardinals seemed to want to revitalize the Catholic Church by beginning with her heart—that is, Europe and the great crisis of faith within it.[32] After the election of Ratzinger, Cardinal Francis George explained that his brother cardinals cast their votes for Ratzinger because of his knowledge of the history and culture of the West, from which arose the greatest challenges facing the Church.[33]

There clearly was a variety of opinions among the cardinals about the most pressing issues facing the Church. For some, the problems were intra-ecclesial, such as finding a new balance between collegiality and papal primacy. For others, it was the role of the Church in the world and the capacity to present the faith to the world.

Vatican observers unanimously believed that the presumed coalition for Ratzinger was tighter, more numerous, and more transcontinental (spanning from South American to Oceania, and from North America to Europe) than other coalitions.[34] Among Ratzinger's supporters was the cardinal archbishop of Cologne, Joachim Meisner, who, confiding in Moynihan, said that he had in mind an intelligent candidate among a dozen or so professors, but someone with the piety of a child receiving first communion.[35] All of this was going on even though Ratzinger apparently made

---

31   Giulio Anselmi and Dario Cresto-Dina, "Martini: perché ho scelto Ratzinger. Siamo diversi, ma sarà un grande Papa," in *La Repubblica*, 26 April 2005.

32   Cf. John Allen, *The Rise of Benedict XVI*, 76; Macro Politi, *Joseph Ratzinger. Crisi di un papato*, 36; Aldo Maria Valli, *Benedetto XVI. Il pontificato interrotto* (Milan: Mondadori, 2013), 22; Giancarlo Zizola, *L'elezione di papa Ratzinger*, 509.

33   Cf. Marco Politi, *Joseph Ratzinger. Crisi di un papato*, 24–25.

34   Cf. John Allen, *The Rise of Benedict XVI*, 91 and 111; Marco Politi, *Joseph Ratzinger. Crisi di un papato*, 36–37; George Weigel, *God's Choice*, 132–133, 135.

35   Cf. Robert Moynihan, *The Last Farewell*, 24.

no effort to garner support for himself.[36] To the contrary, the cardinals knew well that he had asked John Paul II to allow him retire more than once.[37] Ratzinger nonetheless seemed to possess all the qualities the cardinals were looking for in the next pope.[38]

In conclaves of years past, Catholic imperial courts had a determining influence on elections in that they could exercise a *ius exclusivae* and veto any candidate whom they thought was opposed to their national interests. The last conclave in which a court could invoke such a right was in 1903. Since that time, political powers have not had any direct influence on the voting, but only indirect. Hence any such influence is difficult to detect. In the twentieth and twenty-first centuries, the more powerful and influential force has been the mass media. International politics apparently did not have any direct influence on the conclave of 2005. At most, there may have been a meeting or two between the United States' President George Bush and the American cardinals.[39]

In the press, there were competing campaigns for the possible, if not always probable, *papabili*. There may have even been an attempt to block the election of Ratzinger. Among those associated with this drive in Italy were Marco Politi of *La Repubblica* and Luigi Accattoli of *Corriere della Sera*. In London, the *Sunday Times* ran a series of unfounded stories about Ratzinger and the Hitler Youth. A similar campaign took place against Cardinal Jorge Mario Bergoglio (who also numbered among the *papabili*[40]) on the

36   Cf. John Allen, *The Rise of Benedict XVI*, 69; Bernard Lecomte, *I misteri del Vaticano* (San Paolo: Cinisello Balsamo, 2010), 319 (originally published as *Les Secrets du Vatican*, Perrin, Paris 2009); George Weigel, *God's Choice*, 118.
37   Cf. Marco Politi, *Joseph Ratzinger. Crisi di un papato*, 23; George Weigel, *God's Choice*, 205.
38   Cf. John Allen, *The Rise of Benedict XVI*, 81; Giancarlo Zizola, *L'elezione di papa Ratzinger*, 505–506.
39   Cf. Giulio Anselmi, *Intra omnes*, 539; George Weigel, *God's Choice*, 94.
40   Cf. M. Politi, *Joseph Ratzinger. Crisi di un papato*, 35; Giancarlo Vecchi, "Conclave tra 11 giorni. 'Sarà breve'"; George Weigel, *God's Choice*, 138.

part of John Allen, who, in an interview with CNN, suggested that the cardinal had collaborated with the ruling military *junta* in Argentina in the 1970s.[41] Other media campaigns were conducted against Cardinals Angelo Scola, Ivan Dias, and Angelo Sodano.[42]

In the days running up to the conclave, increasing attention was focused on Ratzinger, both at the popular level (at least three different internet sites were founded to promote his election[43]) and in the College of Cardinals. Having received numerous bishops and cardinals in Rome during his tenure as Prefect of the Congregation for the Doctrine of the Faith, Ratzinger was one of the few familiar to nearly all of them, and he himself knew all their names.[44]

The conclave was preceded by a Mass *pro eligendo Pontifice* celebrated by the Cardinal Dean, who was Ratzinger himself. In his homily of 18 April 2005, he summarized what he saw as the most urgent issues of the day. They are worth remembering here in full:

> How many winds of doctrine have we known in recent decades, how many ideological currents, how many ways of thinking. The small boat of the thought of many Christians has often been tossed about by these waves—flung from one extreme to another: from Marxism to liberalism, even to libertinism; from collectivism to radical individualism; from atheism to a vague religious mysticism; from agnosticism to syncretism and so forth. Every day new sects spring up, and what Saint Paul says about human deception and the trickery that strives to entice people into error (cf. Eph. 4:14) comes true. Today, having a clear faith based on the Creed of

---

41 Cf. George Weigel, *God's Choice*, 185; 138–139.
42 Cf. John Allen, *The Rise of Benedict XVI*, 88–89.
43 Cf. Marco Politi, "Cardinali divisi su Ratzinger," *La Repubblica*, 14 April 2005.
44 Cf. John Allen, *The Rise of Benedict XVI*, 74; 86–88; 112.

the Church is often labeled as fundamentalism. Whereas relativism, that is, letting oneself be "tossed here and there, carried about by every wind of doctrine," seems the only attitude that can cope with modern times. We are building a dictatorship of relativism that does not recognize anything as definitive and whose ultimate goal consists solely of one's own ego and desires. We, however, have a different goal: the Son of God, the true man. He is the measure of true humanism. An 'adult' faith is not a faith that follows the trends of fashion and the latest novelty; a mature adult faith is deeply rooted in friendship with Christ. It is this friendship that opens us up to all that is good and gives us a criterion by which to distinguish the true from the false, deceit from truth. We must develop this adult faith; we must guide the flock of Christ to this faith. And it is this faith—and faith alone—that creates unity and is fulfilled in love. On this theme, Saint Paul offers us as a fundamental formula for Christian existence some beautiful words, in contrast to the continual vicissitudes of those who, like children, are tossed about by the waves: make truth in love. Truth and love coincide in Christ.[45]

Ratzinger laid out a clear path for the college, indicating the challenges facing the Church. What did the cardinals think of it? Did they acknowledge those problems in the Church and in the world? Or did they have a different view of things?

Some have interpreted the Cardinal Dean's homily as a way for him to put forth his own candidacy. Alberto Melloni asks whether his homily was a sort of final demonstration to conservative cardinals that he was a man of Vatican II, or the attempt of a curial cardinal to set the agenda for the next pontificate, or the

45   Joseph Ratzinger, Homily for the Mass *pro eligendo romano Pontifice*, 18 April 2005, *Acta Apostolicae Sedis*, n. 97 (2005): 685–689.

explicit attempt of a leading candidate to eliminate possible con-
tenders.[46] For others, the Cardinal Dean was simply showing the
world what the mainstays of Catholicism were and his sharing
reflections on them. In any case, whoever wanted to vote for him
could no longer say he didn't know what Ratzinger supported.[47]

The problems confronting the Church in 2005

Despite the long reign of John Paul II, there were still many pressing issues that had to be dealt with. In Wojtyła's later years, some
journalists began to list the main themes relevant to the life of the
Church regarding which the cardinals had to take a position
sooner or later—namely, collegiality, ecumenical dialogue, interreligious dialogue, the shortage of priests, the participation of the
laity in ecclesial responsibilities, the role of women, a decentral-
ization of power in the Church, globalization, sexual mores, and
the challenges of bioethics, abortion, and contraception.[48]

As the Wojtyła era came to a close, there was an ongoing intra-
ecclesial problem regarding the Lefebvrite schism stemming from
an excommunication issued in 1988 and characterized by the
Lefebvrites rejection of legitimate developments in Catholic doctrine. In fact, there were many "anonymous" schisms—individual
and organized—that called into question the need to accept

46   Cf. Alberto Melloni, "Incipit di un pontificato," *Il Mulino*, n. 54
     (2005): 520. The same author has also published an analysis of the
     conclave and the initial days of the pontificate: Alberto Melloni,
     *L'inizio di papa Ratzinger. Lezioni sul conclave del 2005 e sull'incipit del
     pontificato di Benedetto XVI* (Turin: Giulio Einaudi, 2006).
47   Cf. J. Allen, *The Rise of Benedict XVI*, 84; Chantal-Paul Colonge, *Be-
     noît XVI. La joie de croire* (Paris: Cerf, 2011), 278; M. Politi, *Joseph Rat-
     zinger. Crisi di un papato*, 38–39; Peter Seewald, *Benedicto XVI. Una
     mirada cercana* (Madrid: Ediciones Palabra, 2006), 48 (original edi-
     tion: *Benedikt XVI. Ein Porträt aus der Nähe* [Berline: Ullstein, 2005]);
     George Weigel, *God's Choice*, 169–171.
48   Cf. M. Politi, *Joseph Ratzinger. Crisi di un papato*, 14; John Allen, *Con-
     clave*, 40–68; Greg Tobin, *Selecting the Pope. Uncovering the Mysteries
     of Papal Election* (New York: Barnes & Noble Books, 2003), 89–94.

magisterial teaching—be it papal or collegial—in matters of faith, morals, doctrine, and the Church's relationship with the modern world.[49] We might think of several middle-European initiatives born out of an inferiority complex to Protestantism resulting in the demand for women priests, despite John Paul II's teaching in the Apostolic Letter *Ordinatio Sacerdotalis* (1994) that declared the impossibility of widening the priestly ministry, a declaration considered magisterially definitive. We might think of those who tried to bypass the fundamental theological assertions made by the Congregation for the Doctrine of the Faith in the document *Dominus Iesus* (2000) regarding the unicity and salvific universality of Christ and the Church. We might think of dissent on a practical level in the area of moral theology, not only in sexual matters, but more broadly in the area of bioethics tracing all the way back to the criticisms of Paul VI's Encyclical Letter *Humanae Vitae* of 1968. We might think of pastoral practices toward the divorced and remarried that were often at odds with the living tradition of Church teaching. There was the urgent and deplorable issue that surfaced during the latter third of John Paul II's pontificate—namely, the sexual abuse of minors by not a few priests that had created scandal and dismay in society and in the Church, and the hierarchy's incapacity of dealing with the problem or of finding a solution.

Regarding the exercise of power in the Church at the level of the hierarchy, there was tension between those who wanted day-to-day collegiality, those who emphasized a greater sharing of evangelical responsibility and zeal among the faithful but downplayed the search for effective solutions to long-standing problems, and those who continued to adhere to a Roman centralism that remained rather effective in the globalized world but ineffective in its capacity to facilitate greater consultation. Adequate space still had not been found for a balance of power between bishops and clergy. Over the last century, this led to an increase of power in the former as never before witnessed in the history of the Church.

49   Cf. M. Politi, *Joseph Ratzinger. Crisi di un papato*, 184.

As for the relationship between the Church and the world, debate continued as to how to present the faith to non-believers and non-practicing Catholics, the role of the Church in the public square, or rather how the Church should act in the arenas of legislation and socio-political life. The Church wanted to free itself from increasing marginalization, but no one seemed to know how to do it. While Catholic "associationism" represented by groups such as Catholic Action and its various offshoots had waned, there were signs of vitality in new movements such as Communion and Liberation, the Neocatechumenal Way, the Focolari, the Renewal of the Spirit, and others. But the latter were also gradually losing momentum, and there was dismay among members of the hierarchy who found them difficult to control. Quite simply, was the world outside the Church to be won over in order to change it? Was the Church to reconquer it? Should she let it go or just join it?

John Paul II left a complex legacy. Understanding it requires in-depth knowledge of situations within the Church and the thinking of the world at large. Martyrdom in Asia, the challenges of the poverty-stricken, young, persecuted churches in Africa, and the withering, socially driven churches of South America seemed problems of the past, but they were as relevant as ever. At the level of sheer numbers, in fact, the majority of the college was northern by culture and therefore sensitive to that immediate context: of the 117 electors, 58 were European, 14 were North American, and 1 Australian—amounting to 62.4 percent—and if we count the one Mexican and one Filipino who were over the age limit for voting, the percentage climbs to 63.5%.[50] If we want to look more closely at percentages, we will better understand the sectors of influence within the College of Cardinals. Europeans accounted for 50.4% of the voting cardinals (17% Italians), 17.4% came from Latin America, 12.2% from North America, 8.7% from Asia, and 9.6% from Africa. Only two came from Oceania

---

50   Cf. Alberto Melloni, *Il conclave. Storia dell'elezione del Papa* (Bologna: Il Mulino, 2005), 178.

(constituting 1.7%). Furthermore, if we look at other components, no fewer than 24 cardinals were "curial."[51] They span the continents but are generally marked by a mindset we might more or less call "Roman." The world of religious life was represented by 20 cardinals (17.4% of the electorate), and two cardinals belonged to Opus Dei.[52] There were also cardinals associated with religious movements. This was a relatively new phenomenon, and although this kind of association was rather clear for some (Scola, for example, was a card-carrying member of Communion and Liberation), for others it was opaque (we can think of those loosely associated with the Focolarini).

In reality, if we look closely, we see that the suggestive comments made by cardinals, as well as Ratzinger's homily and the problems he and others identified in 2005, point to themes and problems that harken back to the two pre-conclave sessions of 1978, affirming that there was a line of continuity in assessments and analyses made by the cardinals regarding the Church, the world, and the Church in the world, as if there were a constant refrain that echoed from one conclave to the next.

The 1978 precedent: continuity

In August of 1978, the year of three popes, we can similarly identify several groups. Some maintained a more "progressive" post-Vatican II agenda emphasizing themes of justice, human rights, and an episcopal collegiality to be exercised more manifestly through the Synod of Bishops as a deliberative body. Some bishops (more specifically, members of the Institute for Religious Sciences in Bologna), enjoying strong support in powerful ecclesial circles, circulated a memo among the cardinals that asked for a revision of the papal office based on a reaffirmation of the need for preferential treatment of the poor and particularly the poor

51   Cf. Alberto Melloni, *Il conclave. Storia dell'elezione del Papa*, 178.
52   Cf. George Weigel, *God's Choice*, 112.

within the Church,[53] urging the new pope to use "poor means comprehensible to the poor." They also asked for an "effective implementation of collegiality," "a respect for choices made by local communities," and in the political arena they asked for a suppression of "a politics of intervention" typical of the papacy in recent centuries. On the other side, there were the so-called "conservative" cardinals seeking a candidate able to ensure the restoration of orthodoxy, to direct a process of theological renewal from above, and to reestablish an order of discipline within the Church. Finally, the majority of cardinal-electors were so-called "moderates," seeking a candidate with enough pastoral experience to carry on the implementation of Vatican II and overcome ecclesial divisions, and adhere to the need for ecclesiastical disciple (particularly with regard to the obedience of priests).[54] On 26 August 1978, the Patriarch of Venice Albino Luciani was elected pope, a man known for his equilibrium and discipline.

The brief pontificate of John Paul I navigated a course between continuity and discontinuity. There were new developments in the way the papal office was exercised, but also continuity in the implementation of Vatican II. In a certain sense, the choice of a double name—"John" and "Paul"—symbolized a synthesis of the different opinions among the cardinals. As the historian Jankowiak notes, the name conveyed a clear sense of two diverse tendencies in the Church. Luciani tried to "align the 'progressive and traditional qualities' of the Church with respect to John XXIII and Paul VI."[55]

---

53   "Per un rinnovamento del servizio papale nella Chiesa alla fine del XX secolo," in Giuseppe Alberigo (ed.), *L'officina Bolognese: 1953– 2003* (Bologna: EDB, 2004), 199–213. A more developed form of the article appears in: Alberto Melloni, *Sette proposte per il Conclave. Attualità e limiti di un memorandum* (Bologna: EDB, 2013).

54   Cf. Giovanni Vian, *Giovanni Paolo I*, in Antonio Menniti Ippolito (ed.), *Enciclopedia dei Papi*, Vol. III (Rome: Istituto della Enciclopedia Italiana, 2000), 678.

55   Francois Jankowiak, *Qui sibi nomen imposuit…Les noms de Pierre ou le choix du nom pontifical aux époques moderne et contemporaine*, in Ber-

The same dynamic was at work just a few weeks later in the next conclave. A young Cardinal Ratzinger, then Archbishop of Munich and Freising, in an interview with the *Frankfurter Allgemeine Zeitung* in October of 1978, expressed concern about "leftist pressures" among the cardinals.[56] He then gave an even clearer indication of his concerns on the eve of the conclave, when, according to Andea Riccardi, he said, "The election of the pope should not be influenced by discussions of Italian politics or in terms of a historic compromise. Some cardinals were afraid that such a contingent agreement would turn into an alliance on a larger scale, as Catholics on the left had hoped."[57] Ratzinger's intervention and more generally the attitude of the German-speaking cardinals—expressed in a public statement—represented an opening and a debt of gratitude to the cardinals of central-eastern Europe who were dealing with the troubles of communist regimes.[58]

The real question was more precisely the future of the Church. A heavy air hung about the internal public controversies in the community of believers regarding church hierarchy, tradition, liturgy, forms of religious life, and the Magisterium. A crisis in the Church arose in the wake Paul VI's publication of the 1968 Encyclical Letter *Humanae Vitae*. The ensuring crisis was evident in the drop of vocations to the priesthood and consecrated life, the growing abandonment of priestly ministry, and opposition to priestly celibacy and a distinctive priestly identity. In the end, the problem was the Church and her vitality, which was now highly questionable due to a growing sense of dissatisfaction. Ratzinger had already addressed this problem clearly in the summer of 1968, opening his Preface to the first edition of *Introduction to Christianity* with these words: "The question of the real content

---

nard d'Alteroche (et al.), *Mélanges en l'honneur d'Anne Lefebvre-Teillard* (Paris: Éditions Panthéon-Assas, 2009), 549.

56   *Frankfurter Allgemeine Zeitung*, 8 October 1978.

57   Cf. Ibid., 163.

58   Cf. Alberto Melloni, *Il conclave. Storia dell'elezione del Papa*, 143–144.

and meaning of the Christian faith is enveloped today in a greater fog of uncertainty than at almost any earlier period in history."[59] He subsequently reaffirmed his assessment after becoming pope in an interview with Riccardi while reflecting on the two conclaves of 1978. In reference to the election of John Paul II, he said:

> When he was elected pope, the main problem to confront was how to get out of the Church's crisis at that time. There was a need to adhere completely to the Second Vatican Council. There also had to be a purification of the Council's reception. What was needed was not so much a structural reform, but a deep spiritual reform.[60]

Thus, the Polish cleric Karol Wojtyła was elected. He would go on to keep liberation theology at bay—a task already begun by Paul VI—and to restore confidence in the Church, particularly in the youth through the beautiful tradition of World Youth Days that always strived for a rich and well-crafted catechetical focus.

Hence, we find a consistency of concern in the conclaves of the twentieth and twenty-first centuries. A surprising revelation of the various interpretations of the main crises facing the Church can be found once again in an interview with Ratzinger during John Paul II's illness, published on 19 November 2004. The then-Prefect of the Congregation for the Doctrine of the Faith moved with great agility and balance between a recognition of the pluralistic context of ideas and the need to reinforce Catholic teaching, and the demand for collegiality and a reaffirmation of papal authority: "Through time, a way will be found to create an effective and deep collaboration between bishops and the pope because such collaboration will be absolutely necessary to respond

59   Joseph Ratzinger, *Introduction to Christianity* (San Francisco: Ignatius Press, 1990), 11.
60   Andrea Riccardi, *Giovanni Paolo II*, 168.

to the challenges of the modern world."[61] This perspective was clearly evident in the well-noted reflections Ratzinger composed for the Way of the Cross in 2005, in which he spoke of "filth," "arrogance," and "self-sufficiency" within the Church, especially among the clergy.[62]

In the three conclaves between 1978 and 2005, the central questions facing the Church, according to the cardinals, were the Church and her future, her teaching, and the discipline of clergy.

The conclave of 2005

In response to the consistent concerns that arose during the preconclave and conclave periods, the cardinals had to project broad themes onto a single individual. This was done during the delicate days of the conclave itself, from which point we would have to retrace the logic of how any particular cardinal votes and why a particular cardinal receives votes. Inevitably, this entails the dynamics of how groups or "parties" are formed. In the end, only one winner will emerge to impart his first papal blessing from the balcony.

No matter how useful it may be to simplify and clarify issues—especially in the world of journalism—by using the notion of parties or groups that are often applied to the Roman Curia and the College of Cardinals, the concept is actually misleading and quite difficult to utilize, not only because the men who make up the cardinal electors are constantly shifting (there is an age limit of eighty as well as the unpredictable factor of death), but the men themselves also change interiorly as time goes on. Furthermore, the idea of a party is weak if understood in a monolithic and inflexible way. There are undoubtedly alliances and pressure

---

61   Marco Politi, "Il laicismo nuova ideologia l'Europa non emargini Dio," in *La Repubblica*, 19 November 2004.

62   Joseph Ratzinger, *Via Crucis*, Good Friday, 2005: https://www.vatican.va/news_services/liturgy/2005/documents/ns_lit_doc_200 50325_via-crucis_en.html.

groups, but these also vary over time and depend on specific is-sues in question. The term can be justified only with respect to individual conclaves, during which it may only help to explain any gap that opens up between sides, ultimately leading to a dis-tinction between those electing and those being elected.

The conclave of 2005 must be viewed in a continuous line with the conclaves that preceded it, both in the way it was organ-ized and in the ecclesial tensions that led to narrowing the delib-erations down to one ideal candidate. Just like the two conclaves of 1978, there was immense media coverage exerting significant pressure on the cardinals, particularly during the nine days of mourning for the deceased pontiff. The central points that guided the discussions centered themselves around a rebalancing of in-ternal power within the Church between the episcopate and the papacy. Several residential cardinals favored a strengthening of the episcopate—that is, strengthening their powers in local gov-ernance. Another driving issue was the role of the Church in the modern world, or how to address coming to terms with the mod-ern ethical climate and a full reassertion of Church doctrine and morals. The diversity of opinions and formation of alliances also revolved around individual characteristics of the candidates and their personalities, as well as friendships and antagonisms within the college.

It ended up being one of the shortest conclaves in history, showing that agreement among the electors was reached fairly easily despite speculation about how it was achieved. Ratzinger had already been chosen by the fourth ballot. The only conclaves having fewer rounds of voting were for Leo XIII (1878) and Pius XII (1939), both of whom were elected on the third ballot.

To better understand the swiftness with which Ratzinger was elected, we can use a few stories in the media to retrace the course of events. Such information, or course, was offered anonymously and is therefore not easily verifiable. History alone will reveal how accurate it really is. But these stories are all we have at this point, so we must trust both the journalists and the honesty of the cardinals who chose to talk, whatever their reasons may have been. One of the first reconstructions of events within the Sistine Chapel was published by Lucio Brunelli, whom many consider a trustworthy source.[63] Based on the apparent ill will of the report, however, which relied heavily on a sort of "diary" of one of the cardinals, some commentators conclude that it was offered by one of Ratzinger's "militant" opponents "who wanted to show that Ratzinger's victory was in no way achieved by a 'plebiscite,' that it was not certain victory until the very end, that it was favored by the fact that he was then Cardinal Dean, that the times were ripe for a 'new'—perhaps Latin American—pope, and that because of these mitigating factors Benedict XVI should perhaps resign."[64] In any case, the testimony seems to represent a limited opinion that must be supplemented with other indiscreet revelations disseminated through the media or entrusted to professional historians.

Of the 117 eligible electors in 2005, 115 entered the conclave. Because a two-thirds majority was needed at the time, 77 votes would have been needed to elect a new pope. If we do the math, we see that a minority of 39 electors could have blocked the conclave for about ten days. The eventual majority of 75 cardinals (without counting the leading vote recipient) would thus depend on that minority, in such a way that it might be used as a bargaining chip to attempt mediation resulting in as agreeable an election as might be possible.

On 18 April 2005, at 4:33 p.m., the cardinal electors began their slow procession from the Hall of Blessings to the Sistine Chapel, chanting the Litany of Saints as they went. Having arrived in that sacred space, underneath Michelangelo's *Last Judgment*, the *Veni Creator Spiritus* was intoned, after which each and every cardinal

63   Cf. Lucio Brunelli, "Così elegemmo papa Ratzinger," *Limes*, n. 4 (2005): 291–300: http://temi.repubblica.it/limes/cosi-eleggemmo-papa-ratzinger/5959.
64   Sandro Magister, "Codici vaticani. Il mio conclave lo riscrivo così," in *chiesa.espressonline.it*, 7 October 2005: http://chiesa.espresso.re-pubblica.it/articolo/40137.

professed the ritual oath, which, among other things, asserts that they "promise, pledge and swear that whichever of us by divine disposition is elected Roman Pontiff will commit himself faithfully to carrying out the *munus Petrinum* of Pastor of the Universal Church and will not fail to affirm and defend strenuously the spiritual and temporal rights and the liberty of the Holy See."[65] At 5:24 p.m., the Master of Pontifical Ceremonies, Piero Martini, pronounced the *extra omnes*. After an initial consultation among the cardinals, the decision was made to begin immediately with the first vote. According to Brunelli's source, the result was the following: Joseph Ratzinger, 47; Jorge Mario Bergoglio, 10; Carlo Maria Martini, 9; Camillo Ruini, 6, Angelo Sodano, 4; Oscar Rodríguez Maradiaga, 3; Dionigi Tettamanzi, 2; others, 34.

According to this reconstruction of events, the result in favor of Ratzinger was more than flattering. It would indeed lead us to believe that he already had groups of supporters behind him who had not yet succeeded in his election, but were at least in a position to bargain for a candidate whom they did not find objectionable. Moreover, the range of votes was clear. The meetings at the Villa Nazareth were not able to solidify a significant alternative to the Prefect of the Holy Office. Indeed, it seemed they were hardly even a cohesive group if there was at least a dozen of them participating in those gatherings. Borgolio's position is rather surprising. He only had a few votes, but these were nonetheless significant given that he was an "outsider" to the larger dynamics of the Catholic Church. The votes given to Ruini and Sodano were not insignificant, indicating that they, although not in a position to win personally, each carried an important number of swing votes. In any case, Ratzinger was only 30 votes short of winning.

On the following morning, the 19 April 2005, at 9:30 a.m., the second round of voting began. The result was allegedly the following: Joseph Ratzinger, 65; Jorge Mario Bergoglio, 35; Carlo Maria Martini, 0; Camillo Ruini, 0; Angelo Sodano, 4; Dionigi

---

65 John Paul II, Apostolic Constitution *Universi Dominici Gregis*, art. 53.

Tettamanzi, 2; others, 9. Ratzinger had already surpassed the absolute majority. There are also significant shifts in voting in comparison with the previous day. The voting blocks for Ruini and Martini had shifted, presumably in favor of Ratzinger and Borgolio. There are also several dispersed votes. It seems that the group supporting Borgolio was large enough to stall the conclave, and it eventually reached a peak of 39 votes, making it large enough to push for a compromise candidate to defeat Ratzinger. The group supporting the Cardinal Dean constituted more than a sufficient number to put up a blockade, but it was in fact already pointed toward a decisive majority.

The third round of voting took place at 11:00 a.m. The alleged result was the following: Joseph Ratzinger, 72; Jorge Mario Bergoglio, 40; Dionigi Tettamanzi, 0; Castrillón, 1; others, 2.

These numbers indicate that the group in favor of Borgolio had now garnered enough votes to keep the needed majority in check for over a week and thus force the voting into an absolute majority. In the meantime, however, there was time to cause attrition and division within the two main groups. The history of conclaves shows that this is not uncommon. Among the three dispersed votes were undoubtedly those of Ratzinger and Bergolio, who cannot and should not vote for themselves. According to some sources, Ratzinger cast his vote for Biffi.[66] Others however allege that he voted for Bergoglio.[67]

At 4:30 p.m. the fourth ballot was taken: Joseph Ratzinger, 84; Jorge Mario Bergoglio, 26; Christoph Schönborn, 1; Biffi, 1; Bernard Law, 1; others 2.

Ratzinger was elected, having garnered votes from the Bergoglio camp. This made it one of the fastest elections in the history of the papacy, significantly faster than the eight rounds of

66 Cf. "Conclave 2005, quando Ratzinger voleva eleggere papa il cardinale Biffi," in *Il Fatto quotidiano*, 18 April 2012: http://www.ilfattoquotidiano.it/2012/04/18/conclave-2005-quando-ratzinger-voleva-eleggere-papa-cardinale-biffi/205400/.
67 Cf. Marco Politi, *Joseph Ratzinger. Crisi di un papato*, 41.

voting needed to elect John Paul II and eleven to elect John XXIII. We still do not know the reason for which the minority suddenly desisted. Was it to preserve Church unity? Was it because not all of the electors were convinced the alternative candidate was the right one? Was it because Bergoglio was only a token candidate? Some observers believe Bergoglio himself withdrew from the running, claiming he was not up to the task.[68]

Besides Brunelli's reconstruction of events, there were other indiscreet leaks by cardinals to the press that might help fill in the picture. According to Giancarlo Zizola, Carlo Maria Martini received more votes than Joseph Ratzinger in the first round. He allegedly received around forty. On the following day, Martini requested that his votes be cast in favor of Ratzinger instead, who would then have had more than the sixty votes he had in the fourth round of balloting, garnering ninety-five by the afternoon. This was a significantly large majority, with the other votes dispersed among several candidates.[69] John Allen, basing his assessment on the testimony of no fewer than eight cardinals, wrote that the competition between Ratzinger and Bergoglio was less important than others had reported, in that the votes accumulated by the German cardinal were never seriously challenged and the Argentinian was never seriously considered a viable alternative. Indeed, Allen reports that Bergoglio was actually a supporter of Ratzinger. He speaks of an increasing base of support for Ratzinger (forty on the first ballot, fifty on the second, more than fifty-eight on the third, and around one hundred on the fourth) that was matched by no other cardinal. Martini apparently did not attract much support, even at the beginning, meaning that reports that he had requested his votes be shifted to Ratzinger seem unfounded. This reconstruction also has Bergoglio second among

---

68   Cf. Luigi Accattoli, "Bergoglio si tirò indietro e Ratzinger fu eletto Papa," in *Corriere della sera*, 23 September 2005: http://archiviostorico.corriere.it/2005/September/23/Bergoglio_tiro_indietro_Ratzinger_eletto_co_9_050923057.shtml.

69   Cf. Gianfranco Zizola, *L'elezione di papa Ratzinger*, 502–503.

the leaders but never having enough votes to propel him towards election.[70]

George Weigel's reconstruction, also dating back to 2005 and largely based on the brevity of the conclave, is based on a presumably wide consensus about Ratzinger from the very beginning. According to Weigel, Martini, having only four votes, was persuaded to vote for the Dean of the College along with those who had voted for Ruini. Cardinal Bergoglio and his supporters would have made a similar switch. According to this scenario, Ratzinger would have had fifty votes, rising to seventy by Tuesday morning, leading to an eventual victory with a majority of over one hundred votes.[71]

Also writing in 2005, Peter Seewald alleged that Martini had initially received more votes than Ratzinger, who fell significantly short of the needed two-thirds majority on the third ballot, only to reemerge and carry the victory with a final count of 98 or 107 votes.[72]

In 2010, Bernard Lecomte, basing himself on Brunelli's reconstruction, added a few particulars: Bergoglio openly professed his desire not to be pope, Ratzinger and Martini apparently had a conversation over lunch between the third and fourth ballots, and Cormac Murphy-O'Connor, after the conclave, reported that some of the cardinals decided to cast their votes for their German brother-cardinal "for the sake of Church unity."[73]

In 2011, Marco Politi reviewed the data collected by Brunelli and attributed the sudden election of the Cardinal Dean in the fourth round to the persuasive force of the pro-Ratzinger party, which argued that the consistently strong numbers in favor of their candidate indicated that, if he were to withdraw, it would mean a long, drawn-out, and difficult conclave.[74]

---

70 Cf. John Allen, *The Rise of Benedict XVI*, 102–106.
71 Cf. George Weigel, *God's Choice*, 148, 172–176.
72 Cf. Peter Seewald, *Benedicto XVI. Una mirada cercana*, op. cit.
73 Bernard Lecomte, *I misteri del Vaticano*, 320–325.
74 Cf. Marco Politi, *Joseph Ratzinger. Crisi di un papato*, 39–42.

According to journalist Marco Tosatti's version of the story, Ratzinger had already reached a two-thirds majority in an early ballot, but given the thin majority, he asked for one final ballot to confirm that there was indeed a consistent consensus.[75] Competition between Ratzinger and Bergoglio was also suggested by another external source, the traditionalist and schismatic Bishop Bernard Fellay, superior of the Lefebvrite Fraternity of Saint Pius X.[76]

Finally, Melloni presumes the vote-count reported by Brunelli, but he attributes greater importance to the role of Cardinal Martini, who, at the fourth round, requested that the votes cast for him be cast for Ratzinger instead, giving the German cardinal enough votes to win. Martini, asserts Melloni, feared that if it were not Ratzinger, a "less obvious conservative would have been elected, but one of inferior intellect."[77] Such a shift of votes was also suggested in 2015 by a confidant of Cardinal Martini, the Jesuit priest Father Silvano Fausti,[78] who spoke of a consistent block of votes, initially even greater that what Ratzinger had. This scenario had already been suggested by Seewald in 2005.

We are obviously on shaky ground with these conjectures since there is no way to be sure that the sources are entirely

---

75 Marco Tosatti, "Ecco come andò davvero il Conclave del 2005," in *Vatican Insider,* 10 March 2013: http://vaticaninsider.lastampa.it/vaticano/dettaglio-articolo/articolo/conclave-22761/. Cf. A. Melloni, *Incipit di un pontificato,* 520.

76 "Nel 2005 la sfida con Ratzinger. Bergoglio disse di non sentirsi pronto," *Corriere della sera,* 13 March 2013: http://www.corriere.it/esteri/speciali/2013/conclave/notizie/Bergoglio-sfida-con-Ratzinger-arrivo-secondo_824c3d68-8c2f-11e2-8351-f1dc254821b1.shtml.

77 Alberto Melloni, "Benedetto XVI," in *Il conclave di papa Francesco,* Alberto Melloni (ed.), *Istituto della Enciclopedia Italiana* (Rome, 2013), 23–61, here 38.

78 Cf. Andrea Tornielli, "Martini, la rinuncia di Benedetto e il conclave del 2005," *Vatican Insider,* 17 July 2015: http://vaticaninsider.lastampa.it/vaticano/dettaglio-articolo/articolo/matini-martini-martini-benedetto-xvi-benedict-xvi-benedicto-xvi-42410/. Vido Interview: https://www.youtube.com/watch?t=10&v=30Dl7xZjHY0

reliable. Furthermore, the cardinals who seem to gossip the most belong to the most vehement anti-Ratzingerian factions, which, once again, does not take into the account the swiftness of the election. These loose-tongued cardinals and journalists seem to aim only at delegitimizing Ratzinger's pontificate from the very beginning, ironically portraying it as arising from a fundamental consensus, or at least tied to the influence of certain ecclesial groups. The latter hypothesis, however, is particularly perplexing, since, if we look at the pontificate as a whole, such groups do not seem to have enjoyed greater privilege or a greater number of episcopal nominations. In any case, what really matters is the virtually unanimous consensus that the two leading candidates were Ratzinger and Bergoglio, and that the former consistently had a greater block of votes than the latter.

Once the election was determined to be successful, Cardinal Angelo Sodano (not the Dean, since the Dean had just been elected, and Sodano was first among the cardinals both in rank and seniority) turned to Ratzinger in the name of the entire electoral college and asked if he would accept the election. "No. I cannot. I accept it as the will of God," he allegedly answered.[79] When asked what name he wished to be called by, he answered, "Benedict." From that moment on he was known as Benedict XVI. There are some who say that once his name had been announced in the Chapel, Ratzinger turned toward the crucifix, saying, "What are you doing to me? Now you must assume responsibility! You must guide me! I cannot do it myself."[80]

---

79 "I remember the senior cardinal going up to Cardinal Ratzinger and saying: 'Your Eminence, will you accept to be the supreme pontiff of the Catholic Church?' And we all waited. He said: 'No. I can't.' And then he said: 'I accept as the will of God.'" Sam Jones, "Choosing the pope: Cardinal Murphy-O'Connor recalls the 2005 conclave," in *The Guardian*, 8 March 2013: http://www.theguardian.com/world/2013/mar/08/choosing-the-pope-cardinal-oconnor.

80 Eric Frattini, *I corvi del Vaticano*, with the collaboration of Valeria Moroni (Milan: Sperling & Kupfer, 2013). (Original edition: *Los cuervos del Vaticano*, 2012).

On 27 April 2005, during his first General Audience in Saint Peter's Square, the newly elected pope explained why he had chosen the name "Benedict."[81] It was inspired by Benedict XV, he said, a man of peace who reigned during the First World War, in whose footsteps Ratzinger wished to follow, placing his ministry "at the service of reconciliation and harmony between persons and peoples." He also linked the choice of his name to Saint Benedict of Norcia, who, thanks to his monastic order, "had an enormous influence on the spread of Christianity across the Continent [...] he is a fundamental reference point for European unity and a powerful reminder of the indispensable Christian roots of his culture and civilization." The name suggests that Catholicism and the papacy have a clear role to play in shaping the political vision of the world. Indeed, the idea of "Europe" is central to Ratzinger's vision. Moreover, his reference to peace seemed inevitable following the events of September 11, 2001, and the wars being waged in various parts of the globe in 2005. And in this sense, Ratzinger's vision stretched far beyond the borders of Europe.

Beside the name, the papal coat of arms he chose was replete with meaning. In the middle stands a shell, which in a theological-spiritual sense signifies man's striving to know God despite his finite capabilities (this alludes to Ratzinger's experience as a theologian), and in a wider sense it refers to the tradition of pilgrimage, placing Benedict firmly in the footsteps John Paul II, the pilgrim-pope par excellence. There are two other images on the coat of arms that recall his former ministry as Archbishop of Munich and Freising: they are the head of a Moor, an ancient symbol of the Diocese of Freising, and a burden-laden bear, a symbol of Saint Corbinian, the first bishop of Freising. Hence Benedict's coat of arms is devoid of any allusion to his program of governance. It rather serves as a link to his personal past and a theological program for his life and pontificate—namely, the search for God. A

81 Benedict XVI, *General Audience,* 27 April 2005: http://www.vatican.va/holy_father/benedict_xvi/audiences/2005/documents/hf_ben-xvi_aud_20050427_it.html.

surprising novelty was his renouncement of the heraldic symbol of the tiara, which at one time signified the temporal and spiritual power of the pope and was subsequently expanded to signify the three papal powers of legislation, judgment, and teaching. Rather, Benedict chose to place a simple miter in its place: perhaps recalling his identity as a bishop? Or to suggest a theological vision that linked the papacy more closely to the episcopate? A further novelty was the insertion of a pallium under the shield, which symbolizes the responsibility of the shepherd for his flock, thus becoming a symbol of papal jurisdiction. The coat of arms therefore has a strong theological-pastoral meaning and bears no political overtones.[82]

On the day of the election, around 7:00 p.m., the elected pope appeared on the *Loggia delle benedizioni* and said: "After the great Pope John Paul II, the Cardinals have elected me, a simple and humble laborer in the vineyard of the Lord. The fact that the Lord knows how to work and to act even with inadequate instruments comforts me, and above all I entrust myself to your prayers."[83] The reference to his predecessor was inevitable, as was his mention of the way the Lord works. He was the first pope to ask the public for prayers immediately following his election.

The quickness of the conclave does not mean that the one elected accepted the new office readily or easily, no matter how many supporters there were in the chapel. Benedict himself later recounted to his fellow countrymen on pilgramge to Rome the apprehension and fear he felt in those days and hours:

When, little by little, the trend of the voting led me to understand that, to put it plainly, the axe was going to fall on me, my head began to spin. I was convinced that I had already carried out my life's work and could look

82 Cf. Andrea Cordero Lanza di Montezemolo, "Lo stemma di Papa Benedetto XVI," *L'Osservatore Romano,* 28 April 2005.
83 Benedict XVI, "First Greeting and Apostolic Blessing *Urbi et Orbi,*" 19 April 2005, *L'Osservatore Romano,* 21 April 2005.

forward to ending my days peacefully. With profound conviction I said to the Lord: Do not do this to me! You have younger and better people at your disposal who can face this grave responsibility with greater dynamism and greater strength.

I was then very touched by a brief note written to me by a brother Cardinal. He reminded me that at the Mass in memory of John Paul II, I based my homily, starting from the Gospel, on the Lord's words to Peter by the Lake of Gennesaret: '"Follow me!" I spoke of how again and again, Karol Wojtyła received this call from the Lord, and how each time he had to renounce much and simply say: Yes, I will follow you, even if you lead me where I never wanted to go.

This brother Cardinal wrote to me: Were the Lord to say to you now, "Follow me," then remember what you preached. Do not refuse! Be obedient in the same way that you described the great Pope, who has returned to the house of the Father. This deeply moved me. The ways of the Lord are not easy, but we were not created for an easy life, but for great things, for goodness.

Thus, in the end I had to say "yes." I trust in the Lord and I trust in you, dear friends.[84]

At the end of 2005 and in 2010, Benedict XVI, remembering once again those fateful hours, spoke of the "true shock,"[85] of the "fear," and of his obedient and faithful response,[86] and that within

---

84   Benedict XVI, "Speech to the German pilgrims gathered in Rome for the inauguration ceremony of the Pontificate," 25 April 2005: https://w2.vatican.va/content/benedict-xvi/en/speeches/2005/april/documents/hf_ben-xvi_spe_20050425_german-pilgrims.html.

85   Benedict XVI, *Luce del mondo. Il papa, la Chiesa e i segni dei tempi. Una conversazione con Peter Seewald* (Città del Vaticano: LEV, 2010), 17.

86   Benedict XVI, "Discorso alla Curia romana," 22 December 2005, *Acta Apostolicae Sedis*, n. 98 (2006): 40–53.

the interior reaction there was an intimate spiritual conversation occurring: "What are you doing with me? Now the responsibility is yours. You must lead me! I can't do it. If you wanted me, then you must also help me!"[87]

But the question remains: Why was Ratzinger elected and why so quickly? As we have seen, many commentators have tried to retrace the strategic moves that led to his election, but we must neither forget nor underestimate the horizon of faith, the sense of responsibility toward God, and the universal Church at work within the micro-environment of the "spiritual exercises" that go on during a conclave.[88] These affect the way the cardinals relate to each other and influence their voting.[89] For our part, we can only propose hypotheses. The electors must have weighed the moral, intellectual, and doctrinal authority of the individual carefully. They must have considered the strong connection with the pontificate of John Paul II, choosing a path that would respect continuity at a doctrinal level apart from any difference in the style of governance. They must have carefully considered the age of the individual, wanting to avoid a protracted reign after the long papacy of John Paul II. Undoubtedly, whomever they elected seemed the best person to respond to the ecclesiological and ecclesial issues in the church (i.e., the need for cleansing) and the challenge of secularization on both sides of the Atlantic Ocean. Could it have been anyone else? If we will ever know, it will be a long time before we do. It is relevant to mention the opinion of one controversial American cardinal, Theodore McCarrick, who later resigned from the College of Cardinals and was dismissed

---

87   Benedict XVI, *Luce del mondo*, 18. In English, *Light of the World* (San Francisco: Ignatius Press, 2010).

88   Marco Politi, *Joseph Ratzinger. Crisi di un papato*, 32.

89   Cf. Laurie Goodstein and Ian Fisher, "Cardinals Align as Time Nears to Select Pope," *The New York Times*, 17 April 2005: www.nytimes.com/2005/04/17/international/worldspecial2/17rome.html?_r=0&adxnnl=1&adxnnlx=1398336273-KRc9Cnxkx41ZofCt3mDQRA&pagewanted=all&position=.

from the clerical state on account of sexual misconduct with minors and adults. McCarrick's ability to read circumstances and cleverly conform to them (independently of whether or not he believed in them) allowed him to turn those same circumstances in his favor. McCarrick's comment appeared in a long public interview where he explained the reasons behind Ratzinger's election, reasons which plausibly moved many other cardinals to support him. McCarrick stated:

> I believe the brevity of this conclave was due not only to how struck we were at the genuineness of this man's prayer for our beloved Pope John Paul II; nor only for his humble, gentile, amicable way—yet always full of goodness and dignity—with which he performed his duties as Dean of the College of Cardinals in the days between the death of John Paul and the conclave; but also because, standing next to him, we all began to realize the extraordinary things he had done for the Church in his twenty-five years of service to Pope John Paul II. He fulfilled his duties as the Holy Father's main theologian and the guardian of the doctrine of the faith: a service so treasured by John Paul II and all of us.
>
> With their combined wisdom, the Holy Father and he formed a great team and worked for the good of the Church to guide the faithful. I believe that, as we watched and listened to him, we were convinced that he was not only a great theologian but a man of faith [...]. So when we chose the new pope—the first pope of the third millennium—we found ourselves in the presence of a man who had impressed us by the way he guided us over the course of three weeks. His goodness and holiness reminded us of the extraordinary gifts he had already given to the Church during all those years of close collaboration with John Paul II. In

today's world, he seemed to have the strength and grace needed to guide us into the future.[90]

Undoubtedly, in the wake of Ratzinger's election, there were those who tried to interpret his "victory" from another point of view. For example, in Bruxelles on June 13th, 2005, the above-cited Lefebvrite Bishop Fellay, using two-dimensional language and basing himself on a source he alleged was trustworthy, said, "Benedict XVI was elected in opposition to the progressives." He continued, "for the progressives it was a disaster. All of this gives us hope. Things are going in the right direction because the progressives were beaten."[91] This is a gross over-simplification that fails to take into account the complexities we considered above. There were others in the same vein—although with a much more moderate tone—such as George Weigel, who interpreted the choice as suggesting that "the forty-year effort to compel the Catholic Church to bend its doctrine and moral teaching to the pressures of late modernity is over."[92] It would seem according to these authors that the main guiding issue was the question of the Church's relation to modernity.

Whatever factors we choose to associate with the result, one thing is clear: the entire press community, who previously had never shown sympathy for Ratzinger, was incapable of hiding its adversity either during or after the conclave. Some headlines were downright vulgar or false (as read in, for example, *The Daily Mirror*, *The Sun*, and *Il Manifesto*), and the roster of analysts was unsurprisingly full of voices who had always opposed Ratzinger (Richard McBrien, the Jesuit Patrick Howell, and the theologian Hans Küng), even though some cardinals expressed joy bordering on euphoria

---

90 *Le testimonianze di ventuno cardinali sul nuovo papa*, Part I: http://www.30giorni.it/articoli_id_8812_11.htm.

91 Bernard Fellay, Conference paper, *Quali prospettive per la Chiesa con l'avvento di un nuovo papa?*, Bruxelles, 13 June 2005: http://www.unavox.it/Documenti/doc0127.htm.

92 George Weigel, *God's Choice*, 151

(Meisner, Rivera Carrera, Schönborn), and some offered a balanced, reasonable appraisal of the result (Timothy George, for example, representing Catholic-Evangelical thought in the United States).[93]

The program of the new pontificate

A new pope was made, but it was not clear what direction he would take in his universal governance apart from the expectations of the cardinals. What pressing issues and what new goals would he indicate to the Church?

His predecessors had outlined a program at the outset of their respective pontificates, as well as in their first encyclicals, something that Benedict XVI would choose not to do. Only years later, did it become clear why he chose not to do so. He believed his pontificate would not be a long one; thus, he felt it necessity to focus on the essential message of Catholicism.[94] Later, as Pope emeritus, he stated: "I must try above all else to show what faith means in the contemporary world, and further, to highlight the centrality of faith in God, and give people the courage to have faith, courage to live concretely in the world with faith. Faith, reason, these were all things I recognized as central to my mission, and for these things it was not important to have a long pontificate."[95]

To get a better idea, we might turn to the first public speeches in the opening days of his pontificate. The two most significant may be his first message to the cardinal electors as they concelebrated Mass on 20 April 2005,[96] and the homily at the beginning of his pontificate on 24 April 2005.[97]

---

93 Cf. Weigel, *God's Choice*, 152–154.
94 Cf. Benedict XVI, *Last Testament: In his own words*, with Peter Seewald, (London – Oxford – New York – New Delhi – Sidney: Bloomsbury Publishing, 2017), 3–4, 190, 232.
95 Benedict XVI, *Last Testament*, 4.
96 Benedict XVI, *"Primo messaggio al termine della concelebrazione eucaristica con i cardinali elettori,"* 20 April 2005, *Acta Apostolicae Sedis*, n. 97 (2005): 707–713.
97 Benedict XVI, "Omelia della Messa per l'inizio del ministero pe-

In his first message, Benedict emphasized the connection between his pontificate and John Paul II's, both in terms of focus and content, as if he wanted to assure and console a Catholic world still grieving at the beloved pope's passing. This message also revealed the theological and scriptural expertise of the new pontiff that he was always able to express in a simple, direct style. He spoke of the titles attributed to him as Pontiff, including the Bishop of Rome, the Successor of Peter, the Servant of the Servants of God. He then turned to speak of then Church's collegiality, one of the most relevant topics today according to one group of cardinals, but also a theme dear to Ratzinger's heart, and something he declared in the previously quoted interview. He spoke about collegiality with clear reference to the Church's traditional teaching on the topic and the way it had been exercised by his predecessors:

> Just as, according to the Lord's will, Peter and the other Apostles made up one apostolic college, so in the same way the Successor of Peter and the Bishops, successors of the Apostles—just as the Council taught (cf. *Lumen Gentium*, 22)—must be strictly united to one another. This collegial communion, even given the different roles and functions of the Roman Pontiff and the Bishops, is at the service of the Church and the unity of faith, upon which her effective evangelizing activity in the contemporary world depends. It is this path, which my venerable predecessors trod, that I intend to follow as well, solely concerned with the living presence of Christ in the world.

He also reflected on the Second Vatican Council, his theological outlook, and his experience at the Congregation for the Doctrine of the Faith: "I wish to affirm strongly my desire to continue

trino del vescovo di Roma," 24 April 2005, *Acta Apostolicae Sedis*, n. 97 (2005): 694–699.

implementing the Second Vatican Council in the footsteps of my predecessors, and in faithful continuity with the Church's two-thousand-year tradition." After speaking briefly about the centrality of the Eucharist, he referred to the "correctness of celebrations." He then turned to the theme of ecumenism, which he placed at the heart of his ministry:

> [...] [T]he primary task [of ecumenism] is to work tirelessly to rebuild the full and visible unity of all the followers of Christ. This is its goal, this is its driving force. Therefore, we know that the mere display of good feelings toward one another is not enough. Concrete gestures are needed that will penetrate souls and stir consciences, motivating everyone to that interior conversion that is a presupposition for any progress in ecumenism [...] we must be disposed to do everything in our power to promote the fundamental cause of ecumenism.

For Ratzinger, this is made possible by a "purification of memory."[98]

As expected, Benedict then went on to reaffirm that the Church must repropose Christ to "modern humanity," and that she must place herself in dialogue with various cultures and civilizations.

In his homily at the Mass to commence his Petrine ministry, Benedict XVI returned to the theme of the Church, trying to give hope to Catholics, re-emphasizing that the Church is "alive" and "young" and—with the typical allusion to the Church's universality made by newly elected popes throughout the centuries—

---

98 "This act of the purification of memory, of self-purification, of opening oneself to the Lord's grace, which spurs us on to do good, serves also to make us credible in the eyes of the world." *Gesammelte Schriften*. Vol. 8/1: *Kirche – Zeichen unter den Völkern*, (Freiburg: Herder), 504.

he affirmed that she "holds within herself the future of the world." He then offered a greeting to Christians of other confessions and to Jewish people.

He then said something that caught the attention of those waiting for a mention of the program he had in mind for his pontificate. He alluded to it rhetorically precisely by denying that there was going to be any:

> Dear friends! At this moment there is no need for me to present a program of governance. I was able to give an indication of what I see as my task in my April 20th message, and there will be other opportunities to do so. My real program of governance is not to do my own will, not to pursue my own ideas, but to listen, together with the whole Church, to the word and the will of the Lord, to be guided by Him, so that He himself will lead the Church at this hour. Instead of putting forward a program, I should simply like to comment on the two liturgical symbols which represent the inauguration of the Petrine Ministry. Both of these symbols, moreover, reflect clearly what we heard proclaimed in today's readings.

By commenting on the symbols, he actually presents his "program," which constantly centers on the internal life of the Church rather than external politics. This is in fact what John Paul II did when he invited the leaders of the world to open the doors to Christ. Benedict, however, directs his words inwardly toward the Church. She must always lead people "toward friendship with the Son of God." She must "win men and women over to the Gospel—to God, to Christ, to true life," and to the ecumenical journey.

We can hear in his words an authentic consistency between his intentions and the symbolism on his papal coat of arms. From the outset, his priorities are pastoral and ecclesial.

In short, Benedict indeed had a program but also did not. It is clear that his central concern is always with the Church herself, wounded by the divisions of various confessions and not by a few internal divisions within the Catholic community. Five years after his election, the pope would leave yet another sign of this consistent focus. He will reiterate that a renewal of strength to proclaim the Gospel to the world is one of the programmatic tasks entrusted to him.[99] In the same speech, he spoke of the "drama of our times" during which we need "to remain firmly planted in the Word of God [...] and [...] give Christianity that simplicity and depth without which it cannot achieve its end."[100]

All of this stood as the central theme of his pontificate, at least at the beginning. Would it remain so? Or would he deviate and follow other paths? And how is it possible to reconcile his intentions with the choice of a name that clearly carried political overtones?

99   Cf. Benedict XVI, *Luce del mondo*, 185.
100 Ibid., 101.

CHAPTER TWO
THE ROMAN CURIA

The priorities of the Church and the papacy briefly established, how were they implemented? The pope had at his disposal a structure to serve the needs of his Petrine ministry—namely, the Roman Curia, a conglomerate of dicasteries including the Secretariat of State, various congregations, pontifical councils, tribunals, commissions, and numerous other offices, all of which exist precisely to assist the pope in his governance of the universal Church. This structure is neither unchangeable nor monolithic. It is composed of human beings who have their own ideas and personal preconceptions that may either help or hinder a pope's governance.

The Curia operates according to a fundamental, overarching law (i.e., the Apostolic Constitution *Pastor Bonus* of 1988) and a collection of policies and procedures (i.e., the so-called *Regolamento Generale* of 1992) that defines the respective competencies, powers, and limits of the curial offices. The historical nature of the Curia, however, is more important than the juridical aspect in that the personalities and talents of the prelates and cardinals in charge determine, to a large degree, the ways in which the dicasteries and offices contribute to Church governance. The directives each of those offices receives from the pontiff may also vary and have a key role in how the Curia operates. When it comes to the individuals in charge, the will of a strong temperament may simply predominate over a weaker one. Direct access to the pope is another way of overcoming resistance from other cardinals or bureaucratic red tape.

All of this makes it clear that it is more than just a matter of the pope having a program. It is important that he choose the right people to implement it.

Furthermore, the election of a pope inevitably involves a change—albeit gradual—in the make-up of the Curia. Every pope has his own go-to men who are often provincial friends. With Pius IX, it was the hour of the *marchigiani* (from the Italian province of Le Marche), Leo XIII ushered in the *Gabinetto dei perugini* (Perugian Cabinet), and Pio X favored the Venetians (the boat of Peter had been reduced to a gondola, it was often said). Everyone referred to the teams of Pius XI, John XXIII, and Paul VI as the "Lombard group." With the election of the first non-Italian pope in the modern era, there was a decisive shift away from regional groups toward international representation. The Polish, for example, visibly emerged after the election of John Paul II. Yet there was no German group *per se* after the election of Benedict XVI. Rather, given the amount of time he had spent in the Curia, there was a network of former collaborators, friends, and colleagues. It was less a matter of geographics than a shared vision and supported, when possible, by natural affinity.

When a pope begins his pontificate, however, he finds a team already in place put there by his predecessor. Even if the pontifical constitutions give him the power to remove heads of dicasteries, custom and prudence dissuade a pope from making rash decisions because if he does so he runs the risk of putting people in positions for which they are not adequately prepared, which in turn leads to poor management. Moreover, the business of the Curia is primarily conducted on the basis of precedents. Precedents are not only a useful point of reference, but, depending on the case, they are binding (for example, decisions of a dogmatic and—in a secondary way—disciplinary nature), so experience is of the utmost importance.

Nevertheless, there are rare cases when an avalanche of change occurs. Normally, however, popes tend to reconfirm the heads of dicasteries and replace them one at a time gradually.

Such was the case in Benedict XVI's pontificate, except for a few secondary roles that he changed in the initial months of his reign. The pope maintained the line-up as given to him and then made gradual changes according to the natural expiration dates of respective mandates. This gave him more time to decide how to fill those positions in light of his program. Ratzinger was aware of his limitations, including his limited capacity for governance and certain inabilities as an administrator.[1] As he admitted the end of his pontificate: "I am just in that aspect actually more a professor, someone who deliberates and reflects on intellectual matters. So practical governance is not my forte, and there, I would say, is a certain weakness."[2] Hence he had to make decisions with prudence and wisdom, for it was not easy to identify who was available, free, and capable of good governance. Even though he had worked in the Curia for about twenty-five years, Ratzinger was never really a "man of the Curia." That is, he always remained a bit aloof from the dynamics, the bureaucratic machinery, and the intrigues of the *palazzo*.[3] But nonetheless he had clear ideas of what he wanted to accomplish.

The new pope was the center of international attention given his unique curriculum vitae and his public stance on many issues. Hence the expectations of some that he would initiate a swift and significant curial reform, not as an end in itself, but as the first step toward a wider transformation of the Catholic Church's internal culture so that it might become more Gospel-centered.[4] In 1988, the then-Cardinal Ratzinger clearly expressed his opinion about the direction in which the Church (and consequently the Curia) should go: "Future reforms should therefore aim not at the creation of yet more institutions, but at their reduction."[5] In 1990, responding to a question at a press conference during the meeting of Communion and Liberation in Rimini, he stated:

1   Cf. George Weigel, *God's Choice: Pope Benedict XVI and the Future of the Catholic Church* (New York: Harper Collins, 2005).
2   Benedict XVI, *Last Testament*, 236.
3   Cf. Marco Politi, *Joseph Ratzinger. Crisi di un papato* (Bari: Laterza, 2013), 49.
4   Cf. John L. Allen, Jr. *The Rise of Benedict XVI: The Inside Story of the How the Pope Was Elected and Where He Will Take the Catholic Church* (New York: Doubleday Religion), 199–200.
5   *New Song for the Lord*, cited in Allen, *The Rise of Benedict XVI*, 203.

I have urged an examination of conscience that could well extend to the Roman Curia in the sense that we need to reexamine constantly the extent to which all these dicasteries are necessary, or the extent to which they correspond to their proper goal. We have already had two reforms of the Curia since Vatican II, so there is no need to rule out a third if necessary. But the problem is not simply the Curia. That would be too easy. We must also see if all the Councils created since Vatican II are still necessary.[6]

Even more significant was the vision he expressed during his first speech to the Roman Curia. He said that Vatican II "can always become an even greater force in the ongoing task of reforming the Church."[7] The Church is in a state of continual reform, so the Curia must be as well.

It was hoped that the pope's ideas for reform might be transformed into lasting structural realities, especially in the wake of a pontificate that was not deeply interested in internal administration.[8] Yet before making any structural changes, Benedict needed to identify capable and honest men who could help carry out his program.

The pope's men

Two days after his election, on 21 April 2005, the pope reconfirmed Cardinal Angelo Sodano as Secretary of State, thus following the precedent set by popes since Pius XI (1922), who left the prior Secretary of State in office after he was elected. Such was

6   Press conference given by Joseph Ratzinger in Rimini, 1 September 1990: https://www.meetingrimini.org/default.asp?id=673&item =5190
7   Benedict XVI, "Speech to the Roman Curia," 22 September 2005, *Acta Apostolicae Sedis*, n. 98 (2006): 52.
8   Cf. John Allen, *The Rise of Benedict XVI*, 201.

not the case prior to Pius XI. He and his predecessors changed their chief administrator immediately after being elected so that they might exert control over the Curia as quickly as possible, selecting a trustworthy man for the position or at least someone he could control or someone grateful for the promotion. In addition to Cardinal Sodano, the pope confirmed the Substitute of the Secretariat of State, Leonardo Sandri, and the Secretary for Relations with States, Giovanni Lajolo. The other dicasterial heads (cardinals and archbishops) were confirmed *donec aliter providebatur*— that is, until further notice from the pope. The secretaries of the dicasteries were confirmed at least for the five-year terms they were already serving.[9] In true Ratzingerian style, the changes were made gradually, thus giving rise to the term "a gentle revolution."[10] The first undeniably deliberate decision was the nomination of a successor to the Congregation for the Doctrine of the Faith. Benedict chose the American prelate Willian Joseph Levada (May 13, 2005), who had already been an official in that congregation.

Against this relatively static background, there were apparently a few significant changes in number-two positions within some dicasteries. The pope's selections seem to have been motivated by a shared theological vision rather than any prior personal relationship. A few months into his pontificate, Benedict removed the Secretary at the Congregation for Divine Worship, Domenico Sorrentino, "an ardent supporter of Paul VI's liturgical reform," and made him Bishop of the Diocese of Assisi. He replaced him with the Sri Lankan prelate Malcolm Ranjith (10 December 2005), a man more in line with the pope's thinking. In a similar vein, in February of 2006, Benedict assigned Michael Fitzgerald, President of the Pontifical Council for Interreligious Dialogue, to a post as Apostolic Nuncio in Egypt and a delegate to the Arab League. Some spoke of this as an exile due to a divergence in opinions with

9   *L'attività della Santa Sede nel 2005* (Vatican City: LEV, 2006), 214–215.
10   Gianluigi Nuzzi, *Sua Santità. Le carte segrete di Benedetto XVI* (Milan: Chiarelettere, 2012), 90.

the pope (since the time of John Paul II). Fitzgerald was never replaced since his dicastery seemed destined for absorption into the Pontifical Council for Culture.

In May of 2006, a year after Benedict's election, curial changes in top positions shifted into a higher gear. They began with the appointment of a new Prefect for Propaganda Fide, Ivan Dias, who replaced Crescenzio Sepe, who was nominated Archbishop of Naples. On 22 June 2006, Benedict made his most important nomination by choosing a new Secretary of State who was to take over the following September. The elderly Cardinal Angelo Sodano was to be replaced by Cardinal Tarcisio Bertone, who had no time to ease into the role as he was immediately confronted by a crisis in the Islamic world following a speech Benedict delivered in Regensburg. We shall return to this event later. At any rate, it was a rude awakening for the new Secretary of State.

What is most interesting about the pope's appointment is that he broke the long-standing practice of filling the post with a prelate boasting a distinguished career in the diplomatic service. Bertone neither had a diplomatic career nor did he have any prior experience in the Secretariat of State. His appointment, however, was not unprecedented. The great Secretary of State Ercole Consalvi (1757–1823), Auditor of the Rota and Assessor of the Arms of the Papal States, had no previous diplomatic experience. Neither did the brilliant Jean-Marie Villot (1905–1979), who had a rich pastoral experience but seemed a mere schoolboy next to Paul VI. Placing a non-diplomat at the head of Vatican bureaucracy sent a clear message: Benedict's appointments were motivated not by diplomatic politics but by other concerns. It was no coincidence that the pope chose someone with not only recent pastoral experience as Archbishop of Genova, but also curial responsibilities in the Congregation for the Doctrine of the Faith when he was Secretary and therefore the right-hand man of the then-prefect Ratzinger. Bertone was also a key figure in the revision of canon law as a member of the preparatory commission. A religious priest has not served as Secretary of State since 1836 (Luigi Lambruschini).

With such a choice, Benedict XVI proved that he was not operating according to the usual logic of the curial machine. It was unsurprising that Bertone was considered a spurious transplant and an outsider. Ratzinger probably chose him because of their long-standing working relationship and for his "proven affinity and fidelity."[11] But that which is a virtue to some may be a vice to others. The diplomats from the United States, for example, were not entirely pleased with the choice of Bertone in that they saw a lack of diplomatic experience in him and believed he was a "yes man." Diplomats in general did not like his "pastoral style which often took him far from Rome as he occupied himself more with spiritual problems than with foreign politics and curial administration."[12] Perhaps this is precisely what the pope was looking for. In reality, it was not easy for the diplomats to understand what was behind this "pastoral" diplomacy, or rather this attempt to confront problems from a theological point of view, or, according to others, an "exclusively" theological point of view (an exclusivity that had yet to be seen).[13]

The new Secretary of State immediately showed that he was walking the same line as his mentor. Two weeks before assuming his new responsibilities, he gave an interview in which he revealed his intended *modus operandi* ("I hope to be able to contribute to the task of accenting the spiritual mission of the Church that transcends politics and diplomacy") and expressed the need to reform the Curia, to "reflect on how to make the existing structures aim more effectively at the Church's mission and to evaluate whether things need to be maintained exactly as they are now."[14]

There are some sectors of the Curia in which Bertone was not

---

11   Ibid., 171–172.
12   Ibid., 173.
13   Ibid., 176; Stefania Maurizi, *Dossier Wikileaks. Segreti italiani* (Milan: Bur, 2011), 117.
14   Andrea Tornielli, "Nessuno dimentichi i cristiani del Libano," *Il Giornale*, 29 August 2006.

much appreciated, as he is considered improvisational and inattentive to the administrative machinery of the Church; indeed, he seemed almost aloof, spending much of his time travelling; he appears too conciliatory in the political sphere (labeled an "Italian" politician), and he did not know how to manage the crisis of papal governance.[15] At the same time, it must be acknowledged that it would have been a bit strange for someone to be readily accepted who—at least in his public statements—wanted to restructure the bureaucracy.

Undoubtedly, Bertone's appointment is linked to an indisputable trust the pope had in him. When his pontificate was over, Benedict was able to say publicly: "We trusted one another, we understood each other, and thus, I was on his side."[16] He was referring to the criticism toward Bertone advanced from several quarters, which Benedict read as instrumental criticism: "He had often been at the center of criticism, and I believe that much of that directed to him actually belonged to me."[17]

After the appointment of Bertone to Secretary of State, the season of changes began. A cleric from Piedmont was nominated President of the *Governatorato* right after Bertone's nomination. His name was Giovanni Lajolo (September 15, 2006). Archbishop Dominique Mamberti took his place as Secretary for Relations with States. Consequently, there were other changes at the Secretariat of State. The Under-Secretary for Relations with States, Monsignor Pietro Parolin, was sent to Venezuela as Papal Nuncio. He was succeeded by Monsignor Ettore Ballestrero, a Genoese priest well known to Bertone. The nominations of Mamberti and Ballestrero were not appreciated by the United States Embassy to the Holy See because they were

---

15 Cf. Politi, *Joseph Ratzinger: Crisi di un papato*, 172–173.
16 "Ci fidavamo l'uno dell'altro, ci capivamo, perciò stavo dalla sua parte." Benedetto XVI, *Ultime conversazioni*, Peter Seewald (ed.), (Milano: Corriere della Sera, 2016), 212. In this case, the Italian version of the source has been used because in the English one the Pope's answer is incomplete: Benedict XVI, *Last Testament*, 227.
17 Ibid.

considered lacking in experience.[18] Gabriele Caccia, sent to Lebanon as Nunzio, was replaced by an American, Monsignor Peter Wells. At the same time, Archbishop Leonardo Sandri ceded his spot as Substitute at the Secretariat of State to Fernando Filoni in order to become Prefect of the Congregation for Eastern Churches. In turn, Filoni was replaced by Focolarini priest Archbishop Giovanni Angelo Becciu (May 10, 2011) in order to become Prefect of Propoganda Fide. The year 2006 also saw the significant entry of a religious priest into the Curia with Franciscan Cardinal Cláudio Hummes who was placed at the head of the Congregation for Clergy (October 31), succeeding Cardinal Castrillón Hoyos. The dicastery thus remained in Latin American hands.

There were also important—albeit lower-level—appointments that made a significant impact on the day-to-day management of the Curia and Vatican City State. In October of 2007, the pope nominated a new Master of Ceremonies, Monsignor Guido Marini, whose liturgical taste was similar to Ratzinger's own. In 2008, Vincenzo Di Mauro took the place of Franco Croci as Secretary at the Prefecture for Economic Affairs (he was subsequently nominated Coadjutor Bishop of Vigevano and replaced by Lucio Ángel Vallejo Balda). On 16 July 2009, the diplomatic Archbishop Carlo Maria Viganò became General Secretary of the Governatorato of Vatican City State, replacing Renato Boccardo who was sent to be the new bishop of the Diocese of Spoleto-Norcia). Even at the secondary level, the curial machine was run more and more by men chosen by Benedict.

Now the time had arrived for the gradual but inevitable changes of curial heads. The first nomination of an erudite figure made by the pope was that of the Ambrosian-rite priest, Archbishop Gianfranco Ravasi, to become President of the Pontifical Council for Culture (3 September 2007). Cardinal Agostino Vallini, whom Sodano had jockeyed to become Prefect of the Tribunal of the Apostolic Signatura, was sent to the Vicariato of

18   Maurizi, *Dossier Wikileaks. Segreti italiani*, 117.

Rome and substituted by Raymond Leo Burke, who was theologically close to Benedict XVI (27 June 2008).

An important milestone in the replacement of the curial heads occurred in the fifth year of Benedict's pontificate: Cardinal Peter Turkson, from Ghana, became President of the Pontifical Council for Justice and Peace (24 October 2009), the Swiss Bishop Kurt Koch was appointed President of the Council for the Promotion of Christian Unity (1 July 2010), the Canadian Cardinal Marc Ouellet became Prefect of the Congregation for Bishops (30 June 2010), the curial veteran Mauro Piacenza was placed at the top of the Congregation for Clergy (7 October 2010), the Guinean cardinal Robert Sarah covered the role of President of the Pontifical Council *Cor Unum* (7 October 2010), the Brasilian Focolare cleric João Braz de Aviz assumed duties as head of the Congregation for Institutes of Consecrated Life and Societies of Apostolic Life (4 January 2011), Domenico Calcagno was promoted from Secretary to Prefect of the Administration of the Patrimony of the Holy See (APSA, 7 July 2011), the diplomat Giuseppe Bertello became President of the Governatorato (3 September 2011), and the Piedmontese Giuseppe Versaldi became Prefect of Economic Affairs (21 September 2011).

In the following months, Monsignor Jean-Louis Bruguès, a Dominican, was nominated Librarian and Archivist of the Holy Roman Church (taking the place of the Salesian Raffaele Farina, a friend of Bertone), and in his place as Secretary of the Congregation for Education came the Focolare priest, Vincenzo Zani. Monsignor Vincenzo Paglia of the Community of *Sant'Egidio* became the President of the Pontifical Council for the Family, taking the place of the Focolare cleric Cardinal Ennio Antonelli. Augustine De Noia, Secretary of the Congregation for Divine Worship, became Vice-President of the Pontifical Commission *Ecclesia Dei*, who in turn was replaced by the English priest Arthur Roche. The Tanzanian bishop Protase Rugambwa became adjunct Secretary of *Propoganda Fide,* and the Polish cleric Krzysztof Józef Nykiel left the Holy Office to take the place of Gianfranco Girotti as Regent of the Apostolic Penitentiary (who also came from the Holy

Office and therefore was close to Ratzinger and Bertone). A German cardinal, Gerhard Ludwig Müller, was nominated Prefect of the Congregation for the Doctrine of the Faith on 2 July 2012.

The appointment of Turkson, Koch, Ouellet, and Müller to heads of dicasteries has strong theological significance (even though Turkson never finished a doctoral degree due to his episcopal nomination, but he did complete theological studies in the United States and biblical studies in Rome and had extensive teaching experience in his home country). These appointments differ significantly from other appointments—especially of Italians—that seemed to be motivated by other factors (according to the movements they belonged to, their personal fidelity, or their *cursus honorum*).

In any case, these cardinals and prelates were the pope's men, ideally called to put Benedict XVI's plan of governance into action, though as we shall see it wouldn't play out that way.

It should be noted that the bulk of nominations to top positions were made either following or contemporaneous with crises in the media or in governance, as we shall soon see. It is therefore a legitimate question whether these circumstances urged nominations of those known more for their fidelity than for other characteristics. A conglomerate of names emerges of those tied closely to Secretary of State Bertone, who in the final stages of Benedict's pontificate was personally involved in making appointments to the economic, financial, and state institutions in the Curia and within Vatican City State.

Closely tied to these churchmen were also laypersons, especially in the field of communications. The beginning of the pontificate saw the exit of Joaquín Navarro Valls as Director of the Vatican Press Office. Jesuit priest Federico Lombardi replaced him. The media crisis in the final years of Benedict's pontificate led to the appointment of a young Opus Dei layman to manage the complex world of journalism—namely, an American Greg Burke. Even though it is not a curial office, we must remember that the *Osservatore Romano* was entrusted to the editorship of Professor Giovanni Maria Vian (related to the Montini family) beginning in October of 2007. Another important role was filled by the layman Domenico Giani, whom Benedict appointed Inspector General of the Vatican *Gendarmeria* in early June 2006. Giani was a natural successor in that he had already been serving as Vice-Inspector. The appointment of Swiss Protestant Werner Arber, who had won a Nobel Prize for medicine,[19] to the presidency of the Pontifical Academy of Sciences was highly symbolic. It was the first time that leadership of an Academy was given to a non-Catholic.

Within the convoluted maze of Vatican administration and bureaucracy, the pope has his own "family": the small Pontifical Family made up of his personal secretary Monsignor Georg Gänswein (Ratzinger's right-hand man since his time at the Holy Office), Monsignor Mieczysław Mokrzycki (called "Don Mietek") who had worked as a personal secretary for Benedict's predecessor and who later was appointed Archbishop of Leopoli and thus substituted by the Maltese priest Monsignor Alfred Xuereb, and by lay women from the *Memores Domini* association (a branch of Communion and Liberation) who helped with domestic tasks: Carmela Galiandro, Loredana Patrono, Cristina Cernetti, and Manuela Camagni. The last of these, on November 23, 2010, was tragically killed in a traffic accident as she was crossing the street in Rome.[20] Rossella Teragnoli replaced her in the household. The year 2010 was indeed a bleak year for the pope who was experiencing health problems, disappointments in the Church, and personal suffering. There were other figures such as Paolo Gabriele, who would unexpectedly rise so high as to have access to the pope's desk. Other female figures included Birgit Wansing of the Schönstatt Movement, who helped the pope in writing and editing, and Christine Felder from the Spiritual Family "The Work,"

19 Cf. Pontificia Accademia delle Scienze, *Werner Arber*, President: http://www.pas.va/content/accademia/en/academicians/ordinary/arber.html.

20 Marco Ansaldo, "Lutto e dolore nella 'famiglia papale': morta una delle suore di Ratzinger," *La Repubblica*, 24 November 2010.

who took care of the pope's brother, Monsignor Georg Ratzinger, when he definitively took up residence in Rome, rounding out the "Pontifical family."

The style of governance

Every pope has his own leadership style. Some are meticulous and control every aspect of governance (Pius XII), while others prefer to delegate the bulk of administration to others, reserving only the most serious decisions to themselves (John Paul II). It all depends on the pope's personality and talents.

It was Benedict XVI's custom to study all the paperwork entrusted to him attentively and to reserve final decisions to himself. As is curial custom, he met with his collaborators according to a set schedule: on Monday with the Secretary of State, on Tuesday with the Substitute of the Secretariat of State, on Wednesday with the Secretary for Relations with States, on Thursday with the Prefect of *Propaganda fide,* on Friday with the Prefect of the Congregation for the Doctrine of the Faith, and on Saturday with the Prefect for the Congregation for Bishops.[21] Meetings with the heads of other dicasteries were regular but less frequent. In addition, two times a year, in the spring and in the fall, he held collegial meetings with the all the heads of dicasteries.[22] Nevertheless, some analysts believed that little debate occurred at these meetings. It was more a matter of "obeying" rather than "giving consensus."[23]

Unlike his predecessors, especially John Paul II, Benedict XVI did not regularly invite guests to handle curial business over breakfast or lunch. He met less frequently with papal representatives (nuncios), limiting his personal time with them to protocol meetings and discussing decisions for new assignments. Nevertheless, the diplomats were always in touch with the Secretariat

21   Cf. Politi, *Joseph Ratzinger. Crisi di un papato,* 169.
22   Cf. Ibid., 170.
23   Ibid., 179.

of State. His contact with diocesan bishops was also reduced: *ad limina* visits began to take place every seven rather than every five years, and during those meetings he normally did not meet with them individually (which had been the custom of his predecessor John Paul II).

Benedict XVI followed all the *dossiers* quite closely, but he followed individual persons less so. In one interview, he said: "Decisions regarding persons are difficult because no one can look into the heart of another, and no one is devoid of errors. For this reason, I exercise greater prudence in making them. I find them more intimidating and make them only after much consultation."[24] The pope did trust people, though. He once said that a curial collaborator must have "the right qualities," that he must be "pious," "a true believer," and most especially "a man of courage."[25] These are the same qualities he looked for in candidates for the episcopacy, a topic we will discuss later.

The Roman Curia is not an easy animal to control. Leaks to the media are not infrequent. Such breaches of confidence reflect a lack of reserve and obedience. It seems that within the *palazzo* there are some who wanted and tried to sabotage the pope's program. This does not mean, however, that we must believe the historians and journalists who say the pope was isolated, alone, and negligent in his governance. That would be an easy mistake. Every pope by definition is "alone" in that his is the last word in the chain of command. But he is not alone in the process of making decisions because the central governance of the Church makes use of collegial bodies that examine, study, and evaluate cases submitted for judgment. This is the task of both the permanent bodies of the Holy See (congregations, pontifical councils, commissions, etc.), and the *ad hoc* groups created to deal with a specific problem or current issue. Within the network of competencies that has been refined through centuries of experience are imbedded other less formal

24   Benedict XVI, *Luce del mondo*, 125. In English, *Light of the World* (San Francisco: Ignatius Press, 2010).
25   Ibid., 126.

modes of soliciting advice, collecting information, and gathering opinions that each pope uses according to his preference. The pope is never alone even though the ultimate decision-making must be done by him as head of the Church. In this sense, we can say that every pope experiences solitude in decision-making insofar as it is an inherent characteristic of papa "primacy," but in a specific and proper sense of the word, "solitude" is not an accurate way to describe this process precisely because of the *iter* that precedes all papal decisions.

During moments of crisis and tension, no pope believes it is appropriate to look for a scapegoat among his collaborators, even if they are cardinals and prelates in the Curia. For this reason, every pope is vulnerable since he must accept the fact that he is ultimately "in charge."

The Secretariat of State

As a whole, the Curia is subject to much criticism. *Nihil novi sub sole.* Indeed, in some corners of the Church, there is a deep anti-Roman spirit (just as in others there is an equally robust Roman spirit). But beyond general prejudices, we need to consider the key aspects of the Secretariat of State and the ecclesial climate during the period under consideration if we are to make clear distinctions.

According to many foreign diplomats accredited to the Holy See, the Curia is "Italo-centric, cryptic, and out-of-date."[26] That notwithstanding, the Curia is recognized as an important cultural resource. Politi writes that "the curial personnel are far more cultured than the personnel of any other political body. One notices a literacy, a capacity for reflection, a consideration of arguments,

---

26   Politi, *Joseph Ratzinger. Crisi di un papato,* 173. Various judgements to this effect can be found among the confidential files of the United States' administration published by the international organization *WikiLeaks.* For files divulged in Italy, see the aforementioned: Maurizi, *Dossier Wikileaks,* 117.

and careful attention to the use of words. In the Curia, the secular mindset is eclipsed by more prudent analyses and a serenity of expression."[27]

During the media maelstrom of 2010, analysts were noting not so much the Holy See's incapacity to communicate as its sheer lack of communication. "There was no firm guiding force among the Curial heads, someone to keep a finger on the pulse of the people, someone to offer a clear overview of the international situation, someone to devote energy to the Curia's prime objective."[28] Some journalists noted that for a hundred days, between February and May 2010, "the leadership of the universal Church was under unprecedented pressure."[29] It was rightly observed that "it is not the papacy that sets the agenda and presents itself to the journalistic world, but public opinion and the mass media who constantly judge Church governance."[30] This governance was primarily centered in the Vatican Secretariat of State.

The Secretariat of State is the central organizational office of the Curia. It has a significant impact not only on Vatican diplomacy, but on the central governance of the Catholic Church as a whole.

Indeed, the Secretariat of State's competence lies both in ecclesial and diplomatic issues, the latter of which involves not only political and diplomatic affairs *per se*, but also spiritual and religious matters, which in times past "were not only present, but often predominating the Holy See's approach to dealing with states."[31] Moreover, the Secretariat of State is responsible for the management of all the Curia's activities. At times, the Secretariat deals with business directly rather than delegating it to one of the dicasteries. There have been numerous cases in which matters

27 Politi, *Joseph Ranztinger. Crisi di un papato,* 175.
28 Ibid., 233.
29 Ibid., 235.
30 Ibid.
31 Lajos Pásztor, *La Segreteria di Stato e il suo Archivio 1814–1833,* Vol. 1 (Stuttgart, 1984), Anton Hiersemann, "Päpste und Papsttum," 23, I, 15.

were directly referred to the pope by the Secretary of State, sidelining the competent dicastery completely, which was informed only after the pontiff made a final decision.

The role of the Secretariat of State within the Curia was strengthened considerably during Paul VI's reforms,[32] who defined the Secretariat as "primary [...] to other dicasteries,"[33] and under John Paul II's style of governance, many important executive functions were presumed to be in the power of the Secretary of State.[34] This was the situation into which Benedict XVI's "new men" were inserted, whose tendency was not only to maintain but to strengthen the role and influence of the Secretariat of State both in the Curia and in matters relating to Italy, marginalizing to a great extent the Italian Bishop's Conference beginning in 2007.[35]

There is traditionally a strong link between the pope and the Secretary of State, who often fills the pope in on daily business and stays in regular touch with papal nuncios and apostolic delegates, as well as with ambassadors accredited to the Holy See. The Secretary of State's primary position within the Curia is undeniable. He numbers first among the pope's collaborators as a sort of "prime minister." Enjoying a certain privilege and power, he has the responsibility to "represent and put into action the pope's wishes in every type of affair" entrusted to him.[36]

---

32   Paul VI, Constitution *Regimini Ecclesiae Universae*, 15 August 1967, *Acta Apostolicae Sedis* vol. 59 (1967), 885–928. For the reforms after Vatican II, see Romeo Astorri, "Mélanges de l'École française de Rome – Italie et Méditerranée modernes et contemporaines," *La Segreteria di Stato nelle riforme di Paolo VI e di Giovanni Paolo II*, n. 110 (1988), 501–518.

33   Enrico Galavotti, "Sulle riforme della curia romana nel Novecento," in *Cristianesimo nella storia*, vol. 35 (2014): 880.

34   Ibid., 879–885.

35   Paolo Valvo, "Segreteria di Stato," in Filippo Lovison, *Dizionario Storico Tematico. La Chiesa in Italia*, Vol. II, Roberto Regoli and Maurizio Tagliaferri (eds.), *Dopo l'unità nazionale.*

36   Pásztor, *La Segreteria di Stato e il suo Archivio 1814–1833*, 4.

Nevertheless, it is often difficult to ascertain the extent of the Secretary of State's influence and the centrality of the Secretariat of State within the Curia. Each case must be examined separately. Naturally, individual personalities are hardly a secondary factor.

It is therefore necessary to ascertain carefully the relationship between popes and their respective Secretaries of State, the latter of which have been referred to as "the pope's men" since the time of Cardinal Alfredo Ottaviani. According to Andrea Riccardi, "they represent the crucial and fundamental link between the pope's personal and political will and the structure of Roman government."[37] It is also important not to overlook the spiritual and theological dimension of this web of relationships, friendships, and interests. Whether it be the establishment of new offices in the Curia or changes made to already existing curial entities, be it in their aims and ways of functioning, the relationship between the pope and the Secretary of State is "strictly tied to the needs of the universal Church,"[38] to conciliar history, and to the ecclesiology of the moment.

Even though Benedict started his pontificate by initially keeping his predecessor's secretary—Cardinal Angelo Sodano—his true Secretary of State was Cardinal Tarcisio Bertone, who, as we have already seen, was not always well regarded given his unconventional, non-diplomatic pedigree.

There was constant criticism of Bertone during his mandate. Indeed, they continually increased, both in the media[39] and among cardinals close to Pope Benedict. In the documentary

---

37 Andrea Riccardi, "Les secrétaires d'Etat du Saint-Siège (1814–1979). Sources et méthodes. Introduzione," in *Mélanges de l'École française de Rome – Italie et Méditerranée modernes et contemporaines,* vol. 110 (1998), 443.

38 Lajos Pásztor, *La Curia Romana. Problemi e ricerche per la sua storia nell'età moderna e contemporanea, ad usum studentium* (Rome: Pontificia Università Gregoriana, 1971), 6.

39 For example, see Sandro Magister, *Disastro doppio in Vaticano: di governo e di comunicazione* 4 February 2009: http://chiesa.espresso.repubblica.it/ articolo/214368.

evidence currently available to us, we see that in February 2009 Cardinal Paolo Sardi wrote to the pope complaining about— among other things—"the disorganization and confusion that now reign" within the Curia and especially in the Secretariat of State.[40] The press also reported a meeting that took place between the pope and Cardinals Schönborn, Scola, Bagnasco, and Ruini on 18 April 2009 in which the churchmen expressed concern about the running of the Curia and the role Bertone was playing.[41] The criticism centered on an incapacity for preventing crises and dealing with them whenever they erupted. It was no coincidence that in 2010, after three years of tension in the media and diplomatic world (2006–2009), the pope publicly reiterated his trust in Bertone who had already reached the age of seventy-five (he was born on 2 December 1934), the normal age at which curial members retire. In his first intervention in the matter, Pope Benedict published a letter (dated 15 January 2010) in the *Osservatore Romano* on 22 January 2010, in which he spares no praise for Bertone and reappoints him as head of the Secretariat of State:

> With typical refined consideration, on your seventy-fifth birthday, you desired to place the future of your mandate as Secretary of State into my hands. First of all, I wish to join you in thanking the Lord for the good work you have done in the many years of your priestly and episcopal ministry. Given this opportunity, in fact, it is with deep appreciation that I would like to recall the long road of our collaboration, beginning with your work as a Consultor to the Congregation for the Doctrine of the Faith. I also think of the delicate work you carried out in constructing dialogue with Msgr. Marcel Lefebvre, and I will never forget the visit I made to Vercelli, which reconnected me to a great witness of faith, Saint Eusebius of Vercelli. Called by my beloved Predecessor to render

40   Cf. Nuzzi, *Sua Santità. Le carte segrete di Benedetto XVI*, 161.
41   Cf. Politi, *Joseph Ratzinger. Crisi di un papato*, 174.

service in the Roman Curia, you carried out with competence and generosity the role of Secretary of the Congregation for the Doctrine of the Faith. Those were years of intense work, during which important documents were produced regarding crucial doctrinal and disciplinary matters. I always admired your *sensus fidei*, your doctrinal and canonical preparation, and your *humanitas*, all of which were an enormous help in creating an atmosphere of genuine familiarity aimed at a focused and disciplined work environment. All of these factors motivated me to decide, in the summer of 2006, to nominate you Secretary of State, and they are the reason for which I do not wish to lose your valuable collaboration even in the future. It is a pleasure for me, finally, to extend to you, distinguished Cardinal, my wishes for everything good and prosperous in the Lord, invoking upon you abundant grace in your ministry as my close collaborator.[42]

As journalist Marco Politi rightly observes, this missive reveals a particular psychological trait of Ratzinger that became more pronounced as he grew older—namely, the need to have at his side "an intimate confidant with whom he could have absolute familiarity and who would diligently implement his plans."[43] But we must emphasize another aspect of this letter, this time by way of omission. The praise Benedict lavishes upon the cardinal regards the service he previously had rendered to the Congregation for the Doctrine of the Faith. He makes no mention of the Secretariat of State. And if Bertone is reappointed with this letter, it is on the basis of past merits and not any (for they are not even mentioned) he may have gained as the head of pontifical diplomacy and the management of the Curia.

In the same year, on 1 June 2010 (made public on 30 June

---

42   Benedict XVI, "Lettera al cardinale Tarcisio Bertone, Vaticano, 15 January 2010," *L'Osservatore Romano*, 22 January 2010.
43   Politi, *Joseph Ratzinger. Crisi di un papato*, 174.

2010), the pope sent another letter to the cardinal on the occasion of his fiftieth anniversary of priestly ordination. An appropriate rhetorical style is used in this instance, too, and the language is laudatory:

From the moment I discovered a reciprocal and enduring familiarity between us, deriving from the fact that we found ourselves working side-by-side on a daily basis, it is right and fitting that I extend to you heartfelt good-wishes as you complete fifty years of priestly ordination. Furthermore, in addition to this duty—indeed, a duty you have performed admirably—through this letter we wish to convey our thoughts to you so that our intentions may be all the clearer.

As we undergo difficult times at present, we believe that your mind goes back to happier times in the past, when through the imposition of the hands of our venerable brother Albino Mensa, you were promoted to order of priests, surrounded by you family and brother priests. Neither does it escape our attention how much in the following years, having become proficient in juridical matters, you dedicated yourself to teaching and guiding young people with your instruction and writing, both within and outside of the Salesian family circle.

Hence it is no wonder that you held an important position and earned the esteem of Our Predecessor, the Venerable Servant of God, appointed you Archbishop of Vercelli, and that you became a faithful herald of divine gifts there. Subsequently, according to the same Pontiff's wish, you assumed the tasks of Secretary of the Congregation for the Doctrine of the Faith, where we formed a happy friendship in our common work.

In Genoa, too, to whose Church you dedicated your apostolic efforts, many tell of the signs of your zealous pastoral ministry, from which we particularly acknowledge the fruits which that ecclesial community enjoyed, for which you received an even higher title through your induction into the College of Cardinals.

Moving to more recent times, we wished to make you a close collaborator, appointing you Secretary of State, with whom we have shared important decisions and tasks. Without doubt, you are striving with great effort and expertise to participate in our pastoral plans for the universal Church and our initiatives for the entire world, so that the family of God may be strengthened and the world may become more harmonious.[44]

In this letter, Bertone, the butt of criticism and jealousy among many cardinals and diplomats, was supported and protected by the pope. Remarks made within the diplomatic ranks of the United States were particularly pointed: Bertone, who does not know English, was said to be "rather egotistical" and "ambitious."[45] This letter, like the first, contains very little about Bertone's work as Secretary of State. Indeed, the letter mentions appreciation for his participation in Benedict's "pastoral plans" and no less precise "initiatives for the entire world." But is there any mention of his management of the Curia and leadership in papal diplomacy? Is this just an omission once again?

In any case, under Bertone, the Secretariat of State began to exert stronger control over curial business. *Via* a rescript issued on 7 February 2011,[46] it was decided that, if heads of dicasteries were in need of special faculties from the pope, they had to request them through the Secretariat of State. Did any of these moves toward greater centralization make things more efficient? Whatever the outcome, they were certainly aimed at avoiding a dispersion of energy and resources.

44   "Benedict XVI to Cardinal Tarcisio Bertone," *L'Osservatore Romano*, 30 June 2010.
45   Maurizi, *Dossier Wikileaks*, 117.
46   Secretariat of State, "Rescritto 'ex audientia SS.mi' di approvazione dell'articolo 126 bis del Regolamento generale della Curia Romana," 7 February 2001, *Acta Apostolicae Sedis*, n. 103 (2011), 127–128.

In the spring of 2011, some sectors of the Curia, by means of Monsignor Gänswein, expressed concern over the poor quality of management: "inferior norms" stood in contradiction to specific points of the Apostolic Constitution *Pastor Bonus* regarding the Curia, thus delegitimizing "superior norms." A note making its way to the papal apartment complained of the "*demoralization of the pope's collaborators*" at the highest levels, and of honest officials who loved the Church and its mission." It also raised concerns over "a sense of powerlessness on the part of many, and unnecessary connivance on the part of others. Such an atmosphere leads to complicity on the part of still others for personal ends (career advancement, hidden and unbridled monetary gain, the legitimization of wastefulness, etc.)."[47]

The Curia is obviously much larger than the Secretariat of State. Otherwise, it would only be concerned with politics, but this is not the case. With a pope who had once been Prefect of the Congregation for the Doctrine of the Faith, the Curia (and therefore the Secretariat of State) was quite interested in cultural and theological issues. The very vision (and revision) of dicasterial structures was affected by that breadth of vision, to which it had to give an account and live up to. There is no mistake that in the speeches the pope gave at the annual Christmas gathering of his closest collaborators and high-ranking curial, diplomatic, and Vatican personnel, he particularly emphasized pastoral questions rather than administrative or "curial" questions. Benedict XVI wanted to widen the pastoral horizon of the curial machinery rather than having it turn in on itself, even though that is a temptation for any large bureaucratic machine (i.e., the risk of a myopic self-centeredness).

Other dicasteries

With a view toward organizing and simplifying the Curia, Benedict XVI a year after his election began to streamline things. In

47   Nuzzi, *Sua Santità. Le carte segrete di Benedetto XVI*, 179–180.

March of 2006, he merged the Pontifical Council for Interreligious Dialogue with the Pontifical Council for Culture so that they would fall under the purview of the same president, Cardinal Paul Poupard. This change reflected the pope's wider vision, according to which interreligious dialogue should be inserted into the wider spectrum of dialogue for peace between peoples and nations—i.e., within a cultural and political arena. In March of 2006, the Holy Father also joined the Pontifical Council for Pastoral Care of Migrants and Itinerant People with the Pontifical Council for Peace and Justice under the presidency of Cardinal Renato Raffaele Martino. It seemed Benedict's reform program had begun.

Such changes, however, were short in coming even though as cardinal, Ratzinger had advocated for streamlining the Curia for some time. In 2007, autonomy was given back to the Council for Interreligious Dialogue, and in 2009 it was bestowed upon the Pontifical Council for Pastoral Care of Migrants and Itinerant People. Did the nomination of Bertone as Secretary of State cause Benedict to rethink his simplification of Vatican bureaucracy? Or did Bertone's entrance on the scene lead the pope to turn his attention elsewhere? In short, was the wave of Benedict's reform already in retreat? With regard to interreligious dialogue, the reinstitution of the dicastery needs to be read in light of the crisis with Islam provoked by the pope's speech in Regensburg in September of 2006. It was clear that a dicastery dedicated exclusively to interreligious dialogue was in fact necessary, and its autonomy well deserved. To understand the aims of the reinstituted dicastery, we need to look more closely at its new president, Jean-Louis Tauran. Interreligious dialogue could no longer be viewed merely through a cultural lens (as it was in 2006), but a political lens (in the wake of crises among Muslim governments). The motive for reconsidering the need for a dicastery for migrants is less clear. Was it just a matter of having a place to assign friends, benefactors, and others seeking positions? Or was there a greater recognition of the urgency of migration issues?

Another adjustment to the Curia took place in 2009. The Pontifical Commission *Ecclesia Dei*, created by John Paul II in 1988 for dealing with matters pertaining to dialogue with the traditionalist and schismatic Lefebvrites, was internally restructured and tied strictly to the Congregation for the Doctrine of the Faith (whose prefect would also serve as president of the commission). The reason for this change, Benedict explained, was that dialogue with the Lefebvrites had reached a point where the issues were primarily of a doctrinal rather than a liturgical nature.[48]

One of the simplifications that endured was the insertion of the Pontifical Commission for the Cultural Heritage of the Church (*Beni Culturali*) into the Pontifical Council for Culture (2012) in such a way that Cardinal Gianfranco Ravasi would become the president of both.[49] The same year saw the establishment of the *Pontificia Academia Latinitatis*, which fell under the same Pontifical Commission.[50] It seems that the dicastery for culture was the center-point of most of Benedict's modifications of the Curia, giving it more and more power.

Those changes, however, only amounted to fine tuning because they were made in view of concrete and contingent circumstances. A more substantial act of reform, however, corresponded to a wish that had been brought up in the conclave of 2005 and shared by the pope—namely, the institution of a dicastery completely pastoral in scope, tied to the notable waning of the practice

48 Cf. Benedict XVI, "Motu Proprio *Ecclesiae Unitatem*," 2 July 2009, *Acta Apostolicae Sedis*, n. 101 (2009), 710–711. The English version is available at: http://w2.vatican.va/content/benedict-xvi/en/apost_letters/documents/hf_ben-xvi_apl_20090702_ecclesiae-unitatem.html.

49 Cf. Benedict XVI, "Motu Proprio *Pulchritudinis Fidei*," 30 July 2012, Acta Apostolicae Sedis, n. 104 (2012): 631–632: https://w2.vatican.va/content/benedict-xvi/la/motu_proprio/documents/hf_ben-xvi_motu-proprio_20120730_pulchri-tudinis-fidei.html.

50 Cf. Benedict XVI, "Apostolic Letter in the form of *motu proprio Latina lingua*," 10 November 2012, *Acta Apostolicae Sedis*, n. 104 (2012): 991–995. The English version is available at: http://w2.vatican.va/content/benedict-xvi/en/motu_proprio/documents/hf_ben-xvi_motu-proprio_20121110_latina-lingua.html.

of the faith in areas of the world where it once had been strong. The foundation of the new dicastery, the Pontifical Council for the Promotion of the New Evangelization, with the president being Archbishop Rino Fisichella, a noted theologian with a pastoral profile and highly skilled at communicating with the media, reveals the urgency with which Pope Ratzinger took the cause of the New Evangelization. At the center of his priorities were faith and the crisis of faith. The new dicastery was commissioned to keep the question of faith alive and not let it be marginalized by society. Indeed, the dicastery was not entrusted with a bureaucratic or administrative function, but rather a vital mission at the center of Pope Benedict's concerns. It was founded in direct response to a question he had raised to the Curia publicly in December of 2011: "How are we supposed to proclaim the Gospel today? How can faith, as a living, breathing reality, become a reality today?"[51] According to the pope, the Church needed to confront "the great spiritual battle" in which Christianity (and not simply Catholicism) must embrace "what is good and right about modernity," and at the same time it must separate and distinguish itself from what is becoming a "counter-religion."[52] Benedict places this theme at the center of the present and future Church. He underscores the theme by establishing this dicastery.

Prelates outside the curial circle also drew attention to the Church's crucial task of evangelization, such as the cardinal archbishop of Paris, according to whom Benedict XVI created the Pontifical Council for the New Evangelization in order to respond to the critical "functioning of the Church," and in this way he joins the pastoral projects launched by Paul VI after the Second Vatican Council.[53]

---

51 Benedict XVI, "Discorso alla Curia romana," 22 December 2011, *Acta Apostolicae Sedis*, n. 104 (2012): 35.

52 Benedict XVI, *Luce del mondo*, 87. In English, *Light of the World* (San Francisco: Ignatius Press, 2010).

53 "Il est vrai que l'organisation de la Curie a plusieurs siècles. Elle n'est certainement pas adaptée en toute chose au fonctionnement actuel de l'Eglise. Après le concile, quand le pape Paul VI a voulu mettre

The establishment of a new dicastery should make us think. If at the beginning of Benedict XVI's pontificate there were supposed to be a thinning of the Vatican bureaucratic machinery, in the end it was not only maintained, but increased. Some changes involved the entity of Vatican City State. On 7 October 2008, the Vatican police force (*la Gendarmeria*) became a part of Interpol.[54] This allowed the Vatican to be more closely involved with international cooperation to fight crime.

Benedict's spirit of reform, aimed at reigniting Catholicism throughout the world, was often distracted by problems within the Curia. The internal and international political activity of the Holy See was shaken by a leak of classified information to the media in what became known as *Vatileaks*. The pope had to clean up the mess after sections of the Curia released this classified information. On 31 March 2012, Benedict appointed a commission of Cardinals to look into the matter, presided over by the Spanish cardinal Julián Herranz. Among its members were the Slovakian Jozef Tomko and the Italian Salvatore De Giorgi (both of whom had reached the retirement age of eighty and therefore had more free time). The conclusions of the commission were never made public. In this tense atmosphere, on 2 July 2012, Benedict XVI addressed a letter to Bertone[55] in which he thanked him for his close collaboration and wise counsel. Once more, the pope had to come to the aid of his Secretary of State in public view. It was a clear reversal of roles.

en route des projets nouveaux, il a été oligé de créer des organismes pour cela. De même, Benoît XVI vient créer un Conseil pontifical pour la nouvelle évangélisation." Clémence Houdaille, *Radio Notre Dame*, 21 June 2012: https://www.paris.catholique.fr/Les-fuites-au-Vatican-un-trouble.html.

54 Cf. Eric Frattini, *I corvi del Vaticano*, in collaboration with Valeria Moroni (Milan: Sperling & Kupfer, 2013), 224. (Original edition: *Los cuervos del Vaticano*, 2012). Interpol, Vatican City State: https://www.interpol.int/Who-we-are/Member-countries/Europe/VATICAN-CITY-STATE.

55 Cf. Benedict XVI, "Lettera a cardinale Tarcisio Bertone," Vatican City State, 2 July 2012, in *L'Osservatore Romano*, 5 July 2012.

The relative competencies

The big changes were not the only significant ones. There were also smaller, though no less significant, changes whose importance was felt in the long run—namely, the changes in assignments of competency to the various dicasteries.[56]

The first one regarded petitions for dispensation from priestly obligations, the responsibility for which was passed from the Congregation for Divine Worship and the Discipline of the Sacraments to the Congregation for Clergy (21 June 2005),[57] which was subsequently in a position to open a fourth office to handle its various tasks (28 December 2007).[58] Since this decision was announced just two months after Benedict's election, it is clear that the groundwork was laid in the prior pontificate.

A second legislative intervention regarded the establishment of and provision for ecclesiastical territories in Europe and Asian countries of the ex-Soviet Union (4 April 2006).[59] This reordering was necessary due to the new situation in Europe after the fall of communism. According to the new arrangement, competence for Russia, Byelorussia, Ukraine, Armenia, Azerbaijan, Georgia, Moldova, Kazakhstan, Kyrgyzstan, Tajikistan, Turkmenistan, and Uzbekistan was passed from the Congregation for Eastern Churches to the Secretariat of State. The latter (rather than the Congregation for Bishops) now had responsibility for both the Latin and Eastern ecclesiastical jurisdictions in Bosnia-Herzegovina, Serbia-Montenegro, Macedonia, and

---

56 Cf. Lorenzo Lorusso, "Le modifiche di Benedetto XVI alla Constituzione Apostolica *Pastor Bonus*: un ponte verso ulteriori riforme," in *Iura Orientalia*, 10 (2014): 67–88.

57 Cf. Lorenzo Lorusso, "Le modifiche di Benedetto XVI," 71–72.

58 Cf. *L'Attività della Santa Sede 2008* (Vatican City: LEV, 2009), 559.

59 Secretariat of State, ""Rescriptum ex audientia," 4 January 2006, *Acta Apostolicae Sedis*, n. 98 (2006): 65–66. Cf. Lorenzo Lorusso, "Costituzione e provvisione delle circoscrizioni ecclesiastiche in europa: riordino delle competenze della Congregazione per le Chiese Orientali. Il Rescriptum ex Audentia," *Ius Missionale*, n. 2 (2008): 235–266.

Albania.[60] As a result, *Propaganda fide* turned over its wide-ranging competence in Europe to the Congregation for Eastern Churches. Such shifts in competence are not unusual among the dicasteries of Roman Curia due to ongoing religious and political demographics. When areas of competency become blurred, the pope may step into clarify them, since the curial dicasteries are ultimately at his service in serving the universal Church.

The Pontifical Commission *Ecclesia Dei*, on the other hand, was entrusted with a wider range of responsibilities, as is evident from the Instruction *Universae Ecclesiae*, approved by the pope on 8 April 2011 but carrying the formal date of 30 April 2011, the liturgical Memorial of Saint Pius V.[61] In the wake of the liturgical reform promoted by the Motu Proprio *"Summorum Pontificum"* in 2007, and the permanent dialogue with the Lefebvrites, the Commission enjoyed a greater range of freedom and competence.[62] It was entrusted with ordinary vicarious power in matters related to its competence, and in a special way of keeping vigil over the observance and application of the provisions listed in *Summorum Pontificum*. It was given the authority to make decisions on recourses against bishops' individual administrative provisions or similar ordinaries whenever they were at odds with the motu proprio. The commission was also entrusted with preparing future editions of liturgical texts regarding the *forma extraordinaria* of the Roman Rite. It was precisely by virtue of such faculties that the commission published an instruction regarding the competence of bishops in guiding the use of the Extraordinary Form, the rights and obligations of the faithful, and the role of the priest, in addition to questions regarding liturgy and catechesis.

60 Cf. Lorusso, "Le modifiche di Benedetto XVI," 71–72.
61 Cf. Pontificia Commissione Ecclesia Dei, "Istruzione Universae ecclesiae sull'applicazione della Lettera Apostolica motu proprio datae *Summorum Pontificum* di Benedetto XVI," *L'Osservatore Romano*, 14 May 2011.
62 Cf. Agostino Montan, "L'istruzione Universae ecclesiae nella prospettiva del motu proprio *Summorum Pontificum*. Implicazioni giuridiche," *Rivista Liturgica*, n. 98 (2011): 893–916.

A few months later, on 30 August 2011, with the Motu Proprio *Quaerit Semper,* the Holy Father modified the Apostolic Constitution *Pastor Bonus.*[63] He transferred some of the competencies of the Congregation for Divine Worship and the Discipline of the Sacraments to the new office responsible for processing *ratum sed non consummatum* marriage cases and cases regarding the nullity of sacred orders opened at the *Rota Romana* tribunal.[64] The purpose of this transfer was to allow the Congregation to devote time and energy "principally to giving new life to the promotion of the liturgy in the Church as desired by Vatican II."[65]

Again in 2011, suggestions were made to the pope *via* the pope's personal secretary Georg Gänswein—this time by Ettore Gotti Tedeschi—for the establishment of a "sort of Minister of the Economy [...] whose purview would be to oversee the economic activities already in course, and to develop them anew and to account for expenditures and revenue."[66] But nothing came of this.

In January of 2013, a month before Pope Benedict made public his intention to resign, he was still actively engaged in designing a more reasonable structure to the Curia, making an additional change to the competencies of the respective offices. By means of a motu proprio entitled *Fides per doctrinam,* dated 16 January 2013,[67]

63 Cf. Benedict XVI, "Lettera Apostolica in forma di motu proprio *Quaerit semper,*" 30 August 2011, *Acta Apostolica Sedis,* n. 103 (2011): 569–571.

64 Cf. Antoni Stankiewicz, "Un'innovazione storica," *L'Osservatore Romano,* 28 September 2011; Matteo Nacci, "Le novità del motu proprio *Quaerit semper* e gli insegnamenti della storia sulla missione della Rota Romana," *Apollinaris,* n. 84 (2011): 563–580; Rafael Rodriguez Chacón, "*Quaerit semper:* Una interesante posibilidad de cambio de óptica desde la reorganización de las competencias," REDC, n. 69 (212): 148; Joaquín Llobell, "La competenza e la procedura per la dispensa 'supe quolibet' nel motu proprio *Quaerit semper,*"in *Ius Ecclesiæ,* n. 24 (202): 481.

65 Lorusso, "Le modifice di Benedetto XVI," 74.

66 Frattini, *I corvi del Vaticano,* 218–219.

67 Benedict XVI, "Motu Proprio *Fides per doctrinam,*" 16 January 2013, *Acta Apostolicae Sedis,* n. 105 (2013): 136–139.

a further change was made to *Pastor Bonus* that transferred responsibilities for catechesis from the Congregation for Clergy to the Pontifical Council for the Promotion of the New Evangelization, seeing as the latter was already responsible for the use of the *Catechism of the Catholic Church*. This was a very reasonable change. But while losing one area of competence, the Congregation for Clergy gained another. On the same day, in fact, in a Motu Proprio Apostolic Letter entitled *Ministrorum Institutio,* he transferred the responsibility of overseeing seminaries from the Congregation for Catholic Education to the Congregation for Clergy.[68] That began a situation in which two different offices were responsible for seminaries—that is, the Congregation for Catholic Education for the intellectual formation of seminarians, and the Congregation for Clergy for the internal life of seminaries. This raises a question: was the change made to enhance the coherency of priestly training and priestly life by placing seminary life under the Congregation for Clergy, or was this just a matter of competition between Roman congregations?

We should note that the rationale Benedict gave for these changes to *Pastor Bonus* was that new needs had arisen from the Second Vatican Council—that is, these changes were motivated by a clear and specific theological vision.

The congregations most affected by these changes were those for Divine Worship and Clergy, which, together with the Pontifical Council for Culture (seemingly the pope's "go to" dicastery), seemed to represent most clearly the ways in which the Holy See needed to respond to the Church and to the world. Moreover, if we consider carefully the general program of Benedict XVI's pontificate, faith, the liturgy (i.e., faith as celebrated), the priesthood (wounded by some of its members), and cultural dialogue constituted the primary engines driving papal action.

---

68   Benedict XVI, "Motu Proprio *Ministrorum institutio*," 16 January 2013, *Acta Apostolicae Sedis*, n. 105 (2013): 130–135.

Finances

One point of Benedict's reform, launched early but short-lived, was financial management. He was obligated to do something about finances since John Paul II left the issue to his successors. Here, too, Benedict's strategy was to choose the right individuals, be they clerical or laity, who had the wherewithal to manage the Vatican's financial institutions: the Administration of the Patrimony of the Apostolic See, the Governatorato of Vatican City State, the Prefecture of Economic Affairs, the Congregation for the Evangelization of Peoples (Propaganda Fide), and the Institute for Works of Religion (IOR, the only "bank" within Vatican territory). Shortly before his retirement, Secretary of State Cardinal Angelo Sodano placed his right-hand man, Monsignor Piero Pioppo, in charge of the latter as Prelate of the IOR (July 2006), a position that had been vacant since 1994. The pope's new men, the so-called "Ratzi-bankers," administering a budget of more than six billion euros a year, included the Prefect of Propaganda Fide Indian Cardinal Ivan Dias, a man of remarkable integrity and spirituality, and the Scalabrian priest and canonist Velasio De Paolis who was in charge of the Prefecture for Canonical affairs (from 2008). These two were advised by new consultors in their respective discasteries. Cardinal Attilio Nicora remained in charge of APSA. Bertone did not replace him with one of his own men—Domenic Calcagno—until July of 2011. At the Governatorato and IOR there were other insertions of "Ratzi-bankers" such as Ettore Gotti Tedeschi, Archbishop Carlo Maria Viganò, and Giuseppe Sciacca.

The first significant public step Benedict XVI took toward restructuring the IOR was made on 23 September 2009, when the Supervisory Commission of Cardinals for the Institute, presided over by Bertone, updated the Board of Superintendence by appointing four new members (Carl Anderson, Supreme Knight of the Knights of Columbus; Giovanni De Censi, president of *Credito Valtellinese*; Ronaldo Hermann Schmitz of *Deutsche Bank*; and

Manuel Soto Serrano, vice-president of *Indra Sistemas*) and entrusting the presidency to Ettore Gotti Tedeschi, a well-known banker of international repute (president of Santander Consumer Bank and a professor of financial strategy at the Catholic University of Milan), who took the place of Angelo Caloia, caught in the quagmire of leaks showing his involvement—or at least lack of oversight—in Italian bribes brought into the IOR.[69]

A year after Gotti Tedeschi took charge (September 2010), allegations by Rome's attorney general that the IOR was involved in questionable, non-transparent financial activities on Italian soil began to appear in newspapers all over the world.[70] International pressure led Gotti Tedeschi to advocate strict reform measures at the IOR, a call heeded and encouraged by Benedict XVI.[71] Later, Gotti Tedeschi declared that the pope wanted the IOR to "comply with international standards of financial transparency" in "an exemplary way," in order to "guarantee the Church's credibility as a universal moral authority."[72]

On 30 December 2010, Benedict XVI promulgated a law, effective 1 April 2010, preventing and combatting "the laundering of money from criminal activity and the funding of terrorism,"[73] setting up at the same time an independent and autonomous Financial Information Authority and granting it the right to investigate every Vatican office. Again, looking back, Gotti Tedeschi

69   Cf. Gianluigi Nuzzi, *Vaticano S.A.* (Milan: Chiarelettere, 2009).
70   Cf. Nuzzi, *Sua Santità. Le carte segrete di Benedetto XVI*, 99–103; Frattini, *I corvi del Vaticano*, 94–95, 98f.
71   Cf. Nuzzi, *Sua Santità. Le carte segrete di Benedetto XVI*, 102; Frattini, *I corvi del Vaticano*, 125–127.
72   Ettore Gotti Tedeschi, "What Cardinal Pell Needs to Know," in *The Catholic Herald*, 8 January 2015: http://www.catholicherald. co.uk/issues/january-9th-2015/what-cardinal-pell-needs-to-know-about-the-vaticans-finances/.
73   Pontifical Commission for Vatican City State, "Legge 127," 30 December 2010, in *Acta Apostolicae Sedis*, "Supplemento per le leggi e disposizioni dello Stato della Città del Vaticano," n. 81 (2010): 167–201.

recalled "the efforts, the conflicts, and the challenges we faced in 2011 when we began to implement the anti-money-laundering law and the AIF started its work."[74]

The motivation for these measures primarily came from outside as a way order to render the IOR worthy of inclusion in Moneyval's "White List" of nations considered financially reliable, but it was equally utilized on the inside by those (like Tedeschi and others who adhered closely to the pope's reforms) who wanted greater transparency in Vatican finances. The external motivation reinforced the reforming will of the pope and those people close to him.

The pope appointed Cardinal Attilio Nicora (19 January 2011) president of the newly constituted AIF. During this same year, however, the President of the Vatican Tribunal, Giuseppe Dalla Torre, prevented the law from going into force before 1 April 2011. On 25 January 2012, by means of a decree (number CLIX)[75] promulgated by Cardinal Giuseppe Bertello, the President of the *Governatorato* of Vatican City State, and supported by Bertone,[76] the December 2010 law was changed in order to place more limits on the AIF's competencies and to subject its investigative powers to the *nulla osta* of the Secretariat of State and a future *Regolamento* of the *Governatorato*. In a confidential memo, Nicora admitted that "the changes to the law [...] were a real step backwards,"[77]

---

74 Ettore Gotti Tedeschi, "What Cardinal Pell Needs to Know," in *The Catholic Herald*, 8 January 2015: http://www.catholicherald. co.uk/issues/january-9th-2015/what-cardinal-pell-needs-to-know-about-the-vaticans-finances/.

75 President of the *Governaterato* of Vatican City State, "Decreto CLIX," 25 January 2012, *Acta Apostolicae Sedis*, "Supplemento per le leggi e disposizioni dello Stato della Città del Vaticano," n. 83 (2012): 173–223. This was approved on 24 April 2012 by the President of the Governatorato of Vatican City State. See "Legge CLXVI," *Acta Apostolicae Sedis*, "Supplemento per le leggi e disposizioni dello Stato della Città del Vaticano," n. 83 (2012).

76 Cf. Politi, *Joseph Ratzinger: Crisi di un papato*, 273.

77 Frattini, *I corvi del Vaticano*, op. cit., 114.

because in the end they confused the role of regulation with the role of being a regulator.[78]

Newspapers reported that those involved with the IOR took different stances toward to the steps to increase financial transparency.[79] Those in favor included Director of the AIR Cardinal Nicora, attorney Francesco De Pasquale, and president Gotti Tedeschi. Those opposed included Cardinal Bertone and the Director of IOR, Paolo Cipriani (appointed in 2007 by Benedict).[80] Some spoke of an "all-out civil war" or at least an "underground battle."[81]

It was in the thick of this mess—in the weeks following the ratification of the January 2012 decree on 24 April 2012—that serious actions were taken against the president of the IOR, who was the primary proponent for greater transparency.[82] Shortly after the reappointment of Gotti Tedeschi at the end of May, two members of the Board of Supervisors, Anderson and Schmitz (vice-president), asked Bertone separately to revoke Gotti Tedeschi's mandate, accusing him of indifference and ineffectiveness. Schmitz's letter was part of a previous chain of correspondence regarding the IOR's "extremely fragile and risky situation."[83] In other words, steps had already been taken well before they were made known. From the documents published subsequently, it was clear that Bertone had been alerted of the lack of confidence in the IOR president on the part of some members of the board. (On 22 May 2012, Schmitz wrote to the Secretary of State: "As you are aware, at the meeting of the IOR Board on May 24th this week, there will be a motion to take a no-confidence vote

78 Cf. Ettore Gotti Tedeschi, "What Cardinal Pell Needs to Know," in *The Catholic Herald*, 8 January 2015: http://www.catholicherald.co.uk/issues/january-9th-2015/what-cardinal-pell-needs-to-know-about-the-vaticans-finances/.
79 Cf. Politi, *Joseph Ratzinger. Crisi di un papato*, op. cit., 274ff.; Frattini, *I corvi del Vaticano*, 92 ss.
80 Cf. Ibid., 107ss.
81 Cf. Ibid., 92.
82 Cf. Ibid., 136ss.
83 Cf. Frattini, *I corvi del Vaticano*, 142.

against President Gotti Tedeschi.")[84]

On 24 May 2012 (the same day that the pope's butler, Paolo Gabriele, was arrested), Gotti Tedeschi learned of the no-confidence vote taken by the IOR's administrative board through a letter published two days later in the *Corriere della Sera*,[85] in which he was criticized for an inability to fulfill the basic duties of the presidency, his lack of prudence and attention, his absence from meetings, the dissemination of presidential documents, and his "progressively erratic personnel (*sic*) behavior." Gotti Tedeschi himself literally feared for his life.[86] It is interesting to hear what Tedeschi's friend, Giuseppe Orsi, president of Finmeccanica, said of the Vatican: "It is an environment like any other involving power: lies, corruption, blackmail."[87] It was clear, as Monsignor Gänswein declared, that the Holy Father was "surprised, very surprised" at the vote of no-confidence against a person so "esteemed" and "loved": "Out of respect for the competencies of those responsible, he decided not to intervene at that time."[88] On 24 May 2012, the papal household was rocked by a storm. The President of the IOR had been kicked out and the papal butler had been arrested for stealing documents. The pope was buffeted by gale force winds. Where should he turn his attention? Where should he intervene?

On 27 May 2012, Anderson publicly denied that the dismissal was due to a lack of transparency.[89] Two days later, the newspaper

---

84 Cf. Ibid, 140–142.
85 Board of Superintendence of the Institute for Religious Works, "Notice and memorandum of vote and resolution of no confidence," 24 May 2012: http://media2.corriere.it/corriere/pdf/2012/Memorandum-IOR260512.pdf.
86 Ibid., 92.
87 Politi, *Joseph Ratzinger. Crisi di un papato*, 275.
88 Franca Giansoldati, Il Messaggero, 22 October 2013: http://www.ilmes-saggero.it/primo_piano/vaticano/padre_georg_papi_francesco-208592. html.
89 Marco Bardazzi, *Vatican Insider*, 27 May 2012: http://vaticaninsider.lastampa.it/inchieste-ed-interviste/dettaglio-articolo/articolo/vatileaks-vaticano-gotti-tedeschi-15427.

of the Italian bishops, the *Avvenire* (a publication well aware of the opinions of Cardinal Nicora), lined itself up in defense of Gotti Tedeschi, whom they asserted was known for his "professionalism, dedication, and generosity in trying to solve all sorts of problems with transparency, always in view of a greater good."[90] On 1 June 2012, the Commission of Cardinals of the IOR had a meeting at which they confirmed the no-confidence vote against Gotti Tedeschi and entrusted the presidential functions *ad interim* to Schmitz, who had been serving as vice-president.

Months later, precisely on 15 February 2013, after Benedict XVI announced his intention to resign from the papacy, Gotti Tedeschi's successor was officially named: Ernst von Freyberg, a German.[91] Given the context, it seemed that a public clearing of Gotti Tedeschi's name was needed, but this is something that never happened.[92]

What are we to make of this affair? It is difficult to say. Was it a missed opportunity for greater transparency? Currently, not enough documentary evidence is available to make a fully informed judgment. When we put what we have together, it seems Benedict was a pope who initiated processes and then abandoned them to follow others, always trying not to intervene too much. Was it a deflated papacy, or, as the coincidence of dates suggests (i.e., it all came to a head on 24 May 2012), was he distracted? Undoubtedly, the pope's men were not following the same line, and this led to disorder and a weakening of Church governance. It is still not clear what the role of Bertone was: did he support the removal of Gotti Tedeschi, or just give into it? One thing is sure. The issue was not handled well from a journalistic or public relations viewpoint, but that is not saying much.

90   Marco Tarquinio, "Il direttore risponde," *Avvenire*, 29 May 2012.
91   Communication from the Press Office of the Holy See, 15 February 2013: https://press.vatican.va/content/salastampa/it/bollettino/pubbli- co/2013/02/15/0101/00269.html.
92   Cf. Gotti Tedeschi, *Ecco cosa avrebbe bisogno di sapere il Cardinal Pell*, op. cit.

Another problem with Vatican finances involved contracts made by the Governatorato—i.e., the administrative entity of Vatican City State—but not drawn up with a satisfactory level of transparency in that they always involved the same companies, even though costs were significantly higher.[93] The criteria for choosing these companies were not clear. For example, the Governatorato spends approximately 550,000.00 Euro per year on the annual erecting of the nativity scene and Christmas tree in Saint Peter's Square, in addition to other nativity scenes and decorations throughout Vatican City State. The president of the Governatorato appointed in September of 2006, Cardinal Lajolo, was replaced in 2011 by another *piemontese* (i.e., a cleric from Piedmont), Giuseppe Bertello, while the office of Secretary of the Governatorato changed hands several times and was always occupied by someone trying to rationalize the Governatorato's expenses. Initially it fell to the ex-diplomat Renato Boccardo and then to career diplomat Carlo Maria Viganò, who in turn was replaced by the canonist Giuseppe Sciacca (3 September 2011), who had been serving as auditor at the *Rota* tribunal. When Viganò learned that he was going to receive a prestigious appointment to the papal nunciature in the United States, he began to write letters to the Secretary of State, asking to remain in his position, explaining how much he had done to curb expenditures and balance the budget.[94] In one of those letters, he also reminded Bertone of his promise that he would be succeed Cardinal Lajolo as President of the Governatorato (which would entail receiving a cardinal's hat). Then, when he felt his career was at stake and his work disregarded, he began to denounce openly the bad fiscal practices he had discovered and was trying to fix. He also denounced the meddling of third parties, such as Marco Simeon, a young manager favored by Bertone, whom Viganò considered a slanderer, or the unacceptable

93   Cf. Frattini, *I corvi del Vaticano*, 152.
94   Cf. Nuzzi, *Sua Santità. Le carte segrete di Benedetto XVI*, 53–85; Frattini, *I corvi del Vaticano*, 153–161.

behavior of insiders such as Paolo Nicolini at the Vatican Museums. The press was already critical of the archbishop, questioning his capacity to govern. Viganò responded to this criticism in a face-to-face conversation with Bertone.[95] These internal tensions at the Governatorato were in fact the reason Bertone decided to transfer Viganò.[96] The denouncement of Viganò led the pope to establish a special commission *super partes* to investigate what was behind it. Viganò was originally pleased with this commission, but when it had finished its work, the archbishop asked for another juridical body to look into the matter.[97] In the end, Viganò was transferred to the United States and was succeeded at the Governatorato by Giuseppe Sciacca, a close confidant of Benedict XVI. Sciacca continued Viganò's discipline of curbing expenditures and balancing the books. The affair came into the public eye after documents had been purloined. According to Lajolo, Viganò "began his job with suspicions that were revealed to be unfounded, and consequently he started off on the wrong foot." His letters "put forth a very negative assessment; but [...] they bear the mark of a wounded soul."[98] All the evidence simply points to a consistent attempt to improve operations, a line the Holy Father himself was pursuing despite the fact that some of those he trusted were apparently following a different course. At the same time, there were those who were working to hinder economic transparency at the Vatican, a situation that did not help the Holy Father's attempt to improve operations.

95 Nuzzi, *Sua Santità. Le carte segrete di Benedetto XVI*, 56.
96 Cf. "Le finanze del Vaticano non decollano: cercasi governatore," *Il Giornale*, 12 March 2011. This is cited in Nuzzi, *Sua Santità. Le carte segrete di Benedetto XVI*, 53–54.
97 Cf. Nuzzi, *Sua Santità. Le carte segrete di Benedetto XVI*, 57.
98 Interview of Cardinal Lajolo by Fabio Marchese Ragona, "Stanze Vaticane," 8 March 2012: http://stanzevaticane.tgcom24.it/2012/03/08/le-lettere-di-mons-vigano-le-spese-del-governatorato-e-il-vatileaks-intervista-al-card-lajolo-in-azione-forze-ostili-alla-chiesa/.

Plot within the palace

The second part of Benedict's pontificate suffered from an ongoing leak of documents.[99] In some areas, not only was the Curia resistant to the Pontiff's reforms, but some officials were scheming to have documents mysteriously end up in the hands of Italian journalists.

In the end, the fault lay with the butler. Nothing new here. It's the plot of a hundred mystery novels. Paolo Gabriele, the pope's butler, who was arrested and arraigned in 2012, admitted that he was responsible for stealing, photocopying, and circulating confidential documents kept with the pope and his personal secretary. The admitted motive was to reveal certain delicate moves made to favor one type of Church reform or another, either without the pope's knowledge or with little or misleading information.

The revealed documents revolve around a few specific episodes—namely, power struggles between cardinals (e.g., Bertone and Tettamanzi), corruption, decisions within the "Vatican Bank" (IOR), and provisions in the case of the pope's death. With regard to the latter, a *memorandum* was released by Cardinal Castrillón Hoyos in February 2012 according to which Cardinal Romeo, during a meeting in China, asserted that the pope did not have more than twelve months to live—and, in fact, twelve months later, he was not a "living" (i.e., reigning) pope. The Cardinal from palermo, in fact, had never sufficiently explained the reasons for his trip to China and the meetings he had there. In any case, of greater interest to the media were documents that put Bertone in a bad light. The Cardinal Secretary of State did not appear to be a reformer or a guardian of curial transparency.[100] But

99   Cf. Nuzzi, *Sua Santità. Le carte segrete di Benedetto XVI*, op. cit.; Politi, *Joseph Ratzinger. Crisi di un papato*, 264–284.

100 Cf. Nuzzi, *Sua Santità. Le carte segrete di Benedetto XVI*. There was also a television broadcast convering this entitled *Gli Intoccabili* carried by the Italian network *la7*. See also Frattini, *I corvi del Vaticano*, 244–247.

how trustworthy was the information contained in these documents? Did they truly show that there was inadequate attention on the part of the cardinal toward curial administration?

In the middle of this media crisis, on 23 June 2012, the pope summoned a meeting of five cardinals— the Italian Camillo Ruini (at that time Vicar General for the Diocese of Rome), the Canadian Marc Ouellet (Prefect of the Congregation for Bishops), the French Cardinal Jean-Louis Tauran (President of the Pontifical Council for Interreligious Dialogue), the Australian George Pell (Archbishop of Sydney), and the Slovakian Jozef Tomko (Prefect emeritus of the Congregation for the Evangelization of Peoples)—to discuss the situation in the Roman Curia.[101] It is important to note that Bertone, caught in the eye of the storm, was not included. Nothing is known for certain about the business of that meeting.

Precisely at this critical moment when so many were losing faith in and toward the Roman Curia, some residential cardinals began to speak publicly in favor of a reorganization of the Curia. One of these was Cardinal Vingt-Trois of Paris, who, in an interview with *Radio Notre Dame,* said, "It is true that the Roman Curia has been organized differently at different times. And its current structure is certainly not entirely adapted to the needs of today's Church. After the Council, when Pope Paul VI wanted to launch new projects, he was forced to create new bureaucratic entities *ad hoc*. Similarly, Benedict XVI created the Pontifical Council for the New Evangelization. This might be a step forward in one sense, but it is not a functional reform of the system as a whole." He went on to say, "Every dicastery functions on its own and communication between them is often slow or nonexistent, unless

101 For example, see Sergio Rame, "Il papa convoca i cardinali," *Il Giornale*, 23 June 2012; "Vatileaks, il papa convoca i cardinali," *La Stampa*, 23 June 2012. The most important statement was made by Vatican spokesman Fr. Federico Lombardi, Director of the Holy See Press Office, 25 June 2012: http://www.news.va/it/news/direttore-sala-stampa-circa-riunio-ne-del-papa-con. See also, Frattini, *I corvi del Vaticano*, 232.

something comes up in a conversation between two cardinals."[102] Vingt-Trois reflects a common disappointment with the disorganization of the Curia and a desire for a more general intervention rather than a mere patch job.

Interviews with those involved reveal that there were about twenty individuals in favor of leaking and divulging documents.[103] In those chaotic days, some improbable names were brought forth by certain media outlets (Bishop Josef Clemens, Cardinal Paolo Sardi, and the German Ingrid Stampa),[104] but the people who were actually involved were never mentioned. In fact, not all of the leaked documents could be traced back to the pope's personal secretary.[105] In the end, only one man was convicted. Virtually nothing is known about the others except that they were minimally complicit in matters of little relevance (i.e., they primarily thwarted Vatican investigations) by assisting an information technology specialist, Claudio Sciarpelletti. Otherwise, all responsibility lay with the butler. There are many doubts surrounding this case. Could a single individual, who began work as a janitor, have organized this kind of racket? Many people in Rome were asking the question, especially considering the numerous contradictions emerging from the testimony given in the Vatican courtroom.[106] The case has never been completely resolved.

Conclusions

Even if Benedict began his pontificate by doing little more than combining dicasteries, it seems he went in another direction by

---

102 For the original French interview, see Clémence Houdaille, *Radio Notre Dame,* 21 June 2012: http://www.paris.catholique.fr/Les-fuites-au-Vatican-un-trouble.html. See also, Politi, *Joseph Ratzinger: Crisi di un papato,* op. cit., 275; Frattini, *I corvi del Vaticano,* 233–234.
103 Cf. Politi, *Joseph Ratzinger. Crisi di un papato,* op. cit., 270.
104 Cf. Marco Ansaldo, "Svolta sul Corvo del papa *Altri tre sotto inchiesta,*" *La Repubblica,* 23 July 2012.
105 Cf. Politi, *Joseph Ratzinger. Crisi di un papato,* op. cit., 277.
106 Cf. Politi, *Joseph Ratzinger. Crisi di un papato,* op. cit., 282.

establishing new Vatican offices, in particular the Pontifical Council for the New Evangelization and the Financial Information Authority, which were created in response to pastoral needs and the need for fiscal transparency. At the same time, the competencies of other dicasteries were reconsidered, though it is not clear if this was done according to an overarching plan or simply as *ad hoc* responses (to financial issues, for example) or as responses to individuals proposing or advocating for certain changes (heads of dicasteries, for example). In any event, the shuffling of competencies blurred the need for unification and greater cohesion in the Roman Curia.

As Enrico Galavotti notes, Benedict XVI, unlike his predecessors, "did not implement any specific reformation program for the Curia. He did not even officially establish a commission to study the matter."[107] All of Benedict's changes seem to have been *ad hoc*. Galavotti writes that this is due to the fact that Benedict XVI conceived his pontificate "as a programmatic implementation of the teachings of John Paul II." In a second reading of his pontificate in 2016, Benedict XVI declared that he did not have a mind for organizational reform. Moreover, he thought that another general reform of the Curia was not necessary: "And it wasn't necessary either, because there was John Paul II's reform of the Curia, *Pastor bonus*. To turn everything on its head so promptly did not seem right to me. It's correct that I couldn't take charge of any big, long-term organizational projects, but I deemed that it wasn't the right moment."[108] Moreover, the previous century saw no less than three general reforms of the Curia, and these were done 320 years after the reforms of Sixtus V in 1588. Moreover, Ratzinger seemed to apply the principle of ongoing reform (we will discuss this in the next chapter), a principle usually reserved for theological and liturgical matters.

Benedict seemed to act as a silent implementor of preceding pontificates. With respect to John Paul II, he followed a "striking

107 Galavotti, *Sulle riforme della curia romana nel Novecento*, 887.
108 Benedict XVI, *Last Testament*, 192.

continuity of teaching in juridical matters."[109] According to Galvotti, he moved away from Paul VI, thus imitating his Polish predecessor in a style of governance that "put distance between the pontiff and the Curia."[110] Perhaps it is more accurate to say that these popes used a less monarchical approach than Montini, whose style was new with respect to the collegial style used in the Roman Curia in more recent times, a development that would already have seen in the pontificates of Pius XI and Pius XII. In fact, Paul VI's reforms "expanded the powers of the pope over the Curia."[111] Paul VI's reforms, in fact, tended toward a more monarchical administrative model,[112] but John Paul II and Benedict XVI, given their different temperaments and leadership styles, preferred a different model of governance—that is, they governed through delegation after having made their overall vision clear (except for matters dear to their hearts, which they minutely followed). Perhaps it was the distance between the Curia conceived as a centralized mechanism of governance and the popes' less administrative and bureaucratic personalities that was the main cause of friction under both John Paul and Benedict.

There was a significant problem in the criteria used to nominate curial leaders, especially in cases in which individuals appointed by the pope were in direct conflict with one another, thus hindering attempts at reform and leading to accusations of infidelity to the pope's program. In financial institutions, there seems to have been widespread confusion, or better yet a lot of headbutting between different factions of laity and clergy.

Changes to the Curia were not as visible in the creation of new entities or the adjustment of old ones as they were in appointments made to positions of leadership. Benedict's hand was

---

109 Lorusso, "Le modifiche di Benedetto XVI alla Costituzione Apostolica *Pastor Bonus*," op. cit., 81.
110 Galavotti, *Sulle riforme della curia romana nel novecento*, op. cit., 887.
111 Ibid., 883.
112 Cf. Galavotti, *Sulle riforme della curia romana nel novecento*, op. cit., 884.

certainly visible in the case of offices associated with the content of the faith. The appointments of Tauran to the Pontifical Council for Interreligious Dialogue and Koch to Ecumenism were particularly significant. These appointments relieved some of the underlying tension that had existed between these Pontifical Councils and the Congregation for the Doctrine of the Faith.

Even though the pope appointed individuals who clearly reflected his thinking, and some with whom he shared a deep human and intellectual friendship (Bock, Müller, and Ouellet, for example), other appointments clearly were the work of Bertone (especially in finance and administration). The tendency to grant positions to insiders was a particular weakness in that it did not seem to widen the base of ecclesial consent. It seems that a few appointments, however, were made with a view to integrating different strains of Catholicism. Consider the appointments of Focolare members such Brazilian Cardinal João Braz de Aviz as Prefect of the Congregation for Religious, Giovanni Angelo Becciu as Substitute of the Secretariat of State (a position of the highest importance), and Monsignor Vincenzo Zani as Secretary for Catholic Education; or the appointment of Vincenzo Paglia, a member of the community of Saint Egidio, to the Pontifical Council for the Family. In the end, it is hard to overestimate how closely competence and loyalty were valued together. The integration of Catholic currents that underlay many operating decisions would be made more manifest as time went on, especially in episcopal appointments.

This *modus operandi* might be better understood in light of the historical context of the pontificate, which was on the defensive from the beginning, even though Benedict had big plans that we will discuss later. Already during the pre-conclave period, the cardinals and prelates belonging to the "San Gallo" group who were preparing to put up a fight against Ratzinger and everything he stood for (namely, the spirit of John Paul II and the possibility it would continue through him). Indeed, throughout the history of the papacy voices have been raised against certain popes (which we will consider briefly) and the mass media are always breathing down the pope's neck and the necks of those around him. In such an environment, a pope will inevitably look for trustworthy collaborators. Unfortunately, however, there is not always good coordination among the pope's collaborators, and they are not always known for their brilliance.

In the end, the pontificate became the object of journalistic snooping and popular pamphleteering, as is readily seen in the cardinal commissions that were set up to deal with the mess. The Curia was under pressure and was compromised.

The Curia—a body that was not directly elected by the cardinals in the conclave of 2005—had become a self-standing entity, a problem to be solved. The pope had made substantial reforms, but these were overshadowed by peripheral, even trivial concerns.

In any case, this was the Curia, and these were the individuals chosen to collaborate with Benedict XVI to govern the universal Church. It was not an easy game.

CHAPTER THREE
THE MAGISTERIAL GOVERNANCE OF THE CHURCH

Being a professor-pope, Benedict XVI exercised the Petrine ministry with rigorous reasoning and the personal traits one would expect from an intellectual. His personality had public consequences. A professor—especially a theologian—will inevitably act on the basis of a well-reasoned plan rooted in coherent presuppositions. Thinking always comes first. In what follows, I will attempt to synthesize Ratzinger's thinking. But rather than getting bogged down in the various modes in which it is expressed—encyclicals, letters, speeches, *Angelus* addresses (the last are best understood in the context of the time they were given, since the first part of the address regards questions of faith and the second part politics), homilies, interviews, etc.[1]—I will rather examine specific themes.

Benedict XVI introduced a new pontifical way of speaking. For the first time in history, the pope was writing and speaking openly not only as someone sitting on the Chair of Peter, but also as a private—and deliberately private—individual. His books on Jesus stand out as an example. The cover bears the name not only of "Benedict XVI," but also "Joseph Ratzinger."[2] In the book, the pope

1　There are already numerous publications that address these modes of expression. See, for example, Paolo Sartor, Simona Borello, "Benedetto XVI omileta: Logos, Pathos, Ethos" in *La Scuola Cattolica*, 141 (2013): 623–647.

2　Joseph Ratzinger (Benedict XVI), *Jesus of Nazareth* (New York: Doubleday, 2007); *Jesus of Nazareth: Holy Week* (Huntington: Our Sunday Visitor, 2011); *Jesus of Nazareth: The Infancy Narratives* (Colorado Springs: Image Books, 2012).

explicitly asks permission to express his personal opinions and opens his thought to scholarly criticism. He sits on the Chair of Peter with complete openness and fearlessness to entertain opposing opinions.[3] He engages in a new way of communicating not only with Catholics, but other believers and non-believers. Another example of this new communicative mode is an interview Benedict gave to Peter Seewald in 2010 (the first "personal and direct"[4] interview with a pope), the precedents of which are found in John Paul II (who, however, only received and responded to questions in writing), and dialogue between Paul VI and Jean Guitton (which were neither interviews nor explicitly intended for public dissemination).

In public speeches, Benedict clearly indicated his priorities from the outset. As with other pontificates, these most urgent matters influenced his future governance. Melloni notes the following central themes in the first months of the pontificate: "[T]he implementation of Vatican II in full continuity with the Church's tradition, a primary emphasis on the centrality of the Eucharist, the need to reinvigorate a sense of each one's personal apostolic vocation within the ecclesial community, and a commitment to restoring the unity of Christians and promoting dialogue between Christians and other religions, especially with Judaism and Islam, as well as with non-believers."[5] But hadn't these themes taken a back seat? How did they compare with really big problems? The list clearly indicates the intra-ecclesial problems typical of the post-Vatican II period. To understand them, we have to situate them within the big problems of the contemporary Church as perceived by Cardinal Ratzinger.

Benedict XVI has a very particular personality. Not being a man of governance in the usual sense of the word, he had to find

3   In the foreword, he writes: "It goes without saying that this book is in no way an exercise of the magisterium, but is solely an expression of my personal search 'for the face of the Lord.' Everyone is free, then, to contradict me." Xxiii–xxiv.

4   Cf. Benedict XVI, *Luce del mondo*, 8.

5   Alberto Melloni, *Benedetto XVI*, in *Enciclopedia dei papi*, on-line: http:// www.treccani.it/enciclopedia/benedetto-xvi_(Enciclopedia-dei-Papi)/.

a way to govern the Church and the Roman Curia in a way more in line with his personality. He is not a man of administration, just as his friend John Paul II was not, and therefore he had to find trustworthy individuals to whom he could delegate tasks that would help him achieve his goals. He is, however, a man of "power"—that is, a man well aware of his responsibility—and he did not seek to shirk away from it. We can see this in a bird's-eye view of his pontificate. He launched initiatives that were most dear to him and handled delicate matters personally. He opened new doors to the liturgy, gave new impetus to ecumenism, and initiated a period of reform in the Church. He also exercised authority in areas where his brother bishops were reluctant (liturgy and dialogue with the Lefevbrites, for example). He was always a step ahead of the others. And then it had to be the others, particularly his closest collaborators, to implement the details of his projects. This is probably where the weakness lies in this grand pontificate: a pope who was strong, but one using a structure that was not always up to carrying out his plans, though one that nonetheless enjoyed the trust of its leader. The pope was forced to show trust in "his" men of governance. This amounted to a strong pope and a weak papacy.

Not everyone followed his ecclesial vision. There were bishops, priests, members of the laity, and theologians who put it at arm's length. There was a parting of ways between those who regarded him and those who chose not to heed him, and it was as if two parallel Churches emerged.[6] What had already occurred in the pontificate of Paul VI and continued into John Paul II's had still not been overcome. The Church continued to lack unity.

The Catholic Church by the numbers

The life of the Church varies from continent to continent and from one place to another. The population of (baptized) Catholics is not

6   Cf. Marco Politi, *Joseph Ratzinger. Crisi di un papato*, Laterza, Bari 2013², 310.

distributed evenly throughout the world. The most reliable statistics we have date from only 1969.[7] In that year, 17.6% of the
world's population was Catholic. Approximately a decade later
(1980), that percentage jumped to 17.9%. It sunk to 17.7% in 1990
and to 17.3% in 2000, a percentage that remained constant until
Benedict XVI. When Benedict stepped down in 2013, the Catholic
population stood at 17.5%. We can take this as the average global
percentage in the decades spanning from Paul VI to Benedict
XVI—that is, in the years since Vatican II. Even if the percentage
remained roughly equal during that time, the number of human
beings in general increased. In fact, between 1969 and 2012 the
world's population doubled, growing from around 3.5 billion to
more than 7 billion. The same holds for the total number of
Catholics, which doubled from roughly 633,000,000 million in
1969 to 1,228,621,000 in 2012. We also must point out shifts in the
distribution of the world's population. In fact, between 1969 and
2012, the population of Africa grew by about 208%, Asia by 109%,
the Americas by 89.5%, but Europe by 3%. There are significant
differences in the balance of population between continents.

The growth and shifts in population distribution have also
had a significant impact on regional and continental Catholic
populations. Between 1969 and 2012, the percentage of Catholics
in Africa grew from 11% to 18.6%, in America from 55.3% to
63.3%, in Asia from 2.3% to 3.2%, in Europe from 38.3% to 39.9%,
and in Oceania from 23.3% to 26%. But what impact did these
numbers have on the continental distribution of Catholics? It is
not enough to consider only percentages; we must also look at
how they panned out across the globe. Let's again consider each
side of the chronological spectrum. Here are the figures in 1969:
Africa held 6% of the world's Catholic population, America
43.7%, Asia 10.9%, Europe 23.4%, and Oceania 0.8%. Europe had
lost its predominance in the number of Catholics, but not in its
spiritual, theological, financial, and intellectual weight. Another

7   The figures used here are reported in the volumes of the *Annuarium
     Statisticum Ecclesiae* (Vatican City: LEV, 1969—2013).

factor ought to be considered when viewing these statistics. How many of these Catholics were practicing their faith? In the West, it is absolutely essential to distinguish between baptized and practicing Catholics. While the former reflects the phenomenon of "belief without belonging,"[8] a further distinction must be made between those who adhere to the Church's magisterium and those who pick and choose what to believe and what to reject. The sociological definition of someone who practices the faith is someone who regularly attends a place of worship. For example, at the beginning of the twenty-first century, studies show that the percentage of Catholics who practiced in Italy is 18.5% and in Poland around 26%.[9] So, at this point in history, the numbers in the Western world seem to have decreased the most.

In addition to these percentages, we must look at other figures, especially when it comes to the number of baptized Catholics who have entered the priesthood and religious life. Taking into consideration the newly ordained, those who had left the priesthood willingly (that number is shrinking, both absolutely and as a percentage of active priests) and those who had died, the number of active diocesan priests in the world was 269,607 in 1969. When John Paul II was elected in 1978, the number was 258,451. That figure rose continually during John Paul II's pontificate, reaching 265,781 in 2000; 269,762 in 2005; and 279,561 in 2012. This steady increase was due in large part to Africa, which between 2005 and 2012 had increased its number of diocesan priests (many of whom are quite young) by a third, as well as Latin America and Asia, both of which increased their diocesan clergy by 20%. Oceania remained relatively stable during this period, while North America saw a decrease of 10% and Europe of

---

8   Franco Garelli, *Religione all'italiana. L'anima del paese messa a nudo* (Bologna: Il Mulino, 2011), especially 23–26.

9   Cf. Massimo Introvigne, "Effetto francesco. La parola al sociologo delle religioni," *Settimo Cielo*, ed. Sandro Magister, 9 January 2016, http://magister.blogautore.espresso.repubblica.it/2016/01/09/effetto-francesco-la-parola-al-sociologo-delle-religioni/.

5%. Nevertheless, Europe continued to have the greatest concentration of diocesan clergy: 51.5% in 2005 and 46.3% in 2012. This makes it clear why a revitalization of faith-life is so important on that continent. It is still the heart of Catholicism, at least when it comes to Church hierarchy. In the future, it will be important to develop a stronger base in other geographical areas. In fact, if diocesan priestly ordinations between 2005 and 2012 numbered about 6,700, this did not correspond to a change in distribution. While the number of ordinations in Europe dropped from 1,979 in 2005 to 1,717 in 2012, Africa was the only continent to see an increase (from 1,205 to 1,535). More modest increases were seen in America, Asia, and Oceania.

Things are a bit different when it comes to priestly ordinations in religious life. A slow and steady decrease has been consistent worldwide. In 1969, the number stood at 168,694. It was 155,516 at the beginning of John Paul II's pontificate in 1978; 128,755 in 2005; and 126,313 in 2012 (1.9% less than at the beginning of Benedict XVI's pontificate). The steady decline began during the pontificate of Paul VI, showing that men's religious life had truly entered a period of crisis. During Benedict XVI's time, the number of religious priests sunk by 10% in Europe, 6.4% in the Americas (North America alone sunk by 15.6%), and 6% in Oceania, whereas in Asia there was an increase of 22.4% and 18.4% in Africa. Similar figures hold for non-ordained male religious.

For a prudential judgment regarding this situation, we have to consider a few other elements. There was no significant decrease in the ratio of priests to practicing Catholics. It has even been claimed that between 1960 and 2010, the number of priests in Germany with respect to practicing Catholics in that country had in fact doubled.[10] But those figures remain to be verified.

Another factor to consider is women religious. If we look at the number of professed religious women (in institutes of pontifical right), we see a steady decrease worldwide. In 1970, there were

10   Cf. Benedict XVI, *Luce del mondo,* 208. In English, *Light of the World* (San Francisco: Ignatius Press, 2010).

1,004,304 women religious. That number shrank to 763,098 in 1978; 606,181 in 2005 (626,559 if we include the so-called secular institutes); and 542,534 in 2012 (560,626 if we include secular institutes). If these numbers make us stop and think, so do the percentages. From 1970 to 2005, there was a 39.6% decrease in the number of women religious, and the period from 2005 to the end of Benedict XVI's pontificate saw a decrease of 10.5% (the same percentages hold when we include members of secular institutes). The decrease was again most notable in Western countries. Here are the figures if we look at Benedict XVI's pontificate: -18.4% in Europe (which has only 39% of the world's religious women), -14.7% in the Americas (a fall of 22.5% in North America alone), -17.5% in Oceania, and increases of +13% percent in Africa and +7.5% in Asia. These statistics show that the future belongs to Africa and Asia, and Europe appears to be most in need of serious first-aid. Religious life is in a state of crisis in the West, especially for women. What are the causes? What cure did Ratzinger have in mind?

First of all, we must not forget that it was to *this* Church that Benedict and his collaborators had to direct their attention. If the Church is called to show the face of Christ to the world by means of its own faith-life with an explicit Catholic identity (manifested visibly in the liturgy), then this duty must also be applied to the pope's selection of cardinals (i.e., his closest collaborators) in such a way as to support his initiatives both at the level of the Curia and in the local Church, based on a "political" program of exemplary holiness supported by a renewal in religious life and greater involvement on the part of the laity. The role of the pope is crucial in this. He witnesses to the Church through his own personality and the priorities he establishes for the Church.

The centrality of faith

The pope typically governs the Church in an original and unique way, not only through a detailed program, but also with a wider vision conveyed through the preaching of the Word. His governance is predominately magisterial in nature, conveyed primarily through speeches and homilies covering a wide range of topics, leaving the detailed articulation of doctrine to others (i.e., his closest collaborators and local episcopal conferences).

The overarching emphasis of the pope's doctrinal speeches is "an essential and pure Christianity with no layers or accretions. An intimate faith lived concretely and publicly."[11] He desired to overcome the public perception of the Catholic faith as a set of rules and restrictions, and therefore he sought to present the core message of Christianity as "God is love." He would give the name *Deus Caritas Est* to his first encyclical (25 December 2005). He reminds us that at the origin of faith there is an act of love, an encounter with Christ, as he writes in the opening of the encyclical: "Being Christian is not the result of an ethical choice or a lofty idea, but the encounter with an event, a person, which gives life a new horizon and a decisive direction."[12] He goes on to present a fascinating and consoling portrait of Christianity. He describes a Christian as someone who chooses a life of charity in a practical commitment within a community of love, the Church. A Christian loves when he no longer looks out for himself but takes care of others, knowing how to sacrifice himself to do so. The pope unites the themes of love and justice in this encyclical. Within ten days of its publication, there were over a million copies sold in Italy alone.[13]

His second encyclical, *Spe Salvi* (30 November 2007), touches on a fundamental theme within Christian faith—namely, hope. The pope passes from a theoretical reflection to a concrete exposition of the theme. The encyclical is framed eschatologically with a heavy emphasis on the greatest Christian hope: eternal life. The pontiff counters the secularization of hope by giving new vigor to its profound Christian meaning.

In the same vein, the pope wrote a social encyclical entitled *Caritas in Veritate* (29 June 2009) that aims to redefine relationships

---

11 Politi, *Joseph Ratzinger. Crisi di un papato*, 50.
12 *Deus Caritas Est*, n. 1.
13 Politi, *Joseph Ratzinger. Crisi di un papato*, op. cit., 52.

in economics, production, and finance in terms of the universal common good within the ethical framework of responsibility and social justice and according to the principles of solidarity and subsidiarity. The pope proposes a vision according to which the norm for loving one's neighbor arises out of God's will rather than our own selfish desires.[14] Various criticism was directed at the encyclical by the so-called "theo-cons," primarily in the United States.[15] Particular criticism was made of passages in which the pope speaks of the "market." For example, the theo-cons were troubled by Benedict XVI's restatement of Paul VI's invitation for "people to give serious attention to the damage that can be caused to one's home country by the transfer abroad of capital purely for personal advantage" (40), and the assertion that globalization has led to a "downsizing of social security systems" (25). The main problem is that while *Centesimus Annus* seems to place capitalism firmly within a Christian worldview, the new encyclical takes a "more cautious and reserved" stance towards capitalism, "even making some criticism" of it.[16] The "center-left" also had some criticism for the encyclical's approach (especially in the second part).[17] For the most part, however, the encyclical was accepted with acclaim.

Among efforts to show the beauty of the Church, the pope strove to show that her face is none other than Christ's. This was the impetus behind the three volumes he published under the title *Jesus of Nazareth*. The challenge for the Church today is to rediscover God, and therefore the pope felt personally motivated to participate in this project in the way he knew best—that is, by writing both as pope and as a scholar. The central question for the Church and for him was "faith" viewed as a response to God's

---

14 Cf. Benedict XVI, *Luce del mondo*, 77. In English, *Light of the World* (San Francisco: Ignatius Press, 2010).

15 Cf. Paolo Rodari and Andrea Tornielli, *Attacco a Ratzinger. Accuse e scandali, profezie e complotti contro Benedetto XVI* (Milan: Piemme, 2010), 142–150.

16 Ibid., 147.

17 Ibid., 147–149.

love for each and every person. Ratzinger always had a "beautiful Christianity" in mind[18] in which faith, as the pope said to the clergy of Bressanone, "is based on natural virtues: honesty, joy, a willingness to listen to your neighbor, the capacity to forgive, generosity, goodness, and cordiality between persons."[19] This, as he confessed to Peter Seewald, is how he had always viewed his personal responsibility. A pope is "responsible for making sure that the faith that keeps people together is believed, that it remains alive, and that its identity is inviolate."[20] A pope's great challenge—indeed the challenge of the entire Church—is to "bring to light God's priority again."[21] For Benedict XVI, believers "need something like islands where faith in God and the interior simplicity of Christianity are alive and radiant; oases, Noah's arks, to which man can always come back for refuge."[22] The pope's main concerns are not organizational. He rather focuses on what is essential for the life of faith and the community. He articulates this faith within a harmonious vision of its connection with reason. This, in fact, is the topic that predominates in most of his speeches and writings. Indeed, it became the fundamental theme of his entire pontificate.

Benedict believes that the category of "mission" is the best way to understand the responsibility of communicating the faith. In a speech to the Roman Curia in which he recalled meeting the Latin American bishops in Aparecida in 2007, Benedict emphasized the Church's need to engage willingly in this mission; a mission aimed at spreading "forces for good without which all our programs of social order do not become reality but—in the onslaught of the extremely powerful pressure of other interests

18   Politi, *Joseph Ratzinger. Crisi di un papato*, op. cit., 287.
19   Benedict XVI, "Incontro con il clero della diocese di Bolzano-Bressanone," 6 August 2008, *Acta Apostolicae Sedis*, n. 100 (2008): 625–641.
20   Cf. Benedict XVI, *Luce del mondo*, 22. In English, *Light of the World* (San Francisco: Ignatius Press, 2010).
21   Ibid., 100.
22   Ibid., 242–243.

contrary to peace and justice—remain no more than abstract theories."[23] He suggests that the continent is in a crisis of faith that needs a Church attentive to many forms of poverty, but who is unable to respond to them: the number of Catholics is simply declining too rapidly.

Benedict's magisterial approach to Church governance naturally led him to launch initiatives with a particular programmatic and pastoral focus. Whenever a pope designates "extraordinary" or "Jubilee" years, he gives us a special insight into his priorities. In fact, such universal initiatives—because they have practical, organizational, social, and spiritual significance at the local level—are often more revealing than encyclicals and speeches. That is why special attention must be given to the special Jubilee years dedicated to Saint Paul (2008–2009), the Priesthood (2009–2010), and the Faith (2012–2013), as they indicate key peak moments within a pontificate. By means of these Jubilee years, the pope wanted to lead people to listen, live, and proclaim the Word of God.[24]

Along these lines, it is also important to remember the meeting of the Synod of Bishops dedicated to the Word of God (2008), which would culminate in the pope's publication of the Apostolic Exhortation *Verbum Domini* in 2010. This document builds on the foundation of Vatican II's *Dei Verbum*, proposing a sort of "Christology of the Word": Jesus is the "Word of God," and it is to Him that all the "words" offered by God to humanity since the beginning of the world refer, especially the words of Sacred Scripture, which the Church considers the "word" inspired by the Holy Spirit.

At the same time, Benedict XVI kept alive an important and original creation of John Paul II: World Youth Day. Even if it was not in Benedict's nature to make himself the center of attention, and even if he avoided large crowds, he nonetheless understood

23 Benedict XVI, Speech to the Roman Curia, 21 December 2007, *Acta Apostolicae Sedis*, n. 100 (2008): 26–34.
24 Cf. Benedict XVI, *Luce del mondo*, 114.

the significance of World Youth Day. As he explained in 2011, the celebrations of World Youth Day are an original, revitalized way of being Christian where participants have "a new experience of catholicity, of the Church's universality." They show young people the beauty of belonging to the Church, "despite all the trials and times of darkness." From these celebrations, the young Church "derives a new way of living our humanity, our Christianity."[25]

The wide range of topics Pope Benedict covered in his public speeches did not distract him from the business of day-to-day administration. An example of this are the modifications made to the Code of Canon Law with regard to marriage and sacred orders.[26]

Benedict XVI and theology

It is the task of theology to present the beauty of the faith to the world today. A theologian pope thus finds himself in a unique position to make a lasting contribution to theology.

During the pontificate of John Paul II, a significant theological development with deep pastoral implications began to develop around the theme of magisterial authority and the obedience due to that authority.[27] The faith of believing Catholics—be they traditionalists undoggedly faithful to Rome, or members of new ecclesiastical movements—is lived out in obedience to the pope,.[28]

In an address to the International Theological Commission on 1 December 2005, the pope affirmed:

25 Benedict XVI, *Discorso alla Curia romana e alla famiglia pontificia*, 22 December 2011, *Acta Apostolicae Sedis*, n. 104 (2012): 34–40.
26 Benedict XVI, Motu Proprio *Omnium in Mentem*, 26 October 2006, *Acta Apostolicae Sedis*, n. 102 (2010): 8–10.
27 Congregation for the Doctrine of the Faith, *Doctrinal Commentary on the Concluding Formula of the Professio Fidei*, 29 June 1998.
28 Cf. Giovanni Miccoli, *La Chiesa dell'anticoncilio. I tradizionalisti alla riconquista di Roma* (Rome: Laterza, 2011), 342–343.

The theologian's work [...] must take place in communion with the living voice of the Church, that is, with the living Magisterium of the Church and under her authority. [...] Here one might object: but is theology thus defined still a science and in conformity with our reason and its freedom? Yes. Not only are rationality, a scientific approach, and thinking in communion with the Church not exclusive of one another, but they go together. The Holy Spirit guides the Church to all truth (cf. Jn 16: 13); the Church is at the service of truth and her guidance is an education in truth.[29]

Theology is never carried out on totally neutral ground. This means the Congregation for the Doctrine of the Faith is not merely concerned with promoting theology, but defending and correcting it (not controlling it). During Benedict's pontificate, the work of only two theologians was censured. The first was Jon Sobrino, a Jesuit priest, whose Christology was determined problematic.[30] In the notification regarding his work, the Congregation stated that

theological reflection cannot have a foundation other than the faith of the Church. Only starting from ecclesial faith, in communion with the Magisterium, can the theologian acquire a deeper understanding of the Word of God contained in Scripture and transmitted by the living Tradition of the Church. Thus, the truth revealed by God himself in Jesus Christ, and transmitted by the

---

29 Benedict XVI, Address to Members of the International Theological Commission, 1 December 2005, *Acta Apostolicae Sedis*, n. 97 (2005): 1039–1041.

30 Congregation for the Doctrine of the Faith, Notification on the works of Father Jon Sobrino, SJ, 26 November 2006. See *Acta Apostolicae Sedis*, 99 (2007): 181–194.

Church, constitutes the ultimate normative principle of theology. Nothing else may surpass it.[31]

The other theologian whose work prompted a notification was Sister Margaret A. Farley.[32] The problem with her moral theology lay in her incorrect "understanding of the role of the Church's Magisterium as the teaching authority of the bishops united with the Successor of Peter."

In the twentieth and twenty-first centuries, ecclesiological thinking produced contrasting visions of the role of the Roman Pontiff, bishops, episcopal conferences, and the laity. Every theologian readily referred to Vatican II, which developed the theological foundation of Vatican I. But reference to a single historical event does not ensure a unified theological interpretation. On the contrary, various overlapping and contrasting ecclesiologies emerged after 1965, which in fact indicated different visions of where power lies within the Church. Even though many bishops and theologians clearly articulated what the Church needed, there were undeniably conflicting opinions regarding teaching authority and power of governance within the Church. This resulted in a divergence of magisterial discipline and individual practice. The Archbishop of Trieste, Giampaolo Crepaldi, even spoke of "two pastoral programs that are very different in themselves, to the extent that they almost no longer understand one another, as if they were expressions of two different Churches, causing insecurity and error in many faithful."[33]

Let's move from dogmatic questions to moral and disciplinary questions. What is the situation today?

31 Ibid.
32 Congregation for the Doctrine of the Faith, Notification on the book *Just Love. A Framework for Christian Sexual* Ethics by Sr. Margaret A. Farley, R.S.M., 30 March 2012. See *Acta Apostolicae Sedis*, 104 (2012): 505–512.
33 Giampaolo Crepaldi, "Anti-Popes and Dangers of a Parallel Magisterium," *Zenit*, 21 March 2010: https://zenit.org/articles/anti-popes-and-dangers-of-a-parallel-magisterium/.

Pope Benedict XVI gave a fundamental interpretation of the tension within the Church's self-understanding by offering his own hermeneutic of Vatican II. Particularly significant was his first Christmas address to the Roman Curia (22 December 2005).[34] In that speech, he identifies a Church developing through the centuries, "yet always remaining the same, the one subject." He thus anchored the Council in the Church's Tradition and living Magisterium. When faced with decisions at an inopportune time, contingent situations, Benedict asserted, call for contingent responses. Thus, it is necessary to get to the core of pontifical declarations by understanding their underlying principles. Admittedly, these principles are not always readily grasped. Sometimes, the initial impact of a papal teaching can be more dramatic than the actual text. At other times, the Holy See and the Church fail to articulate principles to the degree necessary.

This speech touched on the value and dynamics of Vatican II as interpreted by Benedict XVI. He offered these reflections not only to the Curia, but to the Church at large. The point of the speech was not so much to juxtapose the "hermeneutic of discontinuity and rupture" and the hermeneutic of continuity, but rather to compare the "hermeneutic of discontinuity" with the "hermeneutic of reform." This is indeed an important difference. The word "reform" is both "suggestive and problematic, as well as fruitful."[35] How should it be understood? The pope puts it this way: it is a "renewal in the continuity of the one subject-Church that the Lord has given us. She is a subject that increases over time and develops, yet always remains the same, the one subject of the journeying People of God. The hermeneutic of discontinuity risks ending in a split between the pre-conciliar Church and the post-conciliar Church." Benedict says in the same speech:

34 Benedict XVI ,"Discorso alla Curia romana," 22 December 2005, *Acta Apostolicae Sedis*, n. 98 (2006): 40–53.
35 Giuseppe Lorizio, "Il Pontificato interrotto. Spunti per un bilancio teologico," *Studium*, n. 109 (2013): 418.

The hermeneutic of discontinuity is countered by the hermeneutic of reform, as presented first by Pope John XXIII in the Speech inaugurating the Council on 11 October 1962 and later by Pope Paul VI in his Discourse for the Council's conclusion on 7 December 1965. Here I shall cite only John XXIII's well-known words, which unequivocally express this hermeneutic when he says that the Council wishes "to transmit the doctrine, pure and integral, without any attenuation or distortion." He continues: "Our duty is not only to guard this precious treasure, as if we were concerned only with antiquity, but to dedicate ourselves with an earnest will and without fear to that work that our age demands of us [...]." It is necessary that "adherence to all the teaching of the Church in its entirety and preciseness [...]" be presented in "faithful and perfect conformity to the authentic doctrine, which, however, should be studied and expounded through the methods of research and through the literary forms of modern thought. The substance of the ancient doctrine of the deposit of faith is one thing, and the way in which it is presented is another [...]" retaining the same meaning and message.

Cardinal Ruini has stated that this interpretation of the Council is the "only theologically and pastorally fruitful one."[36] The pope's speech provoked debates in many disciplines, including liturgical theology. For Church history, it presented useful categories, given that continuity, discontinuity, and reform are constantly used today to describe human action within time. Yet their theological import is significantly different from their historical meaning.

The liturgy and its innovative restoration

One of the projects in which Benedict XVI took a special interest was liturgy, insofar as it is intrinsically and essentially tied to

36   Politi, *Joseph Ratzinger. Crisi di un papato*, 85.

faith—that is, to its proclamation and celebration. Cardinal Ratzinger's views on the subject were well known.[37] For example, in a famous interview given to Vittorio Messori in 1985, the then-Cardinal Ratzinger expressed taedium and dismay at the current state of Catholic worship, which, he said had been reduced to "the level of a parish tea party" and the "intelligibility of a popular newspaper," in such a way that it had become confusing, boring, banal, and run-of-the-mill.[38] Also notable was Cardinal Ratzinger's book entitled *The Spirit of the Liturgy*. Released in Germany in 2000, the book took its inspiration from the noted theologian Romano Guardini, whom Ratzinger admired. It is no surprise that once he became pope, Ratzinger got busy with fixing up a few liturgical matters. Shortly after being elected, he appointed a new Secretary to the Congregation for Divine Worship, Archbishop Ranjith, and a new papal Master of Ceremonies (2007), Monsignor Guido Marini.

There is a clear connection between Ratzinger's theological thinking (much influenced by the German liturgical movement and Romano Guardini[39]) and his exercise of the Petrine ministry. We can see the background of this in his speech to the Roman Curia in December of 2005, in which he articulated his understanding of Vatican II and the post-conciliar period (hints of which we also see in the last speech of his pontificate[40]). The pope's fundamental assertion is that a correct interpretation of the Church in today's era must be tied to the logic of "reform," acknowledging continuity with the past and avoiding abrupt breaks from it (i.e., strict "discontinuity"). The Latin liturgy must

---

37 Joseph Ratzinger, *Opera omnia*, vol. XI, *Teologia della liturgia. La fondazione sacramentale dell'esistenza Cristiana* (Vatican City: LEV, 2010).

38 Vittorio Messori, *The Ratzinger Report* (San Francisco: Ignatius Press, 1983), 121.

39 Emery de Gaál, *The Theology of Pope Benedict XVI: The Christocentric Shift* (New York: Palgrave Macmillan, 2010), 39.

40 Benedict XVI, Meeting with the Parish Priests and the Clergy of Rome, 14 February 2013. See *Acta Apostolicae Sedis*, 105 (2013): 283–294.

follow the same logic. According to Ratzinger, the crisis of the Church and the crisis of faith are in strict correlation with the "collapse of the liturgy, which at times is even celebrated *etsi Deus non daretur:* as if it is no consequence to the liturgy whether God exists and whether he speaks to us and listens to us."[41] To reinvigorate the faith, therefore, a liturgical renewal is absolutely essential.

The first thing Benedict did to spark this renewal occurred on 22 February 2007, when he published an Apostolic Exhortation on the liturgy entitled *Sacramentum Caritatis,* which represented the fruit of the bishops' discussions and suggestions in the preceding Synod (October 2005) dedicated to the theme of the Eucharist. This was the first major document released during his pontificate. The Apostolic Exhortation closely followed John Paul II's teaching on the liturgy (expounded in the Apostolic Letter *Mane Nobiscum Domine* and the Encyclical Letter *Ecclesia de Eucharistia*) and was clearly in line with *The Spirit of the Liturgy.* It must also be read in conjunction with *Deus Caritas Est* in that there is an inseparable link between Christian love and the Eucharist. The document, albeit highly theological, does not fail to touch on concrete aspects of the liturgy—namely, respect for the liturgical books, gestures, silence, words, music, posture, and dress. He takes a firm position on sacred architecture (which must impart a unity to the various parts of the sanctuary), liturgical music (giving pride of place to Gregorian chant), the structure of the liturgical celebration (from a well-prepared homily to a modest exchange of peace and more). He even denounces liturgical abuses and proposes a greater use of Latin, especially in massive, multi-national celebrations and in the liturgical formation of seminarians. Reactions to Benedict's proposal to recover the Latin language were many and varied, ranging from strong approval (by the English Latin Society, for example[42]) to a complete lack of

---

41   Joseph Ratzinger, *La mia vita: autobiografia* (San Paolo: Cinisello Balsamo, 1997), 115.

42   Shawn Tribe "British Declaration in Support of the Liberalization of the 1962 Missale Romanum," in *New Liturgical Movement*, 29 Ja-

understanding (some thought pope was making a huge mistake[43]). In this arena, we must also remember his establishment of the Pontifical Academy *Latinitas* (10 November 2012).

The pope was more directly involved in liturgical matters than in other matters, and this involvement was proactive and creative. He saw no contradiction between approving, supporting, and defending the so-called "extraordinary form" (see the Motu Proprio *Summorum Pontificum*, 7 July 2007[44]) and allowing for the customs of the Neo-Catechumenal Way (even if certain practices are still open to question). These are two very different liturgical styles, but they are both Catholic. It is precisely the Holy See that guarantees their catholicity, such that these styles—dissimilar as they are—act as a sort of centripetal force of unity.

Without going into the specifics of *Summorum Pontificum*—a document we will examine more closely when we talk about Christian unity—suffice it to say that it gave greater latitude for celebrating the so-called Tridentine Mass—now referred to as the "Extraordinary Form" of the Roman Rite—on the basis of "continuity," a theological concept invoked by the pope on several occasions, as we have seen.

We should recall that before assuming the Chair of Peter, at the end of the 1990s, Ratzinger had already clearly stated his thoughts on the matter:

> I am of the opinion, to be sure, that the old rite should
> be granted much more generously to all those who de-
> sire it. It's impossible to see what could be dangerous
> or unacceptable about that. A community is calling its
> very being into question when it suddenly declares that
> what until now was its holiest and highest possession

nuary 2007. Accessed at http://www.newliturgicalmovement.org/2007/01/british-declaration-in-support-of.html#.U2yFF4F_uEO.

43   James Carrol, "Pope Benedict's Mistake," *Boston Globe*, 16 July 2007.
44   Benedict XVI, "Motu Proprio *Summorum Pontificum*," 7 July 2007, *Acta Apostolicae Sedis*, n. 99 (2007): 777–781.

is strictly forbidden and when it makes the longing for
it seem downright indecent.[45]

Cardinal Ratzinger was clearly willing to speak in defense of
the Tridentine Mass.[46]

With the promulgation of the new Motu Proprio, the Tridentine
Mass could be celebrated by any priest, at any time, in any season
of the liturgical year according to a format known as *sine populo*,
and the faithful could participate in such masses at their own discretion. In parishes where there is a stable group of faithful adher-
ing to the traditional form, the pastor is invited to provide for their
needs on a regular basis. If the pastor fails to meet their needs, they
may turn to the local bishop, and if the local bishop fails to find a
way of providing them the Extraordinary Form of the Mass, the
faithful may turn to the Pontifical Commission *Ecclesia Dei*.

Some bishops were enthusiastically in favor of the Motu Proprio, others groaned at the mention of it, and still others took a
public stance against it.[47] Several tried to pit bishops against bishops and pastors against theologians, even though there were
many in the latter group who were openly favorable to the Motu
Proprio.[48] The consensus in favor was stronger among young
priests and seminarians. Within the space of a few months, quite
a few publications appeared in opposition to the pope's decree.[49]

---

45 Joseph Cardinal Ratzinger, *Salt of the Earth* (San Francisco: Ignatius
    Press, 1997), 176.
46 David G. Bonagura Jr., "The Future of the Roman Rite: Reading Be-
    nedict in Light of Ratzinger," in *Antiphon*, 13 (2009): 228–246.
47 Cf. Alberto Carosa, "L'opposizione al motu proprio *Summorum Pon-
    tificum*," in *Fede e Cultura* (Verona, 2010); Andrea Grillo, *Oltre Pio V.
    La riforma liturgica nel conflitto di interpretazioni* (Brescia: Queriniana,
    2007).
48 Cf. Agostino Montan, "L'istruzione Universae Ecclesiae nella pro-
    spettiva del motu proprio Summorum Pontificum," in *Rivista Li-
    turgica*, 98 (2011): 895.
49 C Cf. Paul Bovens, "Chronique inachevée des publications autour
    de la Lettre apostolique en forme de motu proprio *Summorum Pon-*

After a long hiatus, the liturgy was suddenly once again a main topic of discussion in the Church.

Even if the pope's interventions in liturgical matters were not meant to impose uniformity, he nonetheless wanted to overcome what he defined as the "confusion" and "fragmentation" of the liturgy.[50] Over time, he envisioned a peaceful coexistence of the ordinary and extraordinary forms. Cardinal Koch openly commented on this vision: "Benedict XVI knows well that, in the long run, we will not be satisfied with the simultaneous, parallel existence of the Ordinary and Extraordinary Forms of the Roman Rite, and that the Church will need a single, common rite."[51] If Koch is right, there will likely be a gradual, reciprocal fusion of the two forms. However, this did not happen in the years following the Motu Proprio.

In any case, between 2007 and 2010, the greatest number of requests for the celebration of the older form came from Europe, North America, and Australia. There was also a significant number of requests from Latin American countries, but only a few from Asia and Africa.[52] The issue, therefore, seemed most prevalent in the Western world. In hindsight, it seems like a lot of racket over a minor issue, but if we look closely at the impact it had on significant areas of the Catholic population, the issue is hardly minor.

Benedict's efforts to renew the liturgy were also being carried out on a theological level, which entailed a reexamination of the vernacular translations of the Roman Rite. Here, too, Ratzinger's imprint is clear. At the consecration of the wine, the English translation once read: "Take this, all of you, and drink from it: this is the cup of my blood, the blood of the new and everlasting

---

tificum de Benoît XVI," *Ehemerides Theologicae Lovanienses*, n. 84 (2008): 529–536.

50 Ratzinger, *Opera omnia*, vol. XI, *Teologia della liturgia*, op. cit., 758.

51 Kurt Koch, "Dalla liturgia antica un ponte ecumenico," *L'Osservatore Romano*, 15 May 2011.

52 Cf. Montan, *L'istruzione Universae ecclesiae nella prospettiva del motu proprio* Summorum Pontificum, op. cit., 899.

covenant. It will be shed for you and *for all* so that sins may be forgiven. Do this in memory of me." In 2006, the formula was changed: "Take this, all of you, and drink from it: for this is the chalice of my Blood, the Blood of the new and eternal covenant, which will be poured out for you and *for many* for the forgiveness of sins. Do this in memory of me." The Spanish translation was similarly changed, but there was no need to change the French, since it was already in conformity with the Latin (*"pour vous et la multitude"*).[53] The Italian was also not immediately changed because the translation was already under review by the national bishops' conference and the Congregation for Divine Worship. The changes to the English and Spanish raised considerable controversy. The pope directly intervened in the German discussion of how to translate *pro multis* with a letter written to the bishops in 2012, urging them to change the translation.[54] He wanted to persuade them rather than impose it. This reveals a particular Ratzingerian trait that ended up being both a strength and a weakness in his pontificate.

We should note that Benedict XVI was carrying out his liturgical reforms in gestures as well as with words. Beginning in 2008, Holy Communion was distributed directly on the tongue rather than in the hand during pontifical liturgies, and communicants

53 Congregazione per il Culto Divino e la Disciplina dei Sacramenti, "Circolare a tutti i presidenti delle Conferenze episcopali nazionali, Sulla traduzione in volgare dell'espressione *pro multis* contenuta nella formula della Consacrazione del Prezioso Sangue, nel Canone della S. messa," 17 October 2006, *Notitiae*, n. 43 (2006): 441–443 (in other languages, 444–458); Congregazione per il Culto Divino e la Disciplina dei Sacramenti, *Vox Clara* Committee, press release, 28–29 April 2010, *L'Osservatore Romano*, English language edition, 5 May 2010; Gianni Valente "Come tradurre pro multis. La lettera della Congregazione per il Culto divino e la Disciplina dei sacramenti," *30Giorni*, n. 4 (2010). Accessed at: http://www.30giorni.it/articoli_id_22502_l1.htm.
54 Benedict XVI "Lettera al presidente della Conferenza episcopale tedesca," 14 April 2012, *L'Osservatore Romano*, German language edition, 11 May 2012.

received kneeling rather than standing.[55] This reflected the pope's deep conviction that the liturgy should reflect God's true presence in the sacrament, and that He should be adored.

We should make it clear that Benedict's liturgical reforms reflect ideas he already held as a cardinal, and that they are not limited to the directives of *Summorum Pontificum*. Taken collectively, these changes certainly aimed to draw back many traditionalists, precisely by showing that they could be in union with more contemporary styles of Catholic worship. It was an attempt at balance, but a balance with a clear theological underpinning rather than merely weighing Church politics.

New demographics in the College of Cardinals

All that we have said regarding Ratzinger's understanding of "faith" (detectable in his theological and liturgical vision) applies to his day-to-day governance of the Church and the intra-ecclesial relationships that guide his decision-making. That is why it is important to consider his appointments to the College of Cardinals and his relationships with them. The College of Cardinals is a key body in the Church, both because of the advice it gives the pope on important matters, and because it is responsible for electing his successor. Benedict XVI modified the process of papal elections slightly by making small changes to John Paul II's norms published in 1996. In 2007, he reestablished the rule of a two-thirds majority of cardinal electors gathered in the conclave needed to elect a pope, rather than a simple majority (which was already allowed after a set period of unsuccessful ballots[56]). Benedict wanted to avoid the possible election of an overly divisive

---

55   Cf. Ufficio delle Celebrazioni Liturgiche del Sommo Pontefice, "La Comunione ricevuta sulla lingua e in ginocchio." Accessed at: http://www.vatican.va/news_services/liturgy/details/ns_lit_doc_20091117_comunione_it.html.

56   Benedict XVI, "Motu Proprio *de aliquibus mutationibus in normis de electione Romani Pontificis*," 11 June 2007, *Acta Apostolicae Sedis*, n. 99 (2007): 776–777.

candidate who would be thwarted in achieving his goals. In 2013, a few months before he stepped down from the papacy, he made further, minor modifications and clarified a few passages in the document.[57]

A pope must always keep the College of Cardinals at a sufficient number as members age and die. This is not a simple, straightforward task. The famous *Pasquino* ("talking statue") in Rome once displayed an epigram in the nineteenth century that sums up the situation: *La difficoltà non sta in der fabbricà i cappelli, ma in der trovà le teste de appiccicajieli* (the difficulty is not in making the hats, but in finding the heads to stick them on).[58]

Membership in the College of Cardinals ultimately depends on whom the pope wants to admit. He announces his choices in anticipation of an upcoming consistory. There are certain paths that normally lead to a red had, including a *cursus honorum* in the Roman Curia (either as a curial official or a diplomat) or by being an archbishop of a significant cardinalature see. Certain ecclesiastical sees traditionally have had a cardinal-archbishop, such as large, capital cities or historically important sees.[59] Some curial appointments inevitably lead to the College of Cardinals. Although it is not written in stone, it is almost automatic after a long service in the Roman Curia that an official will be made a cardinal. Hence

---

57   Benedict XVI, "Motu Proprio *Normas nonnullas*," 22 February 2013, *Acta Apostolicae Sedis*, n. 105 (2013): 253–257.

58   Jean LeBlanc, *Dictionnaire biographiques des cardinaux du XIXe siècle: contribution à l'histoire du Sacré Collège sous les pontificats de Pie VII, Léon XII, Pie VIII, Grégoire XVI, Pie IX et Léon XIII, 1800–1903* (Montreal: Wilson & Lafleur Ltée, 2007), 71.

59   These include Venice, Naples, Bologna, Toledo, Lisbon, Bordeaux, Esztergom, Vienna, Mechelen, Lyon, Westminster, Prauge, Paris, Cologne, and others. A study of cardinalature appointments between 1851 and 1929 in ecclesial sees that regularly have a cardinal archbishop (99 dioceses), it emerges that only a part of them (between 13 and 24 sees) have reserved the right of appointing their shepherd to the College of Cardinals. Cf. Philip A. Viton, "'Obligatory' Cardinalatial Appointments, 1851–1929," *Archivum Historiae Pontificiae*, 21 (1983): 275–294, particularly 284.

a pope does not generally have to choose which curial officials he will make cardinals. The same holds for archbishops of important residential sees. But his selection of those outside these parameters is quite free. In these cases, it is his responsibility to get to know those candidates well and assess their worthiness for carrying out their duties within the College.[60] Membership in the College of Cardinals is not necessarily permanent. There have been times when cardinals were stripped of the honor.[61]

There were five consistories in Benedict XVI's pontificate in which ninety new members[62] (sixteen non-voting[63]) were inducted into the College of Cardinals (March 2006, November 2007, November 2010, February 2012, and November 2012). These appointments had a significant impact on ecclesiastical geopolitics.

As with every pontificate, is not always easy to decipher the reasons for which Benedict made the cardinalature appointments he did. More specifically, it is not easy to discern the influence

60   Cf. John F. Broderick, "The Sacred College of Cardinals: Size and Geographical Composition (1099–1986)," *Archivum Historiae Pontificiae*, n. 25 (1987), 10; Joël-Benoît d'Onorio, *Le Pape e le gouvernement de l'Eglise* (Paris: Fleurrus-Tardy, 1992), 424.

61   Cf. D'Onorio, *Le Pape e le gouvernement de l'eglise* o cit. 427 ; claude Prudhomme, *Stratégie missionnaire du Saint-Siège sous Léon XIII (1878–1903). Centralisation romaine et défis culturels, ecole française de Rome*, Rome 1994, (Collection de l'Ecole française de Rome, 186), 147.

62   Cf. Nicolas Diat, *L'homme qui ne voulait pas être pape. Histoire secrète d'un règne* (Paris: Albin Michel, 2014), 367–379.

63   Cf. Hans-Joachim Kracht, *Lexicon der Kardinäle 1058–2010*, Vol. 1, *Kardinäle unter Benedikt XVI. Kardinäle 1058–2010: Buchstabe A*; vol. 2, *Am 18.2. und am 24.11.2012 Kreierte Kardinäle, Kardinäle 1058–2010: Buchstabe B*, in collaboration with Pamela Santoni (Cologne: Erzbischöflische Diözesan-und Dombibliothek, 2012–2013) (Libelli Rhenani, 45). An informative and synthetic overview (in Italian) of Benedict's composition of the College of Cardinals can be found at https://it.wikipedia.org/wiki/Evoluzione_del_collegio_cardinalizio_durante_il_pontificato_di_Benedict_XVI, and https://it.wikipedia.org/wiki/Concistori_di_papa_Benedict_XVI.

that the Secretary of State had on these decisions. Journalists at the time speculated that Cardinal Bertone enjoyed the full trust of the pope, even when it came to compiling lists of candidates for the College or Cardinals.[64]

For example, the media considered the consistory of 18 February 2012 an overwhelming success for Cardinal Bertone.[65] Some even referred to it as the *concistoro bertoniano*.[66] The inequilibrium of that consistory may have prompted Benedict to convoke a new one for the following November (he was also probably thinking of his plans to retire, even though the rest of the world knew nothing about it at the time). This consistory was revolutionary in that, for the first time in history, there were no Italians or Europeans on the list. But let's look at these events in chronological order.

In March of 2006, the pope created fifteen cardinals, three of whom were beyond the age of eighty and therefore ineligible to elect the next pope. The *prima creatura* (i.e., this is how the first cardinal appointed by a pope is customarily referred to) was Ratzinger's successor at the Congregation for the Doctrine of the Faith, William Joseph Levada.

In November of 2007, the pope created twenty-three cardinals, of which five were ineligible to vote. In November of 2010, he created twenty-four cardinals, of which twenty were eligible to vote and four were not. These last appointments more clearly reflected the pope's personality and thinking. Angelo Amato, for example, the new Prefect for the Congregation of Saints, had been Secretary of the Congregation for the Doctrine of the Faith when Ratzinger was Prefect. We can also think of Robert Sarah, President of the Pontifical Council *Cor Unum*; the American canonist Raymond Burke, Prefect for the Tribunal of the *Segnatura Apostolica*; the Swiss theologian Kurt Koch, President of the Council for the Promotion of Christian Unity; the Italian curial official

---

64   Cf. Diat, *L'homme qui ne voulait pas être pape*, 367.
65   Cf. Politi, *Joseph Ratzinger: Crisi di un papato*, 266.
66   "Le consistoire bertonien," in Diat, *L'homme qui ne voulait pas être pape*, 371.

Mauro Piacenza, Prefect of the Congregation for Clergy; the Archbishop of Colombo (Sri Lanka) Malcolm Ranjith; and the Archbishop of Munich, Reinhard Marx. Among the cardinals elected beyond the voting age of eighty we have other examples of individuals whom the pope highly esteemed and with whom he cultivated personal friendships: the historian Walter Brandmüller (an expert on the councils), a Belgian historian of religions, Julien Ries, and the musician, musicologist, and composer Domenico Bartolucci (*maestro perpetuo* of the Sistine Choir), who at the time was the oldest man ever to have been made a cardinal.

In the aforementioned consistory of February 2012, the pope created twenty-two new cardinals, of whom four were beyond the age of eighty. There were seven Italians in the group. Eight of those elected were members of the Curia: Giuseppe Bertello (Governor of Vatican City State), Domenico Calcagno (President of APSA), Giuseppe Versaldi (Prefect of the Economic Affairs of the Holy See), Fernando Filoni (Prefect of Propaganda fide), Francesco Coccopalmiero (President of the Pontifical Council for Legislative Texts), Antonio Veglio (President of the Pontifical Council for Migrants), and João Braz de Aviz (Prefect of the Congregation for Religious Life). Also within the curial inner-circle was retired Spanish nuncio Santos Abril y Castello (Archpriest of the Basilica of Saint Mary Major). The seventh Italian on the list was Archbishop of Florence Giuseppe Betori, a friend of Cardinal Ruini. Among the residential archbishops appointed, we should mention Archbishop Timothy Dolan of New York, a man known for his dynamic personality and ability to reconcile international differences (the Italians referred to him as a "Yankee" who broke every cardinalature stereotype). Of the eighteen new elector-cardinals, ten came from within the curial bureaucracy. Most of the Italians were considered loyal to Cardinal Bertone. Among those beyond the voting age were German theologian Karl Josef Becker, a Jesuit who taught at the Pontifical Gregorian University and served as a consultor to the Congregation for the Doctrine of the Faith for years.

At the "reparatory" consistory of November 2012, all six cardinals seem to have been chosen personally by the pope: the

American James Harvey (once Prefect of the Pontifical Household and then appointed Archpriest of the Basilica of Saint Paul Outside the Walls), the Lebanese Maronite Patriarch Bechara Boutros Raï, the Indian Baselios Cleemis Thottunkal (Primate of the Catholic Syro-Malankara Church), the Nigerian John Olorunfemi Onaiyekan (Archbishop of Abuja), the Columbian Rubén Salazar Gomez (Archbishop of Bogotà), and the Filipino Luis Antonio Tagle (Archbishop of Manila).

Looking at these nominations collectively, we can draw a few general conclusions. Already beginning with the consistory of 2012, the majority of cardinal-electors had been appointed by Benedict, who would therefore have had a considerable impact on any eventual conclave.

Of the seventy-four cardinal-electors nominated by Benedict, 52.7% were European (thirty-nine, to be exact, of whom twenty-one were Italian, meaning 28.4% of the total), 14.9% were North American (eleven, including one Mexican and nine from the United States), 9.45% from Central and South America (seven cardinals), 13.5% from Asia (10 cardinals), 9.45% from Africa (7 cardinals), and 0% from Oceania. If we consider all ninety of the cardinals nominated—that is, if we include the non-electors—the picture does not change much: 58% were European (52 cardinals, of which twenty-six were Italian, making up 29% of the total), 12.1% were from North America (11 cardinals), 8.9% from Central and South America (8 cardinals), 12.1% from Asia (11 cardinals), 8.9% from Africa (8 cardinals), and 0% from Oceana. There is a clear European stamp on the College of Cardinals, with the non-voting members reaching as high as 81% European.

Geographical factors within the College of Cardinals must be taken with a grain of salt. In a way, appointments from within the Roman Curia transcend any national categorization. Those working in the Curia or diplomatic corps have a mindset often referred to as the *spirito romano* ("Roman spirit"), which is more commanding than one's geographical background. Dante wryly captured this when he wrote, *"di quella Roma onde Cristo è romano"* ("of that

Rome where Christ is a Roman").[67] In other words, ideological factors are sometimes weightier than national factors. Cardinals with an academic background are an example of this. In fact, sixteen of the non-electors are retired professors (Vanhoye, Navarrete, Betti, Sgreccia, Brandmüller, Bartolucci, Ries, Grech, and Becker), with the rest being two diplomats (Cordero Lanza di Montezemolo and Coppa) and five pastors (Poreku Dery, Emmanuel III Delly, Karlic, Estepa Llaurens, and Muresan). A career in the diplomatic corps also speaks much louder than one's birthplace or pastoral service. Some cardinals hailing from "marginal" countries, in fact, carried out their *cursus honorum* within the Secretariat of State or within papal nunciatures, not counting those cardinals who worked for some period of time in Roman dicasteries. Furthermore, many of the cardinals appointed by Benedict did their priestly formation in Rome or at least imbibed the "Roman spirit" at the local seminaries in which they studied. The atmosphere within these limited circles is indeed "Catholic," but in a restricted, Roman sense.

Of the eight Latin Americans nominated, three were Brazilian, and all three spent their careers in the Roman Curia (Claudio Hummes, Odilo Scherer, and João Braz de Aviz). What is the most important factor to consider in these three? Curial service, cultural background, or membership in a religious community or movement? Clearly, we have to look closely at the personal biography of each individual cardinal, paying particular attention to how and where they were formed in their youth.

Another group of cardinals comes from a very particular theological, disciplinary, and spiritual atmosphere—namely, the Eastern Catholic tradition. These include three patriarchs (Chaldean, Coptic, and Maronite) and two Major-Archbishops (Syro-Malabar and Syro-Malankar). Over the last few decades, it has become the norm to include these patriarchs within the Sacred College of Cardinals, despite marginal voices who have expressed reservations about the practice (asserting that "patriarch" is a more theologically robust category than "cardinal").

67   Dante Alighieri, *Purgatorio*, Canto XXXII, v. 102.

Moreover, we cannot forget that some cardinals belong to religious families. Only thirteen of the new cardinals are religious, of which three are Jesuits, three Salesians and two Franciscans. These amounts to 14.4% of the new cardinals, a figure that has become typical since the nineteenth century. There are also some cardinals who belong to ecclesial movements or who are sympathetic to religious spiritualities, but it is hard to provide an exact or even an approximate number.

Even though beyond the scope of this book, there is other data about the cardinals important to consider, including their social and family background, their cultural formation, their academic training (especially in theology), and their success in pastoral ministry.

Reviewing the names of the nominees, one French commentator wrote:

> The cardinals created by Benedict XVI are a reflection of his pontificate. There are those who are similar to Joseph Ratzinger, sharing his lofty vision of a purified Church. There are career churchmen who unabashedly use every means at their disposal to get ahead. There are shadow men who work daily without any desire for recognition. If we put together all five consistories under him, we see *gravitas* and grace, Pharisee-ism and holiness, a respect for history and a fascination with what is of the moment.[68]

---

68 "Les cardinaux créés par Benoît XVI sont à l'image de son pontificat. Il y a les prélats qui ressemblent à Joseph Ratzinger, partageant avec fidélité sa vision élevée d'une Église purifiée, les ecclésiastiques carriéristes qui profiteront de tous les moyens à leur dispositions, sans vergogne, et les hommes de l'ombre, qui travaillent quotidiennement sans se soucier d'apparaître ou non en pleine lumière. Tout au long de cinq consistoires donnés à l'Église, il y a la pesanteur et la grâce, le pharisaïsme et la sainteté, l'histoire et le moment." Diat, *L'homme qui ne voulait pas être pape*, op. cit., 372.

Perhaps the same could be said about many pontificates, if not all.

The College of Cardinals has been studied closely throughout history and has been interpreted in every way possible. In recent times, journalists have tenuously tried to divvy it up into little groups: the "diplomats," the "Bertonians," the "Ambrosians,", the "Ratzingerians," the "Focolarini," the "Roman party," the "pastoral party," the "Opus Dei contingent," the "foreigners," and the "masons" (that is, those who, although seemingly having nothing to do with Freemasonry, act according to a power structure that closely resembles it").[69] These subdivisions, although they make curious and fascinating distinctions, have only a limited capacity to help us understand the College, because one and the same person can belong to different groups simultaneously, to the point that belonging in any particular one of them hardly tells us anything at all.

Within the College or Cardinals, it is important to distinguish those members who are able to exert some influence upon major Church decisions. These are obviously the cardinals who live in Rome and who are members of various congregations and tribunals within the Roman Curia, sometimes becoming Prefects of those dicasteries. Indeed, decisions made in these deliberative bodies have an impact that resounds throughout the entire Church. Curial cardinals are the pope's primary collaborators, and they consequently form a "residual" class within the College.[70] However, if we rely on the limited documentation currently available, we are unable to carry out an exhaustive study of how this class influences Church governance. We can only rely on rumors and oral reports.

69 Eric Frattini, *I corvi del Vaticano*, with the collaboration of Valeria Moroni, Sperling & Kupfer, Milano, 2013 (Original edition: *Los cuervos del Vaticano*, 2012), 258.
70 "We regard curial cardinals (along with discretionary diocesan appointments) as forming a 'residual' class of cardinals." Viton, "'Obligatory' Cardinalatial Appointments, 1851–1929," op. cit., 277.

Cardinals residing in Rome also heavily influence the appointment of bishops, about which we will speak in the next chapter, given that Benedict's pontificate presents some exceptional cases that deserve special consideration.

Religious life

Even if only a few cardinals belong to religious congregations or orders, we must remember that these entities continue to have an enormous impact on the life of the Church, despite the problems with religious life in the twentieth and twenty-first centuries that we discussed earlier. In a few cases, these problems include scandals of embezzlement and moral depravity. But there are also more subtle problems touching upon the very raison d'être of communal living in a world increasingly individualistic; a world that jeopardizes the very existence of the Church's oldest and most venerable religious orders and congregations, including smaller institutes (especially women's) founded in the 1800s and 1900s. Nevertheless, new forms of religious life, as fragile as they are, speak to its enduring vitality.[71] If we look at census figures for new communities, we see unparalleled and increasing energy (there were over 775 new foundations between 1911 and 2010).[72] The data available to us is increasing and changing constantly as religious life spreads more evenly across the globe.[73] Between 1911

71   On this topic, see Roberto Fusco, Giancarlo Rocca (ed.), *Nuove forme di vita consacrata* (Vatican City: Urbaniana University Press, 2010); Roberto Fusco, Giancarlo Rocca, Stefano Vita (ed.), *La svolta dell'innovazione. Le nuove forme di vita consacrat*a (Vatican City: Urbaniana University Press, 2015).

72   For more reflections on new ecclesial communities, see Giancarlo Rocca (ed.), *Primo censimento delle nuove comunità* (Vatican City: Urbaniana University Press, 2010), particularly 9–11.

73   A more recent census completed in 2015 shows that the total number of new communities between the beginning of the twentieth and twenty-first centuries has increased to another 77 that had previously not appeared in a census. Cf. Giancarlo Rocca, *Nuovi Istituti,*

and 1950, there were only twenty or so new communities founded. This grew by leaps and bounds in the decade spanning 1970–1980 (with 190 new foundations) and 1980–1990 (with 222 new foundations). The United States of America leads in these new foundations (205 have been accredited), followed by Italy (200), France (161), Canada (47), Brazil (44), and Spain (2). Altogether, these new foundations span forty countries. Most of these are in the West, just as Church leadership continues to be concentrated in the West. For every hundred or so new institutes of consecrated life, there are about ten that close. In the wake of Vatican II, the trend of new institutes was to get back to the roots of communal Christian living with as few rules as possible. But the following decades have also witnessed serious internal reforms to the structures of older institutes. The most innovative communities are mixed—composed of men and women—under an overarching rule. There are also more traditional institutes that have collaborating branches for men and women acting as a single spiritual family. Newer forms of consecrated life also involve laity, even married couples, who are fully active in the institute and take part in apostolic works.

Ratzinger's relationship to religious life—and more specifically monastic life—is already evident in the name he chose as pope, as well as in his Wednesday catechesis, a large portion of which was dedicated to monastic life (within the more general topic of the fathers of the Church).[74] A salient moment came in a speech Benedict gave in 2008 at the Collège des Bernardins (once a Cistercian monastery) in Paris.[75] He sketched out the ideal of monastic life in Europe and explained its spiritual and intellectual contribution to the continent's cultural development. This interpretation is at the

in Fusco, Rocca, Vita (ed.), *La svolta dell'innovazione. Le nuove forme di vita consacrata*, op. cit., 277–308.

74 Borja Vivanco Díaz, "Monaquismo en el magisterio de Benedicto XVI," *Studia monastica*, n. 57 (2015): 197–218.

75 Benedict XVI, "Discorso in occasione dell'incontro con il mondo della cultura al Collège des Bernardins, Parigi," 12 September 2008, *Acta Apostolicae Sedis*, n. 100 (2008): 721–730.

heart of Benedict's enormous respect for monasticism. He ties the origin and development of Europe's cultural identity to the monastic dynamism of the Middle Ages.

If religious life has been so important historically, what are we to say about it today? The pope interprets the significance of consecrated life within the wider horizon of contemporary culture and the crisis of faith. The pope has touched on this theme multiple times, urging religious men and women to embark—individually and communally—on the deliberately chosen path of a rigorous faith lived fully and courageously in freely witnessing to Christ.[76] What we have said on other matters also applies here: the pope avails himself of his teaching authority to interact with religious, proposing a clear, Christological way to them.[77] In his speeches to religious men and women, Benedict XVI, beside expressing his highest esteem for their state of life,[78] constantly invites them to examine what is essential to their existence—that is, a vigorous faith life lived out in wisdom and humility (the way of the cross).[79] The pope invites all religious to a radical renewal in Christ. The crisis, however, remains, and it is not just a crisis of numbers, but of the relationship of religious life to the life of the Church.

Hence the pope's support of reforms such as that of the Legionnaires of Christ after the heinous crimes of their founder,

76   Cf. Francesco Lambiasi, "Prefazione," in *Come ceri accesi. La vita consacrata secondo papa Benedetto,* Maria Marcellina Pedico, ed. (Roma: Centro Studi Usmi, 2013), 6–8.
77   Pier Giordano Cabra, "Il pontificato di Benedetto XVI e la vita consacrata (2005–2013)," in Pedico (ed.), *Come ceri accesi. La vita consacrata secondo papa Benedetto,* op. cit., 17–25; Giuseppe Costa, "La trilogia su *Gesù di Nazaret* di Benedetto XVI. Una bussola cristologica per la vita consacrata," in Pedico (ed.), *Come ceri accesi. La vita consacrata secondo papa Benedetto,* op. cit., 27–31.
78   Maria Gabriella Bortot, "Bellezza e stima per la vita consacrata. Le Omelie della Giornata del 2 febbraio," in Pedico (ed.), *Come ceri accesi. La vita consacrata secondo papa Benedetto,* op. cit., 49–54.
79   Maria Marcellina Pedico, "Presentazione," in Pedico (ed.), *Come ceri accesi. La vita consacrata secondo papa Benedetto,* op. cit., 11–13.

Marcial Maciel, became public.[80] The pope took a direct interest in the reform of the Legion. He appointed Cardinal Velasio de Paolis to oversee it. Cardinal de Paolis was assisted by Monsignors Mario Marchesi and Brian Farrell, as well as by Jesuit Father Gianfranco Ghirlanda, and Father Agostino Montan, S.C. Whenever Benedict found that institutes were not living up to the expectations of religious life, he was not afraid to suppress new movements that speciously seemed fruitful, such as the Monastic Family Fraternity of Jesus (2010).[81] Other new entities needed help from going down wrong paths, such as the Community of the Beatitudes, which was dissolved in order to be reestablished under the guidance of the Extraordinary Pontifical Commissioner, Dominican Brother Henry Donneaud, in the wake of revelations of sexual abuse committed by their founder and a few other members of the group.[82]

Another crisis that arose and came to the public's attention regarded women's religious life in the United States. In 2008, the Vatican Congregation for Institutes of Consecrated Life and Societies of Apostolic Life, headed by Cardinal Franc Rodé, began an apostolic visitation to investigate the quality of women's religious life in the United States, not including cloistered communities.[83] The visit was prompted by the apparent crisis among women's

80   Cf. Paolo Rodari, Andrea Tornielli, *Attacco a Ratzinger. Accuse e scandali, profezie e complotti contro Benedetto XVI* (Milan: Piemme, 2010), 217–230; Gianluigi Nuzzi, *Sua Santità. Le carte segrete di Benedetto XVI* (Milan: Chiarelettere, 2012), 196–204.
81   Sandro Magister, *Il professor Ratzinger? Troppo buono*, 26 August 2011. Accessed at: : http://chiesa.espresso.repubblica.it/articolo/1349175.
82   Cf. "Intervista di Anne-Bénédicte Hoffner a Henry Donneaud," in *La Croix*, 1st December 2011: http://www.la-croix.com/Actualite/France/-Henry-donneaud-Les-Beatitudes-meritent-de-vivre-a-condition-de-se-puri- fier-_EP_-2011-12-01-74245.
83   Cf. Ludovica Eugenio, "Roma contro la Leadership Conference of Women Religious," in Mauro Castagnaro and Ludovica Eugenio, *Il dissenso soffocato: un'agenda per papa Francesco* (Bari: Edizioni la Meridiana, 2013), 203–237.

religious communities in the States. Between 1945 and 2008, membership in women's communities fell by 45%, and the average age of active religious women was around seventy.[84] Looking at statistics alone, other figures stick out: there were about 180,000 active religious women and cloistered nuns in 1965, and in 2009, there were only 59,000.[85] These numbers, however, can be misleading, depending on whom we include (those who have made temporary vows, solemn vows, or novices? Do we include only communities of pontifical rite, or also those of diocesan rite?). The religious women belonging to the Leadership Conference of Women Religious (L.C.W.R.)—an organization that did not experience the same drop in numbers as did the overall number of religious (60,642 in 2007, dropping to 46,451 in 2011[86])—were surprised by the apostolic visitation and expressed confusion over its scope and aims.[87] Their dismay was shared by other organizations such as the National Coalition of American Nuns (N.C.A.N.), who believed the visitation was "disorganized, questionable, and partial," in addition to being "unnecessary."[88] Sister Clare Millea, a member of another organization of religious the United States—the Council of Major Superiors of Women Religious (C.M.S.W.R.)—was charged with overseeing the visitation. N.C.A.N. considered her to represent the "old style" of religious life.[89]

It was Sister Millea's responsibility to organize the details of the visitation and, at the end of the process (which included personal dialogues with superior generals, responses to questionnaires, and on-site visits), to send Cardinal Rodé a confidential report of her findings.

A little later, the main cooperative body of religious women in the United States, the Leadership Conference of Women

84   Ibid., 205.
85   Cf. Ibid., 214.
86   Cf. Ibid., 227.
87   Cf. Ibid., 206.
88   Ibid., 207.
89   Ibid., 207.

Religious (L.C.W.R.), to which 95% of religious belong, was under examination by the Congregation for the Doctrine of the Faith between February 2009 and April 2012. The congregation was troubled by both the theological teaching (especially in ecclesiology and soteriology) and the moral teaching (especially in human sexuality and issues involving life and death) of the organization.[90] This meant that religious women in the United States were under observation by two Roman dicasteries.

Oversight of the investigation was entrusted to Bishop Leonard Blaire of Toledo, Ohio, a member of the doctrinal commission of the United States Conference of Catholic Bishops. The first step in the process was to send out a questionnaire to every superior general in order to get a comprehensive picture of the state of religious life throughout the country. This would be followed by an on-site visit.

In taking these steps, Benedict XVI and the Roman Curia were concerned with "basic matters of Catholic faith and moral practice,"[91] rather than the peripheral issues of consecrated life. The congregation recognized that there were "serious doctrinal problems that affect many in Consecrated Life," marked by a diminution of the "fundamental Christological center and focus of religious consecration" and consequently of a "constant and lively sense of the Church."[92] In January of 2011, following Bishop Blair's investigation, the Cardinal members of the Congregation for the Doctrine of the Faith acknowledged that "the current doctrinal and pastoral situation of the L.C.W.R. is grave and a matter of serious concern, also given the influence the L.C.W.R. has on religious Congregations in other parts of the world." Consequently, the Cardinals suggested that the Holy See make a canonical intervention to enact a

90 Cf. Politi, *Joseph Ratzinger. Crisi di un papato*, op. cit., 315.
91 Prefect of the Congregation for the Doctrine of the Faith, "Doctrinal Assessment of the Leadership Conference of Women Religious," 18 April 2012: http://www.vatican.va/roman_curia/congregations/cfaith/documents/rc_con_cfaith_doc_20120418_assessment-lcwr_en.html
92 Ibid.

reform of the L.C.W.R. The pope approved the resolution and decided to appoint an archbishop delegate (assisted by a group of consultors) to deal with the problems. The delegate chosen was Peter Sartain, Archbishop of Seattle, who acted as a bridge between the L.C.W.R., the United States Conference of Catholic Bishops, and the Holy See in carrying out a renewal of the organization through a revision of its statues, projects, and programs. The delicate points involved questions of faith and dissent toward the Church's Magisterium, sometimes in the form of an open unwillingness to accept its teaching. In particular, the organization was in opposition to John Paul II's teaching on the prohibition of the ordination of women in *Ordinatio Sacerdotalis*, and held dubious positions on the right to life. The president of L.C.W.R. was "shocked" by the Vatican intervention and considered its evaluation a collection of "unfounded accusations."[93]

Archbishop Sartain noted that, in the past, there had been friction between the American bishops and religious, between one congregation and another, and between factions within individual religious congregations regarding Church teaching, discipline, lifestyle, and mission.[94] The Vatican should therefore take the visitation as an opportunity to facilitate reconciliation. Moreover, women religious generally are not as concerned with doctrinal questions as with their lifestyles. In short, it was hard to bridge communication across the Atlantic. Each side went its own way. There were meetings nonetheless, both in Rome and in the United States. At a meeting in Baltimore in the fall of 2012, Archbishop Sartain was assisted by Bishops Blair and Paprocki, who seemed less willing to budge on the importance of doctrinal issues. The end of Benedict XVI's pontificate still did not see a resolution to this case.

What is most striking about Rome's intervention in this affair is that the topics under discussion were at the heart of Benedict's

---

93   Eugenio, "Roma contro la Leadership Conference of Women Religious," op. cit., 223, 230.

94   Cf. Ibid., 232.

pontificate, and they exemplify the wider crisis in the Church about how to conceive the Church's nature. On the one hand, Rome and the North American episcopate represented a new brand of Catholicism, loyal to the pope, attentive to doctrine and morals and flourishing in new vocations—and on the other hand a brand of Catholicism mostly concerned with social issues and most often marked by ecclesial dissent. It is no accident that the L.C.W.R. was awarded the Pax Christi U.S.A. prize in 2010 for its commitment to peace and justice (the recognition speech was delivered by Auxiliary Bishop Gabino Zavala, president of the American section who subsequently had to resign because he had fathered two children)[95] and in 2013 it received a prize from the Herbert Haag Foundation in Germany—presided over by Hans Küng—for hailing "freedom in the Church."[96] The issue of women religious in America is simply a microcosm of the larger problem of a Catholic Christian's core identity and the role of the Church in the world. This was an overarching tension that imbued the entire pontificate of Benedict XVI.

Ecclesial movements

Another important part of understanding the priorities of Pope Benedict's pontificate can be found in a driving force in the Catholic world that began to emerge in the second half of the twentieth century—namely, ecclesial movements.[97] These bodies brought together dedicated Catholic laity burning with a desire for a deeper faith that would help them witness Christ to the world in a way similar to religious and priests carrying out the new evangelization. These movements often found support from the successor of Peter in a way they didn't find support from the

95   Cf. Ibid., 217–218.
96   Cf. Ibid., 236–237.
97   Cf. Guzmán Carriquiry Lecour, "Movimenti ecclesiali," in Gianfranco Calabrese, Philip Goyret, Orazio Francesco Piazza (ed.), *Dizionario di ecclesiologia* (Roma: Città Nuova, 2010), 938–947.

local bishop in many cases. Bishops were divided on the question of their importance. Some accepted them with enthusiasm (depending on the particular movement in question) whereas others did everything to keep their distance.

The relationship between ecclesial movements and the Church is a crucial factor in how Christianity will develop in the future. Membership in the Church at large has become more abstract, and traditional ways of living a communal life are less relevant than they once were. Sometimes they are downright ignored. The old European continent has seen sharp drops in the active engagement of the Catholic laity. In Germany alone, it has become commonplace for baptized Catholics to abandon the faith through a formal act (*Kirchenaustritt*). In 2006, 84,000 Catholics formally left the Church in that country. There were 93,000 who left in 2007; 121,000 in 2008; and 181,000 in 2010. The election of a German pope did little to stop the hemorrhage; in fact, the rate doubled.[98] The entire European situation is complicated. In 2005, 18% of the European Union citizenry declared itself atheist. Only 52% declared itself believing. Knowledge of Christian teaching among the youth has been drastically reduced.[99] The Church is dealing both with a problem of non-belief, and with a problem of believers choosing to believe whatever they want. Younger generations tend to detach ethics from religion. We are living in a time when faith has become highly individualistic. The freedom of the individual is placed over the Church as an institution. The vibrancy of Catholicism is now seen primarily in smaller entities. During a flight from Rome to Prague, Benedict XVI expressed it in this way:

> I would say that usually it is creative minorities who determine the future, and in this regard the Catholic Church must understand that she is a creative minority with a heritage of values that are not things of the past,

98   Politi, *Joseph Ratzinger. Crisi di un papato,* op. cit., 136.
99   Cf. Ibid., 288.

but a very lively and relevant reality. The Church must modernize, she must be present in public debate, in our struggle for a true concept of freedom and peace.[100]

Included in this creativity are ecclesial movements, which can be viewed as the Church's avant-garde face to the contemporary world, an opportunity for the intense spiritual formation of practicing Catholics, and a force for the new evangelization in a world of unbelief. Participants in ecclesial movements generally feel as if they are taking part in a new charism under the inspiration of a charismatic leader. It is difficult to draw up a definitive list of ecclesial movements because they are in various stages of development. Some have received canonical recognition, others simply perceive themselves as a group/movement, others are simply a sociological phenomenon. But if we had to make a list of the better known movements today, it would include the "Work of Mary" (Focolare Movement), Communion and Liberation, the John XXIII Community, the Community of Sant'Egidio, the Neocatechumenal Way (although members prefer not to call it a "movement"), the Renewal in the Spirit, the Cursillos in Christianity, the Apostolic Movement of Schönstatt, l'Arche, and, according to some, Opus Dei.[101] Even if there is reason to exclude the last of these due to its unique history and canonical status, its sociological underpinnings and internal structure make it reasonable to include it.[102] In any case, it is best

---

100 Interview of the Holy Father Benedict XVI during the flight to the Czech Republic, 26 September 2009: https://w2.vatican.va/content/benedict-xvi/en/speeches/2009/september/documents/hf_ben-xvi_spe_20090926_interview.html
101 Angelo Manfredi, "Movimenti ecclesiali," in Filippo Lovison (dir.), *Dizionario Storico Tematico. La Chiesa in Italia*, vol. II, Roberto Regoli, Maurizio Tagliaferri (ed.), *Dopo l'unità nazionale*: http://www.storiadellachiesa.it/glossary/movimenti-ecclesiali-e-la-chiesa-in-italia/.
102 Cf. Antoni Stankiewicz, "Le prelature personali e i fenomeni associativi," in Sandro Gherro (ed.), *Le prelature personali nella normativa*

to consider the first real ecclesial movement to be the Work of Mary (Focolare Movement).

Benedict XVI began to cultivate a special relationship with ecclesial movements from the beginning of his pontificate. At the beginning of the 1970s, during his time as professor, Ratzinger had experiences with the Neocatechumenal Way, Communion and Liberation, and the Focolare Movement. He said that his encounter with each was "a marvelous experience."[103] He believed that their "energy," "enthusiasm," faith, and "joy in the faith" were a response to what theologian Karl Rahner and others called a "wintertime for the Church"—that is, she was in a "cold" and "tired" state of inertia.[104] At the same time, Ratzinger did not hesitate to recognize certain "immature" elements in the movements such as a sense of exclusivity, one-sidedness, and a difficulty of inserting themselves in the life of the local Church. In any case, by 1985 he already considered these movements a sign of vitality, faith, and hope for the universal Church.[105]

In May of 1998, Cardinal Ratzinger delivered the inaugural address to the World Meeting of Ecclesial Movements, in which he discussed their theological and historical place in the Church and acknowledged their remarkable enthusiasm for the faith and their vocations to serve the Church at the universal level.[106] This

e nella vita della Chiesa. Venezia—Scuola Grande di San Rocco—25 e 26 giugno 2001 (Padua: CEDAM, 2002), 137–163; José L. Gutiérrez, "La Prelatura del Opus Dei y los movimientos eclesiales. Aspectos eclesiológicos y canónicos." Accessed at: http:// prelaturaspersonales.org/wp-content/uploads/2012/10/JL-Gutierrez-La-Prelatura-dellOpus-dei-e-i-movimenti-ecclesiali.pdf.

103 Joseph Ratzinger, "I movimenti ecclesiali e la loro collocazione teologica," in Pontificium Consilium pro Laicis, *I movimenti nella Chiesa. Atti del Congresso mondiale dei movimenti ecclesiali, Roma, 27–29 May 1998* (Citta del Vaticano, 1999), 23.

104 Ibid., 23–24.

105 Cf. Joseph Ratzinger, *The Ratzinger Report* (San Francisco: Ignatius Press, 1985), 42–44.

106 Cf. Joseph Ratzinger, "I movimenti ecclesiali e la loro collocazione teologica," 23–51.

was Ratzinger's view of the ecclesiological significance of movements, which more generally (even in past centuries) "progressed side-by-side" with the pope.[107] Ratzinger affirmed: "[T]he papacy did not create movements, but it was their essential support within the Church's structure, their ecclesial bedrock."[108] In some passages of the text, the then-Prefect of the Congregation for the Doctrine of the Faith defined movements of the twentieth century as a "gift" to the entire Church. According to some commentators, the German cardinal, in a way not dissimilar to John Paul II, cultivated "movements as a sort of bulwark against the problems of the post-conciliar Church."[109]

Ratzinger carried this vision into the papacy in 2005. He constantly encouraged the work of movements by receiving them in audiences, as he did with Communion and Liberation in March of 2007, and by supporting them with ecclesial structures, as with the approval of the statutes (2008) of the Catechetical Directory (2012) of the Neocatechumenal Way.[110] This action demonstrated that the Holy See prefers to insert movements into the ecclesial body through statues and not through a "legal framework."[111]

The pope also showed his esteem for ecclesial movements by promoting many of their members to various levels within the Church hierarchy. Moreover, as we have already seen, he filled several curial posts with individuals associated with the Focolare Movement and the Community of Sant'Egidio (whom American diplomats considered a "trustworthy interlocutor" and an entity from which one could obtain funds for personal initiatives[112]).

107 Ibid., 40.
108 Ibid., 39.
109 Massimo Faggioli, *Nello spirito del Concilio. Movimenti ecclesiali e recezione del Vaticano II* (San Paolo: Cinisello Balsamo, 2013), 44.
110 Cf. Bernhard Sven Anuth, "L'istituzionalizzazione del Cammino neocatecumenale," *Il Regno-Documenti*, n. 9 (2013), 296–320.
111 Faggioli, *Nello spirito del Concilio. Movimenti ecclesiali e recezione del Vaticano II*, op. cit., 50.
112 Stefania Maurizi, *Dossier Wikileaks. Segreti italiani* (Milano: Bur, 2011), 136.

Others he appointed local bishops. The number of bishops belonging to or associated with movements became visible (something John Paul II already begun) in meetings and audiences with movements in that a significant amount of time was dedicated to greeting the bishops and their guests personally (*baciamano*).[113] A similar protocol was observed for religious congregations.

On 22 May 2006, on the occasion of the Second World Congress of ecclesial movements and new communities, Benedict XVI, in his message, acknowledged the strength of the movements to build a more just social order in an increasingly more barbarous world.[114] A few days later, on the vigil of Pentecost, the pope recognized the providential role of movements,[115] just as John Paul II had (even if, according to some observers, Benedict XVI expressed less enthusiasm[116]).

Benedict XVI linked the birth of these new ecclesial movements to a great Catholic rebirth.[117] He made it clear that, in his mind, movements are intended for the entire Church. Their particular contributions can be found in the spiritual support they offer, through which, in his opinion, young people are "seized by the enthusiasm of having acknowledged Christ as the Son of God and of bringing him into the world."[118]

After having struggled for recognition in the twentieth century, ecclesial movements have reached a point where their members are involved in some of the Church's most important decisions. They are not merely one resource among many, but an

---

113 Hubertus Blaumeiser, Helmut Sievers (ed.), *Chiesa-comunione. Paolo VI e Giovanni Paolo II ai vescovi amici del movimento dei focolari* (Roma: Citta`Nuova, 2002).

114 Benedict XVI, Message, 22 May 2006, in *Acta Apostolicae Sedis* 98 (2006): 455–458.

115 Benedict XVI, Homily, 3 June 2006, in *Acta Apostolicae Sedis* 98 (2006): 503–510.

116 Cf. Faggioli, *Nello spirito del Concilio. Movimenti ecclesiali e recezione del Vaticano II* o cit., 53.

117 Cf. Benedict XVI, *Luce del mondo*, op. cit., 89.

118 Ibid., 100.

essential element in the life of the Church, younger and more dynamic than older religious associations and religious orders. This allows them to offer profound spiritual inspiration to society as a model of communion that can help many Christians live faith more vivaciously and fruitfully. Given their cultural and theological sophistication and their effective models for action within the Church and in society, the movements described thus far are a potent response to the European ecclesial crisis as perceived by recent popes, who in turn cannot help but support them and include them in evangelization efforts coordinated at the level of the Roman Curia. Hence it is no surprise to see during Benedict's time the establishment of the Pontifical Council for the New Evangelization. The particular attention that Benedict gave to Europe was front and center in this initiative.[119] Both Benedict XVI and John Paul II, however, show a very different stance toward other small Christian communities—the so-called *communità de base*—which are very popular in Latin America.

The influence and strength of movements outside of Europe, however, should not be underestimated. The Renewal in the Spirit, for example, born in the United States, spread quickly and widely throughout the entire world. The need for movements in the Church cannot be restricted merely to the European crisis. Communion and Liberation has a strong presence in Latin America, and the Neocatechumenal Way has found a home on every continent. Thus, it would be a mistake to reduce movements to ecclesial-political instruments that Christianity might use to reconquer Europe. That would completely miss their true nature. The missionary goal of ecclesial movements is only one aim among many.

For its own part, in light of these other ecclesial movements, among the other ways that the Curia likewise nourishes the long-term health of the Church is by offering models of holiness and courageous Christian witness. This is why she is involved in the

119 Cf. Faggioli, *Nello spirito del Concilio. Movimenti ecclesiali e recezione del Vaticano II*, op. cit., 52–53.

causes of saints and blessed, something often referred to as the "politics of holiness."

The politics of holiness: canonizations and beatifications

John Paul II left an enormous legacy of holiness. He is responsible for 1,341 beatifications and 482 canonizations.[120] In comparison, Paul VI bequeathed only 23 blessed and 83 saints.[121] Benedict, an older pope, is between these two with 870 blessed (733 martyrs and 97 confessors of the faith) and 44 saints (one of whom— Hildegard of Bingen—was proclaimed through an "equivalent canonization").[122] The number of beatifications under Pope Benedict is markedly higher than those under Paul VI, and this within only eight years. However, if we consider the reforms of John Paul II (how he simplified and streamlined the processes for beatification and canonization in 1983 with the Constitution *Divinus Perfectionis Magister*), the numbers are not all as striking, especially if we consider how many of them were martyrs.

In 1989, during a public speech in Seregno in the province of Milan, Cardinal Ratzinger said that among those more recently beatified and canonized, there were "saints who perhaps had something to say to a certain group, but they don't really speak

120 Cf. Angelo Amato, "Donne beate e sante nel pontificato di Benedetto XVI," in *Come ceri accesi. La vita consacrata secondo papa Benedetto*, op. op. cit., 56. Other figures (1,345 beatifications and 483 canonizations) are listed in Valentina Ciciliot, "Le beatificazioni e le canonizzazioni di Giovanni Paolo II come strumenti di governo della Chiesa," *Humanitas*, n. 1, a. 65 (2010):118–142. Cf. http://www.academia.edu/1211051/Le_beatificazioni_e_le_canonizzazioni_di_Giovanni_Paolo_II, as well as U. Zuccarello, "Le canonizzazioni e beatificazioni di Giovanni Paolo II . Quale politica papale della santità?" *Società e Storia*, 109 (2005): 541–658.
121 Cf. Amato, "Donne beate e sante nel pontificato di Benedetto XVI," op. cit., 56
122 Cf. Ibid. For a quick look at the list, see: https://it.wikipedia.org/wiki/Beatificazioni_del_pontificato_di_Benedetto_XVI; https:// it.wikipedia.org/wiki/Canonizzazioni_celebrate_da_Benedetto_XVI.

to the majority of believers."[123] He expressed a desire to give "priority" to saints whose lives delivered a more universal message. Also noteworthy is a letter Ratzinger sent to the Congregation for the Causes of Saints after having been elected pope (24 April 2006), in which he directed the congregation to limit the number of canonizations and beatifications and reformulated the inquisition process at the local level.[124] Why, then, were hundreds of names added to the list during his pontificate? Undoubtedly, there were many causes from the prior pontificate well underway, especially martyrs—those who witnessed the faith with their very blood—who are striking examples of holiness for the universal Church—precisely what Ratzinger wanted. Conversely, there were fewer "confessors of the faith," even in light of the changes John Paul II had made to the process.

The pope has a lofty and vivid vision of what it means to be a saint. He spoke of this in his first homily—that is, at his inaugural Mass—in which he called them "friends of God" by whom we are "surrounded, led, and guided."[125]

In an attempt to streamline the process of beatification and canonization, Benedict XVI also gave attention to the symbolism of the ceremony and distilled it to its essential core. Just a few months after his election, he decided to entrust beatifications to a papal representative (normally the Prefect of the Congregation for the Causes of Saints) rather than celebrating those ceremonies himself. He also stipulated that beatifications preferably be celebrated in the diocese that promoted the cause.[126] By stripping

---

123 Ciciliot, "Le beatificazioni e le canonizzazioni di Giovanni Paolo II," op. cit., 139. The author reports an interview with Cardinal Ratzinger appearing in *30Giorni*, n. 5 (1989): 18–23.

124 Congregation for the Causes of Saints, *Instruction* Sanctorum Mater, 17 May 2007, in *Acta Apostolicae Sedis*, 99 (2007): 465–510.

125 Benedict XVI, *Omelia per l'inizio del ministero petrino*, 24 April 2005, *Acta Apostolicae Sedis*, 97 (2005): 707–712.

126 Congregation for the Causes of Saints, *Comunicato*, 29 September 2005: http://www.vatican.va/roman_curia/congregations/csaints/docu-ments/rc_con_csaints_doc_20050929_comunicato_it.html.

down the beatification ceremony in this way, it was easier to distinguish it from canonizations. The local celebration of the former also helped to decentralize the Church.

The personal support of the pope is obviously important in the politics of holiness. The individuals he advances have something to say about his program. "The pope can foster a cause or block it. He can speed up its *iter* or let it move slowly according to its natural course. Canonizations, on the other hand, move forward according to a linear logic, as if they are obligated to advance as soon as a miracle has already been assigned to the blessed."[127] For example, we see that in the "hagiographical panorama of Wojtyła, the typical model of holiness he proposed reflected the most urgent parts of his message."[128] We see less of this in Benedict XVI, precisely because of the reduction in the public face of beatifications, now entrusted to his Prefect for the Congregation for the Causes of Saints. There are perhaps two exceptions that clearly show the pope's preference—perhaps also his weakness—for one towering intellectual—John Henry Newman (beatified during Benedict's visit to England in 2010)—and one personal friend—namely, John Paul II (beatified in Rome in 2011). We can consider the former Ratzinger's ideal intellectual friend, and the latter as a model for the world of theology. He spoke of the former in his end-of-the-year speech to the Curia in 2010,[129] noting Newman's three conversions as well as his clear reference to the importance of conscience. Furthermore, the pope's beatification of Newman illustrates his fight against rationalistic theology.[130] Ratzinger personally intervened in only a few causes for saints, such as in the decree declaring the virtues of Pius XII (2010), whose beatification was vociferously opposed by

127 Ciciliot, "Le beatificazioni e le canonizzazioni di Giovanni Paolo II come strumenti di governo della Chiesa," op. cit., 139.
128 Ibid.
129 Benedict XVI, Address to the Roman Rota, 20 December 2010, *Acta Apostolicae Sedis*, 103 (2011): 33–41.
130 Roland Hureaux, "Benoît XVI, théologien de la raison," *Liberté politique*, 60, (2013): 78.

forces inside and outside the Church, and in opening the beatification process for John Paul II (a significant gesture given that he knew John Paul so well and was his direct successor). Particularly noteworthy was also Benedict's single "equipollent" or "equivalent" canonization—i.e., a process that is not confined to the usual *iter*—of the Benedictine sister Hildegard of Bingen (2012), an extraordinary individual and likely a favorite of Pope Benedict.

The breakdown of beatifications is also worth consideration. Among the 870 beatified, one is a pope (John Paul II), three cardinals, seven bishops, 59 diocesan priests, 497 men religious, 89 women religious, 145 lay men, and 69 lay women. Of the 44 canonized saints, four are bishops, four priests, 17 men religious, 16 women religious, one lay man, and two lay women.[131] Whereas Pope John Paul II naturally had an affinity for holiness in his home country of Poland, Benedict XVI beatified only ten Germans and canonized only two. Ratzinger promoted the "internationalization" of holiness, so to speak.

In line with John Paul II, the most striking group of holy men and women is composed of martyrs: 773 blessed were martyrs (89% of the entire group), and only one saint (2% of the total)—namely, the Filippino catechist, Pedro Calungsod. Most of these martyrs died under communism, Nazism, or the Spanish Civil War: world events too historically or politically sensitive to receive attention in the 1960s and 1970s. Just like John Paul II, Benedict XVI wished to emphasize that, in the twentieth century, the face of the Church was particularly brilliant in her martyrs, and that their witness would have enduring significance in the twenty-first century.

The traditional model of priests and religious being the Church's main protagonists prevailed, especially given the predominance of male religious. There were only 89 female blessed (10% of the group) and 16 female saints (36%). Cardinal Angelo Amato nevertheless claimed that there was a "considerable

131 Cf. Amato, "Donne beate e sante nel pontificato di Benedetto XVI," op. cit., 56.

number" of women. It is not entirely clear to whom he was refer-ring and to what time period.

The names of several founders of male and female congrega-tions appear on the list. Since, as we have seen, religious life in its traditional form has been in a state of on-going crisis into the twenty-first century, the Church continues to extol models of ho-liness that give witness to the ideal of consecrated life. But is it truly an attempt to bring religious life out of the crisis, or is it an attempt to put it at arm's length? It could simply be a matter of appeasing the spiritual sons and daughters of these founders (i.e., the current members of the congregations they founded). If reli-gious men and women are encouraged to emerge from the crisis through new examples of holiness, so too are members of ecclesial movements. We can take, for example, the laywoman Chiara Luce Badano, a member of the Focolare Movement. Aging Catholic As-sociations also have a representative—the layman, Blessed Giuseppe Toniolo—who, among other things, was the founder of the Italian Catholic University Federation (FUCI). There is an ever-increasing presence of lay people among the blessed and saints (24.6% of the blessed, 7% of saints), predominantly martyrs, but nevertheless representative of untraditional *itinera*, such as the joint beatification of Mr. and Mrs. Martin (2008), parents of Saint Therese of Lisieux.

The work of several curial offices reinforces the various spir-itualities emerging at the beginning of the twenty-first century. Everyone can easily find a patron saint protector. The variety of backgrounds they represent satisfies a wide range of devotional preferences. There is one, however, that particularly transcends traits of personal holiness. It touches instead upon a characteristic that became extremely important in the 1800s—that is, devotion to the pope.

Devotion to the pope

In more recent times, devotion to the pope emerges as a key characteristic of religious life. It is "categorical and constitutive"[132] of contemporary Catholicism, and its icono-graphical figures are Pius VII and Pius IX—that is, the two popes who suffered precisely because of the Petrine office. We need only recall the pilgrimages to Rome and the appeals for "Peter's Pence." Obedience to the pope became a stable element both in practical norms and in *ad hoc* questions.[133] "Papism" thus became a distinguishing characteristic of the organized mobilization of Catholics.

Attachment to the pope in priests and bishops grew through the active promotion of studies in Rome, the creation of "monsignors," and the internationalization of the College of Cardinals.[134] The attachment of the laity to the pope was fostered through papal voyages, the image of the pope in mass media, papal audiences in Rome, and nominations for traditional pontifical honors.

In recent times, John Paul II's near "martyrdom"—i.e., the attempt on his life in 1981—in addition to his prolonged illness, magnified the figure and role of the pope enormously.

This trend continued during the pontificate of Benedict XVI. The numbers speak for themselves. In the last years of John Paul II's pontificate, participation in papal events in Rome swelled beyond 2,500,000 persons (2,615,110 in 2003, and 2,231,800 in

---

132 Giovanni Miccoli, *Chiesa e società in Italia dal Concilio Vaticano I (1870) al pontificato di Giovanni XXIII*, in *Storia d'Italia*, vol. 5/2, *I documenti* (Turin: Einaudi, 1973), 1508. Cf. Roberto Regoli, "Tramonto delle Chiese 'nazionali' e nuovo giorno del Papato? La lunga epoca dei cambiamenti," in Péter Tusor, Matteo Sanfilippo (ed.), *Il Papato e le Chiese locali. Studi / The Papacy and the local Churches. Studies* (Viterbo: Sette Città, 2014), 379–406.

133 Cf. Giovanni Vian, *La riforma della Chiesa per la restaurazione cristiana della società: le visite apostoliche delle diocesi e dei seminari d'Italia promosse durante il pontificato di Pio X: 1903–1914* (Rome: Herder, 1998), 938.

134 Roberto Regoli, "L'élite cardinalizia dopo la fine dello Stato Pontificio," *Archivum Historiae Pontificiae*, n. 47 (2009): 63–87.

2004).[135] In the first year of Benedict XVI's pontificate, the faithful present at papal events grew to nearly three million (2,855,500). In his second year, the number increased to 3,222,820, but then sank to 2,830,100 in 2007. Numbers oscillated from then onward, but hovered around the same figure: 2,215,000 in 2008; 2,243,900 in 2009; 2,553,800 in 2011 (unfortunately, the figures for 2010 were never released); and 2,351,200 in 2012.[136] In short, Benedict XVI ended up welcoming the same number of faithful as his predecessor.

However, the Peter's Pence collection (*l'obolo di san Pietro*) decreased during Benedict's pontificate: from $100,000,000 in 2006 (a record due to two impressive personal gifts), $82,500,000 in

135 Press Office of the Holy See, *Dati statistici circa la partecipazione di fedeli a incontri con Giovanni Paolo II nel corso dell'Anno 2003*. Accessed at: http://www.vatican.va/news_services/press/documentazione/documents/pontificato_gpii/incontri-gpii_statistiche_2003_it.html; Holy See Press Office, *Dati statistici circa la partecipazione di fedeli a incontri con Giovanni Paolo II nel corso dell'Anno 2004*: http://www.vatican.va/news_services/press/documentazione/documents/pontificato_gpii/incontri-gpii_statistiche_2004_it.html.
136 Cf. *Partecipazione di fedeli alle udienze generali e agli incontri in Vaticano con il Santo Padre Benedetto XVI, dati statistici*: https://press.vatican.va/content/salastampa/it/bollettino/pubblico/2005/12/28/0655/01706.html;https://press.vatican.va/content/salastampa/it/bollettino/pubblico/2006/12/28/0683/01908.html; https://press.vatican.va/content/salastampa/it/bollettino/pubblico/2007/12/29/0700/01871.html; http://press.vatican.va/content/salastampa/it/bollettino/pubblico/2008/12/29/0815/02005.html;https://press.vatican.va/content/salastampa/it/bollettino/pubblico/2010/01/05/0007/00010.html; "Nel 2011 circa 2.600.000 fedeli hanno partecipato ai diversi incontri con il papa," in *Zenit*, 6 January 2012: http://it.zenit.org/articles/nel-2011-circa-2-600-000-fedeli-hanno-partecipato-ai-diversi-incontri-con-il-papa/; "Più di 2 milioni di fedeli agli incontri con il papa nel 2012," in *Zenit*, 8 January 2013: http://it.zenit.org/articles/piu-di-2-milioni-di-fedeli-agli-incontri-con-il-papa-nel-2012/.

2009, and $67,000,000 in 2010.[137] This drop was due in part to a slowing of the global economy, as well as the billowing sexual abuse crisis among the clergy, especially in the United States and in Europe, particularly in Germany (revealed at the beginning of 2010).[138] In other words, in the two countries who traditionally contributed the most in fundraising.

Support for Benedict wavered in the European polls.[139] Public polls are helpful in determining how "popular" the pope is in society at large, but not necessarily within the Church (that is, among practicing Catholics and not just seasonal Catholics). This is because other dynamics are obviously at work in society, but these dynamics do not help gauge devotion to the pope within the "Church militant." For example, while the Vatican was bogged down with its public-image crisis in 2010, a groundswell of faithful announced the celebration of "Pope's Day" in Rome on May 16. On this day, 150,000 faithful gathered in Saint Peter's Square to express their affinity and affection for Benedict XVI.[140] His popularity within the Church was increasing precisely at a time when he was widely considered to be under attack and immersed in insolvable problems. And there were still problems on the horizon for the aging pope.

137 Cf. Nuzzi, *Sua Santità. Le carte segrete di Benedetto XVI*, op. cit., 87.
138 Politi, *Joseph Ratzinger. Crisi di un papato*, op. cit., 208–211.
139 Ibid., 194.
140 Ibid., 247.

CHAPTER FOUR
THE INCREASING URGENCY OF
UNIVERSAL GOVERNANCE

As he carries out his mission, a pope must not only attend to the agenda he set out to accomplish, but must also be ready for the unexpected. More often than not, rather than having the time and energy to dedicate to his premeditated program, Benedict had to deal with more urgent matters, for example the pedophilia crisis. Even in areas where it seemed he might have a chance to implement his plan—such as in episcopal nominations—pressing matters arose that severely limited his freedom.

What ultimately counts as urgent is often not what was originally a priority for the pope. Priorities are projected, strategized, and diligently undertaken. Urgent matters come up quickly and suddenly. Sometimes priorities and urgent matters coincide, but not always. Timely responses to crises of faith are priorities, and more often than not they pop up suddenly and without warning. The pedophilia crisis exploded toward the end of John Paul II's pontificate, and it had to be treated as a priority.

During the pontificate and emeritus season of Benedict XVI there has been much talk about the issue of clergy sexual abuse of minors, about how this pope handled it, and about how his efforts should ultimately be evaluated.

In general, the major issue (especially in the English-speaking world) is not only pedophilia in itself, but the ways in which the Church has dealt with it. In other words: have some in the Church covered up the crimes of pedophile priests? In dealing with this topic, we need to take care not to be led into error. For decades, in fact, there has been a conflict within the Catholic Church concerning courses of action. This is nothing new in a two-millennia history, but what is unique in recent years is the fact that the issue of sexual abuse is no longer being addressed in itself but in view of the future.[1]

On the one hand, there are those who (like Ratzinger) connect the abuse crisis to the moral liberalism of the second half of the twentieth century, highlighting personal responsibility for the crimes;[2] and there are those who, on the other hand, link abuse to a systemic crisis and ultimately speak of institutional irresponsibility (such as the members of the commissions of inquiry into pedophilia in the German and French churches[3]). In the latter case, sexual abuse is used to institutionally change the Church on essential points. Consider the demands of the German synodal plan (initiated during the pontificate of Francis[4]), which, on the

1 Roberto Regoli, "Pope Benedict, Sex Abuse and the Catholic Church's Future," *Wall Street Journal*, 18 February 2022.
2 Benedict XVI, "The Church and the Scandal of Sexual Abuse," 11 April 2019, https://www.catholicworldreport.com/2019/04/10/full-text-of-benedict-xvi-the-church-and-the-scandal-of-sexual-abuse/. There is an important examination of this text in Livio Melina, *Chiesa sotto accusa. Un commento agli Appunti di Benedetto XVI*, ed. Tracey Rowland and preface by Georg Gänswein (Siena: Cantagalli, 2020). The original text is in German and was published in the monthly journal *Klerusblatt*.
3 For France, we must first of all turn to the documentation produced by the commission on sexual abuse that was established by the French bishops: Commission indépendante sur les abus sexuels dans l'Église, October 2021, at https://www.ciase.fr/rapport-final/. For Germany, documentation is sparse, but there are many journalistic articles that synthesize the moment. To provide an essential source: Daniele Piccini, "Abusi sui minori a Colonia, spunta un nuovo rapporto con 300 casi," in *AciStampa*, March 26, 2021: https://www.acistampa.com/story/abusi-sui-minori-a-colonia-spunta-un-nuovo-rapporto-con-300-casi-16649.
4 In September of 2018 the German Bishops Conference commissioned a study on sexual abuse in German dioceses in three German universities. The study showed that from 1946 to 2014 in the German dioceses, 3,677 minors were victims of abuse committed

basis of curtailing abuse, calls for rethinking what is not at all related to abuse—namely, priestly life, power and the separation of powers in the Church, women and ministries in the Church, and the sexual aspect of life. The issue increasingly tends to be less about the abuse in itself and more about what model of Church to propose in the future. Yet the abuse must be addressed in itself and not instrumentalized, otherwise there emerges an abuse of abuse; furthermore, we lose a sense of gravity toward it and do not find effective measures for truly preventing it. For this reason, we will approach the issue here with a properly historical viewpoint, without engaging the skirmishes between various leadership factions in the Church.

The sexual abuse of minors: Rome is forced to deal with the local incompetency of local authorities

No news rattled the Church more than the clerical abuse of minors. Studies have shown that the horrendous crime of sexual abuse occurs in families, neighborhoods, schools and other educational institutions, sports clubs, recreational facilities, cultural centers, as well as religious environments. Most abuse is perpetrated by family members. Some studies have produced alarming statistics, showing that abuse against minors has

> by 1,670 religious. From this data, Cardinal Reinhard Marx, then-president of the German Bishops Conference, launched a synodal initiative with the task of reforming the Church in Germany, which actually began in January 2020. Starting from the knowledge of abuse, they decided to institute a program that within internal debates led to other radical proposals. Cf. D. Piccini, "Abusi sui minori a Colonia, spunta un nuovo rapporto con 300 casi." An important step came with the report of the March 2019 plenary of the Bishops Conference in March 2019: *Pressebericht des Vorsitzenden der Deutschen Bischofskonferenz, Kardinal Reinhard Marx, anlässlich der Pressekonferenz zum Abschluss der Frühjahrs-Vollversammlung der Deutschen Bischofskonferenz*, Lingen March 2019 https://www.dbk.de/fileadmin/redaktion/diverse_downloads/presse_2019/2019-040-Pressebericht-FVV-Lingen.pdf.

occurred in "60% of families, and it pervades all environments, especially in institutions that are relatively cut off from the world."[5]

There are still those who deny its existence, claiming it can never reach epidemic proportions. Granted, studies conducted up to the present are limited, but the data is alarming nonetheless. For example, if we look at the figures of sexual abuse in India alone, furnished by the Ministry of Women and Child Development in 2007, we find that 53.22% of children under the age of eighteen have suffered from sexual abuse.[6] Equally striking is the national investigation that took place in Australia between 2013 and 2017, which shows how over the years the problem of sexual abuse of minors has reached various institutions and all sectors of society.[7]

The most rigorous and reliable studies to date regard the Catholic Church since she has been at the center of the polemic in the twentieth and twenty-first centuries. Hence the figures we have give us a good idea of what has occurred in the Catholic Church, but not necessarily in the rest of the world. This is why the numbers are incomplete and need to be filled in by more comprehensive research. The problem of sexual abuse against minors did not receive serious international attention until the 1980s, probably because it was too much a taboo subject to talk about openly prior to that.

As far as we know, at the beginning of the twenty-first century (according to data provided by the sociologist Philip Jenkins) the rate of priests convicted for abuse against minors varies, by geographic area, from 0.2% to 1.7% of the total convicted, while for Protestant

5   Marco Politi, *Joseph Ratzinger. Crisi di un papato* (Bari: Laterza, 2013), 211.

6   Loveleen Kacker, *Preface*, in Ministry of Women and Child Development – Government of India, *Study on Child Abuse: India 2007* (New Delhi: Kriti, 2007), VI.

7   Royal Commission into Institutional Responses to Child Sexual Abuse, *Final Report*, 15 December 2017, vols. 1–16: https://www.childabuseroyalcommission.gov.au/final-report.

pastors it ranges from 2% to 3%.[8] In data for some German territories, members of the Church convicted for sexual abuse correspond to 0.1% of the total. In other data for the USA (limited to 2008) Catholic priests account for 0.03% of criminals involved in cases of pedophilia.[9] If these are the overall figures, it is helpful to now go into detail regarding the numbers linked explicitly to the Catholic Church.

The Catholic Church is to thank for some of the most serious studies done on sexual abuse to date. These studies were conducted with a clear, precise, and comprehensive methodology and were primarily focused on the period between 1950 and 2010. We have reliable statistics on the number of accused and the number of allegations. The first major study was commissioned by the United States Conference of Catholic Bishops in 2002 to the John Jay College of Criminal Justice in New York. The years under examination ran from 1950 to 2002.[10] During that period, 4,392 priests were accused. That amounts to 4% of the priests active during that time. More specifically, 4.3% of diocesan clergy and 2.5% of religious clergy. The 1960s and 1980s were peak years for accusations. And 68% of those accused were ordained between 1950 and 1979, 21.3% before 1950, and the rest were ordained after 1979. The victims were 81% male and 19% female. Additionally, 40% of the victims were between the ages of 11 and 14. One third of the reports against priests were filed between 2002 and 2003, and two thirds after 1993. This initial investigation was followed by a second in 2006, and a third in 2011,[11] which included data collected up to 2010.

8   Cf. Paolo Rodari and Andrea Tornielli, *Attacco a Ratzinger. Accuse e scandali, profezie e complotti contro Benedetto XVI* (Milan: Piemme, 2010), 258.

9   Cf. Peter Seewald, *Benedetto XVI. Una vita* (Milan: Garzanti, 2020), 1056.

10   John Jay College of Criminal Justice of The City University of New York, *The Nature and Scope of Sexual Abuse of Minors by Catholic Priests and Deacons in the United States 1950–2002*, John Jay College of Criminal Justice, New York 2004.

11   John Jay College of Criminal Justice of The City University of New York, *The Nature and Scope of Sexual Abuse of Minors by Catholic*

A similar study was also conducted in the Netherlands. As in the United States, the study was motivated primarily by media pressure and an initiative by the local bishops' conference in collaboration with the conference for Dutch religious. The reports were produced, the second of which was released only in Dutch.[12] The first report, released in December of 2011, included data from 1945 to 2010. The second report focused particularly on the abuse of females within women's congregations. The data of the second report was scarce and inconclusive. However, the second report did include an addendum to the first report, which had lacked data from the Dominican order. The most difficult years were the 1950s, in which the average rate of abuse in the Catholic Church was higher than the national average. The first report neither distinguished between those accused and those convicted, nor were the crimes reported committed only by priests. Nevertheless, the results of the investigation were clear. The sexual abuse of minors in the Catholic Church in Holland between 1945 and 2010 is relatively low when calculated as a percentage, but it is a serious problem in terms of sheer numbers.[13] With respect to bishops and religious superiors, in many instances they had taken insufficient steps after

Priests and Deacons in the United States 1950–2002. Supplementary Report, John Jay College of Criminal Justice, New York 2006; John Jay College of Criminal Justice of The City University of New York, *The Causes and Context of Sexual Abuse of Minors by Catholic Priests in the United States, 1950–2010*, John Jay College of Criminal Justice, New York, 2011.

12   The first report: Commission of Inquiry, *Onderzoek, Seksueel misbruik van minderjarigen in de RK Kerk*, 2011: http://www.onderzoekrk.nl/english-summery.html. The second report: Wim Deetman, *Seksueel mi- sbruik van en geweld tegen meisjes in de rooms-katholieke kerk. een vervolgonderzoek*, Uitgeverij Balans. Amsterdam 2013. Available online: http://www.onderzoekrk.nl/vervolgon-derzoek/eindrapport.html.

13   A translation into Italian was made by Introvigne, Marchesini: *Pedofilia: una battaglia che la Chiesa sta vincendo: con un approfondimento storico, filosofico, clinico*, op. cit., 41.

receiving reports of abuse, and they paid insufficient attention to victims."[14]

Whereas the approach in the reports mentioned thus far has been documentary and historical, episcopates in other countries have chosen a different metric. In France, for example, the Independent Commission of Sexual Abuse in the Church—the so-called CIASE (*Commission indépendante sur les abus sexuels dans l'Église*) or the Sauvé Commission (after the name of the president of the organization), which was charged with the issue by the local bishops' conference—has preferred an approach of data projections over a simple historical investigation.[15] If for the 1950–2020 period, the historical method (that is, starting from verifiable documents) yielded a number of pedophilia victims between 4,832 and 27,808, the method of projections starting from 118 cases of anonymous complaints led to an estimation that as many as 330,000 people may be involved—but this is a hypothetical and unverifiable figure. This projection approach has been sharply criticized because it leads to fragile, equivocal results that are easy to dismantle, that is,`these results are ultimately unreliable. The first criticism on this front came from the French Catholic academic world.[16]

Other nations produced regional studies, usually commissioned by individual dioceses. Consider the well-known report

14   "Bishops and other Church authorities were not ignorant of the problem of sexual abuse. Moreover, in the view of the Commission of Inquiry, in many cases they failed to take adequate action and paid too little attention to victims." Commission of Inquiry, *Onderzoek, Seksueel misbruik van minderjarigen in de RK Kerk*, 2011: http://www.onderzoekrk.nl/filead- min/commissiedeetman/ data/downloads/eindrapport/20111216/Samenvatting_eindrapport_Engelstalig.pdf, 20 of the report.
15   Cf. Commission indépendante sur les abus sexuels dans l'Église, October 2021, at https://www.ciase.fr/rapport-final/.
16   Cf. Analyse du rapport de la Commission indépendante sur les abus sexuels dans l'Église (CIASE): https://www.youscribe.com/ BookReader/Index/3257401/?documentId=4290283.

on the Diocese of Cloyne in Ireland.[17] In Germany in the 2010s, the issue was addressed in local cases, which involved various law firms. Germany is of special interest, as it is the homeland of Pope Benedict XVI. The Archdiocese of Cologne had first requested a report from the Westpfahl Spilker Wastl Law Firm but then blocked it at the behest of Cardinal Rainer Maria Woelki because it would present legal loopholes and a violation of the rights of those involved.[18] This same law firm denied in Cologne, however, was called upon by the Archdiocese of Munich to research the period from 1945 to 2019. The team's work, which was made public in 2022, gave rise to the accusation against then-Cardinal Ratzinger that he covered up four pedophilia accusations against priests when he was archbishop of Munich. In some of these cases it is believed that Ratzinger could not have been unaware. This is was rather weakly argued, and was not based on evidence.

The case that received the most media attention is that of Peter Hullermann, which dates back to 1980, even though it had already been publicly known for years (at least since 2010, when the documents were made public). From published letters we know that Hullermann, after having committed abuse in Rhineland, was taken to a facility in the diocese of Munich to undergo psychotherapy at his bishop's request. We also know that

17 Report by the Commission of Investigation into Catholic Diocese of Cloyne, December 2010: https://www.justice.ie/en/JELR/Pages/Cloyne-Rpt.
18 Cf. Daniele Piccini, "Abusi sui minori a Colonia, spunta un nuovo rapporto con 300 casi"; Nico Spuntoni, "Report su abusi, Woelki ne esce pulito (ma più debole)," in *La Nuova Bussola Quotidiana*, March 21, 2021: https://lanuovabq.it/it/report-su-abusi-woelki-ne-esce-pulito-ma-piu-debole; Giovanni Marcotullio, "Chiesa e abusi: l'attacco finale a Ratzinger," in *Aleteia*, January 21, 2022: https://it.aleteia.org/2022/01/21/20-gennaio-2022-munchen-westpfahl-spilker-wastl-ratzinger/; Nico Spuntoni, "Abusi, Ratzinger al contrattacco: 'Su di me propaganda,'" in *La Nuova Bussola Quotidiana*, January 21, 2022: https://lanuovabq.it/it/abusi-ratzinger-al-contrattacco-su-di-me-propaganda.

about a month later he was involved in pastoral work that again put him in contact with minors, thus enabling him to carry out other abuses in the following years. According to the statement drafted by Ratzinger, he did not know that the priest from the Diocese of Essen was being transferred to Munich for psychotherapeutic treatment as a result of sexual abuse he allegedly committed. Only a generic "risk" (*Gefährung*) was known, but it was not specified. Based on the testimonies collected in each case, however, it was not Ratzinger who decided to engage him in pastoral work, but rather Monsignor Gerhard Gruberan, the vicar general of the diocese (an office that enjoys more power in Germany than in other parts of the world).

In 2022, this reception resurfaced as an accusation against Ratzinger[19] because in his 82-page statement of defense against the charge of covering up for four priests accused of pedophilia, he had erroneously denied his presence in the meeting regarding Hullerman's acceptance. Upon examination of the facts, it became clear that this was a transcription error on the part of Pope Benedict's legal team. An understandable error given that the team had not been put in a position to do their best work. In fact, the Diocese of Munich allowed only one man to access the 8,000-page documentation, did not allow him to have a copy, kept the copy online only, and did not enable him to take advantage of the search function normally used in PDF documents. This confusion over a piece of data, or this error (as some may prefer), for which Benedict XVI has apologized, took nothing away from the substance of the matter and did not affect Ratzinger's Defensive Statement because, as mentioned earlier, the truth had been publicly known since at least 2010 (and perhaps even since 1986 when Hullermann was sentenced to probation for child abuse).

It was in this context that in February 2022 Pope Emeritus Benedict XVI wrote a letter to the Catholics of the world in response to the accusations made against him. The letter expresses

---

19   Cf. Regoli, "Pope Benedict, Sex Abuse and the Catholic Church's Future," op. cit.

his sorrow and his acceptance of responsibility for the blame of abuse, of the "most grievous fault."[20] This does not so much concern personal fault, but a response of his conscience in the face of the "great responsibilities" that he exercised in the Catholic Church. Benedict XVI's response belongs on a spiritual and meta-historical level.

We have opened this long parenthetical about the year 2022 to provide a more complete narrative of the abuse cases in Germany, but now it is time to get back to the ecclesial dynamics and awareness in the years of Benedict XVI's pontificate.

In still other nations, information is scare and fragmented. Data was also provided by Fr. Lombardi, S.J., director of the Vatican press office, but the information given only pertained to Austria, where there were 17 charges registered against church authorities against 510 charges in other sectors of society.[21] In 2002, Cardinal Ratzinger, at the time Prefect of the Congregation for the Doctrine of the Faith, claimed that at the international level, "the rate of sexual abuse perpetrated by priests is no higher than by others, and perhaps it is even lower."[22]

Other statistics regarding the universal Church were furnished by Monsignor Charles J. Scicluna, Promoter of Justice at the Congregation for the Doctrine of the Faith, in an interview published in the 13 March 2010 edition of the *Avvenire*.[23] According to Scicluna, no reports of abuse were received by the Congregation between 1975 and 1985 because the Congregation had no competency to handle such cases at the time. Then, after John Paull II released the Motu Proprio *Sacramentorum Sanctitatis Tutela* in 2001, according to which pedophilia cases against clergy were

20 Benedict XVI, *Letter regarding the Report on Abuse in the Archdiocese of Munich-Freising,* February 8, 2022: https://press.vatican.va/content/salastampa/it/bollettino/pubblico/2022/02/08/0092/00182.html.
21 Politi, *Joseph Ratzinger. Crisi di un papato,* op. cit., 211.
22 Ibid., 227.
23 Gianni Cardinale, "Intervista. Il 'pm' vaticano: 'Chiesa rigorosa sulla pedofilia,'" in *Avvenire,* 13 March 2010.

reserved exclusively to the Holy Office, cases began to arrive. Between 2001 and 2010, the Congregation handled 3,000 complaints of abuse committed by priests over a period of approximately fifty years—that is, an average of sixty per year, many of which occurred many years prior. The largest number of cases arrived from the United States. In fact, 80% of cases received between 2003–2004 came from the United States, but that figure dropped to 25% in 2009. Between 2007 and 2009, the Congregation received on average 250 cases per year.

Of those cases 10% involved pedophilia strictly speaking (that is, sexual abuse against pre-pubescent minors), 60% against adolescents of the same sex (i.e., ephebophilia), and 30% against adolescents of the opposite sex (i.e., heterosexual relations). Priests accused of pedophilia in the strict sense numbered 300. Only 20% of those accused had undergone a canonical process (penal or administrative), and 10% were dismissed from the clerical state through a direct intervention of the pope due to the gravity of the case and the overwhelming incriminating evidence. Only 10% had asked on their own accord to leave the priesthood and were immediately granted a dispensation. The remaining 60%, given their advanced age, were subjected to restrictions on their priestly ministry (such as revoking the permission to celebrate Mass publicly and hear confessions, and asking the accused to lead a life of seclusion and prayer).

There are no similar systematic studies done by other religions or educational bodies. All of this data came to light after the crisis and because of it. In the beginning, the phenomenon was not well understood, and the best way for the Church to deal with the problem could not be based simply on incomplete information about the past. This meant that the Church had to face a new, unprecedented challenge. There was no prior tried and tested solution. This explains why so much depended on the people appointed to deal with the situation.

In year 2000 and immediately after, the problem exploded in the American media. This was followed by similar explosions in other Western countries in North America, Europe, and Oceania, although things remained relatively quiet in Africa and Asia. Does this mean that the phenomenon only occurred in certain regions because of specific cultural factors? Certainly not. We only need to recall the previously mentioned data collected in India. Furthermore, the Confucian culture predominating in places like Japan and Korea makes it very difficult for people in those countries to speak openly about sexual abuse. The cultural element is indeed key. In many African nations, young women are already married and having children between the ages of 14 and 16. In Angola, boys between the ages of 13 and 16 are initiated into "boys camps" where they are introduced to sexuality in rituals that would be considered abusive in the West.[24]

The allegations that have come to light often occurred decades ago. The issue was particularly poignant during Benedict XVI's pontificate. Historian Giovanni Miccoli speculated that the abuse crisis "was, for various reasons, an opportunistic moment for many people. It was a lucrative time for lawyers who could make millions from representing alleged victims. In the initial years after 2000, it was an opportunity—at least in part—to hinder the American hierarchy, which for the most part was opposed to the wars waged by George W. Bush."[25]

It will be years before we fully understand why the Catholic Church was the sole focal point of outrage over the sexual abuse crisis. Here we should simply mention that the crisis, because of the enormous amount of media attention it received, was an urgent matter not only for local bishops' conferences, but for the Church in Rome as well, which now found herself under more pressure than ever before.

24   Cf. John L. Jr Allen, "Interview with Hans Zollner," *National Catholic Reporter*, 16 February 2013: http://ncronline.org/blogs/ncr-today/jesuit- expert-calls-benedict-great-reformer-sex-abuse.

25   Miccoli continues: "These factors were undoubtedly at play, but they cannot explain sufficiently the breadth and impact of the crisis. Nor are they sufficient for understanding the wide variety of reactions within the Church." Giovanni Miccoli, *La Chiesa dell'anticoncilio. I tradizionalisti alla riconquista di Roma* (Roma – Bari: Laterza, 2011), 384.

Benedict XVI already had to confront the issue as Prefect for the Congregation for the Doctrine of the Faith, where he became known for his hardline stance. His attitude may not have been shared by many in the Curia.

Already in 1988, then-Cardinal Ratzinger questioned the efficacy of the norms of the Code of Canon Law, which had come out just five years earlier, and which attributed the responsibility for this kind of crime to individual dioceses. On February 19, 1988, he wrote to Cardinal José Rosalío Castillo Lara, president of the Pontifical Commission for the Authentic Interpretation of the Code of Canon Law, requesting more rapid and simplified procedures for the reduction to the lay state (discharge from the clerical state) of priests involved in similar crimes, while safeguarding justice and the good of the faithful. This simplification required the passage of an extrajudicial administrative process. Cardinal Castillo Lara responded within a few weeks (on March 10th), recognizing that the question touched on the "responsible exercise of the task of governance,"[26] but at the same time he did not want to simplify the ongoing procedures, so as not to question the fundamental right to defense, nor to neglect "the due exercise of authority, thereby damaging the common good of the faithful." A few months later, however, the new constitution on the Roman Curia, *Pastor Bonus* (June 29) clearly established the exclusive penal jurisdiction of the Congregation for the Doctrine of the Faith also for "offences against the faith and more serious ones [...] in behavior" (art. 52). Ratzinger and his men seemed to be in a position to operate more freely, but the juridical system debated what these crimes actually were. The authority of the bishops was at issue—that is, their jurisdiction was being undermined. Ratzinger remained with his hands tied for many more years, until he managed to get the handling of these

26 Juan Ignacio Arrieta, "Cardinal Ratzinger and the Revision of the Canonical Penal Law System: A Crucial Role," in L'*Osservatore Romano*, December 2, 2010. Also found at: https://www.vatican.va/resources/resources_arrieta-20101202_en.html.

crimes centralized in Rome, overcoming the inability or failure of local episcopates to deal with them. Also at issue was the real efficacy of the operation of the ecclesial penal system and the uniformity of the procedures for handling cases.

At first, the Congregation for the Clergy asserted its competence over this delicate issue, but its approach to the matter was found to lack the required severity. Consequently, cardinal Ratzinger decided to invoke the reclaim of his dicastery,[27] which John Paul II granted. It was precisely on 18 May 2001, with the letter *De delictis gravioribus* implementing the above-mentioned Motu Proprio *Sacramenorum sanctitatis tutela,* that the Congregation for the Doctrine of the Faith was appointed to deal with "sins against the sixth commandment by a cleric against a minor under the age of eighteen" as one of the *delicta graviora*.[28] Before that time it was local diocesan bishops who had to deal with these cases, but no longer. Rome wanted to look closely at the situation and make sure justice was rendered. Furthermore, in order to ensure that more serious crimes received due attention, it was decided that priority would be given to cases in which the victim was younger at the time of abuse. When the text of the letter became public, some criticized it for stipulating that cases were to be processed under pontifical secret, which they interpreted as meaning that the Vatican had something to hide. In reality, though, the pontifical secret is standard practice for all canonical processes in order to ensure the good reputation of everyone involved until a final decision has been made.

Ratzinger did not fall short in making decisions and interventions to confront what he often called an "open wound." Indeed, the experts considered him the "the most determined figure" in

---

27   Benedict XVI, *Last Testament,* 199.
28   *Delictum contra mores, videlicet: delictum contra sextum Decalogi praeceptum cum minore infra aetatem duodeviginti annorum a clerico commissum*: Congregation for the Doctrine of the Faith, "Lettera de delictis gravioribus," 18 May 2001, in *Acta Apostolicae* 93 (2001), 785–788, and particularly 787.

dealing with the mess.[29] He immediately issued two indictments from the Congregation against two notorious priests who up until that time had been protected by certain Vatican churchmen and by a general climate of reticence in the Church.[30] These priests were Luigi (Gino) Burresi, founder of the Servants of the Immaculate Heart of Mary, who was prohibited from exercising his ministry and obliged to retire form public life (27 May 2005), and Marcial Maciel Degollado, founder of the Legionnaires of Christ (obligated, in May of 2006, at the age of eighty, to retire to a life of prayer and penance and to renounce all public ministry).[31] As pope, Benedict would later state that Fr. Maciel was leading "a life that, as we now know, was out of moral bounds—an adventurous, wasted, twisted life."[32] Ratzinger did not want to waste time given the "filth" in the Church, as he wrote in his Way of the Cross meditations in 2005. These decisions not only signaled his reform program, but they also indicated the momentum of his entire pontificate. In fact, he is the one primarily responsible for initiatives to increase transparency in the Roman Curia in matters regarding sexual abuse and overcoming concerns "to preserve the good name of the Church and to avoid scandals."[33]

The pope, even while recognizing attacks of the "enemy" against the Church (especially during the Year of the Priest in 2009–2010[34]) sparked by a lack of oversight by some Church

29   Allen, *Intervista a Hans Zollner,* op. cit.
30   Cf. Miccoli, *La Chiesa dell'anticoncilio. I tradizionalisti alla riconquista di Roma,* op. cit., 386–387.
31   Cf. Sandro Magister, "Fine della storia per il fondatore dei Legionari di Cristo," 19 May 2006: http://chiesa.espresso. repubblica.it/articolo/58361.
32   Benedict XVI, *Luce del mondo,* 64–65. In English, *Light of the World* (San Francisco: Ignatius Press, 2010).
33   Benedict XVI, "Lettera pastorale ai cattolici d'Irlanda. Per sanare le ferite e ricostruire la fiducia tradita," 19 March 2010, *Acta Apostolicae Sedis,* n. 102 (2010): 209–220. See Miccoli, *La Chiesa dell'anticoncilio. I tradizionalisti alla riconquista di Roma,* op. cit., 87.
34   Benedict XVI, *Omelia, Santa messa per la conclusione dell'anno sacerdotale,* 11 June 2010, in *Acta Apostolicae Sedis,* n. 102 (2010): 376–382.

individuals, did not hide problems surfacing in Ireland in 2010, but also in Germany (where there was an attempt to falsely implicate the pope in a single allegation of misconduct while he was Archbishop of Munich[35]), France, and other European nations.

Among the failures that led to the crisis, the pope singled out the inadequacy of Catholic teaching in recent decades:

> We have to reflect on what was insufficient in our education, in our teaching in recent decades: there was, in the 50s, 60s and 70s, the idea of proportionalism in ethics: it held that nothing is bad in itself, but only in proportion to others; with proportionalism it was possible to think for some subjects—one could also be pedophilia—that in some proportion they could be a good thing. Now, it must be stated clearly, this was never Catholic doctrine. There are things which are always bad, and pedophilia is always bad.[36]

In 2010, the pope asserted that the socio-cultural roots of sexual abuse are in the soil of secularization, the abandonment of the sacraments, a weakening of prayer, and the temptation of priests and consecrated men and women to adapt themselves to the thinking of a secularized society.[37] The problem of sexual abuse is the deplorable product of past confusion and turmoil in the Church. In an interview with Peter Seewald, the pope pointed to the climate between the 1950s and 1970s, a time when "a theory was even finally developed [...] that pedophilia should be viewed as something positive."[38] It

---

35 Politi, *Joseph Ratzinger. Crisi di un papato*, op. cit., 214–216.

36 Interview of the Holy Father Benedict XVI during the flight to Australia, 12 July 2008: http://www. vatican.va/holy_father/benedict_xvi/speeches/2008/july/documents/hf_ben-xvi_spe_20080712_interview_it.html.

37 Benedict XVI, *Lettera pastorale ai cattolici d'Irlanda. Per sanare le ferite e ricostruire la fiducia tradita*, op. cit.

38 Benedict XVI, *Luce del mondo*, 63. In English, *Light of the World* (San Francisco: Ignatius Press, 2010).

was a time when a thesis was circulating that "there was nothing evil in itself," but only "relative" evil.

In his meeting with journalists during a flight to Portugal (11 May 2010), the pope said:

> the greatest persecution of the Church comes not from her enemies without, but arises from sin within the Church, and that the Church thus has a deep need to relearn penance, to accept purification, to learn forgiveness on the one hand, but also the need for justice. Forgiveness does not replace justice.[39]

The pope poignantly acknowledged the faults and asked the Church to perform acts of penance and purification in atonement for them. This is particularly evident in a letter sent to the Catholics of Ireland (19 March 2010), in which he severely reprimanded the Irish bishops:

> It cannot be denied that some of you and your predecessors failed, at times grievously, to apply the long-established norms of canon law to the crime of child abuse. Serious mistakes were made in responding to allegations. I recognize how difficult it was to grasp the extent and complexity of the problem [...]. Nevertheless, it must be admitted that grave errors of judgement were made and failures of leadership occurred. All this has seriously undermined your credibility and effectiveness. I appreciate the efforts you have made to remedy past mistakes and to guarantee that they do not happen again. Besides fully implementing the norms of canon law in addressing cases of child abuse, continue to cooperate with the civil authorities in their area of

39 Interview of the Holy Father Benedict XVI with journalists during the flight to Portugal, 11 May 2010.

competence. Clearly, religious superiors should do like-wise.[40]

The pope speaks with remarkable courage and candor in the letter. Turning to victims, he says "when you were courageous enough to speak of what happened to you, no one would listen. Those of you who were abused in residential institutions must have felt that there was no escape from your sufferings." And again, "You have suffered grievously and I am truly sorry. I know that nothing can undo the wrong you have endured. Your trust has been betrayed and your dignity has been violated." The pope speaks of "crimes" and "the gravest of sins." Priests who are guilty must respond to God and "properly instituted tribunals."

In his ecclesial governance, Benedict XVI simultaneously combined two approaches: a pragmatic one and a spiritual one. Both aspects emerge in this letter, although the spiritual approach is the basis and reason for his governing choices. In the text, for example, the pope insists specifically on prayer, adoration, fasting, and penance as necessary ways for establishing the truth, and for facing and overcoming problems.

The letter is not simply representative of the many pastoral interventions Benedict made during his pontificate, nor is it a simple condemnation of sexual abuse committee by local clergy. Rather, it is the first example of a direct condemnation of the way in which the problem was handled by ecclesial authorities concerned only with "avoiding scandal."[41] The pope is just as clear that the local Church must collaborate with local civil authorities (an admonition that was not always heeded by bishops[42]).

40 Benedict XVI, *Lettera pastorale ai cattolici d'Irlanda. Per sanare le ferite e ricostruire la fiducia tradita,* op. cit.
41 Alberto Melloni, *Benedict XVI,* in Alberto Melloni (dir.), *Il conclave di papa Francesco,* Istituto della Enciclopedia Italiana (Roma, 2013), 23–61.
42 Cf. Miccoli, *La Chiesa dell'anticoncilio. I tradizionalisti alla riconquista di Roma,* op. cit., 386.

The Irish episcopate was subsequently subjected to a canonical visit conducted by a papal envoy (November 2010 to June 2011). The results of the visitation were shocking and resulted in the dismissal or resignation of several bishops at the direct behest of the Holy See. Because this was an internal disciplinary problem, the pope sent a man he personally trusted—someone whom he already considered a collaborator at the Congregation for the Doctrine of the Faith—Monsignor Charles Brown—known for his competency and personal integrity. His priorities were obviously more disciplinary and pastoral than diplomatic, which gave him a different profile than the average papal nuncio. The scandal in Ireland had shaken the life of the Church to its very core, as the pope wrote in the above cited letter. The sexual abuse of children in Ireland "contributed in no small measure to the weakening of faith and the loss of respect for the Church and her teachings."[43]

Despite the Vatican's efforts to deal proactively with the problem, the government in Dublin decided to recall its ambassador accredited to the Holy See, claiming that it had to perform a "spending review" to cut costs. In reality, they were not forthcoming about the influence certain groups within the Church had on making the decision.[44] But that is another story.

Regarding the sexual abuse of minors, Benedict XVI remained vigilant, not only in speeches and letters, but in gestures. During his Apostolic Voyages he went out of his way to meet with victims of sexual abuse at the hands of priests. In 2008, during trips to the United States in April and Australia in July, he met with small

---

43 Benedict XVI, *Lettera pastorale ai cattolici d'Irlanda. Per sanare le ferite e ricostruire la fiducia tradita*, op. cit.

44 Introvigne, Marchesini, *Pedofilia: una battaglia che la Chiesa sta vincendo: con un approfondimento storico, filosofico, clinico*, op. cit., 15–16; Sandro Magister, "Campagna d'Irlanda. Il contrattacco di Roma," in *Settimo cielo*, 3 September 2011: http://magister.blogautore.espresso.repubblica.it/2011/09/03/ campagna-dirlanda-il-contrattacco-di-roma/; *Diario Vaticano / La cattolica Irlanda toglie la tripla A al papa*, 5 November 2011 in http://chiesa.espresso. repubblica.it/articolo/1350075.

groups. In 2006 and 2009, he met twice with the bishops in Ireland, who seemed incapable of handling the problem of pedophilia. There was also a famous meeting in Malta in 2010,[45] in which, according to eyewitnesses, the Pope welled up with tears while listening to the stories of abuse victims.[46] The pope's method of dealing with the crisis became exemplary for the entire Church. Other bishops emulated his approach.[47] Sensibilities still differed, however, as shown by the spat in April of 2010 between Cardinal Christoph Schönborn and Cardinal Angelo Sodano. The former publicly criticized the latter for not taking the crisis seriously after Sodano said that pedophilia was "today's buzz." Schönborn also called the handling of the case of Cardinal Hans Hermann Groër— the Archbishop of Vienna who was dismissed in 1995 on accusations of pedophilia—a "cover-up."[48] In June of 2010, Schönborn was essentially told to be a team player to fall in line. It was his "walk to Canossa."[49] In the College of Cardinals under Dean Sodano, and Camerlengo Bertone, there was no space for criticism and ecclesial discipline was vigorously enforced. The statement issued by the Vatican Press Office on 28 June 2010 made this clear:

45   Cf. "Pope Benedict XVI reduced to tears after child abuse meeting in Malta," in *The Guardian*, 18 April 2010.

46   Holy See Press Office, *Comunicato stampa* (Press release), 18 April 2010: http://www.vatican.va/resources/resources_comunicato-abusi-malta_it.html; Agenzia AGI, *Papa: rabbia e odio spazzati via da lacrime Ratzinger*, 18 April 2010: http://archivio.agi.it/articolo/3e0a2be35f7461bb363d683239c10 3c4_20100418_papa-rabbia-e-odio-spazzati-via-da-lacrime-ratzinger/.

47   Cf. "Vescovi europei in merito al dramma degli abusi," *L'Osservatore Romano*, 2 April 2010.

48   "Pedofilia, l'arcivescovo di Vienna accusa Sodano: 'Insabbiò le inchieste,'" in *Corriere della Sera*, 8 May 2010. Accessed at: http://www.corriere.it/politica/10_May_08/papa-pedofilia-vescovo-mixa_1934c78e-5a8a-11df-903e- 00144f02aabe.shtml.

49   Sandro Magister, "Il papa estrae il cartellino giallo per il cardinale Schönborn." Accessed at: http://magister.blogautore.espresso.repubblica.it/2010/06/28/il-papa-estrae-il-cartellino-giallo-al-cardinale-schonborn/

1. Today, the Holy Father received in audience Cardinal Christoph Schönborn, Archbishop of Vienna and President of the Austrian Episcopal Conference. He had asked to report personally to the Supreme Pontiff on the present situation of the Church in Austria. In particular, Cardinal Christoph Schönborn wishes to clarify the exact sense of his recent statements on some aspects of ecclesiastical discipline, as well as some judgments on the attachment had by the Secretariat of State, and in particular by the then-Secretary of State of Pope John Paul II of venerable memory, as regards the late Cardinal Hans Hermann Gröer, Archbishop of Vienna from 1986 to 1995.

2. Subsequently, invited into the meeting were Cardinals Angelo Sodano, Dean of the College of Cardinals, and Tarcisio Bertone, Secretary of State. In the second part of the audience, some widely circulated misunderstandings that were partially due to certain comments made by Cardinal Christoph Schönborn were clarified and resolved, for which he expressed regret over the interpretations given.
In particular:
    a) It is recalled that in the Church, when accusations are made against a Cardinal, the competence [of judgment] rests solely with the Pope; other instances have a function of consultation, always with the proper respect for persons.
    b) The word *chiacchiericcio* ["chatter," "gossip"] was erroneously interpreted as a lack of respect for the victims of sexual abuse, for whom Cardinal Angelo Sodano holds the same sentiments of compassion and condemnation of evil, as expressed in diverse interventions of the Holy Father. That word, pronounced in his Easter address to Pope Benedict XVI, was taken literally from the papal homily of Palm Sunday and referred to the "courage that doesn't let one be intimidated by the chatter of dominant opinions."

3. The Holy Father, recalling with great affection his pastoral visit to Austria, conveyed to Cardinal Christoph Schönborn his greetings and encouragement to the Church in Austria

and to its pastors, entrusting the renewed path of ecclesial communion it has undertaken to the heavenly protection of Mary, so venerated at Mariazell.

Discovering and combatting sexual violence at the local level is the responsibility of the national bishops' conference. The bishops must design a plan of action, which subsequently must be approved by the Congregation for the Doctrine of the Faith. A few countries (the Netherlands, Belgium, Austria, England and Wales, and others) established commissions to investigate claims of sexual abuse. These were put together according to guidelines approved by the bishops of those nations (Scotland, the United States, Canada, Brazil, Chile, Switzerland, France, Slovenia, Malta, New Zealand, Australia, the Philippines, and others).

The Holy See urged bishops to take action. By means of a circular letter published on 15 July 2010, the Congregation for the Doctrine of the Faith issued more stringent and streamlined norms and procedures for fighting pedophilia in the Church, including a lengthening of the statues of limitation, punishment of guilty parties through decrees, and an immediate decision of the pope in cases that were extraordinarily grave. Abuse of the mentally disabled was put on par with the abuse of minors. It was established that, with the authorization of the pope, bishops, cardinals, and patriarchs could also be subject to trial. The criteria for filling positions on diocesan tribunals were also simplified.

These interventions, in addition to those discussed previously, had immediate effects: in 2011 there were 260 priests dismissed from the clerical state, 124 in 2012, and 171 in the two-year period of 2008–2009.[50]

---

50 Andrea Tornielli, "In due anni Benedetto XVI ha dimesso 384 preti per abusi su minori," in *Vatican Insider*, 18 January 2014: http://www.lastampa.it/2014/01/18/vaticaninsider/ita/vaticano/in-due-anni-benedetto-xvi-ha-dimesso-preti-per-abusi-su-minori-rwXe33fZaQxEDMGwiMSmFI/ pagina.html.

In another circular letter dated May of 2011,[51] the Congregation required every bishops' conference to adopt a plan of action and not to leave initiatives to the discretion of individual diocesan bishops. They were asked to follow civil law statues in reporting crimes to state authorities.

A symposium held at the Gregorian University in 2012 was a real milestone in the Church's public relations. It involved bishops from throughout the world representing 110 bishops' conferences, as well as 35 superior generals.[52] It was meant to be an organized response indicating a willingness to follow Vatican directives, demonstrating that bishops throughout the world were cooperating in this endeavor. It presumably helped 75% of national bishops' conferences adopt guidelines to treat the problem of sexual abuse.[53]

Episcopal conferences were constantly urged to take responsibility. Much of the reason reports of sexual abuse of minors were so scandalous is that bishops seemed incapable of dealing with allegations appropriately and failed in their duty of vigilance and protection. These facts indicate a larger crisis in the episcopate throughout the world—that is, a crisis of leadership, which warranted the Holy See's intervention.

There can be no doubt that much effort was spent by Benedict XVI addressing the issue of the sexual abuse of minors during his pontificate. The scandal of Cardinal McCarrick, which brought to the forefront, once again, the failures of Church leadership, and again called into question Benedict's knowledge of abuses perpetrated and his response to them; the report prepared for the

51 Congregation for the Doctrine of the Faith, *Lettera circolare per aiutare le Conferenze episcopali nel preparare linee guida per il trattamento dei casi di abuso sessuale nei confronti di minori da parte dei chierici*, 3 May 2011, *Acta Apostolicae Sedis* 103 (2011): 406–412.
52 Cf. Agenzia SIR, Pedofilia: simposio alla Gregoriana: "Per una risposta globale e coerente," 19 January 2012: http://agensir.it/quotidiano/2012/1/19/ pedofilia-simposio-alla-gregoriana-per-una-risposta-globale-e-coerente/.
53 Cf. Allen, *Intervista a Hans Zollner*, op. cit.

Archdiocese of Munich by the legal firm of Westphal Spilker Wastl has done just that. The case of former Cardinal McCarrick might be offered as an example of Benedict's two-fold approach to the painful issue. First, when confronted with evidence, action was taken—the "McCarrick report" clearly demonstrates that Benedict took actions as pope to limit McCarrick's public ministry. Second, the action taken actively seeks to avoid any further scandal. This approach has been greatly criticized, especially by some in the media.[54]

The heart of Benedict's approach was the conviction he shared in his letter to the Irish Catholics. In addressing the offending priests, Benedict stressed both the spiritual and material realities of the justice they must face: "You betrayed the trust that was placed in you by innocent young people and their parents, and you must answer for it before Almighty God and before properly constituted tribunals."[55] In speaking to victims, Benedict urged them to rediscover Christ's love, "by drawing newer to Christ and participating in the life of the Church—a Church purified by penance and renewed in pastoral charity." Finally, in suggesting a path forward, Benedict stressed the importance of Eucharistic adoration:

> Through intense prayer before the real presence of the
> Lord, you can make reparation for the sins of abuse that

54 Rachel Donadio, Alan Cowel, "Pope Offers Apology, Not Penalty, for Sex Abuse Scandal," in *The New York Times*, 21 March 2010. Accessed at: https://www.nytimes.com/2010/03/21/world/europe/21pope.html; Ian Traynor, Karen McVeigh, Henry McDonald, "Pope Benedict 'complicit in child sex abuse scandal,' say victims' group," in *The Guardian* 11 February 2013: https://amtheguardian.com/world/2013/feb/11/pope-complicit-child-abuse-say-victims; Mitchell Landsberg, "Pope Benedict took action on sex abuse, but some say not enough," in *Los Angeles Times*, 11 February 2013: https://www.latimes.com/world/la-xpm-2013-feb-11-la-fg-pope-sex-abuse-20130212-story.html.
55 Benedict XVI, *Lettera pastorale ai cattolici d'Irlanda. Per sanare le ferite e ricostruire la fiducia tradita*, op. cit.

have done so much harm, at the same time imploring the grace of renewed strength and a deeper sense of mission on the part of all bishops, priests, religious and lay faithful. I am confident that this program will lead to a rebirth of the Church in Ireland in the fullness of God's own truth, for it is the truth that sets us free (cf. Jn 8:32).

Benedict's approach was not one that sought to respond to the secular media. In addressing the immeasurable harm done to individual victims, Benedict sought, as a man of faith, to redress the wounds done to the entire Church. While setting forth strong, clear laws to punish those who would perpetrate this horrible crime, Benedict also set forth a plan of reconciliation, prayer, and adoration that would seek to heal the wounds caused by this most grievous sin.

The papacy and the episcopacy

The twentieth and twenty-first centuries have seen the Church spread more widely across all five continents, making it extremely difficult to know where to draw boundaries.[56] This is a general crisis in society and politics as well. Consequently, the process of recruiting Church personnel is not easy, nor is it easy to identify the best candidates for local and universal Church governance. Bishops are nominated by the pope, but the process is deeply immersed in the local level. At the universal level, there is constant jockeying between Roman centralism and local ecclesial power (dioceses, bishops' conferences, and major superiors of religious congregations).

Cardinal Ratzinger's opinion of episcopal conferences was well known. He said that "they have no theological foundation,"[57] a position that indeed has a strong historical basis.[58] Another

---

56 Politi, *Joseph Ratzinger. Crisi di un papato*, op. cit., 179.
57 Ibid., 9.
58 This is consistent with studies on the birth of episcopal conferences. Cf. Giorgio Feliciani, *Le conferenze episcopali* (Bologna: Il Mulino,

organism in need of explanation is the Synod of Bishops, which periodically gathers a representation of bishops throughout the world to discuss themes proposed by the pope. The synod was created by Paul VI, but it has not really taken off since, and has limited its activity to debates and the publication of summary documents. Benedict XVI took steps to facilitate the action of the synod, encouraging open discussion at the end of each day's work.

The history of the relationship between Rome and the fringe territories of the Church is dynamic and evolving. Tension between the two is constant. It was undoubtedly present during the conclave of 2005. The dynamic tension between the two is best understood if we glance back at history. It would be too large a task to survey the relationship starting in the Middle Ages or in the Modern period, so let us start with Pope Pius VII in the nineteenth century, who began a gradual—albeit not always intended—program of centralizing the Church around the figure of the pope. The various tensions at that time with various liberal states led the Church—and more specifically the pope—to choose her own bishops. This made for an episcopate that was more and more dependent on Rome, a "Roman" episcopate in its formation and mentality, as men chosen for the office had normally been educated in Roman colleges.

Furthermore, beginning with Gregory XVI (1831–1846), popes consciously made use of episcopal meetings to pass and implement the basic points of their pontifical platform in various local

1974); Giorgio Feliciani, "Le conferenze episcopali nelle proposte del cardinale Bonaventura Cerretti al suo rientro a Roma dalla nunziatura di Parigi," in Brigitte Basdevant-Gaudemet, François Jankowiak, Franck Roumy (ed.), *Plenitudo Juris. mélanges en hommage à michèle Bégou-Davia* (Paris: Mare & Martin, 2015), 235–246; Alessandra Marani, *Una nuova istituzione ecclesiastica contro la secolarizzazione. Le conferenze episcopali regionali (1889–1914)* (Rome: Herder, 2009); Roberto Regoli, "Concili italiani. I sinodi provinciali nel XIX secolo," in *Archivum Historiae Pontificiae*, 46 (2008): 131–161.

circumstances.[59] By means of episcopal gatherings, the Holy See wanted to keep abreast of episcopal deliberations in order to ensure obedience to Roman directives. The Holy See used papal representatives—*nuncii*—for this process. *Nuncii* began by following the local business of bishops (under Pius IX), but gradually became managers of the precise implementation of Roman directives (under Leo XIII). In the course of Pius X's pontificate (1903–1914), there were new attempts to strengthen the powers and functions of the pope over bishops.[60] At the universal level, measures were taken by Pius XI (1922–1939) to exert more control over bishops' conferences: they were required to invite the nuncio or apostolic delegate to their meetings (at least indirectly).[61] During the twentieth century, a norm was established that bishops were to be chosen freely and directly by the pope rather than by local governments. The state could intervene only to raise an objection of a political nature regarding the desired candidate. The last nominations to be made by a state were in Spain in 1976, Peru and the Principality of Monaco in 1980, and Haiti in 1984. There are still dioceses in the German-speaking world where there is a collaboration between Church and civil government, or at least where the government has a significant role. In France, the bishop

59 Cf. Alessandra Marani, "Tra sinodi e conferenze episcopali. La definizione del ruolo degli incontri collettivi dei vescovi fra Gregorio XVI e Pio IX," *Cristianesimo nella storia*, n. 17 (1996): 48.
60 Cf. Giovanni Vian, *La riforma della Chiesa per la restaurazione cristiana della società: le visite apostoliche delle diocesi e dei seminari d'Italia promosse durante il pontificato di Pio X: 1903–1914* (Rome: Herder, 1998), 729.
61 Giorgio Feliciani, "Tra diplomazia e pastoralità: nunzi pontifici ed episcopato locale negli anni di Pio XI," in Cosimo Semeraro (ed.), *La sollecitudine ecclesiale di Pio XI. Alla luce delle nuove fonti archivistiche*. Atti del convegno Internazionale di Studio. Vatican City, 26–28 February 2009 (Vatican City: LEV, 2010), 61–77; Roberto Regoli, "Il ruolo della Sacra Congregazione degli Affari ecclesiastici Straordinari durante il pontificato di Pio XI," in Semeraro (ed.), *La sollecitudine ecclesiale di Pio XI. Alla luce delle nuove fonti archivistiche*, op. cit., 183–229.

of Strasbourg and Metz is still nominated by the government, even though papal confirmation is required.

Today we are witnessing a further scaling back of the power of local churches and a further strengthening of the papacy, which, after a century, has reaffirmed its central and primary role in the universal Church.

To understand this development fully, we would do well to consider the Second Vatican Council, which, while it recognized episcopal collegiality, reaffirmed papal primacy (the college of bishops is a college only insofar as the pope is its head). Even since the council, however, there has been a search for new ways to exercise primacy by involving the bishops to a greater extent. It is no accident that, shortly before the close of the council, the Synod of Bishops was instituted (1965) as a sort of compromise consultation with bishops worldwide.

Because of his prior responsibilities, Benedict XVI knew the episcopacy well when he took the reins of the universal Church. His new responsibilities obviously brought new challenges in relating to the episcopacy.

Yet he was not afraid to give direction to the universal Church, spurring her on, sometimes without the bishops' full support. An example can be found in his repeal of the excommunication of four Lefevbrite bishops (21 January 2009), which was barely acceptable to some bishops. Several complained that the Vatican did not consult the bishops before making this decision.[62] The media turmoil in the wake of this action and the general confusion of the Church on this issue made the Holy See feel as if it were being assaulted, and the pope felt that he was under attack. It was during this confusion that Benedict XVI decided to write a letter to Catholic Bishops dated 10 March 2009, expressing his apologies for what had happened.[63] He

---

62 Politi, *Joseph Ratzinger. Crisi di un papato,* op. cit., 135, 161.
63 Benedict XVI, "Lettera ai vescovi della Chiesa Cattolica riguardo alla remissione della scomunica dei 4 vescovi consacrati dall'arcivescovo Lefebvre," 10 March 2009, *Acta Apostolicae Sedis,* n. 101 (2009): 270–276.

acknowledged that there was "vehemence" in the discussion (public, or private, it is not known fully). This text gives us hints of his vision of the pope's role in the Church and in Christianity, and the relationship between the Roman center and the periphery of the Church.

The letter begins with a recognition of, and distinction between, what really happened and the way it was interpreted:

> Many Bishops felt perplexed by an event which came about unexpectedly and was difficult to view positively in the light of the issues and tasks facing the Church today. Even though many Bishops and members of the faithful were disposed in principle to take a positive view of the Pope's concern for reconciliation, the question remained whether such a gesture was fitting in view of the genuinely urgent demands of the life of faith in our time. Some groups, on the other hand, openly accused the Pope of wanting to turn back the clock to before the Council: as a result, an avalanche of protests was unleashed, whose bitterness laid bare wounds deeper than those of the present moment. I therefore feel obliged to offer you, dear Brothers, a word of clarification, which ought to help you understand the concerns which led me and the competent offices of the Holy See to take this step. In this way I hope to contribute to peace in the Church.

He continued to show his bewilderment and perplexity that a "discreet gesture of mercy" was twisted and badly interpreted; that "a gesture of reconciliation with an ecclesial group engaged in a process of separation thus turned into its very antithesis: an apparent step backwards with regard to all the steps of reconciliation between Christians and Jews taken since the Council." This is followed by a revealing comment: "I was saddened by the fact that even Catholics who, after all, might have had a better knowledge of the situation, thought they had to attack me with open hostility." Among those he has in mind were bishops, priests,

175

laity, and theologians. He then reiterates his role in the Church: "The first priority for the Successor of Peter was laid down by the Lord in the Upper Room in the clearest of terms: 'You [...] strengthen your brothers' (Lk 22:32)." He then also repeats his analysis of the Church's mission in today's world:

> In our days, when in vast areas of the world the faith is in danger of dying out like a flame which no longer has fuel, the overriding priority is to make God present in this world and to show men and women the way to God. Not just any god, but the God who spoke on Sinai; to that God whose face we recognize in a love which presses "to the end" (cf. Jn 13:1)—in Jesus Christ, crucified and risen. The real problem at this moment of our history is that God is disappearing from the human horizon, and, with the dimming of the light which comes from God, humanity is losing its bearings, with increasingly evident destructive effects.

He continues by observing, "At times one gets the impression that our society needs to have at least one group to which no tolerance may be shown; which one can easily attack and hate. And should someone dare to approach them—in this case the Pope—he too loses any right to tolerance; he too can be treated hatefully, without misgiving or restraint." Looking at the state of things inside the Church, he cites a passage from Saint Paul: "[...] if you bite and devour one another, take heed that you are not consumed by one another" (Gal 5:15). He closes with this:

> But sad to say, this "biting and devouring" also exists in the Church today, as expression of a poorly understood freedom. Should we be surprised that we too are no better than the Galatians? That at the very least we are threatened by the same temptations? That we must always learn anew the proper use of freedom? And that we must always learn anew the supreme priority, which is love?

176

The letter is noteworthy for several reasons. Above all, it signifies a new development in the relationship between the papacy and the episcopacy. The letter, which some called "dramatic,"[64] was clearly written freely in a spirit of sincerity and responsibility (the pope does not place the responsibility for the crisis on the shoulders of his collaborators, even though they were clearly the ones that should have shouldered it). It is an example of direct, unmediated communication between the pope and bishops. It manifests the pope's role of primacy as the successor of Peter as he goes out to meet his critics, all the while acknowledging and thanking "all the many Bishops who have lately offered me touching tokens of trust and affection, and above all assured me of their prayers," as well as "all the faithful who in these days have given me testimony of their constant fidelity to the Successor of Saint Peter."[65] Does the letter represent a weakness in Benedict's grasp of his role, or a reaffirmation of it? It is undoubtedly an act of humility and responsibility on the part of the pope. But not only that. It surely indicates that a serious crisis was afoot, and he could no longer act through discreet channels. Such a direct and public intervention manifests the incapacity of curial structures to absorb the impact of what was happening. A public crisis now calls for a public response. The pope was forced to expose his mind. He had to do it because the dossier that caused the problem was initiated and brought to completion precisely at the pope's urging.

Episcopal nominations

Perhaps nothing reveals the dynamic relationship between Rome and the rest of the Church more than episcopal nominations. With the few exceptions noted above, such nominations ultimately

---

64 Politi, *Joseph Ratzinger. Crisi di un papato*, op. cit., 138.
65 Benedict XVI, *Lettera ai vescovi della Chiesa Cattolica riguardo alla remissione della scomunica dei 4 vescovi consacrati dall'arcivescovo Lefebvre*, op. cit.

depend on the pope. The greater the incompetency of the local episcopate, the more proactive the pope is in making decisions. Take, for example the apostolic visit to Ireland, where an investigation into seminaries and dioceses resulted in some bishops resigning willingly, while others were forced to resign. In deciding episcopal appointments, Benedict XVI was assisted by the Prefect of the Congregation for Bishops, Cardinal Re, who was succeeded by the Canadian Cardinal Ouellet; and by the Prefect of Propaganda Fidei, Cardinal Dias, who was later replaced by Filoni; as well as the Secretary of State, Cardinal Bertone (who was preceded by Sodano for the first year of Benedict's pontificate). The process of proposing candidates for Eastern Churches follows a very different *iter* that takes place primarily within the Vatican. The nomination process, overseen by the local papal representative (i.e., a nuncio or apostolic delegate), begins at the local level with information provided by bishops, major religious superiors, and laity. This leads to a *terna* (i.e., a list of three names) of candidates for a particular see. Rome takes over from there. The above-mentioned congregations, in conjunction with the Secretary of State, forwards a *terna* to the Holy Father. The pope has the final say. He always has in mind his ideal model of a bishop formed by what is going on in society and the Church at that time.

In his 2010 interview with Peter Seewald, Benedict XVI sketched the essential qualities of a bishop at the beginning of the twentieth century. He said a bishop must be a man of "courage" and demonstrate outstanding qualities of "intelligence, professionalism, and human courtesy." He also must be a proven leader and show a willingness to go against the cultural current.[66] Have the Congregation for Bishops and Propaganda Fidei been able to identify candidates with such qualities? Have bishops shown that they are able to guide their flocks? The officials at Propaganda Fidei believe it is important for candidates to have done their

---

66   Benedict XVI, *Luce del mondo*, 126. In English, *Light of the World* (San Francisco: Ignatius Press, 2010).

priestly formation in Rome or at least somewhere in Europe at a respectable Pontifical or European university.[67]

In any case, the total number of nominations made by Benedict XVI is significant. Of the approximately 3,000 dioceses in the world[68] (if we consider only new nominations and exclude transfers of a bishop from one see to another), there were 90 bishops appointed in 2009 in the geographical areas depending on the Congregation for Bishops: 92 in 2010, and 99 in 2011.[69] In the territories that fall under the responsibility of Propaganda Fidei, 57 new bishops were nominated in 2009,[70] 51 in 2011,[71] yet the number for 2010 is unclear. If we take these years as typical, we can easily understand how a pope, year by year, transforms the face of the local church, even if the system gives a key role to residential bishops in the process. Indeed, in some cases, the pope's intervention can be of a corrective or urgent nature, if Rome so desires. However, such cases are few.

Every pontificate has a few exceptions to the usual *iter*, in which case the *terna* is set aside and Rome chooses its own candidate. We can surmise this might happen if the candidate settled upon seems risky. Two such nominations appeared during Benedict XVI's pontificate.[72] Unfortunately, we know nearly nothing about decisions that seem to have been popular but, in the end, failed to take hold.

The first nomination to end in failure was the Auxiliary Bishop of Linz (Austria), Gerhard Wagner. His nomination was

---

67   Cf. Olivier Sibre, "Le Saint-Siège et l'Asie orientale à l'heure du pape François: au croisement des enjeux missionnaires et diplomatiques," *Outre-Terre. Revue européenne de géopolitique* 45 (2015): 293–317.

68   Cf. Benedict XVI, *Luce del mondo*, 28.

69   Cf. *L'attività della Santa Sede nel 2011* (Città del Vaticano: LEV, 2011), 500.

70   Cf. *L'attività della Santa Sede nel 2009*, (Città del Vaticano: LEV, 2009), 501.

71   Cf. *L'attività della Santa Sede nel 2011*, op. cit., 503.

72   Cf. Politi, *Joseph Ratzinger. Crisi di un papato*, op. cit., 141–159.

published on 31 January 2009, but he subsequently declined the nomination on 2 March 2009 after a media firestorm spread throughout the Catholic world, including the Austrian hierarchy, because the candidate seemed too conservative. Various reports about his past opinions appeared in the media after his nomination—namely, that Harry Potter is an example of Satanism, the tsunami of 26 December 2004 that devastated a large part of southeast Asia was God's punishment upon wealthy, Western tourists, and hurricane Katrina, which submerged New Orleans in 2005, was further punishment for the city's sordid behavior (night clubs, brothels, and abortion clinics), and homosexuality is a disease that needs to be cured. Obviously, his opinions were not widely shared and there was a major pushback. The Church's public image was at stake. Wagner's name did not appear on the *terna* provided by the nuncio, nor did he appear among the preferences indicated by the ordinary bishop of Linz. The bishops' conference vociferously expressed its displeasure at the Vatican's lack of respect for the usual process: "[T]here is no question that the selection of bishops is the pope's prerogative," but nonetheless, "we bishops are convinced that the method prescribed by Canon Law for the selection and examination of candidates works only if procedures are properly observed. This is because the pope must have a thoroughly tested basis upon which he makes his final decision."[73] In this case, the decision seems to have been forced by the Vatican. One of the priests most openly opposed to Wagner was his diocesan brother, Josef Friedl, a pastor and deacon, who, at that time, was cohabitating openly with a woman.

In the end, the opposition won. Was Wagner's nomination an example of the pope rolling the dice? Or is it an example of the pope's failure to stand by his candidate in the face of those who oppose his program? In reality, it is a matter of two churches battling over a single issue (a nomination) that signifies something more. It is not merely a matter of an episcopal nomination, but

73   Politi, *Joseph Ratzinger. Crisi di un papato,* op. cit., 136.

rather which church to favor at the time, or which kind of Catholicism to thwart or encourage in a given moment.

On 6 December 2006, the pope appointed Stanisław Wojciech Wielgus, Bishop of Płock since 1999, to the archepiscopal see of Warsaw. Soon after the appointment was announced, stories circulated in the media about his alleged collaboration with the Polish communist secret service at the end of the 1960s. Although Wielgus initially downplayed the allegations (claiming he was contacted, but never collaborated), and the Polish Conference of Catholic Bishops supported him, the criticism only grew in the following days. Wielgus complained that he was being framed by certain members in the secret service who were trying to damage his reputation (it is not clear why). The Holy See stood its ground and issued a statement through its press office on 21 December 2006, saying that it took into consideration Wielgus's biography when making the appointment, including his past life. This means that the Holy Father has full confidence in His Excellency Stanisław Wielgus, and completely stands by his decision to entrust the Archdiocese of Warsaw to him.[74] In fact, the bishop had previously been required to clarify some of his positions in writing to the Congregation for Bishops because of concerns raised by the Apostolic Nuncio to Poland, Józef Kowalczyk. Under oath, he declared: "I swear to God, One and Three, that during my meetings and conversations with representatives of the police and intelligence, which I had on the occasion of my trips overseas in the 1970s and 1980s, I never stood against the Church, and I have neither done nor said anything against the clergy and lay people."[75]

Gradually, however, previously unknown information began to surface revealing that the bishop indeed had effectively collaborated with the secret service. Wielgus subsequently wrote a letter

---

74 Press Office of the Holy See, *Comunicato circa la nomina del nuovo arcivescovo metropolita di Varsavia*, 21 December 2006: https://press.vatican.va/content/salastampa/it/bollettino/pubblico/2006/12/21/0668/01883.html.

75 Politi, *Joseph Ratzinger. Crisi di un papato*, op. cit., 157.

to the faithful asking their forgiveness: "Today I can state with full conviction that I never reported anyone and I made every attempt not to damage anyone's reputation."[76] In any case, the bishop placed his future in the pope's hands.

The Polish government, under the leadership of the populist and anti-communist premier Jarosław Kaczyński, did not sit on the sidelines as the crisis unfolded in Krakow. The city, in fact, had long been a staunch symbol of resistance to communism and every kind of collaboration with communist authorities. The government sent a dossier on Wielgus to the Vatican, translated into German so that the pope could read the information easily. Only then did the Vatican begin to rethink its support for Wielgus, who by that point was ready to excuse himself from the office, and he held no delusions of peacefully possessing the archepiscopal see entrusted to him. He tearfully announced his resignation to the faithful gathered in the Warsaw cathedral on the day he was supposed to take possession of it.

It is now clear that Wielgus was not on the nuncio's original *terna,* which included Józef Mirosław Zyciński, Bishop of Lublin and a leader among the left-leaning bishops,[77] Józef Michalik, Archbishop of Przemysł and President of the bishops' conference, and Wiktor Skworc, Bishop of Tarnów. Those on the *terna* seemed to have been supported by various pressure groups within the Church, groups of people who themselves had benefited from being on the radar of the old communist secret service.[78] Others who had aspired to the see, according to the press, included Tadeusz Gocłowski, Bishop of Danzica, a liberal, the curial Cardinal Stanisław Ryłko, and the nuncio Kowalczyk. Under so much pressure, the process stalled, and that is when Wielgus, a specialist in medieval philosophy who had once been rector of the university and, at the time of his appointment, bishop of a

76   Ibid., 156.
77   Cf. Sandro Magister, "Caso Wielgus. I perche' delle dimissioni," 11 January 2007: http://chiesa.espresso.repubblica.it/articolo/110361.
78   Cf. Ibid.

small diocese, emerged as a candidate.[79] According to Politi, the pope himself wanted Wielgus, whom he had known during his time in Munich. He was considered a "conservative," as was most of the Polish episcopate at the time. Were there competing visions of the Church at work in this case, as in Linz? Father Adam Boniecki, then-editor of the Polish edition of *L'Osservatore Romano*, boldly stated: "I don't know who, but someone misinformed Pope Ratzinger. This is serious, and someone—either in Poland or the Vatican—should pay."[80] Was it simply a matter of misinformation? The Cardinal Archbishop of Krakow, Stanisław Dziwisz, spoke of political manipulation: "There was certainly a plan by journalists and a political dimension behind this campaign." Were state politics or ecclesial politics primarily behind it? At this point, we simply do not know.

There were other appointments personally made by the pope. Among the better known is the transfer of André Léonard to the Archdiocese of Malines-Bruxelles in 2010. According to the nuncio in Belgium at the time, the German Karl-Josef Rauber, Léonard's name did not appear on the *terna* prepared at the nunciature. In fact, it was absent from both the first and the second lists because he was not considered the right candidate for that particular diocese (Rauber did not give reasons), even though he was "intelligent" and "an interesting philosopher." According to Rauber, Léonard was "extremely loyal to Rome," and in this sense "Rome made sure that someone obedient to her would be selected."[81] Simplifying the story of Magister, it was "the pope personally who selected him."[82] In any case, this nomination was

---

79   Cf. Ibid.

80   Ibid.

81   Francesco Strazzari, "La scelta di Léonard. Intervista con l'ex nunzio Mons. Karl-Josef Rauber," *Il Regno,* n. 4 (2010): 85–86, here p. 86.

82   Sandro Magister, *"De bello germanico.* Ex nunzio tedesco vuota il sacco contro il papa," *Settimo Cielo,* 2 March 2010: http://magister.blogautore.espresso.repubblica.it/2010/03/02/de-bello-germanico-ex-nunzio-tede-sco-vuota-il-sacco-contro-il-papa/.

more successful than others, even though it was vulgarly attacked by some extremists outside the Church (i.e., FEMEN). The archbishop's subsequent ministry focused heavily on reigniting the faith of his flock without hesitation or compromise. Such an approach seems in line with Benedict XVI's pontificate, who sought bishops who would help him in this endeavor.

Difficult relationship with bishops

Not even Rome's control over episcopal nominations and a thorough process at the local level can guarantee that every candidate chosen is a good one. In places where ecclesial factions are at war with one another, it can only be hoped that a passable bishop or at least one not too tied to any specific faction is chosen. The choice is extremely hard in these cases. Moreover, in such a vast Church, the Holy See does not always have direct relations with bishops, despite the fact that hierarchically there is a linear relationship between bishops and the pope. At times, there are serious administrative and/or financial problems at the local level, inept governance, and serious weaknesses in doctrine or morals. This is when Rome faces the choice of dismissing the local bishop, or at least of convincing him to take an early retirement. Some commentators have even written of a "silent purging." According to the Vatican Insider website, between April 2005 and October 2012, there were 77 "mandatory resignations," or about one per month.

Some of these resignations were due to illness (e.g., McRaith of Owensboro and Gloser of Bolzano-Bressanone), and others for aforementioned reasons. A few bishops, however, who had refused to submit their letters of resignation voluntarily, were deposed directly by the Holy See.

Some bishops disappeared from the scene suddenly due to scandalous circumstances. The Argentinian Fernando María Bargalló was caught on vacation with his lover, and the Chilean Marco Antonio Órdenes Fernández was under investigation for serious sexual abuse.

Other bishops had to step down for doctrinal reasons, such as Argentinians Marcelo Angiolo Melani and Juan Carlos Romanín Gallegos, as well as Australians Patrick Percival Power and William Martin Morris, Bishop of Toowoomba. The latter of these caused quite a stir.

In a pastoral letter written in 2006, Morris showed that he was open to "ordaining married, single or widowed men who are chosen and endorsed by their local parish community, welcoming former priests, married or single, back to active ministry, ordaining women, married or single, recognizing Anglican, Lutheran and Uniting Church Orders."[83] He also permitted communal absolution in place of individual confession, for which he was reprimanded by the Holy See and told to cease the practice immediately.[84] Regarding the ordination of women, the pope allegedly sent a memo to Cardinal Re about Morris's case, emphasizing that "Saint John Paul II stated infallibly and irrevocably that the Church has no authority to ordain women to the priesthood."[85] In addition to repeating this teaching in another letter to Morris, he was also reminded of Catholic teaching on Lutheran, Anglican, and Uniting Church ordinations.[86]

But let us look at events in order. In the wake of his 2006 pastoral letter, Morris received an invitation in February 2007 to present his case in Rome at the Congregation for Bishops. When he

83 William M. Morris, "Lettera pastorale per l'Avvento 2006," 17 November 2006, in Mauro Castagnaro and Ludovica Eugenio, (eds.), *Il dissenso soffocato: un'agenda per Papa Francesco* (Bari: Edizioni la Meridiana, 2013), 47.

84 Cf. Gianluigi Nuzzi, *Sua Santità. Le carte segrete di Benedetto XVI,*(Milano: Chiarelettere, 2012), 17; Paul Collins, "Intervista," 3 July 2011, in Castagnaro and Eugenio, eds., *Il dissenso soffocato: un'agenda per papa Francesco,* op. cit., 2; Mauro Castagnaro, "Il *aso morris,*" in Castagnaro and Eugenio, *Il dissenso soffocato: un'agenda per papa Francesco,* op. cit., 12–14.

85 Nuzzi, *Sua Santità. Le carte segrete di Benedetto XVI,* op. cit., 219.

86 Cf. "Risposta di William Morris alla dichiarazione dei vescovi cattolici australiani del 22 October 2011," 24 October 2011, in Morris, *Lettera pastorale per l'Avvento 2006,* op. cit., 70.

refused to respond in a timely matter,[87] Rome ordered an apostolic visit conducted by the American archbishop Charles Chaput,[88] who submitted a report in May of 2007.[89] This led Rome to order Morris to resign, which he refused to do. Between 2007 and 2011, there was further contact between Rome and Morris, including a meeting with Benedict XVI himself in 2009.[90] The final result was that Morris was removed (or, according to Morris, he took an early retirement) because of a doctrinal vision the pope deemed "inadequate" and "insufficient;"[91] a vision that not only was not Catholic, but also divisive in his diocese, according to Cardinal Pell.[92] As the Australian bishops (who initially showed support for Morris, but in the end accepted the Vatican's decision) acknowledged, the problems identified by Rome were "doctrinal and disciplinary."[93] Major religious superiors in Australia surrounded Morris with support.[94] The press was divided. Two conflicting visions of the Church emerged from this affair regarding doctrinal pronouncements on the sacraments. As observers (some

---

87   Collins, *Intervista*, 3 July 2011, op. cit., 76.
88   Cf. William M. Morris, "Lettera pastorale alla diocesi," 30 April 2011, in Castagnaro and Eugenio, *Il dissenso soffocato: un'agenda per papa Francesco*, op. cit., 50.
89   Cf. Castagnaro, "Il caso Morris," op. cit., 17.
90   Cf. Collins, "Intervista," 3 July 2011, op. cit., 78.
91   Nuzzi, *Sua Santità. Le carte segrete di Benedetto XVI*, op. cit., 219.
92   Cf. David Kerr, "Cardinal Pell Says Bishop Morris Sacking a Tragedy but also a Useful Clarification," in *Catholic News Agency*, 28 May 2011: http://www.catholicnewsagency.com/news/cardinal-pell-says-bishop-morris-sacking-a-tragedy-but-also-a-useful-clari-fication/.
93   "Lettera di Mons. Philip Wilson, presidente della Conferenza episcopale australiana, a Mons. Brian Finnigan, amministratore apostolico di Toowoomba," 12 May 2011, in Morris, *Lettera pastorale per l'Avvento 2006*, op. cit., 66.
94   Cf. "Lettera della Conferenza australiana dei superiori degli istituti religiosi a mons. Giuseppe Lazzarotto, nunzio apostolico in Australia," 13 May 2011, in Eugenio Castagnaro, *Il dissenso soffocato: un'agenda per papa Francesco*, op. cit., 58–61.

of whom were friends of Morris) noted, the key question was in regard to the ordination of women and the Church's vision of ministry.[95] It was a matter of subtle and not-so-subtle voices of dissension in the Church that emerge from time to time when they receive media attention. As long as they don't stir the pot too much, they manage to live in relative peace. But because Benedict XVI proposed a program that emphasized the integral beauty of the faith, he could not sit on the sidelines when fundamental doctrinal matters were at stake. Accordingly, his request for Morris to step down was inevitable.

For moral reasons ranging from concubinage, the sexual abuse of minors, and other questionable moral behavior, Tamás Szabó, the military ordinary in Hungary, was forced to step down, as were Central Africans Paulin Pomodino and François-Xavier Yombandje, the Uruguayan Francisco Domingo Barbosa Da Silveira, John Thattumkal, the Canadian Raymond Lahey, the Mexican Alberto Campos Hernández, and Gabino Zavala from the United States. In Norway, the bishop of Trondheim, Georg Müller, resigned in June of 2009. Only in the Spring of 2010 was it revealed that he had been accused of pedophilia.[96] On 23 April 2010, the bishop of Bruges, Roger Vangheluwe, stepped down on account of circumstantial evidence that he was involved in pedophilia.[97]

Isidore Battikha, Syrian Archbishop of the Melkite Greek Catholic Archeparchy of Homs, was forced to resign on 6 September 2010. He was subsequently forced to leave the Middle East and take refuge in Venezuela on account of still unknown accusations.[98]

Sometimes bishops are invited to submit their letters of resignation for other reasons, such as for poor administration of the

95   Cf. Collins, "Intervista," 3 July 2011, op. cit., 80 and 83–84.
96   Cf. Politi, *Joseph Ratzinger. Crisi di un papato*, op. cit., 235.
97   Cf. Ibid., 226.
98   Cf. Nuzzi, *Sua Santita*. *Le carte segrete di Benedetto XVI*, op. cit., 259–263.

Church's temporal goods, or past or present immoral behavior. If they resist, they are deposed. Walter Miza, for example, Bishop of Augusta and the Military Ordinary in Germany, after having been accused of embezzlement, abusive behavior toward minors as a pastor, and the abuse of minors as bishop of Eichstätt, resigned on 21 April 2010 (his letters of resignation were accepted on 8 May 2010).[99] Later the accusations appeared "unfounded,"[100] or at least not fully credible, to the point that Benedict XVI would appoint him as a member of the Pontifical Council for Health Workers (2012).

Benedict's relationship with the Irish bishops after their extreme incompetence in dealing with the clerical sexual abuse of minors came to light remains highly unique. The pope met the Irish bishops several times from the beginning of his papacy. He met with them in October 2006 and again in December 2009 after the publication of the Ryan Report (20 May 2009) and the Murphy Report (26 November 2009). The former regarded religious institutes in Ireland, where over a period of thirty-five years there were 800 religious members guilty of sexual abuse in 200 institutes. The Murphy Report, put together by Yvonne Murphy, regarded sexual abuse perpetrated by the clergy of Dublin between 1975 and 2004. It revealed that there were 320 cases of sexual abuse perpetrated by 46 priests of the diocese.[101] The real problem was in the way the hierarchy mishandled the problem. The archdiocese tried to cover up the problem to protect the Church. At the end of 2009, four bishops resigned (Donald Murray of Limerick, James Moriarty of

99   Cf. Politi, *Joseph Ratzinger. Crisi di un papato,* op. cit., 209; Markus Günther, "Bischof Mixa reicht Rücktrittsgesuch ein," *Augsburger Allgemeine,* 21 April 2010: http://www.augsburger-allgemeine.de/bayern/Bischof-Mixa-reicht-Ruecktrittsgesuch-ein-id7664381.html; "Rücktrittsgesuch angenommen: Vatikan entfernt mixa aus Bischofsamt," in *Spiegel* Online, 8 May 2010: https://www.spiegel.de/panorama/gesellschaft/ruecktrittsgesuch-angenommen-vatikan-entfernt-mixa-aus-bischofsamt-a-693720.html.
100 Paolo Rodari, *Il Foglio,* 17 June 2010.
101 Politi, *Joseph Ratzinger. Crisi di un papato,* op. cit., 206–207.

Kildare, and Raymond Field and Eamonn Walsh, auxiliaries of Dublin, whose letters of resignation would later be refused by the pope because they were found to be not guilty). The Irish episcopate was then placed under a canonical visitation, an extraordinary action on the part of the Holy See. On 24 March 2010, the Bishop of Cloyne, John Magee, former secretary of Paul VI, John Paul I, and John Paul II, resigned.

Not only bishops, but priests were forced to resign as well. In Italy, the following were dismissed from the clerical state: Lelio Cantini of Florence (2008); the highly touted founder of the Community *Incontro*, Pierino Gelmini (2008); Marco Dessì (2010), a missionary priest in Nicaragua; Andrea Agostini (2010), a priest of Bologna who operated a Catholic asylum; and Nello Giraudo (2010), a priest of the diocese of Savona. In the decade of 2001–2010, a hundred canonical cases of dismissal from the clerical state were opened in Italy.[102]

Deserving special consideration is Paraguayan bishop Fernando Lugo, who, running on a far-left platform, was elected president in 2008. Benedict XVI, at first uncertain of how the handle the situation, dismissed Lugo from the clerical state in July of that year.[103] It seems this was the first time something like this has taken place.

Benedict's relationship with bishops was not, of course, limited to appointing them and firing them. He was in contact with them on a daily basis, collaborating and planning with them. In Italy, for example, which Andrea Riccardi labelled "the Church's garden" (perhaps "the pope's garden" would be more accurate), there is a special relationship between the papacy and the bishops.

It is historically accurate and significant to say that today the Italian Church is under the strict control of the Vatican. Given that Cardinal Bertone not only liked running things, but let everyone know he was running things, this control was no secret. On 25

102 Cf. Ibid., 252.
103 Cf. *https://en.wikipedia.org/wiki/Fernando_Lugo.*

March 2007, he wrote to the Italian Conference of Catholic Bishops: "As to the Church's relationship with political institutions, I assure Your Excellency of the cordial collaboration and respectful leadership of the Holy See, as well as my own."[104] It was already clear that this was happening even before Bertone wrote these words.

Among the sensitive correspondence that surfaced during the Vatileaks affair were letters revealing a cold standoff between the Secretary of State and the Cardinal Archbishop of Milan, Dionigi Tettamanzi, in March of 2011. They strongly disagreed over who should exercise control over the Toniolo Institute of Higher Studies (which was responsible for the governance of the Catholic University and its Polyclinic in Rome called *il Gemelli*). Bertone, bolstering himself with papal authority, invited Tettamanzi to submit his letters of resignation from the presidency of the Institute. The Archbishop of Milan, not believing this really reflected the pope's will, went directly to Benedict XVI.[105] Some months later, Tettamanzi was replaced by Cardinal Scola in the natural course of episcopal nominations, but kept his title as president of Toniolo, and only later stepped down to join the advisory board of the Institute. Even though Bertone failed in his attempt to have Tettamanzi step down, he did manage to revise the Institute's Statutes.[106]

In 2011, the Secretary of State also showed interest in acquiring the hospital named *San Raffaele di Milano*, which had gone bankrupt on account of poor management. Again, Bertone met resistance from both Tettamanzi and Scola because of research conducted at the hospital that was in serious conflict with

---

104 "Lettera di Tarcisio Bertone ad Angelo Bagnasco," 25 March 2007, in *L'Osservatore Romano*, 28 March 2007.
105 Cf. Nuzzi, *Sua Santita*. *Le carte segrete di Benedetto XVI*, op. cit., 163–171; Eric Frattini, *I corvi del Vaticano*, with the collaboration of Valeria Moroni (Milan: Sperling & Kupfer, 2013). Spanish original edition (*Los cuervos del Vaticano*, 2012), 21–27.
106 Ibid., 171.

Catholic moral teaching.[107] In 2012, because the Vatican did not come up with a plan to salvage the institute, it was sold at auction to the health-care management system San Donato operated by Giuseppe Rotelli.

The Vatican Secretariat of State was constantly involved in Italian affairs, but their meddling was often unwelcome. As far as we can tell, there was always a discrepancy between the Vatican's obliquely stated objectives and its actual operations in these affairs.

Conclusion

Looking at the way Rome governed affairs under Benedict XVI and the way it categorized them into ordinary, priority, and urgent matters, we can draw some general conclusions.

First of all, Rome's focus was the "West" in the broadest meaning of the term. The crisis that concerned Pope Benedict was the cultural crisis of the West, which was more a social phenomenon than a geographical one. It was a disciplinary crisis, perhaps even more than a doctrinal crisis. If the bishops' inadequacy in handling clerical sexual abuse of minors obliged Rome to intervene and become more centralized, then Rome was not able to fulfill all its plans for a renewal in the hierarchy (we might think of the glaring cases in Europe). The papacy is on top of things, but it has no time to devote to its own projects. Something similar is seen in the case of religious women in the United States. The crisis put up difficult obstacles to the pope's plan of reasserting the classic theme of "faith." In fact, we see that there were conflicting visions of the Church at play and therefore conflicting visions of faith. Benedict XVI's pontificate came at a time when different points of view came to the fore, leading to inevitable conflict. The pope was just another player on the field trying to lead the Church along a better path according to the framework Rome gave him in the post-Vatican II period that began with Paul

107 Ibid., 171–177.

VI. The way that Rome spoke seemed consistent with this for a long time. Benedict XVI's role was to complete the program that had already been in place during that period and to systematize it into a more structured and organic vision. The difficulty, however, was figuring out how to implement the ideas practically (we can think of liturgical matters, for example).

Catholicism more organized in its teaching and in its politics might have confronted the external challenges more easily. One of the greatest of those challenges was the unity of Christians.

CHAPTER FIVE
THE UNITY OF CHRISTIANS

From the beginning of his pontificate, one of Benedict XVI's main priorities was Christian unity. In his first message at the end of the concelebrated Mass with the cardinal electors on 20 April 2005,[1] Benedict already addresses the theme of Christian unity, showing himself to be fully in line with the gains made since Vatican II and the magisterial teaching of his predecessors. In that message, Benedict, speaking of himself in the third person, said the pope "takes on as his primary task the duty to work tirelessly to rebuild the full and visible unity of all Christ's followers. This is his ambition, his impelling duty. He is aware that good intentions do not suffice for this. Concrete gestures that enter hearts and stir consciences are essential, inspiring in everyone that inner conversion that is the prerequisite for all ecumenical progress."

Thus, Benedict followed the path set by his predecessor, John Paul II, whose main theological counselor he had been, such that we might think of him as the theological soul of the Wojtyła era, so to speak. As we shall see, the long-standing issue of how to achieve Christian unity was usually the business of theologians, some of whom had reached high positions of authority in the Vatican (e.g., Kasper, Koch, and Müller). The most important questions, in fact, were in regard to dogmatic themes, even though they were usually connected to disciplinary matters.

To better understand the parameters of Benedict's ecumenical thinking, we can begin with a speech he gave to representatives

---

1   Benedict XVI, "Primo messaggio al termine della concelebrazione eucaristica con i cardinali elettori," 20 April 2005, *Acta Apostolicae Sedis*, n. 97 (2005): 694–699.

of other churches and Christian communities on 19 August 2005 in Cologne[2] during the celebration of World Youth Day. Rejecting the so-called "ecumenism of return," (understood as the denial and rejection of one's own faith history, or a "uniformity in all expressions of theology and spirituality, in liturgical forms and in discipline"), he proposed the way of "dialogue," which is not merely "an exchange of thoughts" or "an academic exercise," but rather "an exchange of gifts." He affirmed, at the same time, that this unity, "we are convinced, indeed subsists in the Catholic Church, without the possibility of ever being lost; the Church in fact has not totally disappeared from the world."

How should we link that vision to the ecumenical practice of the preceding decades during which unity was sought merely in terms of different Christian confessions walking together? In any case, the pope reminded his audience, "We cannot 'bring about' unity by our powers alone. We can only obtain unity as a gift of the Holy Spirit. Consequently, spiritual ecumenism—prayer, conversion and the sanctification of life—constitutes the heart of the meeting and of the ecumenical movement." It is also enlightening to look at Benedict's speech at Regensburg on 12 September 2006.[3] Within his broader reflection on the relationship between religion and reason, he recalled the years he spent teaching in Regensburg and the atmosphere of study and research at two theological faculties at the university, where rationality was the foundation and a way of life. Rational faith is the departure point, just as it is in ecumenical dialogue. Just a few months later, during the week of prayer for Christian unity in January 2007, the Secretary of the Pontifical Council for the Unity of Christians, Monsignor Brian Farrell, drawing up the pope's thought, stated that ecumenical

2   Benedict XVI, "Discorso all'Incontro ecumenico, Colonia," 19 August 2005, *Acta Apostolicae Sedis*, n. 97 (2005): 909–915.

3   Benedict XVI, "Discorso con i rappresentanti della scienza, Regensburg," 12 September 2006, *Acta Apostolicae Sedis*, n. 98 (2006): 728–739. Italian translation: http://w2.vatican.va/content/benedict-xvi/it/speeches/2006/september/documents/hf_ben-xvi_spe_20060912_university-regensburg.html.

dialogue does not consist in diplomatic agreements or in strategies for inter-faith cooperation, but rather in the ability to dialogue rationally.[4] The picture is filled out even more in a speech by the new president of the Pontifical Council for Christian Unity (Koch) who declared that there are two pillars to ecumenical dialogue according to the theological vision of Ratzinger: love and truth.[5] How do we interpret these two pillars?

There are several practical roads that lead to Christian unity. One is to take a pragmatic approach that concentrates on the major ethical-political questions of the day, upon which various Christians might reach agreements on specific issues. We see this approach at work in Catholic-Orthodox relations, and both Benedict XVI and Metropolitan Hilarion have acknowledged this.[6] The latter has spoken of a "strategic alliance" between Catholics and Orthodox on traditional Christian values—namely, "the family, the value of human life from conception to death, the education of children, and the integrity and indissolubility of marriage."[7] In another interview, Hilarion expanded on this idea to include "questions of social and economic ethics" and the "demographic crisis, bioethical questions, the problem of euthanasia,"[8] and

4   Brian Farrell, *Meditazione sul principale strumento del movimento ecumenico*, 22 January 2007: http://www.vatican.va/roman_curia/pontifical_councils/chrstuni/weeks-prayer-doc/rc_pc_chrstuni_doc_20070122_ire- land-farrell_it.html.

5   Giampaolo Mattei, "Amicizia, amore e verità, i cardini del dialogo ecumenico, Intervista all'arcivescovo Kurt Koch, nuovo presidente del Pontificio Consiglio per la promozione dell'unità dei cristiani," *L'Osservatore Romano*, 15 September 2010: www.vatican.va/news_services/or/or_quo/ interviste/2010/212q08a1.html.

6   Cf. Benedict XVI, *Luce del mondo*, 132. In English, *Light of the World* (San Francisco: Ignatius Press, 2010).

7   Hilarion di Volokolamsk, "Lo stato attuale delle relazioni ortodosso-cattoliche," *Studi ecumenici*, n. 29 (2011), here 115.

8   Edward Pentin, "An Interview with metropolitan Hilarion Alfeyev of Volokolamsk, the Chairman of the Russian Orthodox Department of external Church Relations," in *National Catholic Register*, 4 March 2014: http://www.ncregister.com/daily-news/the-pan-or-

many other topics. This way of proceeding has emerged strongly in recent years and can equally be viewed as a *modus operandi* for cooperating with other Christian confessions.

For decades, the more common path toward Christian unity centered around theological dialogue between the heads of different confessions, often resulting in symbolic gestures (such as the 1964 meeting between Paul VI and the Patriarch of Constantinople Athenagoras, which subsequently led on 7 December 1965 to the cancelation of the mutual excommunication of 1054, despite an ongoing lack of mutual understanding and differing points of view), or in the signing of documents that do not always get to the heart of central questions but still involve significant changes in the relationship between two confessions (e.g., the Joint Declaration between Catholics and Lutherans on Justification signed in 1999). Sometimes there is even talk of an ecumenism of "good feelings," to borrow an expression Benedict XVI himself used to describe a general lethargy in doing the work to achieve full unity. We also need to keep in mind that the ecumenical momentum reached in the 1990s began to wane and a kind of weariness crept in. Cardinal Kasper reflected the feelings of many when he referred to "a crisis" and a "new ecumenical winter."[9]

In comparison to John Paul II, Benedict XVI pursued his quest for unity with a newfound freshness and originality, particularly in three areas: Lefebvritism, Anglicanism, and Orthodoxy. Important developments during Benedict's pontificate include the ordinariates created for groups coming over from Anglicanism, contacts with the Orthodox, and a dense albeit inconclusive dialogue with the Lefebvrites. No major developments took shape

thodox-council-ukraine-crisis-and-christian-unity/&sa=U&ei=8kNAU-fZM6fs4wSn4oHQBg&ved=0CAwQFjAD&client=internal-uds-cse&usg=AFQjCNGFHCiYHixO6ZO3FQR-8nu0YYw49SQ.

9   Walter Kasper, "La teologia ecumenica. Situazione attuale," in *In cammino verso l'unità dei cristiani. Bilancio ecumenico a 40 anni dall'Unitatis Redintegratio*, ed. Donato Valentini (Roma: LAS, 2005), 262.

with regard to Protestantism, aside from a few negative reactions of Lutheran leaders to the ecumenical meeting Benedict had in Germany in 2011.[10] Also worth mentioning is Benedict's analysis of Luther's theological research, which was unprecedented in a pope. He presented Luther as a passionate seeker of God, and more specifically of God's mercy.[11]

During the course of the twentieth century, there were basically two roads followed in the Catholic quest for Christian unity. The first can be called "unionism," and the second "ecumenism." Unionism envisions Christian unity as being achieved by the return of non-Catholic Christians (usually considered dissidents and often judged negatively) to Rome as individuals, groups, or churches. Ecumenism is a multifaceted rapprochement of various Christian churches and communities beginning primarily in the middle of the twentieth century, leading to unity among once separated Christians. Ecumenism envisions all churches and communities walking toward a single horizon, while unionism envisions all non-Catholic Christians walking toward Rome (some call ecumenism a "return to and submission to Rome").

Benedict XVI, looking through a classic ecumenical lens, envisions the development of a visible unity that revolves around a real sacramental and hierarchical communion with Rome while respecting the liturgical, disciplinary, and spiritual traditions of those who previously were not in communion with Rome. To arrive at this, Benedict employed the previously tested methods (especially with regard to Orthodoxy and the traditionalist, schismatic world) and new methods (as in Anglicanism, and in some ways with traditionalism).

10   Gianluigi Nuzzi, *Sua Santità. Le carte segrete di Benedetto XVI,*(Milan: Chiarelettere, 2012), 215–217.
11   Benedict XVI, "Discorso ai rappresentanti del Consiglio della *Chiesa evangelica in Germania*," (Erfurt: 23 September 2011). Accessed at: http://w2.vatican.va/content/benedict-xvi/it/speeches/2011/september/documents/hf_ben-xvi_spe_20110923_evangelical-church-erfurt.html.

Two significant documents with ecumenical repercussions were published by the Congregation for the Doctrine of the Faith during Benedict's pontificate. The first, entitled "Responses to some questions regarding certain aspects of the doctrine on the Church" (dated 29 June 2007 but released the following December), deals with the ecclesiological issues at play in ecumenism. Drawing upon Vatican II terminology, this statement characterizes the Catholic Church as the one, sole Church of Christ in the fullest sense and denies the term "church" in favor of "Christian communities" born during the sixteenth-century Reformation.[12] The second document, entitled "Doctrinal Note on some aspects of evangelization," published on 3 December 2007, was intended to clarify the relationship between Christian mission and "a respect for the conscience and religious liberty of all."[13] It recalls the urgency of the mission and the salvific role not only of Christ but of His Church. While traditionalists criticized both documents for their conciliatory spirit, some ecumenists considered them a step backward "in respect to the way Vatican II characterized the relationships between the Catholic Church and other churches and confessions."[14] Judgments vary on these documents depending on one's point of view. Because they deal with hot topics receiving much theological attention, there are strong positions regarding their meaning and significance.

12   Congregation for the Doctrine of the Faith, "Responses to some questions regarding certain aspects of the doctrine on the Church," 29 June 2007, *Acta Apostolicae Sedis*, n. 99 (2007): 604–608. Accessed at: http://www.vatican.va/roman_curia/congregations/cfaith/documents/rc_con_cfaith_doc_20070629_responsa-quaestiones_en.html.

13   Congregation for the Doctrine of the Faith, "Doctrinal Note on some aspects of evangelization," 3 December 2007, *Acta Apostolicae Sedis*, n. 100 (2008): 489–504. Accessed at:bhttp://www.vatican.va/roman_curia/congregations/cfaith/documents/rc_con_cfaith_doc_20071203_nota-evangelizzazione_en.html.

14   Giovanni Miccoli, *La Chiesa dell'anticoncilio. I tradizionalisti alla riconquista di Roma* (Roma – Bari: Laterza, 2011), 325–326.

Lefebvrism and traditionalists

The lack of understanding between traditionalists and the rest of the Catholic Church goes back to the time of the Second Vatican Council (1962–1965) and revolves primarily around questions of ecumenism, interreligious dialogue, religious liberty and collegiality, as well as the liturgy at the time of its post-conciliar instantiation. The movement includes individuals and groups who do not accept legitimate developments in Catholic doctrine. (Something similar happened in 1870 when a small group of so-called 'old Catholics' dissented from certain aspects of the ecclesiological teaching of Vatican I). The champion of the traditionalist world was Marcel Lefebvre, who pushed his agenda to the point of tearing the Church's fabric apart, so much so that Pope Paul VI suspended him *a divinis* after he illicitly ordained priests. He was subsequently excommunicated *latae sententiae* by John Paul II (1988) following another set of illicit ordinations. (The four bishops he ordained were also excommunicated).

The schism originally occurred when Ratzinger was Prefect of the Congregation for the Doctrine of the Faith, despite his many attempts to prevent it. This explains why mending the rift was not only a theological and ecclesiological priority during his pontificate, but a personal one. It is always preferable to heal a fresh wound than to let it fester.

Hence it was only normal that, shortly after being elected pope, Benedict XVI wanted to reestablish contact with the group of traditionalists belonging to the Fraternity of Saint Pius X, which had been created by the now deceased Marcel Lefebrve, even though the pope had been criticized harshly by them for being a "modernist," and his works shelved among the books of "modernist theologians" in the seminary library at Ecône. The superior general of the Fraternity, Bernard Fellay, harbored an ambiguous attitude toward the new pope. On the one hand, he thought Benedict was the right man to "put things in order" (according to Fellay, Ratzinger, as bishop and cardinal, acted and spoke in "traditional ways"), but on the other, he was critical (as was the whole group) of Ratzinger's lack of Thomistic philosophy, even seeing in him a tendency toward a Hegelian approach. Fellay saw Ratzinger as representing a group of progressive theologians from Vatican II from which he could not detach himself.[15]

That was the backdrop of a meeting taking place on 29 August 2005 at Castel Gandolfo between the pope, Fellay, his personal secretary Monsignor Franz Schmidberger, and Cardinal Castrillón Hoyos.[16] The Holy See's press office issued the following statement: "[T]he meeting took place in an atmosphere of love for the Church and a desire to reach perfect communion. Aware of the difficulties that lie ahead, everyone expressed a desire to move forward step-by-step within a reasonable time frame."[17] In other words, a series of gradual steps was set up to achieve mutually established goals over a longer period of time.

Relations between the Holy See and the Lefebvrites was subsequently handled by the competent Vatican dicastery, the Pontifical Commission *Ecclesia Dei*, which at that time was headed by the Columbian Cardinal Dario Castrillón Hoyos, who, according to sources, was very close to the Fraternity of Pius X. (Fellay affirmed that the Cardinal said: "You are neither heretics nor schismatics."[18])

According to Miccoli, the Fraternity laid down some conditions before proceeding with negotiations: a revocation of the excommunication,[19] and a greater allowance for the celebration of the Mass of Pius V by all priests.[20]

---

15 Bernard Fellay, "Quali prospettive per la Chiesa con l'avvento di un nuovo papa?" Found at: http://www.unavox.it/Documenti/doc0127.htm.

16 Miccoli, *La Chiesa dell'anticoncilio*, op. cit., 10, 292.

17 "Dichiarazione del Direttore della Sala Stampa della Santa Sede Dr Joachin navarro Valls," in Miccoli, *La Chiesa dell'anticoncilio*, op. cit., 292.

18 Fellay, "Quali prospettive per la Chiesa con l'avvento di un nuovo papa?" op. cit.

19 Bernard Fellay, *Lettera ai fedeli*, 24 January 2009, «il Regno Documenti», n. 54, 2009, 71–72. Cf. Miccoli, *La Chiesa dell'anticoncilio* o cit., 8.

20 Fellay, "Quali prospettive per la Chiesa con l'avvento di un nuovo

Rome clearly wanted the discussions with the Fraternity to end in full unity. In the consistory of 23 March 2006, Benedict XVI made it clear that he wanted the dialogue with the Fraternity to move toward full communion.[21] During that consistory, the cardinals expressed a variety of opinions. According to media reports, Cardinal Kasper, who was head of ecumenism, said the following: "Every one of us wants reconciliation [...] the question is whether this is the right time. If they are willing to acknowledge the Council, then a solution can be found." The media also reported that Castrillón Hoyos was more sanguine: "The Church waits for them with open arms. We are on a journey [...] family members have different opinions and different points of view."[22]

The dialogue already began to bear fruit in September 2006 with the establishment of the Bon Pasteur Institute which brought some of the traditionalists back into reconciliation with Rome. Something similar had happened with the Priestly Fraternity of Saint Peter during the time of John Paul II. As he had shown during the pontificate of John Paul II, Benedict XVI was committed to achieving a full reunification and not just a series of partial steps. He would not have been happy with attracting just a few individuals or smaller groups. He wanted to mend the break completely.

Benedict XVI had already been preparing a document to allow for the wider use of the Pius V Missal in the fall of 2006. This caused alarm among the French episcopate, which began to voice concern at its November meeting. The bishops feared a greater allowance for the old Mass might delegitimize Paul VI's liturgical reform and justify the attacks of traditionalists against Vatican Council II. Cardinals Jean-Marie Lustiger and Jean-Pierre

---

papa?" op. cit.; Cf. Miccoli, *La Chiesa dell'anticoncilio,* op. cit., 290, 300, *passim.*

21   Cf. Ibid., 299; *Incontro del Santo Padre con i membri del collegio cardinalizio,* 23 March 2006: https://press.vatican.va/content/sala-stampa/it/bollettino/ pubblico/2006/03/23/0144/00435.html.

22   Marco Politi, *Joseph Ratzinger. Crisi di un papato,* op. cit., 87.

Ricard voiced these concerns directly to the pope in Rome. However, the Secretary of the Congregation for Divine Worship, Malcom Ranjith, spoke of a "growing number of requests for a return to the Tridentine Mass."[23]

Despite these concerns, the pope decided to go ahead with widening the use of the Pius V Missal. On 27 June 2007, in the presence of Cardinals Bertone and Castrillón Hoyos, the pope communicated his decision to some cardinals and bishops in countries that would be most affected by the decision: Ruini and Bagnasco in Italy, Ricard and Barbarin in France, Lehmann in Germany, Koch in Switzerland, Murphy-O'Connor in England, O'-Malley and Burke in the United States, Pell in Australia, and Toppo in India.[24] Then he met with Fellay the following day.

On 7 July 2007, Benedict XVI issued the Motu Proprio *Summorum Pontificum*[25] regarding the use of the Roman liturgy prior to the reforms of 1970, allowing a wider use of John XXIII's Missal, or, as it is often referred to, the Mass of Pius V. The document refers to it as the "Extraordinary Form." As Manlio Sodi points out, it was now the case that "the same rite would be celebrated in two different forms."[26] The document allowed not only for a wider celebration of the Eucharist according to the Extraordinary Form, but also the other sacraments and the breviary. The document announced 14 September 2007 as the starting date for when this more liberal use of the old Missal would begin. The *Ecclesia Dei* Commission was asked to ensure that the new allowances were duly observed. The Motu Proprio was accompanied by a letter from Benedict to bishops worldwide explaining why he decided to make this allowance.[27]

---

23   Ibid.
24   Cf. Politi, *Joseph Ratzinger. Crisi di un papato*, op. cit.
25   Benedict XVI, Motu Proprio *Summorum Pontificum*, 7 July 2007, in *Acta Apostolicae Sedis*, n. 99 (2007): 777–781.
26   "Intervista al direttore di *Rivista Liturgica* da parte dell'agenzia *Zenit*," in *Rivista Liturgica*, n. 94 (2007): 602.
27   Benedict XVI, *Lettera ai vescovi in occasione della lettera* Summorum

Benedict's decision is undoubtedly in line with the liturgical vision presented in the Post-Synodal Exhortation *Sacramentum Caritatis* (2007), in which he asks "that future priests, from their time in the seminary, receive the preparation needed to understand and to celebrate the Mass in Latin, and also to use Latin texts and execute Gregorian chant."[28] Furthermore, Benedict explained that the fruit of Vatican II was the "overall unity of the historical development of the rite itself, without the introduction of artificial discontinuities."[29] At the same time, allowance for a more liberal use of old Missal was clearly a response to the Fraternity and the wider circle of traditionalists throughout the world. Therefore, we can interpret the pope's decision as a move toward the fulfillment of the Fraternity's two requests to facilitate a reconciliation between traditionalists and Rome.[30] It was later made known that four episcopal conferences—France, England, Germany, and part of the United States—expressed grave reservations about the decision prior to the publication of the Motu Proprio.[31] So it is no accident that the Motu Proprio was accompanied by a letter from the pope to bishops justifying his decision. The pope openly states that "it is a matter of coming to an interior reconciliation in the heart of the Church" in order to "maintain or regain reconciliation and unity [...] for all those who truly desire to remain in that unity or to attain it anew."[32]

Pontificum *sull'uso della liturgia romana*, 7 July 2007, *Acta Apostolicae Sedis* n. 99 (2007): 795–799.

28 Benedict XVI, "Post-synodal Apostolic Exhortation *Sacramentum caritatis*," 22 February 2007, *Acta Apostolicae Sedis*, n. 99 (2007): 105–180.

29 Ibid., n. 3.

30 This is the interpretation given by Miccoli, *La Chiesa dell'anticoncilio*, op. cit., 300.

31 "Bilancio del motu Proprio sulla messa tradizionale. Un anno dopo," Interview with Msgr. Bernard Fellay in *Nouvelles de Chrétienté*, n. 111 (2008): www.unavox.it/Documenti/doc0185_Interv_Fellay.

32 Benedict XVI, *Lettera ai vescovi in occasione della lettera* Summorum Pontificum *sull'uso della liturgia romana*, op. cit., 797.

Benedict's far-sighted objective was to probe whether the battle between the Lefebvrites and Rome was merely an argument over the pre-conciliar Mass or rather symptomatic of a more deeply entrenched battle over Vatican II. The pope essentially inserted the Mass of Pius V and the Mass the Paul VI into the same liturgical tradition in order to reinstate a unity of faith and bring the Lefebvrites to the same Catholic *lex credendi*. His strategy was more than just liturgical. It was also theological and political. We can think of it as two different *leges orandi* under one *lex credendi*. In this way, he could dismantle or weaken the traditionalists' objections. By not zeroing in on the Lefebvrites' theological and doctrinal issues, Benedict gave them no room to question his sincerity in allowing for a greater use of the old Missal, and therefore it could not be interpreted as a sign of "weakness."[33] This seems like a strikingly different approach from Paul VI, whose liturgical reforms were rife with theological symbolism. If Paul had introduced this kind of allowance for the old Mass as a sort of "exception" to his reform program, he would have caused an earthquake at the Council and risked making it fall apart.[34]

A further question arises: who used whom? If a wider recognition of the old Mass was laid down by the Lefebvrites as a precondition for further dialogue with Rome to obligate the pope in some way to publish *Summorum Pontificum*, such a precondition seems nonetheless to have been in line with Benedict XVI's own liturgical vision as we discussed in a previous chapter. So, was Benedict being gracious to the Lefebvrites, or did he take advantage of an opportunity to through them promote something that was already within his theological-pastoral vision?

Individual bishops, especially in France and Germany, were already taking a stand and making public criticism of Benedict's decision to allow a more frequent celebration of this Mass.[35] But

---

33 Miccoli, *La Chiesa dell'anticoncilio*, op. cit., 320.
34 Cf. Jean Guitton, *Paolo VI segreto* (Roma: Paoline, 1981), 144–145.
35 Miccoli, *La Chiesa dell'anticoncilio*, op. cit., 300, 317–318.

there was considerable enthusiasm on the part of the traditional-ists.[36]

A little less than a year later, on 4 June 2008, Fellay received a memo from Cardinal Castrillon Hoyos. It was a sort of ultimatum listing a series of conditions and requests to which the Fraternity was required to respond by 30 June 2008.[37] Among the various points made in the memo, the Fraternity had to "avoid the impression that there is Magisterium above the Holy Father and that the Fraternity stands in opposition to the Church," and "to show a willingness to act honestly and in ecclesial charity with respect to the authority of the Vicar of Christ." The reasons for which the ultimatum was given are not known. We can only guess. Was it pressure on the Fraternity to reach an agreement? Or putting up a guard against criticism and insults from the Fraternity?[38] It is not known whether the Fraternity responded by the deadline.

Fellay intervened publicly once more on 23 October 2008 by writing a letter to friend and benefactors, in which he reasserted the classic positions of the Fraternity, and without a resolution to questions regarding the faith (that is, the controversial aspects of Vatican II); the Fraternity would not consider any practical (i.e., canonical) solution. Fellay states clearly: "We cannot, and will not leave any ambiguity subsist on the issue of the acceptance of the Council, of the reforms, of the new attitudes which are either being tolerated or encouraged."[39] There is still distance between the two sides. At times they seem to run as parallel lines. In fact, in a letter to Cardinal Castrillón Hoyos from Fellay, dated 15 December 2008,[40] the Lefebvrite Fraternity reemphasized its acceptance of

36   Ibid., 318–319.
37   "Condizioni risultanti dall'incontro del 4 giugno 2008 tra il cardi-nale Dario Castrillón Hoyos e il vescovo Bernard Fellay." Accessed at:www.unavox.it/Art/Diversi/div091_FSSPX_e_Roma.
38   Miccoli, *La Chiesa dell'anticoncilio*, op. cit., 330.
39   Bernard Fellay, "Letter to Friends and Benefactors," n. 73, 23 Octo-ber 2008: http://archives.sspx.org/superior_generals_news/sup_gen_ltr_73.pdf.
40   So Fellay tells his faithful on 24 January 2009: Cf. Miccoli, *La Chiesa*

the Church's teaching and its adhesion to the Petrine primacy and the rights associated with it: "We firmly believe in the primacy of Peter and his prerogatives, and for this reason the current situation causes us much suffering."[41] Rome's requests were satisfied almost half a year after the deadline. This opened the door for the Vatican to lift the excommunication and acknowledge the need for doctrinal dialogue regarding the status of Vatican II. The Lefebvrites' request would only be accepted after their recognition of the authority and primacy of the pope.

This last point was essential since, according to Benedict, the four bishops were originally excommunicated because they received episcopal ordination without a papal mandate, and therefore they had acted against papal primacy.[42] Benedict said, "[...] their excommunication had nothing to do with Vatican II [...] but had been pronounced on account of an offense against the primacy. [...] [A]lready under John Paul II an assembly of all the heads of the dicasteries, that is, all those in charge of Vatican bureaus, had decided to lift the excommunication in the event a letter of this kind was sent."[43] We can deduce from this how different the pope's viewpoint was from much of Catholic world. The key question was not Vatican II, but Vatican I and its teaching on papal primacy. The question of Vatican II is posed only subsequently when the task is to reach full communion, while others would say this was the primary and overriding issue.[44]

---

dell'anticoncilio, op. cit., 333. Furthermore, see Press Office of the Holy See, *Comunicato sulla remissione della scomunica* latae sententiae *ai vescovi della fraternita`sacerdotale san Pio X*, 24 January 2009. Accessed at: https://press.vatican.va/ content/salastampa/it/bollettino/pubblico/2009/01/24/0056/00146. html.

41 Press Office of the Holy See, *Comunicato sulla remissione della scomunica* latae sententiae *ai vescovi della fraternita`sacerdotale san Pio X*, 24 January 2009, op. cit.

42 Cf. Benedict XVI, *Luce del mondo*, 42. In English, *Light of the World* (San Francisco: Ignatius Press, 2010).

43 Ibid., 174.

44 For example, Massimo Faggioli, "La riforma liturgica conciliare e

After three years of dialogue and Vatican efforts to meet the Lefebvrites' requests, a decree was issued by the Congregation for Bishops on 21 January 2009 (published three days later) lifting the excommunication of the four bishops illicitly ordained by Lefebvre.[45] This was a big step in the long negotiation process.[46] It was overseen by a special Vatican commission consisting of Cardinals Bertone, Hoyos, Levada, Re, and Hummes, as well as by Archbishops Filoni and Coccopalmerio.[47] The decree affirms that the remission was granted because of the "spiritual distress which the parties concerned have voiced as a result of the excommunication," and is based on the "commitment" expressed by the bishops "to spare no effort in exploring as yet unresolved questions through requisite discussions with the authorities of the Holy See in order to reach a prompt, full and satisfactory solution to the original problem." There is a willingness to promote "the Universal Church's unity in charity" and remove "the scandal of division."

The publication of the decree to the general public was accompanied by the previously cited communication of the Vatican's press office that underscored Benedict XVI's desire to "mend the rift with the Fraternity," that is, "to reach as soon as possible a complete reconciliation and full communion."[48] The remission of the excommunication was a step toward full communion. Rome had

il futuro del Vaticano II: a proposito del 'dialogo' coi lefebvriani," in *Horizonte*, n. 24 (2011): 1030–1046. Accessed at: http://periodicos.pucminas.br/index.php/horizonte/article/view/2396/3300.

45 Congregation for Bishops, "Decreto sull'abrogazione della scomunica di quattro vescovi della fraternità S. Pio X," 21 January 2009, *Acta Apostolicae Sedis*, n. 101 (2009): 150–151.

46 Cf. Isabelle de Gaulmyn, "Intervista a Padre Federico Lombardi," *La Croix*, 6 February 2009.

47 Cf. Nuzzi, *Sua Santita. Le carte segrete di Benedetto XVI*, op. cit., 211–215.

48 Press Office of the Holy See, *Comunicato sulla remissione della scomunica latae sententiae ai vescovi della fraternità sacerdotale san Pio X*, 24 January 2009, op. cit.

met all the requests of the Lefebvrites. But in the face of such magnanimity and openness, how did the Lefebvrites respond? With utter silence. The pope was the one taking unilateral steps to resolve the problem.

In the very days surrounding the remission of the excommunication, another event enflamed the discussion and monopolized it. On 21 January 2009, Swedish television aired an interview conducted the previous November with Richard Williamson, one of the four bishops of the Fraternity (who entered directly after leaving the Anglican Church), in which he made comments that seemed to deny the use of gas chambers by the Nazi regime and claimed that the number of Jews killed in concentration camps during World War II had been inflated.[49] Was the timing of the Williamson interview and the lifting of the excommunication a part of some combined strategy to "put the pope in a difficult position" with the help of some "oppositional figures within the Church,"[50] as some commentators suggest? Or does it only look like this in hindsight? Whatever the case may be, discourse in the media shifted from a theological tone to an historical one and began to conflate two issues. The Fraternity kept its distance from Williamson.[51] Benedict XVI himself had to intervene on 28 January 2009 during the Wednesday General Audience, at which he had to clearly and unequivocally say: "May the Shoah be a warning for all against forgetfulness, denial or reductionism."[52] It was an opportune moment for him to explain the meaning of the

49 "Le parole di Williamson," il Regno Documenti, n. 54 (2009), 72–73.
50 Paolo Rodari, andrea Tornielli, Attacco a Ratzinger. Accuse, scandali, profezie e complotti contro Benedetto XVI (Milan: Piemme, 2010), 98. See also, Benedict XVI, Luce del mondo, 176n. In English, Light of the World (San Francisco: Ignatius Press, 2010).
51 Cf. Il Regno Documenti n. 54 (2009): 73. Fellay's interview in Present on 31 January 2009: www.fsspx.org/archives/interview/BF/2009-BF-Present.
52 Benedict XVI, General Audience, 28 January 2009: http://w2.vatican.va/content/benedict-xvi/en/letters/2009/documents/hf_ben-xvi_let_20090310_remissione-scomunica.html.

remission of the excommunication, saying it was a "fulfilment" of the "service to unity" of his Petrine ministry. He said that he "fulfilled this act of paternal compassion because these bishops repeatedly manifested their active suffering for the situation in which they had found themselves." He also made some clarifications in response to concerns that had emerged in the Catholic world. He expressed a wish that his gesture of mercy "will be followed by an earnest commitment on their behalf to complete the necessary further steps to achieve full communion with the Church, thus witnessing true fidelity to, and true recognition of, the Magisterium and the authority of the Pope and the Second Vatican Council."

The Fraternity, in turn, had its own response to the pope's decision. In a thank-you letter to Benedict XVI dated 29 January 2009, the superior general, Archbishop Fellay, took the opportunity to express his own interpretation of the decree which, in his opinion, "rehabilitates in some way the venerable founder of our priestly fraternity" and "renders justice to the priests and faithful throughout the world who are dedicated to the Church's Tradition, so that they may no longer be stigmatized for maintaining the faith of their fathers." Rather inopportunely he adds that while making himself available for further dialogue, he hopes the Fraternity can help the Holy See "to bring an appropriate remedy for the loss of faith within the Church."[53] His attitude shifts from arrogance to brazenness, which was also manifested in a press release of 24 January 2009, in which he said that "we will soon reach a recognition of the rights of the Catholic Tradition," expressing his hope that the dialogues will allow the Fraternity "to expose the fundamental doctrinal reasons which it believes are at the root of the current difficulties in the Church."[54] It was as if the Fraternity wanted to convert the entire Catholic Church. If he wished

53 Miccoli, *La Chiesa dell'anticoncilio*, op. cit., 9. Miccoli refers to *Fideliter* n. 188, March–April 2009: www.laportelatine.org (archives - bulletins et revus).
54 Fellay, *Lettera ai fedeli*, op. cit.

to speak publicly to the pope and to the world, it is no less significant what he says to his own followers. In fact, Fellay spoke even more sharply in a circulated letter dated 24 January 2009 addressed to all the faithful of the Fraternity, in which he recalls his "reservations regarding the Second Vatican Council," reservations that indeed he expressed to Rome the previous December, and he reveals the goal of future dialogue—namely, "to reach a solid restoration of the Church."[55]

Rome and Ecône were essentially speaking in different languages. There were undoubtedly ambiguities, misunderstandings, and contradictions on both sides, as Giovanni Miccoli has noted.[56] Fellay's way of doing things did not make the Catholic leadership comfortable. This was evident in a note issued by the Secretariat of State on 4 February 2009:

> The remission of the excommunication has freed the four bishops from a very serious canonical penalty, but it has not changed the juridical status of the Society of Saint Pius X, which presently does not enjoy any canonical recognition by the Catholic Church. The four bishops, even though they have been released from excommunication, have no canonical function in the Church and do not licitly exercise any ministry within it [...]. A full recognition of the Second Vatican Council and the Magisterium of Popes John XXIII, Paul VI, John Paul I, John Paul II, and Benedict XVI himself is an indispensable condition for any future recognition of the Society of Saint Pius X.[57]

The note concludes by recalling that the Successor of Peter is the one who "watches over the unity" of the Church. The note

---

55 Ibid.
56 Miccoli, *La Chiesa dell'anticoncilio*, especially 17–29, 335ss.
57 "A Note from the Secretariat of State concerning the four prelates of the Society of Saint Pius X," 4 February 2009, *Acta Apostolica Sedis*, n. 101 (2009): 145–146.

also states that, to continue talks with Rome, the society needs to acknowledge the Council and the papal magisterium of the preceding half century

The decision to revoke the excommunication was a source of confusion for the episcopal conferences in countries where the Fraternity was most present (France, Switzerland, and Germany). They feared that a reconciliation would give the impression that the Church was placing Vatican II in doubt.[58] An atmosphere of bafflement and intransigence (although exaggerated by the media) pervaded Catholic journalism, theology, and theological faculties (especially in German speaking countries) who deemed the pope's decision unfortunate.[59] Their reactions were mostly tied to their fear of an attitude of "restorationism" in the Church. With regard to the Lefebvrite issue, two fields of play were constantly crossing and superseding one another: ecumenism and the dreaded backstepping in the Church that was continually challenging the authenticity of conciliar decisions. This is an entirely unique problem that we find in no other ecumenical effort toward dialogue with other churches and communities. Is it that local churches are afraid of looking weak when faced with the demands of the relatively small Fraternity? If so, why weren't there signs of the same fear in other ecumenical dialogues? Are the more recently separated the most insidious group? Such questions are tied mainly to the Church's ecclesiological image. There are some theologians who contrasted the situation with the

58 For the initial reactions of bishops in France, Switzerland, and Germany, see *il Regno Documenti*, n. 54 (2009): 72–75. Austrian bishops also wrote a letter dated 16 February 2009: Alois Schifferle, *Die Pius – Bruderschaft. Informationen – Positionen – Perspektiven* (Kevelaer: Butzon & Bercker, 2009), 27.

59 Miccoli, *La Chiesa dell'anticoncilio,* op. cit., 24–29. The author references Ulrich Ruh, "Sconcerto. Reazioni teologiche dopo la remissione della scomunica," in *Il Regno Attualita,* n. 54 (2009): 311–313; Schifferle, *Die Pius-Bruderschaft,* op. cit., 282ss and 312ss; Til Galrev (ed.), *Der Papst im Kreuzfeuer. zurück zu Pius oder das Konzil fortschreiben?* (Berlin: LIT Verlag, 2009), 225ss.

Church's treatment of liberation theology (why try to embrace the Lefebvrites when liberation theologians were pushed away?).[60] Many did not want to accept the remission of the excommunication without some manifestation of repentance on the part of the excommunicated. No one recalled the lesson offered by Paul VI and the Orthodox in 1964.

Faced with the consternation of some bishops and protests of some theologians, Benedict XVI decided to intervene publicly yet again to help people understand this unusual gesture. He wrote a letter (not an encyclical) to the entire episcopate, dated 10 March 2009.[61] This is a very important text in that it gives us a privileged look at Benedict's way of understanding ecumenism and interreligious dialogue. The pope, in addition to expressing regret for the reactions of some Catholics ("I was saddened by the fact that even Catholics who, after all, might have had a better knowledge of the situation, thought they had to attack me with open hostility"), repeated his objective in lifting the excommunication: "The remission of the excommunication has the same aim as that of the punishment: namely, to invite the four Bishops once more to return." He then goes on to draw attention to some reactions to his gesture: "[U]ntil the doctrinal questions are clarified, the Society has no canonical status in the Church, and its ministers—even though they have been freed of the ecclesiastical penalty—do not legitimately exercise any ministry in the Church." Knowing that the questions at stake were primarily of a doctrinal nature, the pope made it clear that what was needed from the Lefebvrites was "the acceptance of the Second Vatican Council and the post-conciliar magisterium of the popes," and thus alluded to his plans to connect the Pontifical Commission *Ecclesia Dei* to the Congregation for the Doctrine of the Faith. The pope expressed two pointed questions,

---

60   Miccoli, *La Chiesa dell'anticoncilio*, op. vit., 27–28.
61   Benedict XVI, "Lettera ai vescovi della Chiesa Cattolica riguardo alla remissione della scomunica dei 4 vescovi consacrati dall'arcivescovo Lefebvre," 10 March 2009, *Acta Apostolicae Sedis*, n. 101 (2009): 270–276.

one *ad extra* and the other *ad intra*. To the Fraternity, he clearly says: "[Y]ou cannot freeze the Church's magisterial authority from 1962 onward." And to some sectors of Catholics, he says: "[T]hose who tout themselves as staunch defenders of the Council must keep in mind that Vatican II carries within itself the Church's entire doctrinal history. Whoever wants to be obedient to the Council must accept the faith professed throughout the centuries and cannot cut the roots that give life to the tree." The latter statement is not one shared by all Catholics (Miccoli, for example), who see serious consequences "for the relationship between the Church and society."[62]

The second part of the letter expands the horizon. Benedict XVI places his decision within the context of the most important tasks of his pontificate. Almost four years after beginning his Petrine ministry, he recalls and reaffirms the overriding motivation for his service, just as he had said at the beginning of his papacy: that is, to "strengthen your brothers." The goal of Christian unity, ecumenism, "is part of the supreme priority." Even the "small and not-so-small" acts of reconciliation enter into "the Church's real priority." This is how his "quiet gesture of extending a hand" is to be understood. He takes the opportunity to clarify the widest horizon of interreligious dialogue: a commitment to peace is "religious dialogue."

There are those who find Benedict XVI's reasoning hard to accept. Miccoli, for example, believes it is "involuntarily paradoxical." It is paradoxical to include efforts at reconciliation with the Lefebvrites within the scope of the Church's ecumenical mission, "because if there is a group of Christians so intransigently averse to ecumenism in such a way that they even separate themselves from fellow Catholics beginning with Vatican II, then that group is undoubtedly the Fraternity of Saint Pius X."[63] But Benedict's point is different and more inclusive of all. In the same letter, in fact, the pope transcends the theological-ecclesial sphere and pushes toward a more sociological reflection:

62 Miccoli, *La Chiesa dell'anticoncilio*, op. cit., 34.
63 Ibid., 37.

213

Was it, and is it, truly wrong in this case to meet half-way the brother who "has something against you" (cf. Mt 5:23ff.) and to seek reconciliation? Should not civil society also try to forestall forms of extremism and to incorporate their eventual adherents to the extent possible—in the great currents shaping social life, and thus avoid their being segregated, with all its consequences? Can it be completely mistaken to work to break down obstinacy and narrowness, and to make space for what is positive and retrievable for the whole? I myself saw, in the years after 1988, how the return of communities which had been separated from Rome changed their interior attitudes; I saw how returning to the bigger and broader Church enabled them to move beyond one-sided positions and broke down rigidity so that positive energies could emerge for the whole. Can we be totally indifferent about a community which has 491 priests, 215 seminarians, 6 seminaries, 88 schools, 2 university-level institutes, 117 religious brothers, 164 religious sisters and thousands of lay faithful? Should we casually let them drift farther from the Church? I think for example of the 491 priests. We cannot know how mixed their motives may be. All the same, I do not think that they would have chosen the priesthood if, alongside various distorted and unhealthy elements, they did not have a love for Christ and a desire to proclaim him and, with him, the living God. Can we simply exclude them, as representatives of a radical fringe, from our pursuit of reconciliation and unity? What would then become of them?

The Fraternity reacted publicly to Benedict XVI's letter in a statement issued by Fellay on 12 March 2009,[64] in which,

64 "Lungi dal voler arrestare la Tradizione al 1962, noi desideriamo considerare il concilio Vaticano II e l'insegnamento post-conciliare alla

among other things, he replies directly to the pope. In reference to the pope's claim that Tradition cannot be frozen in 1962, Fellay affirms: "Far from wanting to stop Tradition in 1962, we wish to consider the Second Vatican Council and the post-Conciliar magisterium in the light of this Tradition which Saint Vincent of Lérins defined as that 'which has been believed everywhere, always, by all' (Commonitorium), without rupture and in a perfectly homogenous development."

Fellay's assertion certainly fits well in Catholic thinking (his quote of Saint Vincent of Lérins on doctrine and its development is in the Office of Readings from the Liturgy of Hours), but how are we to interpret it? This question is critical.

On 2 July 2009, by means of the Motu Proprio *Ecclesiae Unitatem*, Benedict XVI reorganized the *Ecclesia Dei* Commission, placing it under the Congregation for the Doctrine of the Faith, given that the questions to be handled had become preeminently doctrinal. The new secretary of the Commission was Monsignor Guido Pozzo. On 26 October 2009, the "doctrinal discussions" between the Catholic Church and the Fraternity were initiated.[65] The topics on the table for discussion were summarized in a statement issued by the Pontifical Commission *Ecclesia Dei*:

> In particular, questions to be examined include the notion of Tradition, the Missal of Paul VI, the interpretation of the Second Vatican Council in continuity with Catholic doctrinal Tradition, the themes of the unity of the Church and the Catholic principles of ecumenism,

luce di quella Tradizione che san Vincenzo di Lérins ha definito come 'ciò che è stato creduto sempre, dappertutto e da tutti' (*Commonitorium*), senza rotture e con uno sviluppo perfettamente omogeneo." *Comunicato del Superiore Generale della Fraternità Sacerdotale San Pio X a proposito della Lettera ai Vescovi di S. S. Benedetto XVI del 10.3.09: http://www.unavox.it/Documenti/doc0197_Comun_lett_Papa.htm.*

65 Miccoli, *La Chiesa dell'anticoncilio*, op. cit., 51.

the relationship between Christianity and non-Christian religions, and religious freedom.[66]

Little is known about how the discussions went. There are some hints in personal comments made by members of the Fraternity. Monsignor Alfonso de Galarreta, head of the Fraternity's delegation, in a homily on 19 December 2009, made his point of view clear when he affirmed that doctrinal discussions would take place under one common criterion: "There is one *sine qua non* for these discussions: the Magisterium prior to Vatican II is Tradition, just as the Magisterium is always Tradition."[67] In an interview on 1 March 2010,[68] Monsignor Fellay acknowledged that the Roman contingent (which was composed primarily of conservatives) wanted to save the Council.

On 2 July 2010, Monsignor Pozzo, secretary of the *Ecclesia Dei* Commission, in Wigratzbad, the main headquarters of the Priestly Fraternity of Saint Peter, affirmed that there were no changes to Catholic ecclesiology at Vatican II, as if to meet one of the traditionalists' requirements.

Between 2011 and 2012, the Prefect of the Congregation for the Doctrine of the Faith informed the Lefebvrites of another possibility for achieving unity: the institution of a personal prelature headed by a bishop, together with a profession of obedience to Revelation and the dogmas and teaching of the Church (which would not exclude a discussion of each of its articles).[69] In simple terms: you need to adhere to the Magisterium and then discussions can proceed. From that point onward no other significant steps were taken before the end of Benedict XVI's pontificate.

---

66 "Communiqué de la Commission pontificale ecclesia Dei," 26 October 2009, in Miccoli, *La Chiesa dell'anticoncilio*, op. cit., 52.

67 "Un judgement de Msgr Galarreta sur les entretiens doctrinaux, " in Miccoli, *La Chiesa dell'anticoncilio*, op. cit., 52–53.

68 "Interview de msgr Fellay pour fideliter (1er mars 2010)," in Philippe Levillain, *Rome n'est plus dans Rome* (Paris: Perrin, 2010), 422–424, in Miccoli, *La Chiesa dell'anticoncilio*, op. cit., 328.

69 Cf. Politi, *Joseph Ratzinger. Crisi di un papato*, op. cit., 140.

In short, Benedict XVI's act of rescinding the excommunication in 2009 was essentially the same action Paul VI took with regards to Orthodoxy in 1964. He held the same conviction that the elimination of the ecclesiastical censure would be the best catalyst for true dialogue. The respective reactions to Benedict and Paul VI, however, were much different. In 1964, there was tremendous joy that a pathway had opened up toward dialogue. In 2009, there was an undercurrent of agitation and misunderstanding. Since the Lefebvrite rupture was more recent, perhaps the time was not yet ripe for dialogue.

Rome's successive steps to pursue discussions with the Lefebvrites caused a lot of controversy, as Miccoli lays out in his book.[70] Much of the controversy was caused by fears that the prospect of fully integrating the Fraternity of Saint Pius X would place the Second Vatican Council in question, unduly imposing a "correct interpretation" and singling out its conclusions as too modern (collegiality, ecumenical dialogue, and religious freedom in particular).

The problem for Miccoli is that a rapprochement would have the consequence of a possible reconsideration of "the Church's relationship with society and states" according to the "ideas" and "orientation" of the Fraternity,[71] especially with regards to the Church's relationship with other religions in such a way that the issue would not be "merely an ecclesial affair."[72] Miccoli fears a restoration of the Church and in the Church. He writes, "I believe that this is one of the central problems in the process of restoring the Fraternity back to Rome: which Church are we talking about, and which Church are we dealing with? [...] Which Christianity do we have in mind, and what kind of Christian?"[73] He adds that bringing the Fraternity back would make it look like

70   Miccoli, *La Chiesa dell'anticoncilio*, op. cit.
71   Ibid., 44–45.
72   Ibid., 45.
73   Ibid., 293.

a response to that trivialization of the faith which in Benedict's view is the disaster of our day. These, it seems to me, are the deeper motivations that push the pope to open to the Fraternity in any way possible. [...] [B]ecause it is in the defense of the faith—a faith which is flickering out in the world—that the Fraternity and its priests (simply because of the way they are) can make a contribution and support the Church's mission. From this point of view, I do not believe that it would be wrong to say that Benedict's opening toward them is one of the ways in which he wanted to carry out a "restoration as a recovery of lost values" with respect to conciliar unilateralism, which Cardinal Ratzinger wished since his interview with Vittorio Messori in August 1984.[74]

Even if it seems the Catholic Church was not ready in 2009 to engage in ecumenical dialogue with the Lefebvrites, the Lefebvrites themselves seemed even less ready, missing no occasion to show disrespect for the Catholic Church (and therefore jeopardizing the discussions) and to take distance from her, even showing that they thought they had a mission specific even among Catholics.

Pope Benedict XVI made every attempt and completed every initial step to restore full unity, but his interlocuters were not up to the task, continually wavering between flattery and attacks. To reach that unity, the pope was nevertheless willing to risk tension and turmoil in the Church, convinced of his duty to create communion. In other words, he was either courageous or foolhardy enough to go further than anyone else. But he never enjoyed the fruits of his labor.

Anglicanism: the new category of "personal ordinariates"

The first significant steps toward a dialogue between the Catholic Church and Anglicanism were made under Paul VI im-

74   Ibid., 338.

mediately after Vatican II. Leaving aside attempts to recognize Anglican orders at the time of Leo XIII (who had declared them invalid with the papal bull *Apostolicae Curae* in 1896),[75] we need to go back to 24 March 1966[76] when Paul VI and Michael Ramsey, Archbishop of Canterbury and thus Anglican primate, had a meeting, thus setting out a new path that would first lead to the establishment of the Anglican-Roman Catholic International Commission (ARCIC) in 1967, which over time would lead to further mutual meetings of a theological nature and cooperative publications on theological and dogmatic topics, ultimately arriving at joint declarations signed by the pope and the Anglican primate in 2006.[77]

Already in the early phases of the dialogue, the Anglican communion showed signs of internal division, mostly over the ordination of women and openly professed homosexuals. This division among Anglicans and their shifting teaching made for hard dialogue with Catholics. The Anglican Communion finally broke apart when some groups and churches expressed a desire to safeguard their own doctrinal and moral tradition in continuity with the past.[78]

During the pontificate of John Paul II, numerous members of the Anglican laity and clergy turned to the Catholic Church as a natural source of support during the tumultuous doctrinal and moral changes within the Anglican Communion. The Congregation for the Doctrine of the Faith extended a *Pastoral Dispensation*,

---

75 Leo XIII, "Bolla *Apostolicae Curae*," 13 September 1896, *Acta Sanctae Sedis*, n. 29 (1896–1897): 198–202.

76 Cf. Christopher Hill and Edward J. Yarnold, *Anglicans and Roman Catholics: The Search for Unity* (London: The Society for Promoting Christian Knowledge – Catholic Truth Society, 1994), 10–11.

77 Cf. *Dichiarazione comune del papa Benedetto XVI e dell'arcivescovo di Canterbury Sua Grazia Rowan Williams*, 23 November 2006: http://w2.vatican.va/content/benedict-xvi/it/speeches/2006/november/documents/ hf_ben-xvi_spe_20061123_common-decl.html.

78 Cf. Gianfranco Ghirlanda, "La Costituzione Apostolica *Anglicanorum Coetibus*," *Periodica de re canonica*, n. 99 (2010), 376–378.

also known as a *Pastoral Provision* (1981),[79] to the Anglican clergy and laity who intended to enter into full communion with the Catholic Church, making it possible for members of the clergy (both celibate and married) to be ordained as Catholic priest and incardinated into a diocese. There was also a provision for the erection of personal parishes (and even quasi-parishes) in which these Anglicans could preserve elements of their own liturgical, pastoral, and spiritual Anglican patrimony, and which would welcome individuals coming from within that tradition.[80] While the traditional idea of a parish is a territorial entity within a diocese, a personal parish services a type of community. Indeed, this idea was already in development in the wake of Vatican II.[81]

By the time Benedict XVI was elected pope, tensions within the Anglican Community had worsened. The polarization had reached a point that seemed irreconcilable.

The pope met with the Archbishop of Canterbury, Rowan William, Primate of the Anglican Communion, on 23 November 2006 to commemorate the fortieth anniversary of the meeting between Paul VI and Michael Ramsey. At this meeting, he acknowledged the steps successfully completed over the last forty years, as well as the problems. Benedict XVI even referred to the difficulties over the last three years within the Anglican communion, which caused uncertainties not only internally, but also for dialogue with Catholics.[82] For his part, Williams asserted that the

79 Congregation for the Doctrine of the Faith, "Dichiarazione in merito all'ammissione alla piena comunione con la Chiesa Cattolica di alcuni membri del clero e del laicato appartenenti alla Chiesa episcopaliana (Anglicana)," *L'Osservatore Romano*, 1 April 1981.

80 Cf. Ghirlanda, "La Costituzione Apostolica *Anglicanorum Coetibus*," op. cit., 380.

81 Cf. Anthony Jeremy, "La costituzione apostolica *Anglicanorum Coetibus* e l'ordinariato personale di nostra Signora di Walsingham," in *La costituzione Anglicanorum Coetibus*, Giuseppe Ruggieri (ed.) (Bologna: EDB, 2012), 90. The author refers to the *Code of Canon Law*, can. 515, §1.

82 Cf. Benedict XVI, "Discorso al Dr. Rowan Williams, arcivescovo di

challenges posed by modern society have likewise become problems for the advancement of ecumenism.

On 16 October 2007, some Anglican bishops, confronted with these difficulties and assuring Rome of their complete adherence to the 1992 Catechism,[83] asked to join the Catholic Church in full, corporal, and sacramental communion without renouncing their Anglican identity.[84] They decided to distance themselves from the Anglican Communion because of the deep crisis that was tearing it apart.[85] The Jesuit canonist Gianfranco Ghirlanda has rightly noted that the fractioning of the Anglican Communion (over the ordination of women to the presbyterate and episcopate, as well as the ordination of men and women living in homosexual unions or bestowing their blessing on homosexual unions) is the main element that drove these groups of Anglican faithful to ask for full communion with Rome. "They were convinced of the impossibility to maintain the integrity of the Apostolic Tradition, and therefore the integrity of faith and morals, and the authenticity of ecclesiastical discipline apart from the Petrine ministry."[86] Ghirlanda, however, a consultor at several Vatican dicasteries, does not merely stress this negative point (i.e., union with Catholics simply in order to avoid a liberal agenda), but adds a positive one: these Anglicans believe that the Petrine ministry is "an element desired by Christ for his Church, and therefore the pope alone can effectively act as a center of unity for the Church." Ghirlanda believes that their decision to

Canterbury e primate della Comunione anglicana," 23 November 2006, *Acta Apostolicae Sedis*, n. 98 (2006): 897–899.

83 Cf. Ghirlanda, "La Costituzione Apostolica *Anglicanorum Coetibus*," op. cit., 377.

84 Cf. Denis Pelletier, "La *piena comunione,* il genere e la generosità. Sguardo di uno storico sulla costituzione apostolica *Anglicanorum Coetibus*," in *La costituzione Anglicanorum Coetibus*, (ed.) Ruggieri, op. cit., 16–17.

85 Pelletier, "La *piena comunione,* il genere e la generosità," op. cit., 17.

86 Ghirlanda, "La Costituzione Apostolica *Anglicanorum Coetibus*," op. cit., 382.

join Rome is a "positive element in their maturation toward the fullness of faith."[87] As in the case of dialogue with the Lefebvrites, the first unavoidable step is an acknowledgment of the role of the pope.

For the first time in history, entire communities were asking to be admitted to full communion with Rome.[88] At this point, the procedures stipulated in the pastoral provision of the Congregation for the Doctrine of the Faith were insufficient. It was no longer a matter of individuals or small groups passing over, but large bodies. Rome's method of receiving them now had to be redesigned based on the sheer numbers.

According to the analysis Cardinal Kasper offered to the College of Cardinals (November 2007), questions tied to the ethical realm were now causes of division, not only within Anglicanism, but also in the wider Catholic-Anglican dialogue (a problem that does not arise in dialogue with charismatic and Pentecostal groups).[89]

In the months that followed, the Anglican world continued to seethe with disagreement and broke into even more factions.[90] On 21 October 2009, Benedict XVI's response to some Anglican groups came to light after almost two years, and especially in regard to the "group of Anglicans that freely and legitimately asked to enter the Catholic Church"[91] after the ordination of women and the more liberal attitude toward homosexuality within the Anglican communion. His was a pastoral response to the question "formulated repeatedly by Anglican groups, some

87   Ibid.
88   Cf. Aldo Maria Valli, *Benedetto XVI, Il pontificato interrotto* (Milano: Mondadori, 2013), 234.
89   Cf. Walter Kasper, "Relazione al concistoro cardinalizio, 23 November 2007," *L'Osservatore Romano*, 24 November 2007.
90   Cf. Ghirlanda, "La Costituzione Apostolica *Anglicanorum Coetibus*," op. cit., 379.
91   Giampaolo Mattei, "A colloquio con il cardinale Kasper sulla costituzione *Anglicanorum coetibus*," *L'Osservatore Romano*, 15 November 2009.

of which had already broken off relations with the Anglican Communion."[92]

The response was initially made public by means of a completely unprecedented and new form of joint declaration signed by Vincent Gerard Nichols, Catholic Archbishop of Westminster, and Dr. Rowan Williams, primate of the Anglican Communion and Archbishop of Canterbury.[93] An Apostolic Constitution was announced, *Anglicanorum Coetibus*, which would create a canonical form of accepting those who not only individually, but collectively ("corporately") accepted the Petrine ministry in the Church.[94] This would replace the Pastoral Provision of 1980. The two archbishops placed Rome's decision within the context of the forty-year dialogue between the two churches and declared that the Apostolic Constitution responded "to a number of requests over the past few years to the Holy See from groups of Anglicans who wish to enter into full visible communion with the Roman Catholic Church, and are willing to declare that they share a common Catholic faith and accept the Petrine ministry as willed by Christ for his Church."

The Apostolic Constitution *Anglicanorum Coetibus*[95] (4 November 2009)—whose redactors probably included the aforementioned

92 Michel Van Parys, "La costituzione apostolica *Anglicanorum Coetibus:* valutazione di un ecumenista cattolico," in *La costituzione* Anglicanorum Coetibus, ed. Ruggieri, op. cit., 147.
93 "Dichiarazione congiunta," *L'Osservatore Romano*, 21 October 2009.
94 Congregation for the Doctrine of the Faith, "Nota informativa circa gli Ordinariati personali per anglicani che entrano nella Chiesa cattolica," 20 October 2009, *Acta Apostolicae Sedis*, n. 101 (2009), 939–942.
95 Benedict XVI, "Costituzione apostolica *Anglicanorum Coetibus*," *Acta Apostolicae Sedis*, n. 101 (2009): 985–990. In the daily edition of the *L'Osservatore Romano*, a portion of the norms published by the Congregation for the Doctrine of the Faith on 4 November 2009 appeared. For problems concerning the publication, see Georg Bier, "La costituzione apostolica *Anglicanorum coetibus* e le Norme complementari della Congregazione per la dottrina della fede. Un'analisi canonistica," in "La costituzione *Anglicanorum Coetibus*," ed.

Ghirlanda[96]—accompanied by complementary norms, affirmed that the Church of Christ "subsists" in the Catholic Church and recognized that many elements of "sanctification" and "truth" can be found outside of it,[97] just as Vatican II had taught.[98] In this way it was intended to offer a path toward realizing full communion, both by respecting diversity (of theological, spiritual, liturgical, and pastoral traditions, obviously compatible with Catholicism[99]), and by maintaining the theological foundations of unity.

On a juridical level, the pope decided to welcome these Anglican groups by establishing the so-called "personal ordinariates" based on the model of a military ordinariate (i.e., a juridical entity introduced by John Paul II in 1986 through the Apostolic Constitution *Spirituali militum curae*[100]), according to which the ecclesial structure is not territorial, but personal; that is, the jurisdiction is not bounded by geographical space, but

Ruggieri op. cit., 115, n. 34. For an initial analysis of the norms, see Gianfranco Ghirlanda, "Una normativa essenziale per una struttura canonica flessibile," *L'Osservatore Romano*, 9–10 November 2009. Ghirlanda talked about the implementation of the norms in *La Costituzione Apostolica Anglicanorum Coetibus* op. cit., 373–430. See also by Ghirlanda: "Il significato della costituzione apostolica *Anglicanorum coetibus*," *La Civiltà Cattolica*, n. 160 (2009): 385–392. Commentaries include Juan Ignacio Arrieta, "Gli ordinariati personali," *Ius Ecclesiae*, n. 22 (2010): 151–172; John M. Huels, "*Anglicanorum Coetibus*: Text and Commentary," *Studia canonica*, n. 43 (2009): 389–430; John M. Huels, "Canonical Comments on *Anglicanorum Ccoetibus*," *Worship*, n. 84 (2010): 237–253; Charles Morerod, "*Anglicanorum Coetibus*," *Nova et vetera*, n. 85 (2010): 9–19.

96   Pelletier, "La piena comunione, il genere e la generosità," op. cit., 7.

97   Benedict XVI, Costituzione apostolica *Anglicanorum Coetibus*, op. cit., n. 11.

98   Vatican Council II, Dogmatic Constitution *Lumen gentium*, in *Enchiridion Vaticanum*, vol. I (Bologna: EDB, 1971), n. 8.

99   Cf. Ghirlanda, "La Costituzione Apostolica *Anglicanorum Coetibus*," op. cit., 385–387.

100 John Paul II, Apostolic Constitution *Spirituali militum curae*, 21 April 1986, in *Acta Apostolicae Sedis*, n. 78 (1986): 481–486.

determined by the members themselves (lay faithful, clerics, and members of institutes of religious life or societies of apostolic life) that make up the ordinariate,[101] even though there are provisions for geographical borders (Art. 1, par. 1: "[...] within the confines of the territorial boundaries of a particular Conference of Bishops in consultation with that same Conference"), which can also be reduced (Art. 1, par. 2: "Within the territory of a particular Conference of Bishops, one or more Ordinariates may be erected as needed"). An ordinariate is comparable to a diocese. It has a head—an "ordinary"—personally nominated by the pope. The competent authority for the erection of ordinariates is the Congregation for the Doctrine of the Faith, who up until now has followed the Constitution, and it continues to be through the Congregation that ordinaries will present to the pope reports on the state of their ordinariates. In fact, it seems the Pontifical Council for Christian Unity was sidelined in this decision-making process. The president of the Council, Cardinal Kasper, was involved rather late.[102] Indeed, according to some sources, the Cardinal's opinions didn't enter much into the work.[103] Kasper himself explained that, given the doctrinal implications, the matter falls more naturally under the Congregation for the Doctrine of the Faith,[104] of which he was a member and in whose discussions and decisions he would have been involved. In any case, from the Anglican point of view, "the Congregation for the Doctrine of the Faith and the Pontifical Council for Promoting Christian Unity

---

101 Cf. Pelletier, "La *piena comunione,* il genere e la generosità. Sguardo di uno storico sulla costituzione apostolica *Anglicanorum Coetibus,*" op. cit., 7.

102 Mattei, "A colloquio con il Cardinale Kasper sulla costituzione *Anglicanorum Coetibus,*" op. cit.

103 Cf. Christopher Hill, "What is the Personal Ordinariate? Canonical and Liturgical Observations," in *Ecclesiastical Law Journal,* n. 12 (2010): 202.

104 Mattei, "A colloquio con il cardinale Kasper sulla costituzione Anglicanorum Coetibus" op. cit.

at least appeared to have different understandings of the goal of ecumenism."[105]

In order to join an ordinariate, one has to come directly from the Anglican Church or receive the Christian sacraments of initiation in the jurisdiction of the ordinariate, or have some family connection with a member of the ordinariate and make a profession of faith according to the Catechism of the Catholic Church. The ordinary possesses a "vicariate" power exercised in the name of the pope over the faithful of the ordinariate. He enjoys autonomy from the local diocesan bishop, allowing for the legitimate preservation of the Anglican tradition; in other words, avoiding the assimilation of faithful into the local diocese in such a way that they would lose the richness of their Anglican tradition—something, presumably, that would "weaken the entire Church."[106]

The ordinary must guide the integration of the ordinariate into the Catholic Church.[107] The Constitution and the accompanying norms provide for the preservation of some of the spiritual, liturgical, and pastoral elements of the Anglican patrimony (such as the liturgical books) within the parameters of the discipline of the Latin Church. This also grant faculties to erect personal parishes, as well as new institutes of consecrated life and societies of apostolic life, and the faculty to establish houses of formation for its own seminarians. Seminarians, however, in the doctrinal and pastoral areas, must been formed with other seminarians. The constitution and norms also allow for the ordination not only of celibate men, but also married of Anglican ministers, including bishops (with papal approval to dispense them from the discipline of celibacy in the Latin Church). It needs to be clear that

105 Christopher Hill, "Una valutazione della costituzione *Anglicanorum Coetibus* nella situazione ecumenica attuale," in *La costituzione Anglicanorum Coetibus*, Ruggieri (ed.), op. cit., 168–169.
106 Gianfranco Ghirlanda, "Il significato della costituzione apostolica *Anglicanorum Coetibus*," 9 November 2009: www.zenit.org.
107 Cf. Ghirlanda, *Una normativa essenziale per una struttura canonica flessibile.*

married Anglican bishops who want to join an ordinariate may only be ordained priests. Furthermore, there is an exception allowed with papal approval for married men to be admitted who were *not* previously ordained Anglican ministers.

The configuration of an ordinariate has the advantage of flexibility to adapt to particular situations and the possibility to be organized along the lines of a diocese. Ghirlanda makes it clear that, according to canon 372, paragraph 2, ordinariates cannot be considered "ritual" Churches (such as the Eastern Churches),[108] insofar as the Anglican tradition has a unique status within the Latin Catholic Church. To consider it otherwise would have created ecumenical problems.[109] According to canonist Georg Bier, however, it is precisely canon 372 that juridically grounds the constitution.[110] Furthermore, an ordinariate is not to be confused with a personal prelature like Opus Dei because the latter juridically includes only priests and deacons as members. The laity relate to a personal prelature only to the extent that they collaborate in the apostolic work of its members. In the case of Anglicanism, there is a similarity between an ordinariate and a "diocese," or a "cultural jurisdiction," in addition to a jurisdiction that serves the armed forces.[111]

The Constitution speaks of a reciprocal enrichment of Catholics and Christians coming from Anglicanism. In fact, the ordinariate should "maintain the liturgical, spiritual and pastoral traditions of the Anglican Communion within the Catholic Church, as a precious gift nourishing the faith of the members of the Ordinariate and as a treasure to be shared."[112] Indeed, according to Ghirlanda,

---

108 Cf. Ibid.

109 Ibid.

110 Bier, "La costituzione apostolica *Anglicanorum Coetibus* e le *Norme complementari* della Congregazione per la dottrina della fede. Un'analisi canonistica," op. cit., 118–120, particularly n. 50.

111 Hill, "Una valutazione della costituzione *Anglicanorum Coetibus* nella situazione ecumenica attuale," op. cit., 165–166.

112 Benedict XVI, Apostolic Constitution *Anglicanorum Coetibus*, op. cit., art. III.

the treasure referred to in the document can be considered a gift of Christ to His Church.[113]

The Constitution *Anglicanorum Coetibus* has had—and will have—a number of secondary effects. With regard to the liturgy, for example, the Constitution "legitimizes a diversity of traditions not only within the Catholic Church but also within the Latin Church."[114] Not only will the Latin liturgy have an ordinary Latin form and an extraordinary form, but also a Catholic-Anglican form, not to mention the long-standing Ambrosian form.

How did the Anglican world, the Catholic world, and the wider ecumenical world react to this decision of the Holy See? Let's begin with one fact that has no precedent. For the first time in history, we have a joint declaration between a Christian confession that will welcome new adherents and another that will lose them. This constitutes a unique stage in ecumenism and signifies the fruits of forty years of intense bilateral meetings. One thing is for sure: the joint declaration of 20 October 2009 put an end to the period of uncertainty for some Anglican groups. Bishop John Hepworth, primate of the Traditional Anglican Communion, underscores Pope Benedict XVI's generosity in allowing Anglicans to enter into communion with the Catholic Church without losing the Anglican traditions that are in harmony with the Catholic faith. It was reported that even the Archbishop of Canterbury showed sympathy when presented with the news, even if he was not entirely in agreement with the decision.[115] By the same token, Bishop John Broadhurst, founder of the *Forward*

---

113 Cf. Ghirlanda, "Una normativa essenziale per una struttura canonica flessibile," op. cit.
114 Éditorial, "Des anglicans unis, non absorbés?" in *Istina*, n. 54 (2009): 338.
115 John Hepworth, "Declaración ante el anuncio vaticano de una Constitu- ción Apostólica para entrar en plena comunión con la Iglesia Católica," in Carlos Martínez Oliveras (ed.), *Católicos y Anglicanos ¿Hacia la comunión o el distanciamiento?* (Salamanca: Universidad Pontificia de Salamanca, 2010), 498–499.

in Faith movement, spoke of "Rome's generosity."[116] Mark Fisher, executive secretary of the *Churches in Scotland* movement, said, "the Anglicans who had problems with their Church had had them for a long time. The fact that there was even the possibility of a joint response to those problems on the part of Anglicans and Catholics shows that the dialogue we have been working towards for a long time finally yielded mutual understanding. That's encouraging."[117] Other reactions encouraged both openness and prudence.[118] The overall attitude was: "Let's wait and see."[119]

Not all traditionally minded Anglicans, however, were open to this solution. Those who supported the "Jerusalem Declaration"—that is, those in favor of an official break within the Anglican communion—felt vindicated by the situation. Peter Akinola, the Anglican Bishop of Abuja, declared: "We are convinced that this is not the time to abandon the Anglican Communion. It pains us deeply to think that the current crisis within our dear Anglican Communion made this kind of unprecedented offer from Rome necessary."[120]

As time passed, more and more criticism emerged from the Anglican world under the Archbishop of Canterbury, who longed

116 *Comunicato* of 9 November 2009: www.forwardinfaith.com/artman/ publish/article_497.shtml; Pelletier, "La *piena comunione,* il genere e la generosità," in op. cit., 18.
117 "La Croix," 21 October 2009, in Pelletier, "La *piena comunione,* il genere e la generosità," *op. cit.*, 19.
118 Cf. Christopher Epting, "Comunicado de la Iglesia episcopaliana sobre la Declaración vaticana," in Martínez Oliveras (ed.), *Católicos y Anglicanos ¿Hacia la comunión o el distanciamiento?* op. cit., 500–501.
119 Cf. Nicola Gori, "A colloquio con monsignor Vincent Gerard nichols, presidente della conferenza episcopale d'Inghilterra e Galles, Una comunita' che cresce nel segno dell'ecumenismo," in *L'Osservatore Romano* 31 January 2010; Mario Ponzi, "Fermezza e paternita' per difendere la credibilita' del sacerdote. A colloquio con il cardinale Cláudio Hummes, prefetto della Congregazione per il Clero," in *L'Osservatore Romano,* 13 January 2010.
120 *La Croix,* 13 November 2009, and *Le Monde,* 22 November 2009, op. cit. in Pelletier, "La *piena comunione,* il genere e la generosità," op. cit., 19.

for the days when Cardinal Kasper was in charge of ecumenism. Even Catholics active in initiatives for ecumenical dialogue began to express bewilderment at Benedict XVI's decision.[121] In the autumn of 2010, the Archbishop of Canterbury referred to *Anglicanorum Coetibus* as a "creative pastoral response"[122] to what was a "rather uncomfortable" situation.[123] On the Catholic side, the typical anti-Rome factions attacked the Vatican's decision. Hans Küng, a darling with the media, publicly commented on the affair in an article appearing in a number of European newspapers. He wrote, "the thirst for power on the part of Rome divides Christianity and harms the Church."[124] There was fear of a conservative alliance within Christianity and a conservative spirit galvanizing within the Catholic Church. A "certain hostility" began to emerge in the Catholic Church in England and Wales as well.[125]

Benedict XVI made an Apostolic Visit to England in September 2010, during which he spoke of *Anglicanorum Coetibus* as a "prophetic gesture,"[126] but there still had been no effective application of the Constitution due to a few practical issues. Kurt Koch, the new president of the Pontifical Council for the Promotion of Christian Unity, indicated these aspects.[127] The media suggested

121 Pelletier, "La *piena comunione*, il genere e la generosita," op. cit., 19–21.
122 Hill, "Una valutazione della costituzione *Anglicanorum coetibus* nella situazione ecumenica attuale" op. cit., 171.
123 "I think everyone on the platform was a bit uncomfortable.... I know the Congregation for the Doctrine of the Faith on the whole doesn't go in for much consultation—we were just on the receiving end of that." George Pitcher, "Dr. Rowan Williams: Taking a Break from Canterbury Travails," in *The Telegraph*, 12 December 2009.
124 Ibid.
125 Hill, "Una valutazione della costituzione *Anglicanorum Coetibus* nella situazione ecumenica attuale" op. cit., 159.
126 Benedict XVI, "Discorso ai vescovi di Inghilterra, Galles e Scozia, Birmingham 19 September 2010," *L'Osservatore Romano*, 20–21 September 2010.
127 Gianluca Biccini, "Per il papa del Regno Unito un successo anche in campo ecumenico. Lo afferma l'arcivescovo Koch, presidente del

that they were due to ecumenical tensions that had arisen over the pope's decision.[128] Nevertheless, five Anglican bishops (Andrew Burnham, Keith Newton, John Broadhurst, Edwin Barnes, and David Silk), together with five hundred Anglican faithful, asked to be received into the ordinariate. It is hard to say whether this was the number expected. Small groups in the United States, Australia, and Canada were asking for the erection of an ordinariate in their respective countries.[129]

Having received those requests, the Holy See, a full year after *Anglicanorum Coetibus* was published, and by means of a decree of erection, established the Personal Ordinariate of Our Lady of Walsingham (15 January 2011)[130] covering the territory of the Bishops' Conference of England and Wales, placed under the patronage of Blessed Cardinal John Henry Newman. The faithful who desired to be part of the ordinariate had to manifest the desire in writing and receive adequate catechetical formation.

Another personal ordinariate was erected on 1 January 2012, the Chair of Saint Peter, whose patroness was Our Lady of Walsingham and whose geographical territory was established as coterminal with the jurisdiction of the United States' Conference of Catholic Bishops.[131] Another personal ordinariate was set up

Pontificio Consiglio per la promozione dell'unità dei Cristiani," in *L'Osservatore Romano*, 22 September 2010.

128 Avril Ormsby, "Catholic Church Opens to Anglicans in January," in *Reuters*, 19 November 2010: http://www.reuters.com/article/us-religion-britain- anglicans-idUSTRe6aI37920101119.

129 Avril Ormsby, "First Group of Anglican Bishops to Convert to Rome," in *Reuters*, 8 November 2010: http://www.reuters.com/article/2010/11/08/us-britain-anglicans-conversion-idUSTRe6a72O120101108.

130 Congregation for the Doctrine of the Faith, "Decreto di erezione dell'Ordinariato Personale Our Lady of Walsingham," in *L'Osservatore Romano*, 15 January 2011. See also, *L'Osservatore Romano*, 16 January 2011.

131 Congregation for the Doctrine of the Faith, "Decreto di erezione dell'Ordinariato Personale della Cattedra di San Pietro," 1 January 2012, *L'Osservatore Romano*, English edition, 4 January 2012.

on 15 June 2012 in Australia, called Our Lady of the Southern Cross, entrusted to the patronage of Augustine of Canterbury and covering the territory of the Australian Bishops' Conference.[132] The same entrance requirements as Our Lady of Walsingham were expected of petitioners to these three other ordinariates. Numbers in other parts of the world are considerably smaller due largely to the paucity of Anglicans in those areas.[133]

Some sectors of the Catholic world were not pleased with personal ordinariates as a way of solving the problem and the wide allowances specified in the Constitution because the norms "are not readily conformable with the ecclesiology of Vatican II." They appear to be a "renewed attempt to create a 'uniate' Church" and are grounded in a "post-conciliar Roman practice that is not entirely consistent with the direction of Vatican II ecclesiology."[134] These sectors had problems with the way Benedict XVI's papacy was putting Vatican II into action. In his interview with Seewald, the pope alluded to this as well:

> But it (i.e., the new juridical structure of ordinariates) is at any rate a sign, you might say, of the flexibility of the Catholic Church. We don't want to create new uniate churches, but we do want to offer ways for local church traditions, traditions that have evolved outside the Roman Church, to be brought into communion with the Pope and thus into Catholic communion.[135]

132 Congregation for the Doctrine of the Faith, "Decreto di erezione dell'Ordinariato Personale di Our Lady of the Southern Cross," 15 June 2012, *Acta Apostolicae Sedis*, n. 104 (2012): 599–603.

133 Nicola Gori, "Dialogo ecumenico e impegno di carità, le priorità della Chiesa in Scozia indicate dal cardinale O'Brien," in *L'Osservatore Romano*, 3 February 2010.

134 Giuseppe Ruggieri, "Il movimento ecumenico avanza, segna il passo o retrocede?" in Giuseppe Ruggieri (ed.), *La costituzione anglicanorum coetibus e l'ecumenismo* (Bologna: EDB, 2012), 8–9.

135 Benedict XVI, *Luce del mondo*, 142. In English, *Light of the World* (San Francisco: Ignatius Press, 2010).

Clearly, these represent two ways of interpreting the same phenomenon.

Expanding the horizon of our reflection, we might say that the Catholic Church's opening to some kind of corporate union with Anglicans is indicative of an evolving, post-conciliar ecclesiology, the fruit of new twentieth-century developments going beyond the notion that a particular church must be rooted in a fixed, territorial area.[136] (This is the notion most clearly expressed in the Code of Canon Law, canon 372, par. 2.) In other words, the notion of a geographically top-down ecclesiology in which the universal Church prevails over smaller, particular churches is no longer exclusive. Perhaps the juridical-ecclesiological evolution that led to entities like the personal ordinariate is simply due to a more globalized world.[137] The Constitution *Anglicanorum Coetibus* was essentially a recognition of a personal, particular Church: i.e., a specific portion of the People of God.[138] Perhaps the weak point of the arrangement is that the ordinary—i.e., the head of an ordinariate—does not necessarily need to be a bishop. He also exercises power only vicariously and not personally.[139] The fact that the Constitution also values elements of sanctification and truth outside the Catholic Church is also favorable for ecumenical dialogue, as well as the reaffirmation of the possibility of ordaining married men. Similarly favorable is the Constitution's provision for a governing council that offers advice to the ordinary, as well as the *iter* for nominating new ordinaries (i.e., the pope chooses an ordinary based on a *terna* provided by

136 For a very different interpretation, see Hervé Legrand, "Episcopato, episkopē, chiesa locale e comunione delle Chiese nella costituzione apostolica *Anglicanorum coetibus*," in Ruggieri (ed.), *La costituzione* Anglicanorum coetibus e l'ecumenismo, op. cit., 66–76.
137 Cf. Van Parys, "La costituzione apostolica *Anglicanorum Coetibus*: valutazione di un ecumenista cattolico," op. cit., 152.
138 Cf. Bier, "La costituzione apostolica *Anglicanorum coetibus* e le *Norme complementari* della Congregazione per la dottrina della fede," op. cit., 120—121.
139 Cf. Ibid., 124–125.

the governing council of the ordinariate in need of a new ordinary).[140] These norms, however, are not completely reflective of Anglican norms, which are based heavily on the idea of synodality, stipulating that laity have an equal role in church governance.[141] There are also norms that seem to originate from neither Anglicanism nor Catholicism, such as the consent of the governing council needed for ordinations *in sacris*.[142] For some, the entity of a personal ordinariate should not be considered "an ecumenical model" because it "softens a bit the main ecclesiological model favored by the Catholic Church."[143] For others, it "represents a significant milestone on the way to full unity among Christians."[144] For others still, it represents a firm "no" to ecumenical progress.[145] In any case, ecumenism "in the sense of an understanding between interested churches—or rather ecclesial communities—is neither sought for nor encouraged by *Anglicanorum Coetibus*.[146] The point of reference is the Catechism of the Catholic Church with its required recognition of the dogmas of Vatican I regarding the jurisdiction of the Roman Pontiff and the infallibility of his teaching, in addition to the entire body of

140 Cf. Legrand, "Episcopato, episkopē, chiesa locale e comunione delle Chiese," op. cit., 77–78.

141 Jeremy, *La costituzione apostolica* Anglicanorum coetibus *e l'ordinariato personale di nostra Signora di Walsingham* op. cit., 92.

142 Bier, "La costituzione apostolica *Anglicanorum coetibus* e le *Norme complementari* della Congregazione per la dottrina della fede," op. cit., 95–96. On this point of the *Norme complementari* (Art. 12 §2) there is another interpretative opinion. According to Bier: "The Ordinary must not follow up a certain vote of the governing council, but without this vote he cannot act." Bier, "La costituzione apostolica *Anglicanorum coetibus,* op. cit., 128.

143 Legrand, "Episcopato, episkopē, chiesa locale e comunione delle Chiese," op. cit., 78.

144 Jeremy, *La costituzione apostolica* Anglicanorum coetibus," op. cit., 106.

145 Van Parys, *La costituzione apostolica* Anglicanorum coetibus: *valutazione di un ecumenista cattolico,* op. cit., 147 and 153.

146 Bier, "La costituzione apostolica *Anglicanorum coetibus,* op. cit., 141.

teaching on the sacraments and apostolic succession. As Bier has rightly observed, we are dealing with an "ecumenism of return," for which *Anglicanorum Coetibus* "may perhaps be a model." It "can be accepted or rejected, but it cannot be ignored."[147]

Renewing dialogue with the Orthodox

The seeds of a renewed, mutual dialogue at an official level between the Catholic Church and the Orthodox Churches were planted at Vatican II. A symbolic peak was reached in the aforementioned meeting between Paul VI and the Ecumenical Patriarch of Constantinople, Athenagoras, in 1964 and the subsequent cancellation of the mutual excommunication of 1965. This was followed by a summit meeting in 1979 between Pope John Paul II and the Patriarch of Constantinople, Dimitrios, which resulted in the creation of the Joint International Commission for Theological Dialogue Between the Catholic Church and the Orthodox Church. The commission began its work the following year.[148]

The Orthodox world, however, is not limited to the Patriarchate of Constantinople or the Greek Churches. Another important pole is the Patriarchate of Moscow. The two patriarchates have not moved in the same direction, even though the theological questions in play with Catholics are basically the same (most importantly the primacy of the bishop of Rome). In short, there are two main, parallel poles in the Orthodox world.

The commission's work was interrupted during the pontificate of John Paul II due to tensions between Catholicism and the Russian Orthodox, specifically with regard to the Greek Catholic Ukrainian Church. The problem was that in the 1990s,

---

147 Ibid., 143.
148 Rigas Raftopoulos, "Chiesa cattolica e Chiesa ortodossa di Grecia: le ragioni del dialogo," in *Rivista di Studi Politici*, n. 29 (2007): 101–136; "Il dialogo autentico è qualcosa di sacro, Il Patriarca ecumenico Bartolomeo all'Università cattolica di Lublino," *L'Osservatore Romano*, 25 August 2010.

Greek-Catholics were repossessing places of worship that for-
merly belonged to them, namely, places that the Soviet regime
had given to the Orthodox after World War II. The two confessions were claiming possession of the same patrimony and accusing each other of usurpation.[149] Moreover, the politics of John
Paul II creating new Catholic dioceses in the region of the Russian Patriarchate created resentment among the Orthodox who
felt that the territory under their direct jurisdiction was being
invaded and subjected to proselytism. An impasse was reached
when the commission met in Baltimore in 2000 to discuss the
theme, "The theological and canonical implications of uniatism." The ensuing discussion was complicated and yielded no
agreement. The commission's work could not move forward
and was put on hold.[150]

The work of the commission recommenced under Benedict
XVI and dialogue moved forward. It could not have been otherwise, since, as Benedict said to Seewald, "the place where we are,
if you will, closest to home, and where there is also the most hope
of reunion, is Orthodoxy."[151] It therefore was natural that he
should "battle" for this meeting.[152]

---

149 Cf. Aleksei Judin and Grigorij Protopopov, *Cattolici in Russia e
     Ucraina* (Milan: La Casa di Matriona, 1992); Giovanni Codevilla,
     "Laicità dello Stato e separatismo nella Russia di Putin," in Antonio
     G. Chizzonti (ed.), *Chiesa cattolica ed europa centro-orientale. Libertà
     religiosa e processo di democratizzazione* (Milan: Vita e Pensiero, 2004),
     137–286; Andrea Pacini, "Le Chiese ortodosse e cattoliche in europa
     Orientale e Balcanica. Un'articolazione plurale," in Adriano Roc-
     cucci (ed.), *Chiese e culture nell'est europeo. Prospettive di dialogo* (San
     Paolo: Cinisello Balsamo 2007), 94.
150 Cf. Dimitrios Salachas, "Riconfermata la volontà della Chiesa cat-
     tolica e del- la Chiesa ortodossa di proseguire il dialogo teologico,"
     in *Studi ecumenici*, n. 5, (2007): 101–121, Héctor Vall Vilardell, "Il
     lungo cammino del dialogo tra Chiesa cattolica e la chiesa orto-
     dossa," in *O Odigos*, n. 26 (2007): 1, 7–14.
151 Benedict XVI, *Luce del mondo*, 129. In English, *Light of the World* (San
     Francisco: Ignatius Press, 2010).
152 Ibid., 130.

On 12 September 2005, at a pan-Orthodox meeting in Fanar, it was decided that the work of the Joint International Commission for Theological Dialogue Between the Catholic Church and the Orthodox Church would begin again. After contact with the Pontifical Council for the Promotion of Christian Unity, the first meeting of this new phase was set for 13—16 December 2005 in Rome.[153] The initiative enjoyed the full support of the pope[154] along the lines of the well-established spiritual ecumenism (prayer), with the hope that this dialogue might lead not only to a reunification of the Catholic and Orthodox Churches, but also stand as an example for other ecumenical dialogues underway. The theologian Aimable Musoni believes that the pope's main thinking on dialogue with the Orthodox is based on one, simple idea—namely, the "conviction that today what was possible in the first millennium is not impossible today: as for papal primacy, for example, Rome does not need anything more from the East other than what was formulated and lived in the first millennium." While the West would prepare to recognize the validity of the ecclesial form preserved in the East, the East would refrain from accusing developments in the West during the second millennium as "heretical."[155] According to the historian Giorgio Fedalto, however, the solution of returning to the model of the first millennium "is partly right, but partly wrong,"[156] because today's problems are different.

153 Eleuterio Francesco Fortino, "Dialogo teologico fra cattolici e ortodossi," 22 January 2007: http://www.vatican.va/roman_curia/pontifical_councils/chrstuni/ch_orthodox_docs/rc_pc_chrstuni_doc_20070122_fortino-dialogo_it.html.
154 Cf. Benedict XVI, "Ad Consilium mixtum disponens Dialogum Catholico-Orthodoxum," 15 December 2005, *Acta Apostolicae Sedis*, n. 98 (2006): 38–40.
155 Aimable Musoni, "Le Chiese e la Chiesa. Il modello dell'unità secondo Benedetto XVI," in Manlio Sodi (ed.), *Ubi Petrus ibi ecclesia Sui sentieri del Concilio Vaticano II. Miscellanea offerta a S.S. Benedetto XVI in occasione del suo 80° genetliaco* (Rome: LAS, 2007), 410.
156 Giorgio Fedalto, "E possibile l'unione con le Chiese ortodosse?" in *Vita e Pensiero*, n. 89/5 (2006): 39.

Another significant step in the ecumenical journey was a meeting between Benedict XVI and Bartholomew I, Patriarch of Constantinople, held in Turkey in 2006, during which a joint declaration was signed and, after a brief historical *excursus,* asserted that the efforts of Catholics and Orthodox should be directed toward preserving moral values throughout the world, protecting civil rights and freedoms, countering war and terrorism, and protecting the environment.[157]

The International Commission started to touch on key themes. In Belgrade in 2006, the topic was the primacy of the bishop of Rome embedded in a wider discussion of authority and "conciliarity" in the Church in the wake of documents jointly signed by members of the Commission in the 1980s. Things continued to move forward at an assembly in Ravenna (8–15 October 2007) dedicated to the theme, "Ecclesiological and Canonical Consequences of the Sacramental Nature of the Church: Ecclesial Communion, Conciliarity, and Authority." Cardinal Kasper presented the final document and key points of the discussion to his fellow cardinals during their meeting on 23 November 2007. Despite the absence of the Russian delegation, due to dissensions in the Orthodox world, Kasper emphasized that a first step had been taken by the Orthodox toward recognizing Roman primacy at "a universal level of the Church, and they admitted that there is a *Protos* at this level too—a Primate—that can only exist in the Bishop of Rome according to the *taxis* of the ancient Church." In reference to the Patriarchate of Moscow, the cardinal affirmed that "the ice is finally melting."[158] Kasper was responsible for relaunching a spiritual ecumenism—that is, a spirituality of communion nourished by prayer.

Ecumenical dialogue between Catholicism and Orthodoxy also wavered at times due to tensions in the Orthodox world. The

---

157 Cf. Benedict XVI, "Inter Beatissimum Patrem Benedictum XVI et Patriarcham Bartholomaeum I," 30 November 2006, *Acta Apostolicae Sedis,* n. 98 (2006), 921–924.

158 Kasper, "Relazione al concistoro cardinalizio," 23 November 2007, op. cit.

Russian Orthodox Church excused itself from the commission's discussions in Ravenna in October 2007 in order to protest a decision of Bartholomew I, Patriarch of Constantinople, who had sent representatives from the so-called "Apostolic Church of Estonia," who, in turn, received their autonomy from the Patriarch of Constantinople. Moscow maintained such a decision needed their approval.[159] One of the main problems with the work of the International Commission was precisely the conflict between the Ecumenical Patriarch of Constantinople and the Patriarch of Moscow on the question of the correct Orthodox understanding of the notion of primacy. Such a discussion was necessary before the topic of papal primacy could be approached fruitfully in the dialogue between Catholics and Orthodox.

The strengthening of the dialogue between Rome and Constantinople was evident in the mutual gestures of Ecumenical Patriarch Bartholomew I and the pope during a visit of the former to the Vatican on 28 June 2008 on the Feast of Saints Peter and Paul.[160] It was the first time that the Patriarch of Constantinople went to Rome on this occasion. The patriarch attended the solemn Mass celebrated by the pope, after which both imparted a blessing to the faithful. This gesture, replete with symbolic meaning, was not appreciated by everyone in the Orthodox world.

Several other meetings between Catholics and Greek Orthodox took place. In addition to delegations sent to celebrate various solemnities (e.g., Orthodox went to Rome for the Feast of Saint Andrew on 30 November, and Catholics went to Istanbul for the Feast of Peter and Paul on 29 June), there were other important and symbolic meetings, including one between Benedict XVI and Bartholomew I during the peace pilgrimage to Assisi on 27 October 2011. In his message for the Feast of Saint Andrew, the pope

---

159 Eleuterio Francesco Fortino, "Cattolici e ortodossi a confronto sul ruolo del vescovo di Roma," *L'Osservatore Romano,* 17 October 2009, 6.

160 "Da san Paolo la via per l'unità dei cristiani," in *L'Osservatore Romano,* 29 June 2008.

wrote to the patriarch about the common mission of Christians in nations that once were Christian but are no longer, due to secularism.[161]

Meanwhile, relations between the Catholic Church and the Russian Orthodox Church improved and developed significantly during the pontificate of Benedict XVI. Both Hilarion, Head of the Department for External Church Relations of the Patriarchate of Moscow, and the Patriarch of Moscow and all Russia, Kirill, said as much.[162]

Various meetings also took place at the highest levels. On 21 June 2005, shortly after Benedict XVI was elected, Cardinal Kasper, head of ecumenical relations at the Vatican, made an important visit to the Patriarchate.[163] This was followed by another meeting in May of 2008, paving the way for a new phase in relations. Also worth noting is the face-to-face meeting between Metropolitan Hilarion and Benedict XVI together with some heads of Roman dicasteries, which took place in Rome in September of 2009.[164] Nevertheless, in 2009, Hilarion, speaking of the meeting of the International Commission in Ravenna, admitted that Roman primacy was still the "stumbling block."[165] (The larger problem being, however, that the topic was discussed at the meeting with the presence of the Russian Orthodox.)

On 24 September 2011, during Benedict XVI's apostolic visit

---

161 Benedict XVI, "Ad Bartholomaeum I Patriarcham Constantinopolitanum ob festivitatem Sancti Andreae Apostoli," 23 November 2011, *Acta Apostolicae Sedis*, n. 104 (2012): 1059–1061.

162 Hilarion di Volokolamsk, "Lo stato attuale delle relazioni ortodosso-cattoliche" op. cit., 113; Eleuterio Francesco Fortino, "Il Patriarca Cirillo sottolinea la sintonia con Benedetto XVI," *L'Osservatore Romano*, 4 February 2010.

163 Milan Žust, "Chiesa cattolica e Patriarcato di Mosca," *L'Osservatore Romano*, 22 January 2009.

164 Gianluca Biccini, "A Roma l'arcivescovo Hilarion," *L'Osservatore Romano*, 16 September 2009.

165 Hilarion di Volokolamsk, "Lo stato attuale delle relazioni ortodosso-cattoliche," op. cit., 109.

to Germany, the pope met with members of the Orthodox Bishops' Conference of Germany and representatives of the ancient (i.e., non-Calcedonian) Eastern churches. In his speech, Benedict XVI, acknowledging centuries of division,[166] also summarized the elements of communion, emphasizing the defense of human life from conception to natural death and the values of marriage and the family. He noted the programmatic unity of concerns shared by Orthodox and Catholics on the anthropological—and hence ethical—front.

On 16 October 2012, Metropolitan Hilarion, at the invitation of the Pontifical Council for the Promotion of Christian Unity, participated in the plenary session of the 13th Synod of Catholic Bishops as an observer representing the Russian Orthodox Church.[167] In his speech on that occasion, Hilarion expressed his hope that cooperation between Orthodox and Catholics would grow and thereby more readily respond to new challenges and threats in the modern era. He invited both sides to create a common front in defense of the Christian faith in all those countries where it is oppressed and persecuted, including Egypt, Libya, Afghanistan, Iraq, Syria, and others. The reality is, there is already an understanding on the great principles (including moral ones), as well as on the issues related to marriage and the family.[168]

As historian Adriano Roccucci rightly notes, Rome and Moscow have jointly taken note of the battle against the spread of anti-Christian values and discrimination against Christians in many Islamic countries as they work together to shed light on the relationship between Christianity and Europe.[169] It is no accident

---

166 Cf. Benedict XVI, "Incontro con rappresentanti delle Chiese ortodosse e ortodosse orientali," 24 September 2011, in *Insegnamenti di Benedetto XVI*, vol. VII, 2/2011 (Città del Vaticano: LEV, 2012), 312–315.
167 Russian Orthodox Church, Department of Foreign Relations of the Patriarch of Moscow, 16 October 2012: https://mospat.ru/it/2012/10/16/news73094/.
168 Cf. Benedict XVI, *Last Testament*, 204.
169 Adriano Roccucci, *Vaticano e Chiesa russa: asse cristiano in Europa*

that the question of Europe's Christian roots is deeply relevant to her politics, which are inevitably interwoven with religion. The Putin era is clearly one of "overlapping plans."[170] When there are tensions between the two churches, there are political consequences. For example, during the pontificate of John Paul II, there were multiple reactions to the creation of Latin dioceses in Russia without the previous agreement of the Patriarchate and civil authorities. Not only did the Patriarch break relations with Rome and the civil government criticize the Holy See for its lack of prudence, but "one bishop and four foreign Catholic priests were expelled from Russian territory."[171] On other occasions, Putin was able to compel Rome display signs of courtesy toward the Orthodox (e.g., the return of the icon of the Virgin of Kazan).[172]

While the tendency of John Paul II's pontificate to interweave political and ecclesial issues seemed to hinder ecumenical relations at times, Benedict XVI's pontificate gradually stabilized harmonious relations. The international political climate steered things in this direction. Putin, in fact, "would view the opening of the Patriarchate toward a common defense of Christianity in Europe" as something good given the many economic and military crises as well as the rise of Islamic fundamentalism against the West and Russia.[173] Faced with NATO expansion and feeling surrounded, the Russian Federation sought new alliances. The Holy See did not pull back. To the contrary, it responded in kind. During a trip to Moscow in October of 2005, Archbishop Lajolo, then Secretary for Relations with States at the Secretariat of State, gave an interview in which he expressed an openness to collaboration with Moscow on important themes such as peace in the

(Rome: ISPI, 28 February 2013). Accessed at: http://www.ispion-line.it/it/pubblicazione/ vaticano-e-chiesa-russa-asse-cristiano-europa.

170 Cf. Fausto Fasciani, "Le relazioni tra la Russia di Putin e la Santa Sede," *Rivista di Studi Politici*, n. 20 (2008), 117–133, here 130.
171 Ibid., 121.
172 Ibid., 122.
173 Ibid., 124.

Middle East and coordinated action in international bodies such as the Organization for Security and Co-operation in Europe and the United Nations to eliminate hunger and defend the dignity of the human person. At the same time, he urged respect for the Catholic Church and the right to religious freedom.[174]

It was within this climate that Benedict XVI and Putin met in Rome in 2007. Their talks touched mainly on ecumenical and political topics (e.g., the Middle East, extremism, intolerance, and peace).[175] During this time, it seemed possible to work with the Russian Orthodox by setting political objectives and making political inroads. Theological issues were marginalized. They didn't seem worthy of pursuing. The principal issue was, in fact, more complex, in that there had to be some kind of resolution of the internal Orthodox issues dividing the Orthodox churches.

In general, the lack of understanding between Catholics and Orthodox is not so much of a theological—and particularly an ecclesiological—nature, as a historical and hence political nature. The question of unity will not be resolved by simply finding ways to agree on the exercise of the pope's Petrine ministry and the conciliar/synodal nature of the Church, as it is may be by serenely looking at history (i.e., by "historicizing") and overcoming the myth that the first millennium was one of unity, when in fact it was not at all. In the Church's public speeches, for example, reference is often made to the shock 1054—that is, the year of the mutual excommunications of the Roman and Constantinopolitan churches that presumably shattered the unity of the Church. If we use a simplified and rather impoverished political language, the Church in the early days was really a kind of federated rather than unified Church, and within the individual local churches there were further divisions.

If the initial questions that caused a distance between the Western and Eastern Church were political and cultural, during the pontificate of John Paul II—and even more so during Benedict

174 Cf. Ibid., 125.
175 Cf. Ibid., 127.

XVI—the search for unity was taken up again precisely by sharing common cultural and ethical motivation at the level of international politics. As for theological questions, ecumenism remains "spiritual" at the moment. "Good intentions" alone do not suffice in the twenty-first century when Christians—be they Catholic, Orthodox, or other—are so vulnerable to persecution. Political phenomena (such as secularization and Islamic fundamentalism) push Christians to work ever more closely on an international level.

Conclusions

A new, dynamic ecumenism emerged during Benedict XVI's reign. Various confessional groups entered into effective and visible union with Rome. It should be noted that these steps were essentially made possible because of the personal initiative and action of the pope. Rather than relying on the Pontifical Council for the Promotion of Christian Unity, he worked through the Congregation for the Doctrine of the Faith—that is, through a structure that he not only knew well, but "created" throughout his tenure as prefect. The team at the Holy Office was composed of "his men." He knew them personally and, in many cases, had been the one to hire them. Benedict found a harmony of working styles, goals, and perspectives with these collaborators. The Anglican case is particularly significant in this regard: Cardinal Kasper was primarily in charge of this dialogue until the end of 2007, when the Congregation for the Doctrine of the Faith took over. In the end, it was the Holy Office that proposed the original solution of personal ordinariates.

The criteria for unity essentially fall into two categories: a recognition of papal primacy and an adherence to the 1992 Catechism of the Catholic Church, the latter of which amounts to a crystallized reception of the teaching of Vatican II.

At the beginning of his pontificate, Benedict XVI indicated that there was a need to overcome an ecumenism of "good feelings" in order to "reconstitute the full and visible unity of all the followers of Christ." This is indeed how he acted as he was able to avail himself of the collaboration and support of the Congregation for the Doctrine of the Faith.

On the more critical side, some Catholic commentators have noted that Benedict XVI's approach to ecumenism was really more than a "uniatism" or "unionism,"[176] a sort of "return" of single individuals or subgroups to the "true Church."[177] In reality, Benedict's was a sort of evolving ecumenism that aimed for a visible, tangible unity, which is an *effective* sacramental and hierarchical communion and not merely an *affective* one. The maintenance of the Anglican tradition within the larger Latin tradition is exemplifies reciprocal consideration. The way of acting toward the Anglicans is neither a sort of ecumenism nor a sort of twentieth-century unionism. It is something altogether new. It is a union through a gesture of pastoral solicitude.[178]

When Cardinal Kasper was still president of the Pontifical Council for the Promotion of Christian Unity, he said the following in his speech at the 2007 consistory. Referring to the pope's homily of 20 April 2005, he said that since the first day of his pontificate, Benedict XVI "established the priority of working tirelessly to restore the full and visible unity of all the followers of Christ. He knows well that showing signs of good intentions is not enough. Concrete gestures that penetrate souls and move consciences are necessary. These awaken everyone to the internal conversion that is a presupposition for any progress in ecumenism."[179]

The cardinal spoke of an internal conversion of everyone involved in the ecumenical journey, while the pope indicated a

---

176 Van Parys, "La costituzione apostolica *Anglicanorum Coetibus*: valutazione di un ecumenista cattolico" op. cit., 153.
177 Ruggieri, "Il movimento ecumenico avanza, segna il passo o retrocede?" op. cit., 8
178 "Des anglicans *unis, non asorbés*," op. cit., 337–338.
179 Kasper, "Relazione al concistoro cardinalizio," 23 November 2007, op. cit.

visible unity. Are these two different perceptions only two different viewpoints of the same problem?

In the end, what really counts is that the fully attainted unity with some Anglicans was possible only through an ecumenism of reciprocity. *Anglicanorum Coetibus* allowed the richness of the Anglican tradition to enter into the Catholic Church as a gift of the Church of Christ, and some of the communities coming from Anglicanism can integrate their own patrimony with that of Rome.

The unity of Christians was the central desire of Benedict XVI. We see this thread running through his entire pontificate. As Bier notes:

> To members of the so-called Fraternity of Saint Pius X, the pope showed the way to communion with the Catholic Church. To those who love the Tridentine form of the Roman Rite, he offered the Motu Proprio *Summorum Pontificum*. With the Apostolic Constitution *Anglicanorum Coetibus*, the pope follows the same road [...]. He could not help but make his own contribution to the rebuilding of unity.[180]

A special characteristic of Benedict XVI's pontificate emerges from the accomplishments with the Lefebvrites, the Anglicans, and the Orthodox—namely, the quest, adoption, and pursuit of new ways to unity. These ways are not always unanimously accepted by bishops and theologians, who seem fixed on the words, styles, and actions more typical of earlier decades. This obviously implies a different underlying theology. But is this simply a matter of a conservatism incapable of recognizing theological developments, or merely a case of generational differences? In a certain sense, the elderly Benedict XVI seems younger than other bishops

---

180 Bier, "La costituzione apostolica *Anglicanorum Coetibus* e le *Norme complementari* della Congregazione per la dottrina della fede," op. cit., 137.

and theologians. In other words, he seems more open to new ways. As pope, he showed that he was more accepting than other bishops of groups seeking unity of faith and sacraments. This was Benedict XVI's way of expressing his theological role of being the successor to Peter, knowing how to lead his brothers in the episcopate.

His way of acting also has clear ecclesiological implications. In fact, the Anglo-Catholic ordinariate reinforces the role of the person within the Church and relativizes, weakens, or at least makes more fragile the ecclesiology of the local church (based on the diocese), which is more characteristic of Orthodoxy.[181] This way of proceeding would go on to influence the wider ecclesiological debate on the ontological priority of the universal Church and particular churches, which in the past was an issue that divided Cardinals Ratzinger and Kasper. The latter is obviously underwhelmed by the new way pursued by Benedict.

A clear development is identifiable within the Church as she faces resistance in some Catholic ecumenical circles that now appear more conservative. Those considered innovators just a few decades previously are no longer deemed so innovative. History is full of surprises.

---

181 Cf. "Des anglicans *unis, non asorbés*," op. cit., 338.

CHAPTER SIX
DIALOGUE WITH CULTURE

One of the most salient features of Benedict XVI's pontificate was his handling of the relationship between the Church and the world. In addition to overseeing the Holy See's diplomatic activity (more on that in the next chapter), Benedict worked consistently along certain cultural and political lines whenever he engaged the world in dialogue, compared Christianity to other religions, or expressed the Church's role in the public square. It is clear that the pope devoted unique, personal involvement in these matters. According to Benedict, no single cultural feature ever dominates—be it economics or finance (see *Caritas in Veritate*), science (in the sense of the natural sciences), the arts, or national cultural heritage. Benedict built on the foundation laid by John Paul II, who for his part focused his engagement with the world on the themes of anthropology and the defense of the human person, and thus prepared the grounds for a consistent teaching on politics and bioethics. While the papacy of the nineteenth and twentieth centuries focused on the "social question," in the latter twentieth and twenty-first centuries it confronts a different challenge—namely, the anthropological question, or rather questions regarding man's identity and his role in society.

The central themes that emerged from Benedict's pontificate were human rights and religious freedom, ethics, the promotion of peace, and interreligious dialogue. It was no accident that the last of these was entrusted to the experienced diplomat Cardinal Tauran rather than an academic expert or theologian as in the realm of ecumenical dialogue. New and difficult questions had arisen with regard to the relationship between the Church and modernity.[1] Modernity itself is a complicated topic that cannot be reduced to one, single interpretation. The origins of modernity, generally characterized as the critical autonomy of the subject in the face of preceding traditions, have been explained in several different ways. There is really no single modernizing process because there are in fact several "modernities" (think of the difference between American and European versions of modernity).[2] On a religious level, modernity appears as the challenge of a subject's autonomy, who might give into secularization (i.e., make political power sacrosanct) or laicization (autonomizing the sacred). These two phenomena are actually interrelated, and not easily distinguishable. Our present concern is not to fully unravel the difficult notion of modernity, but to understand Pope Benedict's stance toward it.

First of all, when it comes to progress, it should be noted that the Church and the papacy have consciously and systematically used whatever scientific and technical means (e.g., the press, photography, mass communications, etc.) to pursue her pastoral goals and promote evangelization. In this sense, we can speak of a "modernized papacy" (one thinks of Benedict's use of Twitter, for example). This kind of modernization can be considered functional, aesthetic, and superficial. But the papacy has also been subject to a more substantial modernization in a philosophical, juridical, and political sense. As Carlo Fantappiè has noted, "the 'science' of canon law has been the privileged terrain of a gradual and controlled process of rationalization and secularization which has had many implications. It has extended into other areas that need further investigation (such as Holy Scripture, dogmatics,

1   There is no space here to discuss the wide range of literature on the subject, but we should mention the polemical discussion of Vincenzo Ferrone, *Lo strano illuminismo di Joseph Ratzinger. Chiesa, modernità e diritti dell'uomo* (Rome: Laterza, 2013).
2   ⁶Cf. Charles Taylor, *Gli immaginari sociali moderni* (Roma: Meltemi, 2005), 187.

liturgy, and pastoral theology).”[3] The Church's efforts to galva-
nize the pope's power in the 1800s and the curial reforms in the
1900s were responding to the cultural and political needs of modernization, according to which states become centralized more
and more in their administration and governance. On a pastoral
level, modernization has entailed a uniformity of catechetical
work. So, there have been various elements of modernization in
the Church geared toward protecting and safeguarding the freedom, doctrinal integrity, and authority of the hierarchy.

The action of the Church and the papacy in the face of modernity cannot be reduced to simplistic, binary oppositions such as
reform/restoration, innovation/conservatism, and modernism/
integralism. We must rather keep in mind the reciprocal effects
of each of these and other hybrid forms that allow us to speak of
“conservative reforms” (such as the three curial reforms of the
twentieth century) and innovative restorations (such as the liturgical plurality of the twentieth and twenty-first centuries).

It is within this wider context that we must situate Benedict
XVI. He does not compromise with those Western societies that
prescind from God's truth, for the future would then be nothing
but desolation.[4] At the same time, Benedict XVI knows that it is
important to recognize that the moral truths present in modernity
come to us precisely from Christianity.[5] Modernity is not a mono-
lith. Various elements of value are found within it. According to
Benedict, however, only a theological vision can fully explain the
grounds of those values.

To better grasp Ratzinger's understanding of culture, we must
take a step back and look at the man before he became pope. On
1 April 2005, when he received the Saint Benedict Award at the

3   Carlo Fantappiè, “Prospettive di ricerca,” *Humanitas* n. 64 (2009):
     962.
4   For example, see Benedict XVI, Address to the Roman Rota, 20 De-
     cember 2010, in *Acta Apostolicae Sedis*, n. 103 (2011): 33–41.
5   Cf. Benedict XVI, *Luce del mondo*, 40. In English, *Light of the World*
     (San Francisco: Ignatius Press, 2010).

Monastery of Saint Scholastica in Subiaco, Cardinal Ratzinger gave an important speech on Europe and the crisis of cultures.[6] He spoke of the hegemony of the radical Enlightenment culture that subordinates religion to itself. Such a culture "is essentially defined by the rights of freedom (a concept insufficiently defined) which are still being formulated around the vague notions of a 'prohibition of discrimination,'" inasmuch as "there are also rights of man that oppose one another, such as the conflict between a woman's desire for freedom and the right of the unborn to live."

Cardinal Ratzinger argued that the underlying philosophy of today's Enlightenment culture does not express man's full reason, but only a part of it. It excludes God from public discourse, relegating it to the subjective realm of the conscience. "The real opposition that characterizes today's world is not the opposition between various religious cultures, but between the radical emancipation of man from God, from the roots of life, on the one hand, and from the great religious cultures on the other."

The deepest problem, therefore, is one of relativism, which for Ratzinger is nothing but "dogmatism." Such a culture, he claims, "leads us increasingly to the edge of the abyss, to man's ever greater isolation," and it inevitably leads to an attempt to live and direct one's life *"velut si Deus daretur,"* "as if God existed." Ratzinger therefore proposes a new encounter between Christianity and the Enlightenment:

> Christianity has understood itself as the religion of the *Logos,* as the religion according to reason [...] infosar as it is the religion of the persecuted, the universal religion, transcending different states and peoples, it has denied the

6   Joseph Ratzinger, "L'Europa nella crisi delle culture," 1 April 2005: http://chiesa.espresso.repubblica.it/articolo/27262. Also: *L'Europa di Benedetto. Nella crisi delle culture,* trans. Lorenzo Cappelletti and Silvia Kritzenberger (Città del Vaticano-Siena: LEV and Edizioni Cantagalli, 2005). On-line: http://magisterobenedettoxvi.blogspot.it/2008/02/leuropa-nella-crisi-delle-culture.html.

state the right to regard religion as a part of state ordering, thus postulating the freedom of faith. It has always defined men, all men without distinction, as creatures and images of God, proclaiming for them, in terms of principle, although within the imperative limits of social ordering, the same dignity. In this connection, the Enlightenment is of Christian origin and it is no accident that it was born precisely and exclusively in the realm of the Christian faith, whenever Christianity, against its nature and unfortunately, had become tradition and religion of the state. Notwithstanding the philosophy, insofar as the search for rationality also of our faith, was always a prerogative of Christianity, the voice of reason had been too domesticated. It was and is the merit of the Enlightenment to have again proposed these original values of Christianity and of having given back to reason its own voice. In the Pastoral Constitution *On the Church in the Modern World*, Vatican II underlined again this profound correspondence between Christianity and the Enlightenment, seeking to come to a true conciliation between the Church and modernity, which is the great heritage that both sides must defend. Given all this, it is necessary that both sides engage in self-reflection and be willing to correct themselves.

Ratzinger's thesis was criticized and debated, both on a historical and theoretical level.[7] In any case, from 19 April 2005 onward, what had been the speech of a cardinal instantly became the speech of a pope.

The role of religion in society

Benedict's thinking was more fully disclosed in a famous address he gave in Regensburg in September 2006, which directly

7   Giuseppe Lorizio, "Il Pontificato interrotto. Spunti per un bilancio teologico," in *Studium*, n. 109 (2013): 410.

addressed the question of the relationship between faith and reason, as well as religion and culture. "Not to act in accordance with reason is contrary to God's nature," he said.[8] He fleshed this claim out in subsequent speeches. In 2008 at the White House in Washington, D.C., for example, he asserted that "the principles governing political and social life are intimately linked to a moral order based on the dominion of God the Creator."[9] In a speech to French intellectuals at the Collège des Bernardins in Paris in 2008, he said that the Word of God, which reaches us through human words, must always be interpreted, and only by carefully interpreting it will we avoid fundamentalism. At London's Westminster Hall in 2011, Benedict XVI confronted the question of the role of religion in society, which is recognized in its capacity to individuate "objective moral principles"[10] that reason, and therefore politics, must therefore apply. Religion can preform this function only if it does not degenerate into sectarianism or fundamentalism—that is, if it values "the purifying and structuring role of reason within religion."[11] Reason and faith need each other because they reciprocally purify one other. So, what does this mean for the political and democratic dynamics of the early twenty-first century? It means that a democratic majority is not sufficient to

8   Benedict XVI, "Discorso con i rappresentanti della scienza, Regensburg 12 September 2006," in *Acta Apostolicae Sedis*, n. 98 (2006): 728–739.
9   Benedict XVI, "Speech on the South Lawn (White House), Washington D.C.," 16 April 2008, in *L'Osservatore Romano*, 18 April 2008. English version: https://w2.vatican.va/content/benedict-xvi/en/speeches/2008/april/documents/hf_ben-xvi_spe_20080416_welcome-washington.html.
10 Benedict XVI, Address to Civil Authorities, 17 September 2010, in *Acta Apostolicae Sedis*, n. 102 (2010): 635–639.
11 Benedict XVI, Meeting with representatives of British society, including the diplomatic corps, politicians, academics, and business leaders, 17 September 2010, *Acta Apostlicae Sedis*, n. 102 (2010): 635–639: http://w2.vatican.va/content/benedict-xvi/en/speeches/2010/september/documents/hf_ben-xvi_spe_20100917_societa-civile.html.

ensure good and just legislation.[12] Religion has a role, then, in public life and thus within democratic societies. From this, we begin to deduce Benedict's thinking on the notion of *laïcité*.

In a speech before the Italian President, Carlo Azeglio Ciampi, Benedict XVI said: "Therefore, a healthy secularism (*laicità*) of the State, by virtue of which temporal realities are governed according to their own norms but which does not exclude those ethical references that are ultimately founded in religion, is legitimate."[13] This can be taken as a summation of Benedict XVI's political thinking: the norms of the state must be based on ethical reference points, and these reference points themselves must ultimately be grounded in religion to be fully effective and understood. In this sense, *laïcité* is the condition (i.e., method) that allows religion to have its own space in public debate through a recognition of its cultural significance. *Laïcité* is not so much the neutrality of a state toward religious convictions as it is the condition for various religions to express values that will make a positive (ethical) contribution to society and the state. "Laicism," on the other hand, is the vision of society that confines religion to the life of the individual, thus cutting off religion from civil life. Hence the pope encourages the Church and other Christian communities to intervene in European and international debates, especially with regard to the so-called "non-negotiable" principles:[14] principles not entirely unique to Christians, but to humanity in general. These principles are "rooted in the nature of the human being" and thus "recognizable through the right

12 Benedict XVI, Speech at the Reichstag in Berlin, 22 September 2011, *Acta Apostolicae Sedis*, n. 103 (2011): 663–669

13 Benedict XVI, Address to the President of the Italian Repubblica, Carlo Azeglio Ciampi, 24 June 2005, *Acta Apostolicae Sedis*, n. 97 (2005): 823–826.

14 Benedict XVI, Address to the members of the European People's Party on the occasion of the study days on Europe, *Acta Apostolicae Sedis*, n. 98 (2006): 343–345. English edition: https://www.vatican.va/content/benedict-xvi/en/speeches/2006/march/documents/hf_ben-xvi_spe_20060330_eu-parliamentarians.html.

use of reason."[15] Benedict's vision, which proposes a *laïcité* of the state without severing its roots from religion, is not shared by strict "laicists" because, in their view, lay morals—that is, a-religious morals—are not trustworthy since they too impinge upon the full autonomy of the state.[16]

The basic issue here is the ultimate foundation of human moral action. To put it simply, what value do the morals of non-believers have? The way we answer that question will have deep anthropological and sociological consequences. It is no accident that Benedict XVI's speeches cited herein were made to politicians and not to Catholics as such.

When it comes to Catholics, Benedict XVI penned three encyclicals (*Deus Caritas Est*, 25 December 2005; *Spe Salvi*, 30 November 2007; and *Caritas in Veritate*, 4 December 2009) that treat this theme by taking "politics" seriously (the word is mentioned 13 times in the first encyclical, 8 in the second, and no fewer than 30 times in the third[17]), often treating it in passages that are decidedly theological. *Deus Caritas Est* affirms that a reflection on justice can be greatly assisted by faith if we view faith as a purifying element of reason. In another passage, Benedict XVI argues, "The Church cannot and must not take upon herself the political battle to bring about the most just society possible."[18] Rather, she must "play her part through rational argument." In *Spe Salvi*, the pope once again emphasizes the risk of man relying solely on his own power without God. Man needs God, not only so that he does not lose all hope, but also to use his gift of reason well and

15 Benedict XVI, Speech at the 4th National Conference of the Italian Church, Verona, 19 October 2006, *Acta Apostolicae Sedis*, n. 98 (2006): 804–815; Benedict XVI, Address to the President of the Italian Repubblica, Giorgio Napolitano," 20 November 2006, in *Insegnamenti di Benedetto XVI*, vol. II, 2 (Città del Vaticano: LEV, 2013), 448–652.
16 Giovanni Miccoli, *In difesa della fede. La Chiesa di Giovanni Paolo II e Benedetto XVI* (Milan: Rizzoli, 2007), 337, *passim*.
17 Giacomo Coccolini, "Elementi teologico-politici del magistero di Benedetto XVI," *Rivista di teologia Morale*, n. 178 (2013), 219.
18 *Deus Caritas Est*, 28.

to make it "truly human." He asks for an "openness" of reason to the "saving forces of faith, to the difference between good and evil." In short, "reason needs faith if it is to be completely itself: reason and faith need one another in order to fulfill their true nature and mission."[19] The pope further expounds his thinking in the social encyclical *Caritas in Veritate*, where he writes:

> Secularism (*laicità*) and fundamentalism exclude the possibility of fruitful dialogue and effective cooperation between reason and religious faith. *Reason always stands in need of being purified by faith*: this also holds true for political reason, which must not consider itself omnipotent. For its part, *religion always needs to be purified by reason* in order to show its authentically human face. Any breach in this dialogue comes only at an enormous price to human development.

He addresses Christianity more explicitly when he writes:

> The Christian religion and other religions can offer their contribution to development *only if God has a place in the public realm*, specifically in regard to its cultural, social, economic, and particularly its political dimensions. The Church's social doctrine came into being in order to claim "citizenship status" for the Christian religion.

With these words, Benedict shows that he is a staunch defender of the public dimension of religion, and more specifically of Christianity, as well as the participation of believers in constructing a just and stable social order.

Benedict XVI's general approach to the relationship between faith and reason, Church and state, and Church and society provoked many reactions in the intellectual world. While the radical

---

19   Benedict XVI, Encyclical Letter *Spe Salvi*, 30 November 2007, *Acta Apostolicae Sedis*, n. 99 (2007), 985–1027, n. 23.

neo-Enlightenment crowd never budged, people like Marcello Pera, an Italian philosopher and President of the Italian Senate from 2001 to 2006, decided to explore and compare his own thinking openly with Benedict's. There was also an extraordinary conversation between Ratzinger and the philosopher Jürgen Habermas[20]—which had hints of the former's remarks to French intellectuals at the Collège des Bernardins—as well as an engagement of Italian Marxist intellectuals with Ratzinger's theology (which we will address next). The intellectual world was highly stimulated by this pope who had a capacity to encourage people to see things from a different point of view and even to change their positions.

Benedict XVI's political thinking is strongly formed by the teaching of Vatican II, particularly as iterated by the Declaration *Dignitatis Humanae* and the Constitution *Gaudium et Spes,* as well as in the magisterial teaching since Pope John XXIII. Ratzinger immersed himself more deeply in the theological and theoretical systematization of the role of religion in society, concentrating in a particular way on the European situation, as was most evident during the *sede vacante* period and the conclave of 2005.

Benedict is unique in framing politics within a theological rather than merely philosophical vision. He does so within the specific context of a wider, international debate that broke out after 11 September 2001 surrounding the public role of religion.[21]

---

20   Joseph Ratzinger, Jürgen Habermas, *Etica, religione e stato liberale* (Brescia: Morcelliana, 2004); Benedict XVI (Joseph Ratzinger), Jürgen Habermas, *Ragione e fede in dialogo,* Giancarlo Bosetti (ed.) (Venice: Marsilio, 2005). The comparison between the two found wide echo. For example, the journal *Humanitas,* n. 59 (2004) relaunched their public discussion in Munich on 19 January 2004 on the theme, "The pre-political moral foundations of the liberal State." Moreover, in more recent times, reprints of some debates of that time continue: Vittorio Possenti, "*Stato, Diritto, Religione. Il dialogo tra Jürgen Habermas e Joseph Ratzinger,*" in *Roczniki Filozoficzne,* n. 62 (2014): 71–85.
21   Cf. Coccolini, *Elementi teologico-politici del magistero di Benedetto XVI,*

According to Benedict, Christianity does not really have a "theological politics," but "only a political *ethos*," for which "the *civitas Dei* can never be an empirical, state-like reality,"[22] because the state can only be a *civitas terrena*. That is why, according to Benedict XVI's thinking, it is useless to talk of reestablishing a "Christian regime" in the twenty-first century. In fact, Benedict XVI wants to avoid the risk that Christianity will theologize politics, just as it should not politicize theology.[23] He writes:

> "Render unto Caesar what belongs to Caesar and to God what belongs to God," was Jesus' response to the question about taxes [...]. Jesus' answer deftly moves the argument to a higher plane, gently cautioning against both the politicization of religion and the deification of temporal power, along with the relentless pursuit of wealth.[24]

But this does not mean that the Church should avoid "theologizing man," so to speak. Failing to recognize this leads to many misunderstandings with respect to human rights.[25]

op. cit., 213–226, here 213. For a good presentation of Ratzinger's thinking, see Massimo Borghesi, *Critica della teologia politica. Da Agostino a Peterson: la fine dell'era costantinana* (Genova: Marietti 1820, 2013).

22   Coccolini, *Elementi teologico-politici del magistero di Benedetto XVI*, op. cit., 214.

23   Cf. Ibid, 214.

24   Benedict XVI, "A time for Christians to engage with the world," in *Financial Times*, 20 December 2012: https://w2.vatican.va/content/benedict-xvi/en/speeches/2012/december/documents/hf_ben-xvi_spe_20121220_financial-times.html.

25   On this topic, see Bolgiani, Ferrone, Margiotta Broglio (eds.), *Chiesa cattolica e modernità*, op. cit.; Daniele Menozzi, *Chiesa e diritti umani. Legge naturale e modernità politica dalla Rivoluzione francese ai nostri giorni* (Bologna: Il Mulino, 2012); Marcello Pera, *Diritti umani e cristianesimo. La Chiesa alla prova della modernità* (Venice: Marsilio, 2015).

The Church and human rights

Without falling into a long historical digression, it suffices to say that the Church's position on human rights has evolved through the centuries, especially since the French Revolution. At that time, the Church was understandably wary and critical of the "rights of man" since the Revolution put them on a purely horizontal plane ("the deliberation of the human assembly"), thereby truncating the vertical dimension (i.e., God). Subsequently, however, the Church gradually assimilated the notion of "human rights" in a considerably modified form to the point that the Church now actively advocates on behalf of these rights. The Church's acceptance of the notion of "human rights," however, has led to serious misunderstandings. In fact, since the Church cannot sever human rights from their theological foundation, she finds herself in constant debate with those who attempt to ground them in some other way. This inevitably leads to disagreements over what human rights are, specifically. Although the Church and Western culture concur on a recognition of religious liberty and freedom of conscience, there is great tension over claims to other "rights" that the Church simply cannot recognize. We might think of reproductive rights (i.e., birth control and abortion) and gender (i.e., the self-determination of one's sexual orientation and a recognition of certain public rights,[26] as well as the wider discussion of LGBT rights), and the pressure over internal ecclesial issues such as the admission of women and homosexuals to the priesthood.

There is clearly a widespread misunderstanding about how to delineate rights, and this inevitably leads to conflict because of the connection between rights and religion. Indeed, religious cultures nourish and influence individual and collective behavior and thus strongly shape our juridical conceptions of what human rights are and how they are to be protected.[27] This makes it easy to understand why the media puts such intense pressure on the

26   Menozzi, *Chiesa e diritti umani*, op. cit., 7.
27   Ibid.

Church and the papacy to sign on to a seemingly interminable list of "human rights." Furthermore, because of her theological vision, it is easy to understand why the Church is so intent on protecting a limited list of "non-negotiable rights" rather than an ever-growing list of new rights.

The issue is precisely the "content" of those human rights, or more simply, the "list" of those rights. For the Church of Paul VI (influenced by Maritain and personalism) and John Paul II, the foundation of rights is human dignity, which in turn is rooted in God. The Church bases human rights on natural law, and ultimately places them on a transcendental plane, and this is precisely why the Church is able to present a catalogue of rights—that is, because she knowns and watches over the truth about man, which she receives from divine revelation. This is the only way to guarantee that those rights will not undergo change over time and vary from place to place. In papal teaching, this is why we speak of a "freedom of thought, conscience, religion, expression, and political and cultural pluralism."[28] John Paul II, especially within his anti-communist vision, insists on the right of religious freedom, placing it—or more accurately, reinforcing it— as a typical element in the diplomatic work of the Holy See. During John Paul II's pontificate, heavy emphasis was placed on the right to human life and the absolute respect owed to it. This insistence will increase even more after the fall of the Church's great enemy in the twentieth century: communism. This insistence reached its zenith in the encyclical *Evangelium Vitae* (1995), in which the right to life engages the entire structure of human rights. The call for religious freedom would continue to grow, especially in places where it is not guaranteed or protected, such as in some Islamic countries.

Benedict XVI's teaching would follow the line of his predecessors. He especially drew on John Paul II's teaching that the

---

28   John Paul II, *Discorso al corpo diplomatico*, 13 January 1990, in *Enchiridion della pace*, vol. 2, *Paolo VI. Giovanni Paolo II* (Bologna: EDB, 2005), 3547 (n. 6367).

right to life is the key to understanding all other rights. The Church relentlessly proposed natural law in an ever more stead-fast way as the basis for peaceful human coexistence, and the Church herself was presented as a trustworthy interpreter of the new norms for that existence. In a certain way, it seemed she was the only one who could assume the role of guiding all of humanity.[29]

According to Menozzi, Ratzinger lays claim to a Christian cultural tradition inspired the Universal Declaration of Human Rights adopted by the United Nations' General Assembly in 1948. Menozzi writes that such a claim actually distorts historical reality in that the Church seemed to be constantly opposed to so-called "human rights." Revindicating them in this way would seem a political maneuver. It would "present the Church once more as having a general directive function over human conscience," and it would skip over the contractualistic foundation of human rights in favor of a transcendental legitimization, which is precisely the domain of the Church, and more specifically, her hierarchy.

In a constantly evolving world that prescinds human rights from the realm of the sacred, the Church seeks to be the guarantor and interpreter of those rights, but by doing so she remains in a state of conflict with other sectors of society and with politics, which do not accept the idea of objective morals valid in every time and place, just as the Church does not accept fundamental rights used to safeguard certain autonomous behavior when it comes to sexuality, marriage, genetics, and family life. Benedict XVI insisted on the universality of rights as a way of combatting the tendency to limit them to certain cultures and times. In a speech given before the United Nations' General Assembly on 18 April 2008 in New York,[30] he said:

29   Menozzi, *Chiesa e diritti umani*, op. cit., 259.
30   Benedict XVI, "Address to the Members of the General Assembly of the United Nations Organization; New York," 18 April 2008, *Acta Apo-*

They are based on the natural law inscribed on human hearts and present in different cultures and civilizations. Removing human rights from this context would mean restricting their range and yielding to a relativistic conception, according to which the meaning and interpretation of rights could vary and their universality would be denied in the name of different cultural, political, social and even religious outlooks. This great variety of viewpoints must not be allowed to obscure the fact that not only rights are universal, but so too is the human person, the subject of those rights.

The pope included religious freedom (both individual and communal) among those rights because it "permits men and women to pursue their journey of faith and their search for God in this world."

Three years later, the core message of that speech was echoed in a speech to the German Parliament.[31] In defending the idea of natural rights, Benedict XVI asked the fundamental questions: "How do we recognize what is right? How can we discern between good and evil, between what is truly right and what may appear right?" He then proposes a way:

For most of the matters that need to be regulated by law, the support of the majority can serve as a sufficient criterion. Yet it is evident that for the fundamental issues of law, in which the dignity of man and of humanity is at stake, the majority principle is not enough: everyone in a position of responsibility must personally seek out the criteria to be followed when framing laws.

stolicae Sedis, n. 100 (2008): 331–338. English version: https://www.vatican.va/content/benedict-xvi/en/speeches/2008/april/documents/hf_ben-xvi_spe_20080418_un-visit.html.

31 Benedict XVI, "Discorso al Reichstag di Berlino," 22 September 2011, op. cit.

The pope suggested a sort of conscientious objection to laws considered "irreligious"—namely, those that are fundamentally unreasonable and disrespectful of "the law of truth." In this case, Benedict XVI raised the case of those who joined the resistance to the Nazi regime. He then made a connection to present day:

> Yet when it comes to the decisions of a democratic politician, the question of what now corresponds to the law of truth, what is actually right and may be enacted as law, is less obvious. In terms of the underlying anthropological issues, what is right and may be given the force of law is in no way simply self-evident today.

By means of an historical analysis, albeit a little forced, the pope places the religious world at the foundation of our understanding of what is right and just. Here, we are primarily concerned with what the pope's analysis tells us about his thinking. He says, "decisions regarding what was to be lawful among men were taken with reference to the divinity." Better still, he says, reference to the divinity "has pointed to nature and reason as the true sources of law," and "to the harmony of objective and subjective reason, which naturally presupposes that both spheres are rooted in the creative reason of God." The pope believes that Christianity made a significant theological contribution to that harmony, in that Christian theologians were "on the side of philosophy, and that they acknowledged reason and nature in their interrelation as the universally valid source of law." In short, the pope places the reason of the Creator—that is, the Christian religion specifically and not religion in general—as the basis for natural law. This vision determines the criteria for individuating rights and universal human rights, which in the public square are known as "non-negotiable values." The pope gives examples of these in a speech he delivered to a delegation of European parliamentarians belonging to the Popular European Party—namely, the "protection of life in all its stages, from the first moment of conception until natural death; recognition and promotion of the natural structure of the family (as a union between a man and a woman based on marriage) and its defense from attempts to make it juridically equivalent to radically different forms of union, which in reality harm it and contribute to its destabilization, obscuring its particular character and its irreplaceable social role; the protection of the right of parents to educate their children."[32] Christians are invited to promote these values in the public square.[33] Non-negotiable values are nothing other than the irrevocable ethical demands of a Catholic in public life, just as they are of an Orthodox person, as we see acknowledged in ecumenical undertakings. It is a call for the believer to be consistent.

But where are we to place the so-called "new rights"? Certainly not on the Church's list of rights. In fact, papal speeches take a selective approach to human rights by excluding—or better yet, by not considering—certain demands of the "new rights."

The philosophical world (and not only) has often criticized the Church's magisterial teaching on rights. If the Church wants to safeguard them, she must accept their internal impact as well. It is a question of applying them to herself. The Italian philosopher Marcello Pera asks: "Do human rights also apply *within* the Church? Among its institutions and its faithful?" He sharpens the question in the following way:

> We face a dilemma. Either human rights do not apply to the Church, in which case the Church, as the exception, finds that she is violating at least some human rights. Or human rights apply to the Church was well, in which case human rights demand that some Church

---

32 Benedict XVI, "Address to the members of the European People's Party," 30 March 2006, op. cit.

33 Benedict XVI, "Speech to the General Assembly of Caritas Internationalis," 27 May 2011, *Acta Apostolicae Sedis*, n. 103 (2011): 396–399. English version: https://www.vatican.va/content/benedict-xvi/en/speeches/2011/may/documents/hf_ben-xvi_spe_20110527_caritas.html.

laws be revised. Since in many cases these rules are religious dogmas—or at least they are derived from religious dogmas—human rights end up clashing with
faith. Some contemporary discussions the Church finds
difficult (such as divorce), as well as the push for a "democratic" revision of Canon Law (on the power to
make decisions, for example), or on the modification of
internal procedures (on the secrecy of the Congregation
for the Doctrine of the Faith, for example) are born precisely out of this this: even if they are called so on the
basis of the Gospel, "human rights"—or at least some
of them—are difficult to reconcile with (to use the
weakest expression) many words of the Gospel, or they
outright contradict them. The rights of man and the
rights of a Christian do not always seem to coincide.[34]

This perceived imposition of Catholic thought was criticized
throughout Benedict XVI's pontificate. Pera articulates it in order
to persuade the Magisterium to rethink the way it frames human
rights, but others would prefer that the Magisterium subscribe
completely to the modern program of "rights" and set aside the
Church's declarations of the last century.

It has been difficult for Catholic, neo-Enlightenment, radical,
and *laïcité* positions to find common ground. They have different
conceptions of foundations and values, and a different conception
of the human person. Indeed, perhaps the greatest difficulty in
finding common ground between Catholicism and modernity is
their different anthropologies. We therefore turn to consider this
central question.

The anthropological question

The anthropological question is essentially a cultural question,
and it is closely tied to the problem of ethical relativism. It deals

34   Ibid., 147–148.

with man's identity in the world, his closest relationships, and his wider social network.

The question is important not only for Catholics, but for several other cultural sectors that until now have remained virtually impenetrable to precise anthropological analysis. The anthropological question is, in fact, a perennial one. It touches on issues that are dearest to human life. An adequate response to the question requires a political—and, in the end, a theological—approach.

One attempt at a response can be found in an important publication by Italian Marxist intellectuals in 2011, entitled *Emergenza antropologica: Per una nuova alleanza tra credenti e non credenti* (The anthropological plight: Toward a new alliance between believers and non-believers), edited by philosopher Pietro Barcellona, historian Giuseppe Vacca, philosopher and political scientist Mario Tronti, and sociologist Paolo Sorbi. Barcellona is a convert to Catholicism, and Sorbi is a Catholic.[35] Interestingly, their intervention, published in the form of an open letter, appeared in the pages of *Avvenire*, the daily newspaper of the Italian bishops.[36] It was subsequently printed separately and included contributions by commentators from various cultures.[37] This group of intellectuals (which the press called the "Ratzingerian Marxists") spoke about what they called the "anthropological plight" that arises from the possibility—indeed the reality—of manipulating human life thanks to technical developments and the frenetic rate of globalization. They consider it a "plight," but a plight that manifests—and indeed is—the deepest root of the crisis of democracy. To confront the crisis, the authors propose "a new alliance between men and women, believers and non-believers, religion and

35 Cf. Sandro Magister, "Da Marx a Ratzinger. Il manifesto della svolta," 16 November 2012: http://chiesa.espresso.repubblica.it/articolo/1350361.
36 Pietro Barcellona et al., "Lettera aperta," *Avvenire*, 16 October 2011.
37 Pietro Barcellona, Giuseppe Vacca, Mario Tronti, Paolo Sorbi (ed.), *Emergenza antropologica: per una nuova alleanza tra credenti e non credenti* (Milano: Guerini e Associati, 2012).

politics" that begins with a new definition of *laïcité* that was popular in Italy at the time: i.e., the acknowledgement on the part of the left (including Pierluigi Bersani, secretary of the Italian Democratic Party) "of the public relevance of religious faiths," and an acknowledgment on the part of the Church "of a positive vision of modernity grounded in an alliance between faith and religion." From the authors' point of view, the anthropological question, which had already been at the center of Catholic thinking for some time, must be made part of the left's agenda. The authors reflect on two fundamental themes in Benedict XVI's teaching: the rejection of ethical relativism and the concept of "non-negotiable values." They do not view the condemnation of ethical relativism as a rejection of cultural pluralism, but rather as essentially pertaining "to nihilistic viewpoints of modernity" that permeate the processes of secularization, which tend to drift radically (as happened on the left in the preceding decades). On the other hand, the authors understand the concept of non-negotiable values as a call "to the responsibility of integrating behaviors with the ideals that inspire them" and not as a means to discriminate between believers and non-believers.

The emerging anthropological question is tied to the challenge of scientific-technological progress provoking different ethical constructs. The decisive starting point is our attitude toward human life, which the authors tie to "the dignity of the human person from the moment of conception." Considering the authors' leftist agenda, this is a highly significant assertion. They admit that the most salient characteristic of their proposal is the move "to shift the discussion from the level of rights to the level of responsibilities."[38] The questions they raise stem primarily from the challenges presented by so-called *biopolitica* ("bio-politics"). As Vittorio Possenti wrote in a commentary on the letter, this shows that "when we must determine how to treat a human embryo, we must first decide if we are dealing with a clump of cells or a human person. According to our anthropological stance, the moral consequences

38   Ibid., 11.

of this determination are vastly different and indeed conflictual."[39] Possenti also points to the core of the predominating radical culture "that tries to exalt the human person as an individual with the open intention of safeguarding his rights, but without making any distinction between rights, demands, and desires. The left has allowed itself to be contaminated by this attitude, shielding itself by a defense of rights that ignores any reference to duties."

The authors attempt to forge a project of intellectual and moral reform, advanced by taking seriously the "theology, anthropological vision, and social teaching of Benedict XVI,"[40] within the vision of a new *laïcité*, which they claim Ratzinger has "particularly enriched by developing the idea of an *alliance between faith and reason* as the interpretative key to understanding modernity and the right criterion for confronting the challenges of the current anthropological plight."[41]

The foregoing analysis pushes us to reflect on non-negotiable values (also called undeniable principles), which the Church refined and promoted under John Paul II and Benedict XVI in such as way that she became the spokesperson of a cultural viewpoint that until that time had been marginalized, and indeed unarticulated.

The publication of the letter prompted a lively discussion in Italy that permeated various spheres of culture and helped forge a "shared humanism,"[42] which subsequently flickered out after Benedict XVI resigned. A new springtime of cultural cross-fertilization seems to have been cut short; a cross-fertilization that

---

39 Alessandro Zaccuri, "Tronti e Possenti. Chi ha smantellato l'etica che ci univa?," *Avvenire*, 31 October 2012: http://www.avvenire.it/Cultura/Pagine/CHI-HA-SMANTELLATO-ETICA.aspx. In the same vein, see also Marina Corradi, *Barcellona – Ricci Sindoni. nella crisi, imbarcati come sul Titanic*, in *Avvenire*, 14 November 2012: http://www.avvenire.it/Cultura/Pagine/nella-crisi-imbarcati-come-sul-titanic.aspx.

40 Barcellona, Vacca, Tronti, Sorbi (ed.), *Emergenza antropologica*, op. cit., 12.

41 Ibid., 13.

42 Cf. Ibid., 10.

personally involved Pera—a champion of the liberal world in Italian—and Habermas. The contribution of intellectual—and indeed political—Catholicism in building Western society is a historical fact, however much it is ignored. The crossing of paths between the "Ratzingerian Marxists" and Benedict XVI seems to have been a missed opportunity to set the historical record straight, and then to make history.

Ethical interventions

Besides the conversations with particular groups of individuals, Benedict XVI also made important public political interventions. For example, with regard to Italy, he supported Cardinal Ruini and the Italian Bishops' Conference (CEI) in their cultural and political choice to support a law in the area of assisted fertilization. The proposal was not in line with Catholic moral teaching, but it came about nonetheless as a compromise: a balance between different ethical visions, which was undermined by a 2005 referendum that fell short of Catholic expectations. At that time, the Church in Italy participated in a boycott of the referendum and, in the end, was successful in preventing the referendum from receiving the necessary quorum. This gave the signal that the Church in Italy was still able to influence public moral debate in 2005. Benedict XVI provided his support, just as he encouraged the Spanish bishops in their fight to defend life (against abortion and euthanasia) and in their advocacy for allowing families to choose the means of educating their children. This confirmed key themes of Benedict XVI's magisterial program as the inviolability of life[43] and the preservation of the institution of marriage between a man and a woman.[44]

---

43   Cf. Benedict XVI, Homily upon Assuming Possession of the Basilica of Saint John Lateran, 7 May 2005, *Acta Apostolicae Sedis*, n. 97 (2005): 748–752.

44   Benedict XVI, Homily at the World Meeting of Families, Valencia, 9 July 2006, *Acta Apostolicae Sedis*, n. 98 (2006): 585–589.

This was the framework for his teaching regarding human sexuality. Benedict XVI followed in the footsteps of his predecessors, especially Paul VI (who promulgated the encyclical *Humanae Vitae* in 1968), in that he held contraception to be an act that is not properly human. He reaffirmed this teaching in an in-flight interview during his apostolic voyage to Africa (Cameroon and Angola) on 17 March 2009. The French journalist Philippe Visseyrias, representing *France 2*, asked the pope the following question:

> Your Holiness, among the many ills that beset Africa, one of the most pressing is the spread of AIDS. The position of the Catholic Church on the way to fight it is often considered unrealistic and ineffective. Will you address this theme during the journey?

The pope replied with equal clarity:

> I would say the opposite. I think that the most efficient, most truly present player in the fight against AIDS is the Catholic Church herself, with her movements and her various organizations. I think of the Sant'Egidio community that does so much, visibly and also behind the scenes, in the struggle against AIDS, I think of the Camillians, and so much more besides, I think of all the sisters who take care of the sick. I would say that this problem of AIDS cannot be overcome merely with money, necessary though it is. If there is no human dimension, if Africans do not help (*by responsible behavior*), the problem cannot be solved by the distribution of prophylactics: on the contrary, they increase it. The solution must have two elements: firstly, bringing out the human dimension of sexuality, that is to say a spiritual and human renewal that would bring with it a new way of behaving toward others, and secondly, true friendship offered above all to those who are suffering, a willingness to make sacrifices and to practise self-denial, to be

alongside the suffering. And so these are the factors that help and that lead to real progress: our twofold effort to renew humanity inwardly, to give spiritual and human strength for proper conduct toward our bodies and those of others, and this capacity to suffer with those who are suffering, to remain present in situations of trial. It seems to me that this is the proper response, and the Church does this, thereby offering an enormous and important contribution. We thank all who do so.[45]

The media only paid attention to Benedict's claim that condoms were exacerbating the AIDS epidemic (i.e., "this problem of AIDS cannot be overcome merely with money [...] the problem cannot be overcome by the distribution of prophylactics: on the contrary, they increase it"). Their shallow reporting traveled the globe, inciting protesters who ignored what the pope was praising and what he was actually proposing. Detailed commentaries were offered by scientists, journalists (such as the *New York Times* and *Le Monde*), and governments in France, Germany, and Belgium (where the Parliament issued a condemnation of the pope's words and placed the papal representative at risk of being declared a *persona non grata*[46]), the European Union, and other international organizations accused the pope's claim as being devoid of any scientific basis.[47] The pope's comments perhaps provoked more criticism of the hierarchy's capacity to intervene in these matters concerning "what is natural and what is unnatural, what is scientifically correct and incorrect."[48] There were also outspoken critics inside the Church, not only of what the pope said, but of the Church's moral teaching itself, such as the Auxiliary Bishop

45   "Intervista concessa dal Santo Padre Benedetto XVI ai giornalisti durante il volo verso l'Africa," *Volo Papale*, 17 March 2009, *L'Osservatore Romano*, 18 March 2009.
46   Francesco Strazzari, "La scelta di Léonard. Intervista con l'ex nunzio mons. Karl-Josef Rauber," in *Il Regno Attualità*, n. 4 (2010): 86.
47   Marco Politi, *Joseph Ratzinger. Crisi di un papato*, op. cit., 192–194.
48   Ibid., 193.

of Hamburg, Hans-Jochen Jaschke, and the French bishop, Jean-Michel Di Falco, who said, "the pope should not have said anything about this. It's not his place."[49] On the ground, it was well known that the Jesuits in Congo and the White Fathers in Tanzania included prophylactics in their pastoral fight against AIDS. The Bishops' Conference in Chad and some religious in Zambia and Kenya took a similar approach.[50]

If, in fact, prophylactics reduce the risk of contamination, and fidelity to a single partner reduces it even more, then it is obvious that only abstinence can completely eliminate the illness. In any case, the pope did not merely seek to bicker over percentages. Rather, he wanted to promote an open dialogue about human identity and the anthropological vision of human relationships. For the pope and the magisterial teaching that he represents, the question is not merely how to thwart the sexual transmission of the virus and limit its spread. The pope knows and acknowledges that "there may be a basis in the case of some individuals, as perhaps when a male prostitute uses a condom, where this can be a first step in the direction of a moralization, a first assumption of responsibility, on the way toward recovering an awareness that not everything is allowed and that one cannot do whatever one wants." He says later in the interview, "There can be [...] in the intention of reducing the risk of infection, a first step in a movement toward a different way, a more human way, of living sexuality."[51] At the same time, it is important to remember that the pope did not characterize this situation as a "lesser evil."[52] The point is that he wants to take things a step further and propose a radical change of mindset and life in order to rehumanize sexual

49   Ibid., 195.
50   Ibid., 199.
51   Benedict XVI, *Luce del mondo*, 171. In English, *Light of the World* (San Francisco: Ignatius Press, 2010).
52   Cf. Congregation for the Doctrine of the Faith, *Nota*, in *L'Osservatore Romano*, 22 December 2010. There was a preview of the pope's interview published in *L'Osservatore Romano* on 20 November 2010.

relations. He supports "a humanization of sexuality—that is, a human and spiritual renewal that involves a new way of behaving toward one another. Secondly, a true friendship, especially with those who suffer. An availability, even by making personal sacrifices and renouncing one's desires, to be with the suffering." The key words are "humanization" and "friendship." Scientists, politicians, and church dissenters who criticized the pope were using a triage mentality, doubting that human beings have the power to change, denying that they can cease engaging in risky sexual behavior.

Indeed, it seems that human reproduction is the area in which the Church and modern society are most at conflict. The most pressing issues are the regulation of births, abortion, artificial fertilization, and contraception. Not a few believers have acquiesced to the modern-day mentality that affirms people should act according to their own consciences when making decisions on these matters. The problem is that these consciences are poorly formed. Politi's analysis is not far off the mark, even though the Church would never use his language: "The protests following Ratzinger's comment about prophylactics were essentially a long simmering, explosive reaction against an authoritative dogmatism that repressed human freedom."[53] Besides the hard, unfounded judgment against the Catholic magisterium, Politi places a hermeneutic of facts at the center of his analysis. During Benedict XVI's pontificate, there were numerous powerful explosions between contrasting visions of man and the world present in both society and the Church.

Benedict XVI's pontificate was one that allowed long-standing conflicts to come to the surface. In other words, it facilitated the process of vetting tensions between the Church and modernity without unduly sweetening them. It did the same for various currents within Catholicism, between a papal Catholicism anchored in the magisterium and a "do-it-yourself" Catholicism with a lot of subtle variations in the middle.

53   Politi, *Joseph Ratzinger. Crisi di un papato*, op. cit., 202.

During these years, the strength of the papacy was seen in its ability to spark a new reflection on cultural and global issues in a way that does not allow people to remain standing on the sidelines. New avenues of dialogue opened up not only in philosophy and ethics, but also in Catholicism's relationship with other religions.

Interreligious dialogue and non-believers

In order to understand Benedict XVI's contribution to the different relationships between the Church and other religions, and also between the Church and non-believers, we need to start with a document published by the Congregation for the Doctrine of the Faith at the behest of John Paul II entitled *Dominus Iesus* (2001), regarding the unicity and salvific universality of Christ and the Church. The document addresses not only relativism, but religious syncretism. It was criticized by some Catholics and outsiders for being too restrictive. The then-Cardinal Ratzinger took this opportunity to speak publicly about the document's main themes to clear up some of the confusion. He said, "the document is meant to be an invitation to all Christians to open themselves once more to recognizing Christ Jesus as Lord."[54] He then stressed how important it is for Catholics to remain in constant dialogue with other religious. He writes:

> The document is not merely a reprimand of subjectivist and relativist theses, according to which everyone can become holy in his or her own way [...]. The document affirms with the Council that God gives light to everyone [...]. In this sense, it can be said that there are rituals and prayers in religions that can be a preparation for evangelization. They are opportunities and teaching

54 "Declaration of Joseph Ratzinger," in *Frankfurter Allgemeine Zeitung*, 22 September 2000, translated into Italian in *L'Osservatore Romano*, 8 October 2000.

moments that stir human hearts to open up to God's action. But I should add that this is not the case for all religious rituals. There are, in fact, some religious practices (whoever knows a little about the history of religions cannot help but agree) that drive us away from the light. So interior vigilance and purification are attained through a life that follows one's conscience, that helps to the differences; an opening that in the end means an interior belonging to Christ.

Ratzinger wanted to pave the way for authentic—and not merely superficial—dialogue; a dialogue that from a Catholic point of view aims for belonging to Christ. Not everyone shares this view of what interreligious dialogue is about because it presumes we hope our dialogue partners will change. But this, in fact, is what Paul VI already said in *Ecclesiam Suam*, when he writes: "[I]f, in our desire to respect a man's freedom and dignity, his conversion to the true faith is not the immediate object of our dialogue with him, we nevertheless try to help him and to dispose him for a fuller sharing of ideas and convictions."[55] The conciliar fathers at Vatican II included dialogue among the *praeambula evangelizationis*.[56] Ratzginer would continue in this line of thinking after becoming pope. At the beginning of his pontificate, Benedict XVI affirmed that "the Church wants to continue building bridges of friendship with the followers of all religions, in order to seek the true good of every person and of society as a whole."[57]

---

55 Paul VI, Enclycial Letter *Ecclesiam Suam*, 6 August 1964, *Acta Apostolciae Sedis*, n. 56 (1964): 609–659.
56 Cf. Ilaria Morali, *The Travail of Ideas in the Three Centuries Preceding Vatican II (1650–1964)*, in Karl Josef Becker, Ilaria Morali (eds.), *Catholic engagement with World Religions: A Comprehensive Study* (Maryknoll, NY: Orbis, 2010), 115; Ilaria Morali, "Salvation, Religions, and Dialogue in the Roman magisterium. from Pius IX to Vatican II and Postconciliar Popes," in Becker, Morali (eds.), *Catholic Engagement with World Religions: A Comprehensive Study*, op. cit., 127–132.
57 Benedict XVI, *Address of His Holiness Benedict XVI to the Delegates of*

Benedict's thinking on these issues was directly in line with his predecessors, but he also put a personal stamp on things with his well-known interest in culture and theology, especially the "ferocious battle against relativism"[58] and its ensuing syncretism. In comparison with John Paul II, Benedict XVI was acutely aware of the repercussions of making symbolic gestures with leaders of other religions. They would often be misinterpreted as a source of confusion, as in the case of the first World Day of Prayer in Assisi in October of 1986.[59]

In Benedict's mind, interreligious dialogue must be placed within the wider context of cultural engagement, and it is therefore essentially anthropological at its core. A cultural clash of civilizations can be avoided if the religions that underlie—or at least are informed by—different cultures will enter into meaningful dialogue. A case in point is Benedict's assertion and point of departure that the culture and identity of Europe are both clearly rooted in the Judeo-Christian tradition. He does not make this claim to delve into identity politics or to take an oppositional stance toward other cultures, rather to allow for an authentic engagement between different traditions.

There is a special relationship between the Catholic Church and Judaism because of their shared faith in the God revealed in the Scripture. Pope Benedict XVI took his cue from the theology of Vatican II, deepened by John Paul II, and, like his predecessor, made a visit to the synagogue in Rome (2010). The misunderstandings surrounding Pius XII have not substantially harmed relations between the Church and Judaism because they essentially revolve around political questions and the political (ab)use of his legacy. But how could the Church overcome the dismay caused

other Churches and Ecclesial Communities and of other Religious Traditions, 25 April 2005.

58   Morali, *Salvation, Religions, and Dialogue in the Roman magisterium. from Pius IX to Vatican II and Postconciliar Popes*, op. cit., 140.

59   For the theological context, see Joseph Ratzinger, *Fede, verita`e tolleranza: Il cristianesimo e le religioni del mondo* (Siena: Cantagalli, 2003).

by the Lefebvrite Bishop Williamson and the tension caused by
the wider use of the Tridentine liturgy, including its prayer for
the Jews on Good Friday that some find so offensive today? Pope
Benedict XVI offered ways to overcome all of this in a theology
deeply tied to biblical data and deeply respectful of the Jews, to
the point that he called them "our elder brothers" (a term coined
by John Paul II although not appreciated by everyone) and "fathers in the faith" (a term with deeper biblical roots).[60]

Of course, interreligious dialogue goes well beyond Judaism.
It is considered essential for obtaining true and lasting peace at
the international level.[61] In a world threatened by terrorism, interreligious dialogue (like intercultural dialogue) is presented as
a truly "vital necessity."[62] If it is in fact "vital," it must absolutely
be pursued. But in what way? There are various ways of engaging
in it, and Benedict XVI is clear on this point. Yet a speech he gave
to the Italian bishops in 2007 remains paradigmatic. He says:

> Esteem and respect for all other religions and cultures,
> with the seeds of truth and goodness that are present
> there and that represent a preparation for the Gospel,
> are particularly necessary today in a world that is grow-
> ing ever closer. One cannot, therefore, diminish the
> awareness of the originality, fullness, and oneness of
> the revelation of the true God who in Christ has given
> himself to us definitively, and neither can one tone

---

60 Benedict XVI, *Luce del mondo*, 123 (In English, *Light of the World* [San
    Francisco: Ignatius Press, 2010]); Norbert J. Hofmann, "Benedetto
    XVI e il dialogo con gli ebrei," in *L'Osservatore Romano*, 16 January
    2011.

61 Cf. Benedict XVI, "Speech to Ambassadors of Muslim Nations Ac-
    credited with the Holy See and Other Components of Muslim Com-
    munities in Italy," 25 September 2006, in *Acta Apostolicae Sedis*, n.
    98 (2006): 704–706.

62 Benedict XVI, "Speech to the Diplomatic Corps Accredited with the
    Holy See, 8 January 2007, in *Acta Apostolicae Sedis*, n. 99 (2007): 72–
    81.

down or weaken the missionary vocation of the Church. The relativistic cultural climate that surrounds us makes it ever more important and urgent to root and to bring to maturity within the entire ecclesial body the certainty that Christ, the God with a human face, is our true and only Savior. The book *Jesus of Nazareth*—a very personal book, not by the pope but by a man who is its author—is written with this intention: that we may once again, with the heart and with reason, see that Christ is truly the One whom the human heart awaits.[63]

An essential presupposition of Ratzinger's view of dialogue is that it is "conciliatory," and this implies a denial that other religions might be considered a means to salvation in the same way that Christianity is. On the other hand, according to *Dominus Iesus*, "Equality, which is a presupposition of interreligious dialogue, refers to the equal personal dignity of the parties in dialogue, not to doctrinal content, nor even less to the position of Jesus Christ—who is God himself made man—in relation to the founders of the other religions."[64]

Another speech given in 2008 reveals the pope's deeper hope for interreligious dialogue. During the Tenth Plenary Assembly of the Pontifical Council for Interreligious Dialogue, he said that the objective of dialogue is "the discovery of the truth,"[65] and the motivation for it "is charity, in obedience to the divine mission entrusted to the Church by Our Lord Jesus Christ." Dialogue not

---

63 Benedict XVI, "Speech to Participants of the General Assembly of the Italian Bishops Conference, 24 May 2007: http://w2.vatican.va/content/benedict-xvi/it/speeches/2007/may/documents/hf_ben-xvi_spe_20070524_cei.html.

64 Congregation for the Doctrine of the Faith, Declaration *Dominus Iesus* on the Unicity and Salvific Universality of Jesus Christ and the Church, n. 22.

65 Benedict XVI, "Speech to the Participants of the 10th Plenary Assembly of the Pontifical Council for Interreligious Dialogue, 7 June 2008, *Acta Apostolicae Sedis*, n. 100 (2008): 465–467.

only seeks "areas of collaboration" (such as helping the sick, bringing aid to the victims of natural disaster or violence, and taking care of the elderly and the sick), but Christians are also encouraged "to propose, but not impose, faith in Christ." Dialogue is not meant to be a flurry of words, but a concrete proposal. Although the latter occurs much less frequently.

A better understanding of Ratzinger's authentic thought can be gathered from a private letter he sent to Italian philosopher Marcello Pera in 2008, which later appeared in the preface of a book by Pera. The letter was written on the pope's private stationary without a protocol number, meaning that it was intended as a private piece of correspondence expressing the pope's genuine thoughts, albeit in an informal way. This private text—which only later become public—helps us to understand his thought without the usual political and diplomatic intermediaries. At one point, the letter leaves no room for misunderstanding. The pope writes to the then-President of the Italian Senate:

> You explain very clearly that, strictly speaking, interreligious dialogue is not possible, and you advocate with much more urgency an intercultural dialogue that deepens the cultural consequences of deeply rooted religious decisions. While it is impossible to place one's own faith in parentheses when engaging in intercultural dialogue, it is necessary to confront publicly the cultural consequences of deeply rooted religious decisions. Thus dialogue, mutual correction, and a reciprocal enrichment are possible and necessary.[66]

Such an explanation must not lead us to believe that Ratzinger is taking a reductionist approach. To the contrary. The numbers are clear. Within the eight years of his pontificate, we find 188

---

66 Benedict XVI, *Lettera*, Castel Gandolfo, 4 September 2008, in Marcello Pera, *Perché dobbiamo dirci cristiani. Il liberalismo, l'Europa, l'etica* (Milan: Mondadori, 2008), 10–11.

interventions of Benedict on the topic of interreligious dialogue. This compares to 591 by John Paul in the more than 25 years of his pontificate, and 97 by Paul VI in the span of 15 years.[67] His commitment to interreligious dialogue is clear, perhaps because the pope wanted to clarify some aspects of pastoral practice that had created uncertainty or at least confusion regarding the contents and purpose of the dialogue, especially in the Western context which was either alarmist or ironic, but certainly in an increasingly precarious state due to the web of Islamic terrorism.

After 11 September 2001, armed militant Islam created a widespread sense of unease across the globe and ignited a watershed moment for ongoing conflict between the West and the Islamic world. Moreover, due to the rising tide of migration, Christianity and Islam stood face-to-face on a global and not just regional level.

Benedict XVI had little to say about Islam specifically in his first public speeches after being elected pope. Then, in Cologne (August 2005), he said that a dialogue between Christians and Muslims is a "vital necessity upon which our future depends."[68] He was talking about nothing less than the defense of peace. We need to pay close attention to this wording ("a vital necessity"), which was used to describe the wider and more generic concept of interreligious dialogue. Hence, we cannot say that he was speaking specifically of Islam. Such an approach does not necessarily fall into pacifism or partisan thinking, to the extent that the pope was able to receive in private audience several days later the Italian writer and journalist Oriana Fallaci, known at that time for her attacks against the West that many considered blind and

---

67   Cf. Pontifical Commission for Interreligious Dialogue, *Dialogo interreligioso nell'insegnamento ufficiale della Chiesa cattolica (1963–2013)*, Francesco Gioia (ed.), (Vatican City: LEV, 2013). Also, see Jean-Louis Tauran's speech for the presentation of the book *Dialogo interreligioso nell'insegnamento ufficiale della Chiesa cattolica (1963–2013)*, 12 November 2013: http://press.vatican.va/content/ salastampa/it/bollettino/pubblico/2013/11/12/0740/01668.html.

68   Politi, *Joseph Ratzinger. Crisi di un papato*, op. cit., 71.

cowardly in the face of the Islamic threat. According to John L. Allen, the first year of Benedict XVI's pontificate forges a new type of relation between Catholicism and Islam, which he defined as "severe love."[69] The pope asked more forcefully for a greater firmness of "reciprocity" between Catholics and Muslims—that is, he asked that Christian minorities living in Islamic countries be granted the same religious freedom that Muslims enjoyed in the West.

With these premises and in view of interreligious dialogue, Benedict XVI called for the necessity and urgency of a new union between faith and reason, including a rejection of religiously motivated violence. In the previsouly cited *lectio magistralis* delivered at the University of Regensburg on 12 September 2006, Benedict XVI touched on the relation between religion and reason, condemning the coupling of faith and violence, and the reluctance to cite the reasonableness of faith.[70] The pope wants to deny that violence can be legitimately committed or motivated by religion and to denounce any attempt to reconcile faith in God with violence or to exploit religion for violent means.

In the Regensburg speech, Benedict XVI cited a phrase used by the Byzantian Emperor Manuel II Palaiologos in a letter to a Muslim Persian: "Show me just what Mohammed brought that was new, and there you will find things only evil and inhuman, such as his command to spread by the sword the faith he preached."[71] These were not the pope's words, but words from a letter written centuries earlier. At the end of the speech, the phrase about Mohammed was reported by journalists all over the world as offensive. It provoked an "Islamic rage" in Indonesia, Marocco, Egypt, Afghanistan, Pakistan, and Iraq. There were demonstrations in the streets, vicious slurs, and ransacked churches. The

69 John L. Jr Allen, "Benedetto XVI anno primo: un quadro d'insieme," *Il Regno Documenti*, n. 51 (2006): 213–218.
70 Benedict XVI, "Speech to Scientists," Regensburg, 12 September, 2006 o cit.
71 Ibid.

pope received death threats. Some Christians were killed. Papal nuncios in many countries were called in by their hosting governments. There were public statements by Islamic leaders and governmental ministers (including Turkey, Kuwait, the United Arab Emerites, and in the Maghreb) asking for reparation in the form of a public apology.[72]

The incident received worldwide media attention. As one commentator wrote: "[T]he power of the mass media was clearly demonstrated in this incident, in that the polemic stirred by the pope's words was due precisely to how it was presented by the media."[73] And thus we have a public representation, on the one hand, of the conflict between civilizations and a two religions, and on the other, of a pope who was not sensitive to interreligious dialogue in the way John Paul II seemed to be.

The Italian journalist Politi made this comment: "It only took an hour in Regensburg to tear twenty years of Wojtylian politics toward Islam to pieces"[74]—that is, a politics of embracing Muslims in a sort of spiritual brotherhood. Sami Salem, imam at the Mosque in Rome, followed a similar line.[75] But is this really the case? Is this "papal speech" really driven by political shrewdness or intellectual pride, or does it rather show extraordinary intellectual subtlety and sympathy?[76] Later, there were other reactions from the intellectual community criticizing the pope's historical

72   Cf. Politi, *Joseph Ratzinger. Crisi di un papato,* op. cit., 61–63.
73   Martina Ambrosini, "Papa Benedetto XVI e l'incidente di Ratisbona La rappresentazione dell'Islam e dello 'scontro di civilta' nella stampa italiana," in *Observatorio Journal,* n. 5 (2011): 289–304, here 290.
74   Politi, *Joseph Ratzinger. Crisi di un papato,* op. cit., 63.
75   Marco Politi, "Ratzinger e stato frainteso, reazioni inqualificabili," in *La Repubblica,* 19 September 2006.
76   Cf. Uwe Justus Wenzel, "Fede e ragione, superbia e astuzia. Uno sguardo retrospettivo al discorso di Ratisbona di papa Benedetto XVI," in Knut Wenzel (ed.), *Le religioni e la ragione* (Brescia: Queriniana, 14).

analysis, calling it weak. But a closer look shows the weakness was really their own.[77]

In reality, Benedict XVI wrote this speech for a strictly academic purpose and expected it to be accepted as such, giving little thought to the possible political consequences it might have in light of the fact that he was pope.[78] At the Angelus address on the following 17 September 2006, he expressed regret for the reactions to his speech and made it clear that the incriminating phrase "in no way expresses my personal opinion."[79] He made a similar clarification at the general audience catechesis of 20 September 2006. At the international level, leaders in the West, including George Bush and Condolezza Rice, as well as Muslim leaders Ahmadinejad and Abdullah Ahmad Badawi, made public statements to reassure the world that they understood what the pope meant and pointed to the accuracy of his citation.[80]

On the diplomatic front, the crisis reemerged once again after a meeting between the pope and twenty-two ambassadors from Islamic countries on 25 September 2006, during which the pope assured the ambassadors of the bonds of friendship and solidarity uniting them.[81]

Some time later, between November and December, during a trip to Turkey (which had already been planned for some time),

77 Aref ali Nayed, "Un commento islamico alla lezione di papa Benedetto XVI a Ratisbona," in Wenzel (ed.), *Le religioni e la ragione,* op. cit., 15–46; Kurt Flasch, "Sui padri della chiesa e su altri fondamentalismi. Quanto e` stato tollerante il cristianesimo, quanto e` pronto al dialogo il papa? La chiave sta nella lezione di Ratisbona," in Wenzel (ed.), *Le religioni e la ragione,* op. cit., 47–55.

78 Benedict XVI, *Luce del mondo,* 143. In English, *Light of the World* (San Francisco: Ignatius Press, 2010).

79 Benedict XVI, *Angelus,* Castelgandolfo, 17 September 2006: http://w2.vatican.va/content/benedict-xvi/it/angelus/2006/documents/hf_ ben-xvi_ang_20060917.html.

80 Politi, *Joseph Ratzinger. Crisi di un papato,* op. cit., 68.

81 Cf. Redaction, "Il dialogo interreligioso e interculturale: una necessita` per costruire insieme un mondo di pace," in *L'Osservatore Romano,* 26 September 2006.

the pope took the opportunity to express again the idea that true religion is fundamentally opposed to violence, and he likewise underscored the power of reason. The speeches in Turkey understandably had a reserved tone given the diplomatic concerns. One of the most significant moments during the trip was a visit to the Blue Mosque in Istanbul, during which Benedict made no gesture that might suggest veneration or prayer.

So where does Catholic-Muslim dialogue stand with Benedict XVI? Politi reports that, according to Samir Khalil Samir, a Lebanese Jesuit who knows the pope's thinking well, "the essential idea is that dialogue with Islam...cannot essentially be a theological or religious dialogue." At most, it is a dialogue that draws attention to moral values. In short, it is a "dialogue between different cultures and civilizations."[82] This is the case particularly because of the significantly different conceptions of divine revelation. For Muslims, the Koran is the direct Word of God, whereas for Christians Jesus Christ is the Word of God and Sacred Scripture is an inspired text. Hence the Koran is not open to interpretation, but the Bible is. Because of the profoundly different understanding regarding how God speaks between the two religions, the pope prefers to engage in a cultural rather than a theological dialogue with Islam, with the goal of bringing greater peace to the world.

In any case, the Regensburg incident—or, more precisely, the Regensburg address—led to fruitful contact with the Islamic world and achieved what the pope was hoping it might—namely, a more honest, effective dialogue with Islam on the topics of belief, reason, and violence. The speech actually heightened the dialogue and qualitatively improved it, in that uncomfortable topics were brought into the limelight, and that was precisely what was needed to make the dialogue more authentic. Hence, it ended up being a significant step forward in the initiative launched by John Paul II.

In a later interview, this is precisely what Monsignor Georg Gänswein affirmed when he called the Regensburg speech

---

82   Politi, *Joseph Ratzinger. Crisi di un papato,* op. cit., 70.

"prophetic."[83] Indeed, it was so prophetic that, over time, it created valuable opportunities for initiatives in Catholic-Muslim dialogue that received international attention.

In fact, the speech did anything but close the dialogue between Catholics and Muslims. It opened up a new road to meeting major representatives of the Muslim world. At the Vatican on 6 November 2007, a historic first took place: a meeting between the pope and King Abdullah bin Abd-el-Aziz of Saudia Arabia. In the same year, 139 Muslim intellectuals wrote to the pope (who responded *per* Bertone[84]) and the heads of Christian communities appealing for greater collaboration between the two religions (*A Common Word between Us and You*).[85] Additionally, 309 dignitaries signed the letter.[86] Although the number seems significant, it really only represents a small fraction of the Islamic intellectual world. Nevertheless, the letter did end up generating fruitful discussion within Islam.

The signatories of the letter wanted to draw attention to the values held in common between Islam and Christianity—namely, the unicity of God, God's love, and the call to love our neighbor. Their appeal to "a common word" (which is actually not so common) was celebrated in November of 2008 at a Catholic-Muslim forum held at the Pontifical Gregorian University and in the Vatican. The forum yielded positive results. The representative theologians and experts involved were in accord on issues of the respect for the human person, religious minorities, religious choices and conscience, the public and private practice of one's own religion, and other matters. The forum represented efforts to build a bridge between Catholicism and so-called "moderate" Islam,[87] which was also on display a few months earlier in July at

83   Marco Politi, "L'Islam rischio per l'europa un errore non contrastarlo," in *La Repubblica*, 27 July 2007.
84   *Lettera di Bertone al principe Ghazi bin muhammad bin Talal*, 19 novembre 2007: http://www.vatican.va/roman_curia/secretariat_state/card-bertone/2007/documents/rc_seg-st_20071119_muslim-leaders_it.html.
85   *A Common Word between Us and You*, 13 October 2007.
86   Cf. Politi, *Joseph Ratzinger. Crisi di un papato*, op. cit., 76.
87   Cf. Ibid., 76–77.

the International Congress for Dialogue between the Three Abrahamic Religions in Madrid, promoted by the king of Saudi Arabia, Abdullah, and organized by the World Muslim League, which led to a final declaration signed by the participants.[88]

But something quite different was happening on the ground in many Islamic countries. The dialogue between the Church and some Islamic leaders remained at the level of the elite and had little impact on the lives of the commonfolk. In 2010 and 2011, the pope had to raise his voice one more time against the persecution of Christians in Asia (India, Iraq, and Pakistan) and Africa (Nigeria and Egypt). Bishops in Islamic countries and countries bordering Islamic nations were expressing grave concerns about the persecution of the faithful within their care and the spread of a certain kind of goodwill pacifism among Catholics in the West.

Among the meetings between intellectual elites and instances of local political difficulties, a pragmatic way of mutual understanding was gradually reached on major ethical-political questions that might lead to accords on particular issues. An example can be found in Antonio Mennini's 2012 efforts for an interreligious alliance to support the promotion and juridical recognition of marriage as between a man and a woman, in opposition to the lobby for gay marriage and the adoption of children by gay parents.[89]

More profoundly, the Regensburg address highlighted "the intrinsic link between the way religions interrelate and how they

88   Cf. Giuseppe De Rosa, "La dichiarazione di Madrid. Un passo avanti nel dialogo interreligioso," in *La Civiltà Cattolica*, n. 159 (2008): 280–287.

89   Cf. John Bingham, "Gay marriage: Pope Representatives Calls for Catholic Alliance with Muslim and Jewish Groups," in *The Telegraph*, 27 April 2012: http://www.telegraph.co.uk/news/religion/9232269/Gay-marriage-Pope-representatives-calls-for-Catholic-alliance-with-Muslim-and-Jewish-groups.html; "Archbishop Antonio Mennini, Pope's Representative, Calls for Christians, Jews, Muslims To Unite Against Gay Marriage," in *Huffington Post*, 30 April 2012: http://www.huffington-post.com/2012/04/30/archbishop-christians-jews-muslims-gay-marriage_n_1465661.html.

conceive their discussions of faith and society."[90] That link is rational. Moreover, for the Catholic world, the pope's speech was significant because, even if he didn't intend it, it certainly represented a major shift away from the perceived pacifism of the previous pontificate.

The Church's dialogue with the world also includes dialogue with "non-believers." Engagement with non-believers involves a comparison of different visions of the world and of the human person. Under the leadership of Cardinal Ravasi and now Cardinal José Tolentino de Mendonça, the Pontifical Council for Culture and Education is the Church's principal organ for this engagement. The engagement itself is seen as taking place in the so-called "Courtyard of the Gentiles." The name is borrowed from an area near the second temple of Jerusalem in which everyone—not just Jews—could enter, circumcised or not. It is the place for those to whom "religion is something foreign, to whom God is unknown and who nevertheless do not want to be left merely Godless, but rather to draw near to him, albeit as the Unknown."[91] Not everyone was pleased with this outreach because the Catholic Church believes herself to be the possessor of the fullness of truth, while her dialogue partners carry only partial truths.[92] According to the Church's doctrine it cannot be otherwise.

In any case, Catholic dialogue with "others" is more robust today than it has been in the past. Benedict XVI invited not only religious representatives to the interreligious meeting in Assisi in 2011, but non-believers as well. Unlike previous similar encounters, there was no common prayer (not only because non-believers were present, but also because this practice was more in line with Benedict XVI's theological vision). Yet he extended the range of participants. In an attempt to avoid giving the impression that

90   Knut Wenzel, *Premessa*, in Wenzel (ed.), *Le religioni e la ragione*, op. cit., 7.
91   Benedict XVI, Address to the Roman Curia, 21 December 2009, in *Acta Apostolicae Sedis*, n. 102 (2010): 32–40.
92   Cf. Politi, *Joseph Ratzinger. Crisi di un papato*, op. cit., 305.

the gathering in Assisi was a generic, watered-down gathering of pacifists (as had been the Assisi event in 1986), he chose to invite both non-believers and agnostics. He did not present it as an opportunity for everyone to pray together. It is true that various invocations were offered, but none could be interpreted as "prayer." Religious believers and non-believers came together not to pray, but to express their commitment to world peace.

Thanks to his way of approaching this and similar events, Benedict XVI introduced the idea that, above all, dialogue with non-believers should focus on ethical themes where greater concordance is possible if we start with a shared anthropological vision and a common concern for the dignity of the human person. Indeed, Benedict XVI's concern was the most pressing issue of the day—that is, how do we acknowledge ethical pluralism and recognize different ethical visions. In short, there is simply no way around the plurality of those visions in today's world.

A commitment to peace

The papal magisterium of the twentieth century invested an enormous amount of theological energy to the theme of peace, advocating for it in countless speeches and documents that almost seem to extol pacifism as the ultimate goal. Benedict XVI often referred to this teaching.

Yet even if the Church's rhetoric seemed to delegitimize war as a viable possibility, the 1992 Catechism makes it clear that the idea of a just war (understood as a defensive, proportionate war in response to an offense with the probable outcome of success) is still legitimate. In fact, military personnel continue to receive solicitous pastoral care from bishops, priests, and other persons in ministry. The question of what believers are to make of war and peace is ancient and has been around since the beginning of Christianity. It revolves around the inevitable tension of incarnating the Gospel message. This tension is real and not easily resolved. It is a tension within the believing community between its desire for peace and its participation in warfare; between the attempt in theological, political, and diplomatic discourse to both legitimize and delegitimize the use of violence.

Gilbert Keith Chesterton captures this ambivalence well in his classic book, *Orthodoxy*. He describes the desire for peace and the need to engage in war as permanently coexisting realities:

> It is true that the Church told some men to fight and others not to fight; and it IS true that those who fought were like thunderbolts and those who did not fight were like statues. All this simply means that the Church preferred to use its Supermen and to use its Tolstoyans. There must be SOME good in the life of battle, for so many good men have enjoyed being soldiers. There must be SOME good in the idea of non-resistance, for so many good men seem to enjoy being Quakers. All that the Church did (so far as that goes) was to prevent either of these good things from ousting the other. They existed side by side.[93]

Nevertheless, from World War I until the present day, the Catholic Magisterium has steadfastly asserted the inadmissibility of using religion to justify the use of force.[94]

Particularly beginning with John XXIII and his groundbreaking encyclical *Pacem in Terris* in 1963, popes have invited mankind to find a common path to peace by recognizing the irrationality of war. The above cited World Day of Prayer for Peace hosted by John Paul II in Assisi (1986) marks a highpoint in the papacy's efforts. Rather than having a specific political agenda, the encounter stood as an unparalleled symbol of widespread cooperation to achieve peace. The encounter was held again in 1993 and 2002. These meetings occurred in the critical context of the Balkan War (1992–1993)

93   Gilbert Keith Chesterton, *Orthodoxy*, in *The Everyman Chesterton*, edited by Ian Turnbull Ker (New York: Knopf, 2011), 346.
94   Cf. Daniele Menozzi, *Chiesa, pace e guerra nel novecento. Verso una delegittimazione religiosa dei conflitti* (Bologna: Il Mulino, 2008).

and the Iraq War (2003). In 1993, Cardinal Sodano, representing Pope John Paul II, spoke of the "right of humanitarian intervention," and Archbishop Tauran spoke of the "right/duty of intervention" (August 1992).[95] In 2003, the Holy See kept its distance from the so-called "preventative war."

Papal thinking on this topic remained unchanged after 11 September 2001, the beginning of the so-called global war on terrorism. Refusing to accept the notion of a clash of civilizations, much less a conflict of religions ("any use of religion to support violence is an abuse of it"[96]), Pope John Paul II invited Christians and Muslims to commit themselves to building up a just world of solidarity, bereft of violence. In his mind, religion could never truly be a source of conflict. To the contrary, a world at war is actually the fruit of moral relativism, which can be overcome if human rights and international law are allowed to take root in religious values. God himself is the foundation of peace.

Benedict XVI moved in the same direction, but with even more precise thinking. In the previously discussed Regensburg speech (2006), he condemned the faith-violence pairing and gave religions enlightened by reason a vital role in the quest for peace. Looking over Benedict XVI's teaching in general, we clearly see that he believed a correct relationship between reason and religion was the only way to obtain true and lasting peace. Reason without religion excludes God and leads to totalitarian systems. Religion without reason manipulates God and uses him only as a means for personal aggrandizement. Benedict XVI puts forth two legitimate visions of God—namely, that of *Logos* and that of love, which is the foundation for every refusal of violence.

95 Giuseppe De Rosa, "E cambiato l'atteggiamento del papa nei confronti della guerra?" in *La Civilta Cattolica*, n. 143 (1992): 504–511. John Paul II continued along these lines in his speech to the diplomatic corps, 16 January 1993, denying the "right to indifference" on the part of States; Cf. *Il Regno-documenti*, n. 3 (1993): 68–72, here 72.
96 John Paul II, 1999, in Menozzi, *Chiesa, pace e guerra nel novecento*, op. cit., 315.

Benedict XVI's reflection on this theme reached a highpoint in a speech delivered on 18 February 2007, in which he affirmed that "for Christians, non-violence is not merely tactical behaviour but a person's way of being, the attitude of one who *is so convinced of God's love and power* that he is not afraid to tackle evil with the weapons of love and truth alone."[97] If we had to tease out the ultimate implication of these words, we would have a Catholicism and a Catholic culture not only peaceful, but utterly disarmed. No one, however, seems to have accepted his words at face value.

Even if, within the arc of a century, we arrived at the delegitimization of war and at an effective collaboration between religions for world peace, we still must acknowledge that there has been an active involvement of Catholics in military and security forces and in political discussions of how to defend individual nations. Catholics have taken on the roles of Minister of Defense, President, and King or Queen, all of whom are routinely commanders-in-chief of military forces. Even if, at the level of magisterial teaching, greater and greater distance is taken from the religious legitimization of violence, in practice God is still invoked to bless various military exercises.

All of this is to say that Chesterton's approach to the issue is still alive and well at the beginning of the twenty-first century.

Conclusions

Benedict XVI urged the Church to engage with an ever-growing number of cultural, political, and ethical phenomena. Without excessively worrying about reaching a perfect consensus, the pope launched initiatives that would lead to significant encounters and dialogue regarding man's ultimate identity. In doing so, he would rouse up supporters and naysayers alike. He took on the burden of the latter without allowing them to weigh him down.

The Catholic conceptual framework the pope used to carry

97   Benedict XVI, *Angelus*, 18 February 2007, in *L'Osservatore Romano*, 19–20 February 2007.

out this project was in line with preceding Magisterial teaching, although he now gave it greater systematization (as in the example of the anthropological question), at times opening up new horizons (as in the case with interreligious dialogue). In any case, his system of thought was strictly coherent with what preceded it. But it was provocative in a new way. It is not easy to see in retrospect how well the pope understood the provocations and their ultimate consequences. In any event, Ratzinger's way of speaking leaves no room for indifference, and reached into cultural corners that until then seemed too remote, but in which he was able to spark substantial discussion. His private deliberations about a possible resignation, however, may have stunted the natural development of these new pathways. Does this suggest that his dialoguing was too elite and personal? Only time will tell as his initiatives unfold in the years to come.

In the face of the challenges posed by modernity, Benedict XVI paved the way for an enlightened Catholicism, thinking supported by faith with the courage to offer a contribution to social life within the state and to enhance the recognition of the common good. The proving ground in the twenty-first century lies in the wide-ranging religious, agnostic, and atheistic ethical systems that Benedict invited to a cultural and political collaboration, all centered on the defense of human life against every form of radical libertarian individualism. He advocates for a political-cultural—rather than a religious-theological—collaboration. Collaboration to build up the peaceful coexistence of mankind, however, must also confront the question of how committed Catholicism is to the program of "human rights." Is she fully or partially behind them? A response to this question is complicated, and it is addressed differently by those on the "right" and the "left" (if indeed we are forced to use such categories, even if we find them to often be misleading).

The pope proposed a way of fearlessly and boldly affirming Catholic "reason." He advocated for the recognition of the public role of religion, and of Catholicism in particular. The Holy See is blessed to have the means of engaging in this public dimension through its diplomatic activities, to which we now turn.

CHAPTER SEVEN
PAPAL DIPLOMACY

One of the greatest men to occupy the position of papal Secretary of State, the Roman Cardinal Ercole Consalvi, wrote the following to a papal nuncio in Madrid during a diplomatic crisis in the fall of 1820: "[T]he problem we have to solve is no longer how to avoid every kind of evil, but how to find the least suffering possible."[1]

Not much has changed in papal diplomacy since Consalvi wrote these words. They are perhaps the best description of what papal diplomacy is all about today, even if the general situation is even better now than it was back then.

In fact, over the last century, papal diplomacy has taken on characteristics that allow it to function even in countries where Catholicism has not had much of a role. In these cases, the tools of Vatican diplomacy have been used not only for religious purposes, but to promote peace and justice, bring intellectuals together, and support initiatives for expanding global networks.[2]

---

1   Diplomatic note of Cardinal Ercole Consalvi, Secretary of State, to Monsignor Giacomo Giustiniani, nuncio to Madrid, Rome, 30 November 1820, in *Archivio Storico della Sezione per i Rapporti con gli Stati della Segreteria di Stato, Archivio della Congregazione degli Affari Ecclesiastici Straordinari, Spagna,* 1820, pos. 69–70, fasc. 18, 45v. The reference is provided by Roberto Regoli, "La diplomazia pontificia al tempo di Pio VII. Le istruzioni ai Rappresentanti papali," in Massimo de Leonardis (ed.), *Diplomazia e fede. Le relazioni internazionali della Santa Sede nell'età contemporanea* (Milan: EDUCatt, 2014), 23.

2   Cf. Kagefumi Ueno, "Asia and the Holy See," in *Rivista di Studi Politici Internazionali,* n. 79 (2012): 389–396.

In recent times, the role of religion is gaining more and more recognition, despite every "death-of-God" theory in the West. Carlo Jean, a military and geopolitical expert, writes: "Religions are a decisive element in social life and in shaping relations both domestically and internationally. Religions interact with politics. They are a powerful instrument, but they also pursue their own ends by instrumentalizing politics. In times of crisis, religions are more influential than ever."[3]

These considerations are all the more true for transnational and hierarchically structured religions, and even more so for Catholicism, where Roman centrality is a key consideration for Church unity. Thanks to the papacy, Catholicism is equipped with an ancient, stable, and highly intricate spread of diplomacy.

The network of Vatican diplomacy

Once elected pope, Ratzinger found himself responsible for the span of Vatican diplomacy extending across the globe.[4] At the time, the Holy See maintained diplomatic relations with 174 countries, to which we can add the European Community and the Sovereign Military Order of Malta, as well as special relations with the Russian Federation and the Palestinian Liberation Organization (PLO). It also participates in several international and intergovernmental organizations and bodies (such as the United Nations, the Food and Agriculture Organization, and UNESCO), as well as regional entities (such as the Organization for Security and Co-operation in Europe).

---

3   Carlo Jean, "Ragione e oscurantismo," in *Aspenia*, n. 42 (2008): 32–43, here 32.

4   Cf. Press Office of the Holy See, *Relazioni bilaterali e multilaterali della Santa Sede*: http://www.vatican.va/news_services/press/documentazione/documents/corpodiplomatico_index_it.html; Press Office of the Holy See, *Comunicato*, 9 January 2006: http://press.vatican.va/content/salastampa/it/bollettino/pubblico/2006/01/09/0016/00041.ht ml; Gianni Cardinale, "Il mondo in udienza dal papa," in *Avvenire*, 8 January 2012Accessed at: http://chiesa.espresso.repubblica.it/articolo/1350139.

According to Canon Law, "to the legates of the Roman Pontiff is entrusted the office of representing the Roman Pontiff in a stable manner to particular churches or also to the states and public authorities to which they are sent."[5] Apostolic delegates perform only the first task of representing to a local church, while nuncios perform both functions (both to the state and to the local church).

In conformity with Canon Law, one of the principal tasks of papal representatives is to keep the local churches within their territories connected with the international Catholic network. In fact, some analysts say that, in the last decades, the Church has suffered from a "deficit of universalism" that runs "the risk of legitimizing various national or subnational churches whose language is less and less ecumenical as they become more and more solipsistic."[6] As things move in that direction—a direction often justified by the needs of evangelizing in the light of specific cultural factors—the web of papal representation tries to keep the needs of universalism alive. Faced with so many different forms of Catholicism, the Church must decide whether to approve them or direct them toward an even stronger universalism. The network of papal diplomacy promotes a discussion for more openness while avoiding the absolutization of local churches. Lucio Caracciolo, a political scientist, writes: "the Church is either Catholic—that is, universal—or it is not. A collection of Catholicisms is not the same thing as particularist universalism."[7]

The intricacy of the network makes it very important, and it grew throughout Benedict XVI's pontificate to the point that one diplomat from the United States remarked that Vatican diplomacy "is second only to our own...we have diplomatic ties with 188 nations and they have ties with 177."[8]

---

5   *Code of Canon Law* (1983), can. 363, §1.
6   Lucio Caracciolo, *Prefazione*, in Manlio Graziano, *Il secolo cattolico. La strategia geopolitica della Chiesa* (Bari, Laterza: 2010), IX.
7   Baracciolo, *Prefazione*, op. cit., x.
8   Stefania Maurizi, *Dossier Wikileaks. Segreti italiani* (Milan: BUR, 2011), 141.

The specific relations with some nations became clearer between 2005 and 2013. On the European continent, the Holy See established diplomatic relations with Montenegro in 2006 and appointed a nuncio to the Principality of Monaco, which already enjoyed diplomatic relations with the Holy See. In 2009, the Holy See established full diplomatic ties with the Russian Federation, while in 2011 the nuncio in Slovenia was given the second job of being apostolic delegate to Kosovo. In Africa, the apostolic delegation in Botswana was raised to a nunciature in 2008, and, in the closing days of Benedict XVI's pontificate (22 February 2013), diplomatic relations were announced with South Sudan. In Asia, the Holy See opened diplomatic ties with the United Arab Emirates in 2007. In 2011, a non-residential papal representative was assigned to Vietnam, and, for the first time, a nuncio was appointed to Malaysia. In 2013, just as Benedict XVI was announcing his intention to resign, the network of Vatican diplomacy extended to 180 countries and 7 international organizations.[9]

At the level of multilateral diplomacy, the Holy See became a member of the International Organization for Migration (IOM) in 2011, and assigned a permanent representative to the Organization for the Prohibition of Chemical Weapons (OPCW) in 2012. Papal diplomacy was also extended to international organizations at the local level, including a nuncio assigned to the Association of Southeast Asian Nations (ASEAN) in 2011, and an extra-regional observer assigned to the Central American Integration System (SICA) in 2012.

In some ways, it is more telling where the Holy See does not have diplomatic activity than where it does. The Holy See does not maintain official diplomatic relations with only 13 of the 193 member-states of the United Nations. The Holy See has, however, assigned an apostolic delegate to 10 of those 13. There are only

9   Cf. Dominique Mamberti, "Una diplomazia globale. Le relazioni della Santa Sede nel contesto internazionale e la liberta`della Chiesa in eta`contemporanea," in de Leonardis (ed.), *Fede e diplomazia*, op. cit., 13–20, here 16 and 18.

three nations with no papal representation at all: Afghanistan, the People's Republic of China, and North Korea. Vietnam is a special case in that it has a non-residential papal representative without diplomatic status.[10] Areas where traces of Communism remain appear stony toward the Church even at the beginning of the twenty-first century. But these are remnants of the past, not signs for the future. China is living through a time of remarkable change that is felt in the religious sphere as well.

Even with such a broad network of international relations, the residential presence of the Holy See's diplomatic mission is limited. Just like ambassadors, papal nuncios can be accredited to more than one nation at the same time. Residential ambassadors accredited the Holy See numbered 79 in 2012,[11] while the number of mission heads in the pontifical diplomatic corps who are residential numbered 103 at the beginning of 2013.[12] About half of these are Italians, which is a lower percentage than in the past. Italians made up 83% of the diplomatic corps in 1961 and 73% in 1978.[13] It was John Paul II and Benedict XVI who took a special interest in internationalizing the diplomatic personnel. Between 2005 and 2012, Pope Benedict assigned 36 nuncios as heads of missions for the first time, of which 36% were Italians.[14]

If we look at the total number of nuncios toward the end of Benedict XVI's pontificate, among the 100 heads of missions there were 49 Italians, 25 Europeans (6 Polish, 5 Spanish, 4 French, and 3 Swiss), 13 Asians (6 Indians and 4 from Philippines), 7 from the United States, 4 Africans, 2 Latin Americans, and none from Oceania.[15] Even as the percentage of Italians decreases, the number of representatives from Europe—and more broadly, the West—remains relatively high. If the College of Cardinals appears rather

10   Cf. Ibid., 17.
11   Cf. Cardinale, *Il mondo in udienza dal papa,* op. cit.
12   Cf. Mamberti, *Una diplomazia globale,* op. cit., 17.
13   Cf. Cardinale, *Il mondo in udienza dal papa,* op. cit.
14   Cf. Ibid.
15   Cf. Ibid.

Eurocentric, the diplomatic corps appears even more so, seemingly impermeable to efforts at internationalization. The effects of the geographical factor of papal representation are not secondary given that nuncios have a key role in shaping local churches through their input in episcopal nominations, and not a few nuncios reach the rank of red hat, thereby gaining influence on central decision-making while also making them eligible for the papacy.

But what is the real political impact of papal diplomacy? It is difficult to say, but one thing is for sure. We cannot accurately judge its impact by the limited coverage papal diplomatic activity receives in the press.[16] What really counts are the actual outcomes of this activity. But there are different ways of measuring these outcomes. It is interesting to hear what a retired diplomat, Cardinal Karl-Josef Rauber, had to say about this in 2010:

> Vatican diplomacy is very important, but I notice that its role in international organizations has diminished significantly. Europe and America do not seem to pay much attention to it, but perhaps this is because the Church is going through some rocky times: pedophilia in the United States, Ireland, and now in Berlin. Cardinal Bertone, even though he was an excellent Secretary of the Congregation for the Doctrine of the Faith, does not come from a diplomatic background. The times of Casaroli and Silvestrini were much different. They made historic steps in Vatican diplomacy when faced with the challenges of Communism and the Berlin Wall.[17]

This is clearly a criticism of Sodano and Bertone, but unfortunately it does not get to the heart of the matter. The cardinal seems to allude to an attitude of pulling back. But a pope who

16   Cf. Marco Politi, *Joseph Ratzinger. Crisi di un papato*, op. cit., 184.
17   Francesco Strazzari, "La scelta di Léonard. Intervista con l'ex nunzio mons. Karl-Josef Rauber," in *Il Regno – Attualita*, n. 4 (2010): 86.

blows out candles on his birthday cake at the White House in 2008 does not seem to be pulling back much, nor does a pope who, in the same year, speaks to the United Nations. Rather, it seems the world has changed. The two-sided world of the Cold War era has disappeared. There are now multiple centers of world-power, and the crisis of international stabilization that emerged in 2001 requires leaders to think of new responses, including with regards to political and financial resources as well as new ideas surrounding natural resources and energy. Now the *modus operandi* is less bilateral and more multilateral. But this is still not enough. Non-governmental organizations, like multilateral financial groups, require mental, conceptual, and operational flexibility, something new for the diplomatic world, including papal diplomats.

Vatican diplomacy is in a state of transition at the beginning of the twenty-first century. Even though it utilizes many nunciatures and delegations—not to mention the religious and missionary centers that assist them by providing valuable information—Vatican diplomacy must look carefully at new international challenges and decide what kinds of new initiatives to launch. Otherwise, diplomats will be left standing on the sidelines. For this reason, the institution responsible for preparing future diplomats—the Ecclesiastical Academy—has a symbolic role because in can operate either in a short-sighted or a longsighted way. Those in formation must learn new skills: not only ecclesial, but diplomatic, political, financial, as well as skills in other social sciences. Every period of transition must be accompanied by changes in the formation program. Other historic changes took place in 1829 (the "era of restoration") and in 1879 (the era of a papacy without a state). These might help to guide the intellectual preparation of future Vatican diplomats in order that they may be better equipped to face today's challenges.

During this time of transition, diplomats will have to perform their usual functions, such as managing relations between the pope, bishops, and particular churches. This work seems to predominate over political tasks and requires a different kind of theological—and particularly ecclesiological—care. To show that there is a steady historical trajectory in this task, we can turn to words expressed by the Congregation for Extraordinary Ecclesiastical Affairs in a 1903 *memorandum* released during the pontificate of Pius X:

> Pontifical Representatives are to be ecclesiastics of not only high moral conduct, but exemplary ecclesiastical conduct. It is time to put an end to "salon diplomats" who have little or nothing ecclesiastical about them, who are prone to petty gossip and give a bad name to pontifical diplomacy. A papal representative is above all an ecclesiastic and then a diplomat.[18]

Pius X's description is no less apt in the twenty-first century.

A certain amount of diplomatic activity is also carried out by the pope's own travels. Papal voyages are a way of establishing geopolitical of ecclesiastical priorities, both for the pope's own diplomatic agenda, and for the internal needs of the Church.

If we draw a map of Benedict XVI's travels, we notice that the far East is conspicuously absent while the West is virtually covered. This accords with the needs specified during the conclave. Benedict completed 29 trips within Italy and 22 abroad. Of the latter, 3 were to Africa, 1 to Oceania (i.e., Australia), 3 to the near East (Turkey, Lebanon, and the Holy Land, including Israel, Palestine, and Jordan), 1 in North America (U.S.A.), 3 in Latin American (including Mexico), and 11 in Europe. In some cases he visited a country more than once. Besides Italy, the most visited nations were Germany and Spain (3 visits to each). The pope's travel agenda centered mostly on Europe. Apostolic voyages were a staple in Benedict XVI's activities, and they were the source of many fruits.[19]

---

18 Paolo Valvo, "Da Roma al mondo: l'agenda del nuovo papa. Situazione della Chiesa e prospettive di riforma all'alba del pontificato di Pio X," in *Rivista di Storia della Chiesa in Italia*, n. 67 (2013): 513–533, here 529.

19 Benedict XVI, *Luce del mondo*, 182. In English, *Light of the World* (San Francisco: Ignatius Press, 2010).

John Paul II set a strong precedent for the pope to be a globe-trotter. In evaluating a pontificate, it is important not only to look at the destinations, but the speeches: the words pronounced both abroad and those in Rome in his addresses to diplomats. The written word has an enormous value in diplomacy, and this includes as much the pope's texts and those of his representatives as it does what appears in international agreements (concordats and agreements).

The input of Benedict XVI

At his very first meeting with ambassadors accredited to the Holy See (12 May 2005), Benedict XVI touched on themes that characterized his diplomatic interventions up until the time of his resignation: fraternity, peace, dialogue, human dignity, the common good, and fundamental human rights (the designation "fundamental" is not coincidental). More specifically, the latter are the rights "to life, nourishment, housing, work, and healthcare, the protection of the family and the promotion of social development with respect for the dignity of every man and woman created in the image of God."[20] These rights are ultimately based on a solid theological foundation. Furthermore, the pope only asked that the Church be granted "the legitimate conditions of the freedom to act in order to carry out her mission." This is the classic notion of *libertas Ecclesiae,* a basic tenet in the program of Benedict XVI's predecessors as well. The themes outlined in this early speech came up again and again during the pope's apostolic voyages, in meetings with political leaders, and with ambassadors accredited to the Holy See.

The pope would also go on to deepen the notion of peace, which, as we have already seen, is the key to cultural and inter-religious dialogue, and is also a political and diplomatic concern.

20   Benedict XVI, "Discorso agli ambasciatori del corpo diplomatico accreditato presso la Santa Sede," in *L'Osservatore Romano,* 13 May 2005.

It is no surprise that Benedict considers that both the Church and the diplomatic mission of states have a "common mission" for peace. To obtain it, it is necessary to fight for the truth which, in the pope's mind, leads to and gives a foundation to the right to liberty "both in public and in private life, both in economic and in political relations, as well as in cultural and religious relations."[21] Hence, among the freedoms that the Holy See is interested in promoting are "the freedom of religion...because it regards the most important human relationship: our relationship with God." A commitment to truth opens the way to forgiveness and reconciliation, which are "indispensable elements of peace."

Within this framework, the task of the Holy See is essentially moral and spiritual.[22] Otherwise, she would be unable to perform any of her many other functions. But it is necessary to know whether the international community recognizes this. Even if the Holy See has a legitimate voice, that doesn't mean her voice is heeded.

A point of reference for understanding the role of the Church within the world of international relations is the speech that Benedict XVI gave to the General Assembly of the United Nations in 2008.[23] The pope emphasized the position already expressed by his predecessors (i.e., the human person and human rights as the ethical substratum of international relations) and his personal vision of human rights (already treated in a previous chapter), which must include the right to religious liberty. More peculiar is the support of a new emphasis on the principle of the "responsibility to protect" all "human dignity." Benedict XVI explains it in this way:

> Every State has the primary duty to protect its own population from grave and sustained violations of

---

21 Benedict XVI, "Discorso al corpo diplomatico accreditato presso la Santa Sede," in *L'Osservatore Romano*, 9–10 January 2006.
22 Cf. *Code of Canon Law* (1983), can. 747, §2.
23 Benedict XVI, "Discorso all'assemblea generale dell'ONU, 18 Aprile 2008," in *L'Osservatore Romano*, 20 April 2008.

human rights, as well as from the consequences of humanitarian crises, be they natural or man-made. If States are unable to guarantee such protection, the international community must intervene with the juridical means provided in the United Nations Charter and other international declarations.

This brings nations even closer because relations are now viewed in terms of brotherhood. The pope assures his audience that such relations foster a "dialogue among religions" in service to the common good. Religions, in fact, have the task of proposing "a vision of faith not in terms of intolerance, discrimination and conflict, but in terms of complete respect for truth, coexistence, rights, and reconciliation." Religion's role in the task of building up society is undoubtable.

We might look at a number of other papal speeches to get a fuller view of the pope's vision of international relations, but to summarize the program and foundation of diplomacy in the eight years of Benedict XVI's reign, we will limit ourselves to a talk given by Monsignor Mamberti, Vatican Secretary for Relations with States, during the *sede vacante* period in March of 2013.[24] In line with papal thinking and the diplomatic strategies used in the preceding decades, Archbishop Mamberti says that the Holy See's activities have been directed primarily toward the defense of peace and support for development, and that these are only possible when the Church is granted the freedom to preach, teach, and carry out her mission. Mamberti views these as the basic conditions that allow the Church to speak her own mind about the political order and how it relates to the "fundamental rights of

---

24   Cf. Mamberti, *Una diplomazia globale*, op. cit., 13–20. For an overview regarding papal diplomacy under Pope Benedict XVI, the public speeches of the cardinal secretary of state are available for study: Tarcisio Bertone, *La diplomazia pontificia in un mondo globalizzato*, Vincenzo Buonomo, ed., (Città del Vaticano: Libreria Editrice Vaticana, 2013).

the human person," as well as "the salvation of souls."[25] Mamberti cites Benedict XVI, who presents religious liberty as the "first human right" in that it has a clear social valence that goes beyond the freedom to worship according to one's conscience. A proactive commitment to religious liberty entails combatting religious discrimination, sectarianism, and fundamentalism, which are considered "a falsification of religion itself."[26] This also helps us to understand Benedict XVI's approach to interreligious dialogue.

In the same speech, Mamberti shifts attention from freedom of conscience to the natural law, which the pope understands as the source of "fundamental rights" and "ethical imperatives" based on "non-negotiable values." Another aspect of Vatican diplomacy involves education, which is the primary instrument for combatting corruption, crime, drug-trafficking, demagoguery, and social divisions and tensions. The other guiding factor of Vatican diplomacy is "charity," the linchpin of the Holy See's activity, with a particular commitment to the most vulnerable, especially when it comes to safeguarding the rights of women and children, as well as migrants, refugees, and asylum seekers.[27]

The diplomatic activity of the Holy See is concerned with all the above-mentioned areas. But Mamberti also acknowledges that there is a risk that he calls a "paradox": it seems Vatican diplomacy is focused on "abstract themes" and on "principles alone— i.e., conscience and religious liberty, non-negotiable values, education, and charity." He addresses this issue by affirming that these questions pose real, concrete problems that touch upon the complexity of the human person and his social relations. To the external observer, however, the transition from the abstract to the concrete does not easily appear. Because the objectives aimed at in ecclesiastical diplomacy are principles that transcend time, it is incumbent upon the diplomat to know how to translate them into concrete actions in accord with the specific geographical area,

25 Mamberti, *Una diplomazia globale*, op. cit., 13.
26 Ibid., 14.
27 Ibid., 16.

political reasoning, and cultural needs of a particular people. We now turn to how these principles are translated from continent to continent by analyzing specific countries. In this way, we can see how Bertone, Mamberti, papal nuncios, and diplomatic personnel have historically translated these principles into addressing concrete needs.

The primacy of Europe and Italy

Europe received more attention than any other geographical area during Benedict XVI's pontificate. Indeed, according to American diplomats, the Vatican desires to implement a strategy for reconquering Europe beginning with Poland, understood as "a counterweight to European secularism."[28] Notwithstanding this slightly naïve American approach, the pope—in accord with the elements of his thinking we have explored hitherto—was certainly concerned with the European continent from the time he had been a cardinal. In a speech to the curia in 2006, Benedict XVI gave special attention to Europe, which, he said, "seems to be tired, indeed, it seems to be wishing to take its leave of history." The gravity of his appraisal is hard to miss.

The re-conversion of Europe at the top of Benedict XVI's agenda was already a concern of his predecessors, beginning with Pius XII.[29] Toward the beginning of his pontificate, John Paul II, at a time when the East and West divide was heavily weighing on the continent, said, "I turn to you, old Europe, with this fervent appeal: Find yourself once more! Be yourself! Rediscover your origins. Bring your origins back to life!"[30] Saint John Paul was

28 Maurizi, *Dossier Wikileaks*, op. cit., 121.
29 Cf. Blandine Chelini-Pont, "Papal Thought on Europe and the European Union in the Twentieth Century," in *Religion, State & Society* n. 37 (2009): 131–146; Anthony O'Mahony, "The Vatican and Europe: Political Theology and Ecclesiology in Papal Statements from Pius XII to Benedict XVI," in *International Journal for the Study of the Christian Church*, n. 9/3, (2009): 177–194.
30 John Paull II, Speech, *La vocazione umana e cristiana delle nazioni del*

referring to the Christian origins of Europe, or rather the Judeo-Christian origins he wanted to be recognized in the European Constitution. The former pope did not, however, wish to rewrite the constitution, for he wanted to respect the distinction between the juridical-political and theological aspects of the issue.

The relationship between Europe, the Council of Europe, and the European Union has been a priority in papal diplomacy for some time, but the concrete ways in which that relationship is cultivated need to be tested by actual, concrete cases. Indeed, a strategy for bolstering Christianity's presence in Europe by means of a rapprochement between East and West—i.e., between Orthodoxy and Catholicism—was implemented in a way that would go on to mold Europe's culture and history.[31] A prime example is found in the debates over the legitimacy of publicly displaying a crucifix. When the European Court of Human Rights in Strasbourgh decided to hear a case presented by a Finnish woman residing in Italy who demanded a crucifix be removed from her son's classroom (Lautsi v. Italy), the Vatican quickly mobilized a resistance joined by several other nations.[32] For starters, the Holy See found the ready support of the Italian government. It then went on to recruit twenty other nations to mount an opposition that ultimately won the case. In the end, 21 of the 47 Council of Europe member-states supported the opposition: Italy first, followed by the Russian Federation, Bulgaria, Lithuania, Romania, the Principality of Monaco, Armenia, the Republic of San Marino, Greece, Malta, and Cyprus. These were followed by Albania, Austria, Croatia, Hungary, Macedonia, Moldavia, Poland, Serbia, Slovakia, and Ukraine. The support of Western

continente europeo, Santiago di Compostela, 9 November 1982, in *Insegnamenti di Giovanni Paolo II*, vol. V/3 (Città del Vaticano: LEV, 1982), 1260. The original Spanish text: "Yo [...] te lanzo, vieja Europa, un grito lleno de amor: *Vuelve a encontrarte. Sé tú misma.* Descubre tus orígenes. Aviva tus raíces."

31   Cf. O'Mahony, "The Vatican and Europe," op. cit., 190.
32   Cf. Massimo Franco, *C'era una volta un Vaticano. Perché la Chiesa sta perdendo peso in Occidente* (Milano: Mondadori, 2010), 4, 33–36.

and Scandinavian nations was conspicuously absent. Countries of mid-Eastern Europe prevailed, territories all primarily Orthodox. The Catholic-Orthodox ecumenical initiatives aimed at promoting the common good through a shared ethical and cultural vision —which we discussed in the previous chapter—were already bearing fruit. We should stress once again that the Vatican's strategy was founded more on a cultural rather than a political basis.

At the same time, pontifical diplomacy in Europe was moving along more traditional and tested lines. Rather than launching new initiatives, the Holy See wanted to respond to provocations and problems on an *ad hoc* basis.

Europe generally considered the Holy See a useful entity for mediating conflicts. In January of 2011, the Basque separatist group named ETA ("Basque Country and Freedom") asked the Vatican if it were available to mediate negotiations between itself and the Spanish government.[33] The group received no response because it demanded a truce unilaterally, publicly, and with no mediation. The papal nuncio in Madrid said that the Vatican did not believe it opportune to respond because the Spanish government had previously refused to recognize the group ("It is not up to the ETA to propose a truce, only to break one"[34]). Furthermore, before getting involved, the Vatican, after having consulted with the popular politician Jaime Mayor Oreja, former Minister of the Interior and at that time a European Parliamentarian, preferred to obtain the consensus of both the Spanish government and the ETA. Truth be told, the Holy See may have a missed a unique opportunity to make history.

Countries that are not predominately Catholic also turn to Rome seeking arbitration. Sweden, for example, asked the Holy

---

33 Cf. Gianluigi Nuzzi, *Sua Santità. Le carte segrete di Benedetto XVI* (Milano: Chiarelettere, 2012), 251–256; Eric Frattini, *I corvi del Vaticano,* with the collaboration of Valeria Moroni (Milano: Sperling & Kupfer, 2013), 214–217.
34 Frattini, *I corvi del Vaticano,* op. cit., 217.

See to assist in freeing two journalists detained in Ethiopia. The attempt, however, was unsuccessful in the end.[35]

Sometimes, governments will seek help from the Vatican in controlling the political involvement of priests. In 2011, for example, the Polish government wrote a letter to the Holy See objecting to public interventions made by Father Tadeusz Rydzyk, the undisputed leader of Radio Maryja ("Mary Radio"), who allegedly suggested that Poland was a totalitarian state.[36]

In each of the above cases, the petitioner did not receive a satisfactory response. Did the Vatican simply deem it inopportune to issue a response? Was it a matter of incompetence? Or was the absence of a response a deliberate political choice? In the case of Spain and Sweden, it seems Vatican diplomacy was simply too weak, or at least the petitioners overestimated its power to help.

Two international cases were extraordinarily intense politically. Both involved friction between the episcopate and local governments concerning allegations of abuse against minors. In Belgium, police and local magistrates sequestered the nation's bishops for hours and opened the tombs of deceased cardinals looking for evidence of sexual abuse (24 June 2010).[37] It was a brutal move. The bishops were detained by the police for hours. Cardinal Danneels was repeatedly interrogated at length.[38] The authorities showed no respect for the Church hierarchy in the process. The Holy See could do nothing but raise its voice in protest. On the other hand, the Church's objection to the maltreatment didn't hold much weight since Catholicism was on its way to becoming irrelevant in Belgium. Ireland, once a vibrant Catholic stronghold, went through a time of extreme tension with the Holy See due to the local bishops' poor handling of the sexual abuse crisis. This tension reached a highpoint when the Irish

---

35 Nuzzi, *Sua Santita. Le carte segrete di Benedetto XVI*, op. cit., 263–265.

36 Cf. *ivi*, 266–269.

37 Cf. Franco, *C'era una volta un Vaticano*, op. cit., 6, 23, 112–113.

38 Cf. Mettepenningen, Karim Schelkens, *Godfried Danneels. Biographie* (Antwerpen: Editions Polis, 2015), 471–474.

ambassador to the Holy See in Rome was recalled by the Irish government. We have already discussed this crisis in a previous chapter.

In western Europe, the Holy See's public diplomatic activities were more inconspicuous. We should not forget, however, that nunciatures work hard day in and day out to maintain and promote normal diplomatic relations with these countries. Such relations are usually strengthened inconspicuously except for a few bilaterial understandings that we will address below.

On the European front, we find Russia, a region in which the Holy See has always had considerable interest. Diplomatic relations between the Vatican and Russia have wavered since the late-Middle Ages.[39] Things are not much better today. Stable bilateral relations were established only in 1990, and they are still precarious due to ecumenical tensions between the Vatican and the Orthodox Patriarchate of Moscow. Not only does the patriarchate have an undeniable link to the Kremlin, it is also clearly a part of Putin's political strategy in an increasingly systematic way that rivals even the means employed by his predecessors.[40]

Here, we want to emphasize one point. All of Benedict XVI's diplomatic ideals are reflected in Vatican-Russian relations. He wants to join Europe, Russia, and any other nation in drawing attention to the ethical foundations underlying political action. As was already the case under John Paul II during the wars in Kosovo and Afghanistan, the Vatican and Russia have been engaged in discussions of international issues rather than internal issues—namely, a defense of Christianity in Europe and the Middle East, a reaffirmation of Christian values, an opposition to extremism and international intolerance, a battle against hunger, and the fight for the dignity of the human person. Because of the

---

39 Cf. Fausto Fasciani, "Le relazioni tra la Russia di Putin e la Santa Sede," in *Rivista di Studi Politici*, n. 20 (2008): 117–133.
40 Cf. Felix Stanevskiy, "La chiesa di Putin," in *Aspenia*, n. 42 (2008): 89–95; Claudio Virgi, "Altare e trono: la geopolitica della chiesa ortodossa," in *Aspenia*, n. 4 (2008): 96–104.

close bond between the Orthodox Church and the Russian regime, relations with Moscow could only be three-sided: Vatican-Kremlin-Patriarchate.

From here we must move westward to the Vatican's host country, Italy. Diplomatic relations between the Vatican and Italy are highly unique. Italy has always been a sort of safe haven for the Holy See since both partners take meticulous care to keep the bridge connecting the two sides of the Tiber open.

The appointment of Cardinal Bertone as Secretary of State was a delicate move. Even if the Vatican secretariate of state has always been the main locus for managing relations between the Church and the Italian state (with a certain latitude of delegation given to Cardinal Ruini, President of the Italian Bishops' Conference), it was usually done tacitly. Bertone, however, decided to make it very public. We must ask: was this a sign of weakness or political acumen? Whatever the case may be, in March of 2007, Bertone sent a letter to the new president of the Italian Bishop's Conference, Angelo Bagnasco, explicitly stating the respective roles of the conference and the secretariat of state: "As far as regards relations with political institutions, I assure Your Excellency of the cordial collaboration and respectful guidance offered by the Holy See and me personally."[41] This was an extraordinarily public taming of the Italian Bishops' Conference. The letter, dated 25 March 2007, was not made public by Cardinal Bagnasco or the Italian Bishops' Conference, but by Bertone himself a few days later (despite the meeting of the permanent Council of Bishops on 26 March 2007). This suggests that there had been some misunderstanding or a breakdown in communication.

It seemed as if the secretary of state wanted no competition in managing Italian affairs, a country Bertone considered "seeped in the Christian faith and in which the Chair of Peter has been placed by divine providence." The designated role of the secretariat could not have been clearer. In the same letter, the cardinal

41   "Lettera di Tarcisio Bertone ad Angelo Bagnasco," Città del Vaticano, 25 March 2007, in *L'Osservatore Romano*, 28 March 2007.

secretary of state asked the Italian church to provide young priests for service in the Holy See's diplomatic corps. Was this a proactive attempt to re-Italianize the corps, or simply an attempt to stem the shrinking representation of Italians?

The status of Vatican-Italian bilateral relations is most evident in direct meetings between the two powers. These occur in various ways. One way is represented by a private dinner held at the Vatican, to which Benedict XVI invited the Italian president, Giorgio Napolitano, and his wife (19 January 2009).[42] From documentation provided by the secretariat of state's Dominique Mamberti and Monsignor Antonio Guido Filipazzi (who had been following Italian affairs since 2003), the alleged topics on the agenda included the family (with requests to reduce the tax burden on families, provide appropriate support services for families with infants, and address the sinking birthrate), ethical topics, equal treatment (i.e., fair funding) for Catholic schools, the administrative and legislative parity of untraditional forms of marriage, euthanasia, extraordinary means of life-support, the economic crisis, and welcoming migrants. At the level of international politics, the agenda also included the situation in the Gaza Strip and the Holy Land and the increasingly dire situation in Africa (with specific reference to the Italian nuns who had been raped in Kenya). On the domestic front, it was suggested that the two leaders talk about a speech given by the president of the Chamber of Deputies, Gianfranco Fini, on the racial laws of 1938 (a speech based on "weakly grounded historical analysis"). However, we do not know exactly what themes were discussed over dinner.

A visible moment of mutual understanding occurred in 2010 when Secretary of State Cardinal Bertone, offering a toast at the Italian Embassy to the Holy See, was able to say publicly that "thanks are owed" to the Italian government "for having taken significant steps on behalf of the Church in an atmosphere of

42 Cf. Nuzzi, *Sua Santità. Le carte segrete di Benedetto XVI*, op. cit., 117–122; Frattini, *I corvi del Vaticano* o cit., 210–213.

mutual respect."[43] He was referring to questions regarding exemptions from a payment of a property tax known as the ICI for church buildings, thanks to the maneuvers of the Minister of Finance Tremonti, who had applied pressure on the European Union to relieve the Church of the burden.[44] In the end, however, while Mario Monti was acting prime minister (February 2012), the ICI was levied against ecclesiastical goods and properties with primarily commercial aims (such as hotels, schools, and hospitals).

Because of the Holy See's geographical location in Italy—and Europe in general—herein are the key territories in which the Church of Rome—and, by extension, the universal Church—has needed to work hard to ensure the continual enjoyment of the spiritual and political freedoms necessary to carry out her mission. Hence, it is in these areas that the Holy See has dedicated much of its diplomatic energy. Otherwise, she would risk losing influence—and significant influence—on the rest of the world. But the stakes are high elsewhere too, especially in the most important country in the West, the United States of America.

The United States of America

Diplomatic relations between the Holy See and the United States, formalized under John Paul II, were strengthened and deepened during the pontificate of Benedict XVI, even though they ultimately depend on who happens to occupy the White House at the time.

The pope's visit to North America in 2008 was emblematic of these relations. President George Walker Bush and Benedict XVI prayed together privately at the White House.[45] The pope, celebrating his eighty-first birthday at the White House on 16 April 2008, blew out the candles on an enormous cake while 9,000 guests sang. The two leaders met no less than three times in less than a

---

43 Politi, *Joseph Ratzinger. Crisi di un papato* op. cit., 293.
44 Nuzzi, *Sua Santità. Le carte segrete di Benedetto XVI* op. cit., 108-109; Frattini, *I corvi del Vaticano* op. cit., 221–222.
45 Cf. Franco, *C'era una volta un Vaticano*, op. cit., 48–49.

year. They apparently enjoyed a strong mutual understanding. Among other things, the meetings revealed a strong common interest in protecting Christian minorities in the Middle East.[46] Other salient points on the pope's diplomatic agenda were shared by the Bush administration, including "a respect for the dignity of the human person, the defense and promotion of life, marriage and the family, the education of future generations, human rights and religious liberty, sustainable development and the fight against poverty and disease, especially in Africa."[47] The sexual abuse of minors by members of the American clergy was a major issue of concern on both sides, but it clearly was not the only one.

The tune changed when Barack Obama became president. "Happy Birthday" was an echo of the past. While the first African-American president and the Holy See were in accord on the fight against poverty and on respect for immigrants, there was a serious clash of views on homosexual marriage, abortion, and stem-cell research.[48] The United States Conference of Catholic Bishops (USCCB) did not see eye-to-eye with Washington on healthcare reform and a related "liberal" agenda.[49] In an attempt to keep the channels of communication open with the Holy See, President Obama appointed an ambassador with a theological background, Miguel Humberto Díaz (2009–2012). He seemed to be the right man given that the issues between the Holy See and the Obama administration concerned ethical principles rather than minute details. Díaz knew how to speak "Church-talk."

---

46 Cf. Ibid., 57.
47 Carrie Gress, Kathleen Naab, "Festa di compleanno per il papa alla Casa Bianca," in Zenit, 16 April 2008: https://it.zenit.org/articles/festa-di-compleanno-per-il-papa-alla-casa-bianca/. Cf. *Dichiarazione congiunta di Benedetto XVI e George W. Bush*, 16 April 2008: http://w2.vatican.va/content/benedict-xvi/en/travels/2008/documents/trav_ben-xvi_joint-declaration_20080416.html.
48 Cf. Franco, *C'era una volta un Vaticano*, op. cit., 48.
49 Cf. Massimo Franco, *La crisi dell'impero vaticano. Dalla morte di Giovanni Paolo II alle dimissioni di Benedetto XVI: Perché la Chiesa è diventata il nuovo imputato globale* (Milano: Mondadori, 2013), 34.

Relations between the Holy See and the United States of America were not restricted to bilateral issues, but extended to global action: humanitarian crises, human rights, religious freedom, as well as common interests in specific issues such as the Middle East. Mutual understanding on the latter must be qualified because while the Church was mostly (but not only) concerned with the protection of Christian minorities, the United States was concerned with a geopolitical strategy that included militaristic, propagandistic, commercial, economic, and financial elements that actually placed minorities at risk. If the Holy See and the U.S.A. both wanted to favor religious freedom, the consequences of their respective actions were quite different. For these reasons, the Church wished to avoid any simplistic identification of "Church" and "the West."

Aside from whoever happened to be president, Benedict XVI had positive words to offer the United States regarding the latter's attitude toward Church-state relations. In 2008, he remarked:

> From the dawn of the Republic, America has been…a nation which values the role of religious belief in ensuring a vibrant and ethically sound democratic order…. The American people's historic appreciation of the role of religion in shaping public discourse and in shedding light on the inherent moral dimension of social issues— a role at times contested in the name of a strained understanding of political life and public discourse—is reflected in the efforts of so many of your fellow-citizens and government leaders to ensure legal protection for God's gift of life from conception to natural death, and the safeguarding of the institution of marriage, acknowledged as a stable union between a man and a woman, and that of the family.[50]

50 Benedetto XVI, *Discorso a S.E. Mary Ann Glendon ambasciatore degli Stati Uniti d'America presso la Santa Sede*, 29 February 2008, in L'Osservatore Romano, 1 March 2008.

Thus, the ideals of the American model are offered as an example of a "healthy" *laïcité*—perhaps even as an antidote to European secularism.

The Mediterranean

Many of the same questions characterizing the Holy See's diplomatic activity in Western countries can also be applied to an area closer to the Church of Rome—namely, the Mediterranean, the first and natural basin of Christianity from the beginning. The countries surrounding the Mediterranean are a meeting ground of different continents, cultures, and religions. It is a delicate region due to the confluence of many different peoples and the frequency of serious conflicts. It is the bedrock for the acceptance or rejection of international geopolitics. Most of all, it is where the politics of religion play out most conspicuously.

The region underwent a remarkable change on the threshold of the twenty-first century due to the insurgence of radical Islam in the south and east, and Europe's characterization—even before 11 September 2001—of the Islamic world as the "main antagonist of the West after the fall of Communism."[51] This new instability, first cultural and later political, led to facile and misleading characterizations, which, among other things, arose from American interventions in Afghanistan and Iraq. The Islamic world was identified *tout court* with fundamentalism and, in turn, the "Christian" world was labelled the enemy in its wars with the "West." The general political-cultural context is filled with tension, but outright conflict takes place at the local level.

For many decades the objectives of pontifical diplomacy in the Middle East have dealt mostly with the peaceful coexistence of Christian communities and the protection of Jerusalem and the holy sites (in the sense of guaranteeing a Christian presence in

---

51   Silvio Ferrari, "Verso una nuova politica mediterranea della Santa Sede," in *Rivista di studi politici internazionali*, n. 75/1 (2008): 37–52, here 46.

the place of Christianity's origins).[52] According to the diplomacy of "principles" (i.e., of "abstract themes"), one of the objectives pertains to peace-making in the area, beginning with the Israeli-Palestinian conflict, not only for the previously discussed moral motives, but especially to slacken Christian emigration and to find a viable peace option for Christians, Muslims, and Jews.

The Middle East is a source of grave concern for the Vatican. Christianity, like other religious minorities, has often suffered violence from radical-Islamic forces. We only need recall the death of European missionaries including Andrea Santoro (2006) and Bishop Luigi Padovese (2010) in Turkey. There is also an enormous flow of refugees and migrants from those lands. The countries of the Middle East are not so much partners in Vatican diplomacy as targets of Vatican attempts to maintain peace where it exists and bring it to places where it is absent, thus ensuring Christians the possibility of survival. These lands are also in dialogue with the United States and Russia. That makes it a particularly delicate and urgent case. Extraordinary efforts are secondary to strict necessities.

While Western countries are driven by their self-interests to advocate regime change in the Middle East, the local and universal Church takes a different position. The Holy See's attitude toward the Middle East is in large part based on the feedback it receives from local bishops. Many analysts deemed the 2008 Vatican compromise with authoritarian and non-liberal regimes a failure since it was unable to stem the shrinkage of Christian communities in the area.[53] But the subsequent geopolitical developments in the Mediterranean showed the Holy See was right. Once those regimes criticized by the European public had dissoloved, there was a power vacuum for radical Islam to fill, with devastating results.

Syria has been plagued by an internal war supported by foreign powers since 2011. Following the horrific experience of Saddam Hussien's downfall in Iraq, all heads of Christian churches

52   Cf. Ibid., 39.
53   Cf. Ibid., 37.

"came together in support of Assad."[54] His rule was considered a model for peaceful coexistence of religions and cultures. More precisely, one patriarch considered Syria "a model of secularism open to faith."[55] Basically, it was a question of survival. The negative example is always Iraq. Before its first war with America and Western allies in 1991, there were around two million Christians in Iraq. Within twenty years, that figure was reduced by two-thirds.[56] Basically, there is a legitimate fear that Christians will completely disappear from the region. That fear has a disconcerting face—Salafism.

The Middle East tends to keep its distance from American politics of conquest shrouded in the mantle of "exporting democracy." There is no overlap between American geopolitics and the global strategy of the Vatican. The latter is much closer to Russia. The U.S.A. advances a politics of "conflict" (i.e., chooses to take "hard measures" with some regimes) and grants unconditional support of Israel, whereas the Holy See proposes a "principle of co-existence between Christians and Muslims."[57] The model is Lebanon, even though the country seems more and more in a state of crisis due to foreign influence, and it is virtually inimitable because of its unique status and history (in other countries, Christians are nearly an insignificant minority). At this point, perhaps, the sole example is Jordan. Benedict was clear on the matter, stating, "A Middle East with no or few Christians is no longer the Middle East."[58] Moreover, as many analysts have noted, Christian minorities "have historically been a bridge between Western and Arab cultures" in that territory.[59]

54 Franco, *La crisi dell'impero vaticano*, op. cit., 129.
55 Ibid.
56 Cf. Ibid.
57 Ferrari, "Verso una nuova politica mediterranea della Santa Sede," op. cit., 40.
58 Benedict XVI, Apostolic exhortation *Ecclesia in Medio Oriente*, 14 September 2012, in *Acta Apostolicae Sedis*, n. 104 (2012): 751–796, n. 31.
59 Franco, *La crisi dell'impero vaticano*, op. cit., 134.

One relatively stable country in the region is Turkey, which, because of its integration with NATO, carries considerable weight. Benedict XVI made a visit in 2006, a visit that will be remembered for acts of "reparation" after his Regensburg speech and not for other outstanding reasons. That trip had been planned primarily to promote dialogue with the Patriarchate of Constantinople rather than handle interreligious dialogue or specific political issues.

Israel, of course, is situated in the very center of the region. Relations between Rome and Tel Aviv have been characterized primarily by typically Middle-East issues—importantly, the unique importance of the holy Christian sites in Israel, and the historical (albeit not identical) memory of the Shoah and the Church's aid to the Jews during World War II. Benedict was clear: Israel knows the Vatican supports Israel and supports Judaism throughout the world.[60] He thus reaffirmed the importance of the existence of the state of Israel in the wider context of the peace process. That said, Benedict did not downplay a key important historical question—he firmly acknowledged the heroic virtues of Pope Pius XII, a decisive step toward beatification. Pius XII was accused much later in certain cultural sectors for having remained silent on the explicit denunciation of Nazi war crimes in the persecution of the Jews during World War II. Ratzinger carefully distinguished between external politics and internal ecclesiastical affairs, even in places where there could be public and political repercussions from insisting on such a distinction. Yet Benedict did not shy away from the distinction.

Pontifical diplomacy must always navigate between the conflicting goals of Turkey, radical Islam, Israel, and the Middle East at large. Nevertheless, the Holy See maintains a clearly stated objective of defending local Christian communities and other religious minorities. It is no coincidence that the pope made three voyages to the area (Turkey, Lebanon, and the Holy Land) and

---

60 Cf. Benedict XVI, *Luce del mondo*, 180. In English, *Light of the World* (San Francisco: Ignatius Press, 2010).

convened a special Synod of Bishops on the Middle East (10–24 October 2010). It should be noted that the impact of Vatican diplomacy is rather limited. It always seeks a balance that seems further and further from complete realization. The Vatican stated this objective in 2006: "The Lebanese have the right to see the integrity and sovereignty of their nation. The Israelis have the right to see peace in their state, and the Palestinians have the right for their country to remain free and sovereign."[61]

The last region of the Mediterranean to consider is north Africa, the homeland of some of the great fathers of the Church—among them, Saint Augustine, Saint Cyprian, and others.

There was a sudden change in the West's attitude toward the Maghreb in 2010, with Morocco being the exception. The revolutions in Egypt, Tunisia, and Libya—with the accompanying precarious effects in Algeria—found support in the West, but destabilized the entire region under the media-driven, naïve, and misleading term of "Arab Spring." It was a nice euphemism for military and political initiatives.

This destabilization had serious consequences for local Christian communities. In Tripoli, Bishop Giovanni Martinelli condemned the decisive NATO bombings and supported Gheddafi.[62] There were attacks on Christian churches in Egypt. The greater preoccupation in this turmoil was the transition from political dictatorships to religious ones. The Christians had room to survive in the former, but not in the latter. In that expansive region between 2011 and 2012, a general intolerance broke out that was both anti-Western and anti-Christian. The radical versions of Islam gained a stronger foothold in the region. The Holy See's fears were materializing in plain sight. But what could be done? Very little. By its nature, papal diplomacy is weak, and often falls on deaf ears. All of a sudden, ten years of relative calm fell apart, putting those territories and their

---

61   Holy See Press Office, *Dichiarazione*, in *L'Osservatore Romano*, 21 July 2006.

62   Cf. Franco, *La crisi dell'impero vaticano*, op. cit., 130.

peoples in a state of precariousness and violence until something new came along. Could the Church provide support for the future? It would be very hard if we just considered the numbers in North Africa. The only way to have some influence in dealing with the crisis was through Western governments and their interests.

In any case, the Holy See cannot limit itself to thinking along narrow, political terms. It must always broaden its vision. There cannot really be a "North African politics" and a "Middle Eastern politics." Rather, the Holy See has tried to look at the region in terms of the "Mediterranean," which entails both the relationship between cultural and religious minorities and majorities, and of the phenomenon of immigration.[63] Pontifical politics could not simply focus on the southern Mediterranean, but on the entire Mediterranean in its widest sense, which includes Europe, precisely because of the large number of Muslim immigrants. This is exactly why it made sense to have a diplomat heading the Pontifical Council for Interreligious Dialogue: Cardinal Tauran. At the beginning of Benedict XVI's pontificate, interreligious dialogue seemed to have relevance only in the field of culture. But the aftermath of the Regensburg speech gave it a whole new dimension—an outward political dimension—which by that time was undeniable and indeed necessary. Religions have a responsibility to maintain international equilibrium, an equilibrium that cannot be left to politics or the economy to achieve.

Asia and China

Despite the renewed strength of the Church in the Philippines and the tenacity of the Church in Korea, Benedict XVI was able to visit only the margins of the enormous Asian continent. Altogether, the percentage of Catholics in Asia—like Christians in

63   Cf. Ferrari, *Verso una nuova politica mediterranea della Santa Sede*, op. cit., 37.

general—is relatively low, but it is nonetheless a very ancient presence.[64] It is growing yet remains minute.

One of the major areas of the Holy See's attention is China where there is still no protected freedom to profess one's faith. China remains the Holy See's biggest strategic objective in Asia, as it has been for centuries. There are two communities in the Chinese Catholic Church—the official patriotic institution, which is publicly acknowledged by the government in Beijing, and a clandestine, underground community not recognized by the state. The latter is faithful to Rome and not directly controlled by the regime (indeed, it is repressed by it), and it has limited public visibility. This situation is not dissimilar to the break among the French Church at the end of the 1700s between the governmental institution (whose priests are sanctioned by the constitution), and a hidden community remaining faithful to Rome (served by priests who refused to take an oath to uphold the civil constitution of the clergy). That situation was only resolved thanks to a concordat between Paris and Rome. Might a peaceful solution along similar lines be found in China between Beijing and the Holy See? It would seem governmental approval is needed to achieve peace in the Chinese Church, and yet it was the government's political action that caused the break in the first place.

The ecclesial and not merely political aspect of the affair must not be forgotten because this is what the Curia primarily addresses. In a public interview in 2010, Benedict XVI referred to the situation in China and spoke directly in terms of a "schism" (a term he never used for the Lefebvrites).[65] This is a critical situation demanding an urgent solution.

---

64   Cf. Olivier Sibre, "Le Saint-Siège et l'Asie orientale à l'heure du pape françois: au croisement des enjeux missionnaires et diplomatiques," in *Outre-Terre. Revue européenne de géopolitique*, n. 45 (2015): 293–317.

65   Benedict XVI, *Luce del mondo*, 42. In English, *Light of the World* (San Francisco: Ignatius Press, 2010).

At the beginning of Benedict XVI's pontificate, the Chinese regime gave signs it might gradually open to Rome.[66] Despite the episcopal nominations approved by the government but not by the pope, and despite the oppression of those faithful to Rome, Benedict XVI decided to write a letter to Chinese Catholics on 30 June 2007, pointing to the need for dialogue to overcome divisions.[67] In it, the pope addresses the non-involvement of the Church in China's internal political deliberations. He asks for the last word in episcopal nominations and freedom for the Church's action in educational and charitable works. After the letter was sent, seven men were peacefully ordained to the episcopate with the joint approval of Rome and Beijing. At the same time, the Bishop of Zhengding, Julius Jia Zhiguo, was released after fifteen months of internment. By January of 2007, the Holy See was able to declare that "almost all the bishops officially recognized by the government are by now in full communion with the Holy See."[68]

Cardinal Bertone wrote a letter to Chinese bishops in April of 2008 in which he invites all of them—both patriotic and those faithful to Rome—to meet with one another. Bertone shows signs of openness to the government, an attitude that some Chinese thought was "a step backward," putting the Church in a position of "retreat before the Chinese authorities."[69] This is how things proceeded until the end of 2010, when on November 20th there were new episcopal ordinations without the approval of the Holy See. Some feared that the years of goodwill and reconciliation only served the logic of sniffing bishops out and "labelling them

---

66 Cf. Nuzzi, *Sua Santità. Le carte segrete di Benedetto XVI*, op. cit., 237–244.

67 Benedict XVI, *Lettera ai vescovi, ai presbiteri alle persone consacrate e ai fedeli laici della Chiesa cattolica nella Repubblica Popolare Cinese*, 27 May 2007: https://w2.vatican.va/content/benedict-xvi/it/letters/2007/documents/hf_ben-xvi_let_20070527_china.html.

68 Bernardo Cervellera, "Il vescovo di Pechino, il Vaticano e i compromessi con l'Associazione Patriottica," op. cit.

69 Sandro Magister, *Cattive nuove dalla Cina. A Pechino si è aperta una breccia*, op. cit.

as potentially dangerous to public order."[70] In short, the entire thing was a sham to gather information and oppress more effectively.

There were two different approaches considered in Rome. Each was represented by a different Salesian. The strong line that favored playing hardball with the government was represented by Cardinal Joseph Zen Zekium, Bishop Emeritus of Hong Kong. The line of dialogue and rapprochement was represented by Bertone, put into action practically by Cardinal Dias, Prefect of Propaganda Fide. These competing visions of how to approach the question of dealing with the Chinese government stand in conflict with the other. The question turned to Pope Benedict's own attitude toward China.

Few reliable sources are available to help answer this question. One manner of seeking an answer could be found in the common analogy between the diplomatic approach to the communist regimes in Eastern Europe during the Cold War and contemporary diplomatic strategies in dealing with the Chinese government. It is known that Ratzinger shared John Paul II's criticisms of Cardinal Agostino Casaroli's *Ostpolitik* (that is, the policy adopted in relation to the communist countries of Eastern Europe). Such *Ostpolitik* had been deemed a failure. In fact, Benedict XVI believed that "rather than trying to be reconciled with it [the Chinese question] through conciliatory compromises, one must strongly confront it."[71]

Some scholars take an opposite view on the question. According to the historians Agostino Giovagnoli and Elisa Giunipero, the pope hoped for an agreement between the Holy See and the Chinese Government.[72] This opinion merits consideration, given

70 Nuzzi, *Sua Santità. Le carte segrete di Benedetto XVI*, op. cit., 239.
71 Benedict XVI, *Last Testament*, 170.
72 Agostino Giovagnoli and Elisa Giunipero, "Introduzione," in Agostino Giovagnoli and Elisa Giunipero (eds.), *L'accordo tra Santa Sede e Cina. I cattolici cinesi tra passato e futuro* (Città del Vaticano: Urbaniana University Press, 2019), 22.

Giovagnoli's status as an expert on the question of the Catholic Church and China. The question remains open, however, because of the lack of publicly available first-hand sources.

Based on information gathered on the ground by Monsignor Ante Jozic, a Vatican diplomat at the Study Mission in Hong Kong since 2009, the Holy See ascertained that the Chinese government, through large financial deposits (to individual bishops, dioceses, priests, and sisters in the form of monthly stipends), psychological manipulation, and illegitimate nominations, wanted to change ecclesiastical politics by keeping those faithful to Rome hostage.[73] Nevertheless, in December of 2011, the pope gave approval to the episcopal ordination of Antonio Ji Weizhong. It seemed as if joint nominations (i.e., with the approval of Rome and Beijing) might recommence. But in July of 2012 more bishops were illegitimately ordained (i.e., without the Holy See's consent), and another bilateral crisis broke out. Some say the crisis was caused by new Vatican "intransigence" (i.e., the critiques of Cardinal Zen and the appointment of the Chinese prelate Savio Hon Tai Fai as Secretary of Propaganda Fide).[74]

The Holy See invested a lot of diplomatic energy in China with the help informal contacts with government representatives in Beijing that were created and sustained during Benedict XVI's pontificate. Monsignor Pietro Parolin, then under-Secretary for Relations with States, led a few delegations to China, with the collaboration of Father Antonio Sergianni of the Congregation of Propaganda Fide. A direct and continuous dialogue began between the delegations of the Holy See and China from 2006 to 2009 with meetings held both in Rome and in Beijing.[75] According

---

73 Cf. Ibid., 240–244.

74 Cf. Paolo Valvo, "Quanto dista Pechino da Roma?" in *Il Caffè Geopolitico*, 9 December 2015: http://www.ilcaffegeopolitico.org/36155/quanto-dista-pechino-da-roma; Agostino Giovagnoli, *Santa Sede e Cina dal 1978 al 2018*, in Agostino Giovagnoli and Elisa Giunipero (eds.), *L'accordo tra Santa Sede e Cina. I cattolici cinesi tra passato e futuro* (Città del Vaticano: Urbaniana University Press, 2019), 56–57.

75 Giovagnoli, *Santa Sede e Cina dal 1978 al 2018*, 50.

to some authors, a shared draft of an agreement providing for the role of the pope in the appointment of new bishops was created in July 2009.[76] However, one month later, Parolin was appointed to Apostolic Nunzio in Venezuela, and as a consequence there was a noticeable "discontinuity in the politics of the Holy See" evident in the "hardening" of the Vatican toward the Chines government, which, in turn, provoked the illicit ordinations.[77] Bilateral meetings continued nonetheless. The Vatican delegation was led by Monsignor Ettore Ballestrero (who, for example, met with representatives of the Chinese ruling class in Burgandy in April of 2011), who took the place of Parolin. But responsibilities are mutual, and the Chinese government, in order to exert its power in ecclesial affairs, did not seem interested in considering those too close to Rome as candidates for the episcopacy.

China is an interesting case because it proves that relations between the Holy See and nation-states is never bilateral. It is always trilateral. The third participant is always the local Church. In China, the Church is an object to be struggled with, but also a subject seeking her freedom. Currently, the difficulty lies with the entire internal political situation: Beijing cannot reach agreements with a Church on matters it does not address with other religious minorities. More than anything else, Beijing does not want to loosen its hold on any part of civil society, nor surrender any ground on episcopal ordinations. Doing so would compromise its absolute sovereignty. This is the source of so many misunderstandings. Another significant point regards the patriotic church or the Patriotic Association of Chinese Catholics (founded in 1957)—that is, a group of Catholics tied to the government and their national-communist logic, as well as the National Assembly of Catholic Representatives (whose competence overlaps with those of the College of Bishops). The Patriotic Association is not only a governmental entity, but an organ of the party that plays a decisive role because it is the governmental interface with matters

76   Ibid., 56.
77   Valvo, "Quanto dista Pechino da Roma?" op. cit.

regarding Catholic worship. What is that role? One author writes: "Perhaps the Patriotic Association is a mixed bag, capable of supporting the Chinese Church in its adventures?"[78] Not everyone would agree, since the situation is much more complex and indeed dramatic. On the other hand, in times of division and persecution, it is not easy to find solid ground. Not everyone feels called to martyrdom.

Until the end of Benedict XVI's pontificate, Chinese-Vatican relations continued to have peaks and valleys.

The Far West: Latin America

The history and civil situation of Latin America make it integral to the West. We can practically consider it a "Far West."[79] Its place in the West is due to its use of language and predominate religion and because the continent was the protagonist of the long history of the West, and more specifically the Latin and Catholic West. Beginning with the 1800s, however, movements arose to detach it from Europe and to Americanize the entire area. Lois Zanatta explains that this process stood at the intersection of geography and history.[80] To this long cultural phenomenon is attached a shorter one of a religious nature. Latin American Catholicism is on the wane as Pentecostalism grows. Atheism and forms of Gnosticism are also on the rise. At the same time, the rate of secularization is speeding up, which contributes to an increasing decline in the presence and action of the Catholic Church.

In this expansive region, Vatican diplomacy acts most of all to support the local episcopacy, religious orders, and ecclesial movements in their efforts to evangelize. From time to time, Vatican diplomacy also works to ease tensions between governments

---

78   Francesco Sisci, Francesco Strazzari, *Santa Sede – Cina: L'incomprensione antica, l'interrogativo presente* (Bologna: EDB, 2008), 102.
79   Loris Zanatta, *Storia dell'America Latina contemporanea* (Rome–Bari: Laterza, 2011), 10.
80   Ibid., 12.

and national episcopacies over grievances regarding political and ecclesial freedom. A major case in point is Venezuela. The daily work there consists of monitoring the adjustments of local democracies, still in the phase of a long transition from previous authoritarian regimes, and in supporting the efforts of local churches to offer responses inspired by the Church to enormous social problems. The adaption of political systems regards also their long cultural journey of constructing a national identity, which can sometimes clash with Rome. We might think of the religious populism and the syncretic incorporation of the pre-Columbian rites in Bolivia of Evo Morales. Pontifical diplomacy must then be involved with local churches in matters of a cultural and ideological nature as well.

A more widespread phenomenon in the continent is so-called regional integration, which refers to political and commercial relationships between countries. For this reason, the Holy See has joined international regional organizations in Latin America. Political developments have obliged the Church to get involved in new, multilateral initiatives—including the Economic Commission for Latin America and the Caribbean (ECLAC) and the Organization of American States (OSEA). Brazil is a particularly strong motivating force behind regional accords, holding national governments responsible for confronting the crisis of South American "macro-regioning." Common goals allowed Brazil and Holy See to reach a new diplomatic agreement in 2008.

That said, Latin America remains a "peripheral region in the new international order."[81] Her marginalization is indeed protection from global changes that sometimes produce violent effects. Papal diplomatic action is itself conditioned by this geo-cultural marginality, for which reason the Church's objectives are rather local, undoubtedly integrated between nations, but are not conceived within a broader context.[82] The objectives, moreover, are

81 Zanatta, *Storia dell'America Latina contemporanea*, op. cit., 249.
82 Cf. Alberto Methol Ferré, Alver Metalli, *Il papa e il filosofo* (Siena: Cantagalli, 2014).

tied to the needs of national churches, despite the exception of Cuba and its limitation of religious liberty. The Holy See's efforts to melt the ice between Cuba and the United States peaked toward the end of Benedict's pontificate.

The three papal trips to Latin America had great significance for the national churches there, particularly Brazil in 2007. That visit included a meeting in Aparecida of the Episcopal Conference of Latin America and the Caribbean (CELAM). The pope expressed his support of the local Church in its "continental mission." The speech is noteworthy for drawing a parallel between the establishment of a macroregional political and economic entity (of which we spoke above) and the Church's mission within the entire territory. The appeal for an integration of political and religious spheres is evident in his words, but the motivation is clearly different for each—the Church focuses on evangelization and discipleship, whereas these do not directly factor into the political sphere.

Africa and Oceania

In Africa and Oceania, the pope's interventions remain primarily on an ecclesial and social level. In this sense, with regard to Australia we can think of World Youth Day 2008.

Given the complex make-up of Africa, stress is placed on the Church's need to serve the well-being of the people within individual nations. Such is the line taken in the Apostolic Exhortation *Africae Munus* (19 November 2011)[83] where reconciliation, justice, and peace emerge as the major themes. The political dynamics of the region call for the Holy's Sees direct diplomatic participation. *Africae Munus* was the fruit of a special session of the Synod of Bishops dedicated to Africa (4–25 October 2009). A meeting like this, albeit focused mainly on ecclesial issues, also helps the Holy See to better grasp the local priorities, to which it can then direct

---

83   Benedict XVI, Apostolic Exhortation *Africae Munus*, 19 November 2011, in *Acta Apostolicae Sedis*, n. 104 (2012): 239–314.

its own diplomatic energies (as we saw in the case of the Synod on the Middle East). The papal visits to Africa bring to the fore the work of the local Church, especially its charitable and social outreach in the war on poverty.

Because of the rising tide of anti-Christian Islamic extremism—a new phenomenon whose effects are also felt in the Mediterranean basin—the Holy See is particularly concerned with sub-Saharan Africa. Mali and Kenya have been especially prone to acts of terrorism. In Mali, only the presence of the French military has been able to check Islamic insurgency. Today, the Holy See must not only assist missionary efforts in Africa but also protect already existing Christian communities. These missionary efforts during Benedict's pontificate fell under the competence of Propaganda Fide, whereas political matters involve the Secretariat of State.

Bilateral agreements: A first presentation

Several international agreements were reached during Benedict XVI's pontificate with various nations across the globe on a wide range of issues.[84] The only continent not represented in these agreements is Oceania.

The bulk of these accords were with European countries including France, Germany, Austria, Bosnia-Herzegovina, Italy, Spain, Andorra, Albania, Montenegro, Lithuania, and the European Union (in the last case, the binding entity, properly speaking, was Vatican City State and not the Holy See). It is no accident that the focus of these agreements has been on the West, and

84 The texts of the agreements can be found in *Acta Apostolicae Sedis* and on the Vatican website: //www.vatican.va/roman_curia/ secretariat_state/index_concordati-accordi_it.htm. Often there are also presentations in *L'Osservatore Romano*. In addition, as reference see José T. Martín de Agar, *I concordati dal 2000 al 2009* (Citta` del Vaticano, LEV, 2010); Roland Minnerath, *L'Eglise catholique face aux Etats. Deux siècles de pratique concordataire 1801–2010* (Paris: Cerf, 2012).

especially on European Union countries given the centuries of their common cultural and religious heritage.

Various bilateral agreements were ratified during Benedict XVI's pontificate, including two with France. The first, regarding the church of *Trinità dei Monti* in Rome (12 July 2005), consisted of an *avenant* to the Diplomatic Conventions of 1828 and the *avenants* of 4 May 1974 and 21 September 1999.[85] The second, an agreement to recognize levels of higher education and the ability to grant degrees, was signed on 18 December 2008.[86] Because Germany's Constitution grants a wide range of autonomy to its *Länder*, a series of accords was reached between the Vatican and entities within the German Federation, such as the accord with the Free and Hanseatic City of Hamburg (29 November 2005),[87] a protocol added to the concordat signed with the Free State of Bavaria (19 January 2007), and a accord with the Landtag of Schleswig-Holstein (12 January 2009). There was also an accord to modify the concordat with Lower Saxony on the juridical status of Catholic schools (6 April 2010).[88] Another accord was reached with the Free and Hanseatic City of Hamburg for the establishment of a center for Catholic teaching and formation at the University of Hamburg (18 May 2010).[89] An accord with Lower Saxony to modify the concordat of 26 February 1965 (8 May 2012) was also signed.[90] A lengthy and detailed agreement was ratified

---

85 "Avenant entre le Saint-Siège et la République française, 12 July 2005," in Martín de Agar, *I concordati dal 2000 al 2009*, op. cit., 74–75.

86 "Accord entre le Saint-Siège et la République française," *18 December 2008*, in Acta Apostolicae Sedis, n. 101 (2009): 59–64.

87 *Accordo fra la Santa Sede e la Città Libera e Anseatica di Amburgo, 29 novembre 2005*, in Acta Apostolicae Sedis, n. 98 (2006): 825–847.

88 *Accordo fra la Santa Sede e il Land Niedersachsen, 6 April 2010*, in Acta Apostolicae Sedis n. 102 (2010): 468–471.

89 *Accordo fra la Santa Sede e la Città Libera e Anseatica di Amburgo, 18 May 2010*, in Acta Apostolicae Sedis, n. 104 (2012): 1076–1086.

90 *Accordo fra la Santa Sede e il Land niedersachsen, 8 May 2012*, in *ivi*, 720–721.

with Hamburg in 2005 touching on several important areas in Vatican diplomacy—namely, freedom of religion (i.e., a recognition of religious feast days), religious teaching, the maintenance of cemeteries, the seal of confession, and radio and television. A similar accord was signed with Schleswig-Holstein (2009). Germany is a unique place for these wide-ranging and varied agreements, all of which are made possible by a concordat signed in 1933.

With Austria, there was an exchange of notes regarding the convention of 9 July 1962 pertaining to the organization of schools (8 March–15 November 2006) and the Sixth Additional Accord to the convention on patrimony (5 March 2009).[91] The basic agreement with Bosnia-Herzegovina is a concordat divided into two phases over the course of a year (19 April 2006 and 29 September 2006),[92] which was followed by another agreement regarding the sacramental support of the Catholic faithful serving in the armed forces (8 April 2010).[93] With Bosnia-Herzegovina, the Holy See followed the same line adopted in other ex-Communist countries—attention to religious liberty and respect for human rights in general rather than simply the Church's position within the state.[94] These were even more significant in a country emerging from a rocky history of heavy war where religious status was the factor distinguishing friend from foe. The text of the accord refers to various liberties, including communication between bishops and the Holy See and freedom of the press. The topic is urgent in

91 *Accordo fra la Santa Sede e la Repubblica austriaca, 5 March 2009,* in *Acta Apostolicae Sedis,* n. 102 (2010): 937–938.
92 *Basic agreement between the Holy See and Bosnia and Herzegovina, 19 April 2006 e 29 September 2006,* in *Acta Apostolicae Sedis,* n. 99 (2007): 939–946.
93 *Accordo fra la Santa Sede e la Bosnia ed Herzegovina, 8 April 2010,* in *Acta Apostolicae Sedis,* n. 102 (2010): 544–558.
94 Cf. Germana Carobene, *Il* Basic agreement *tra la Santa Sede e la Bosnia- Erzegovina nel quadro delle dinamiche concordatarie 'post-comuniste,'"* in *Stato, Chiese e pluralismo confessionale,* (www.statoechiese.it), September 2008.

an ex-communist country and was asserted as a way of redressing previous abuses of the legal system.

Due to the peculiar nature of the bilateral and internal relations between the Republic of Italy and the Church, more agreements were signed with this nation than any other during Benedict XVI's reign. The agreements include an exchange of letters between the Italian Prime Minister and the Vatican Secretary of State granting the Church authority to carry out criminal proceedings against ecclesiastics (art. 2, letter b of the Additional Protocol of the 1984 Agreement), 26 July 2006;[95] a protocol to implement articles 4 and 8 of the Customs' Convention between Vatican City State and Italy (15 February 2007)[96]; an exchange of letters between the Prime Minister and the Secretary of State regarding the testimony of cardinals in criminal trials (art. 21 of the Lateran Treaty), 15 February 2008; an exchange of diplomatic notes regarding the immunity of real estate belonging to the Congregation for the Evangelization of Peoples on Via Giosuè Carducci, 2 (11 November 2008–2 March 2009); a protocol of mutual understanding between the Governatorato of Vatican City State and the Italian Minister of Culture regarding the use of the Passetto di Borgo Pio and the Torrino di Avvistamento (14 February 2013).[97] With Spain, there was an exchange of notes regarding an agreement on economic questions dated 3 January 1979 (21–22 December 2006).[98]

95 "Scambio di Lettere tra il Presidente del Consiglio dei ministri, Romano Prodi, e il Cardinale Segretario di Stato di Sua Santita', Angelo Sodano," 26 July 2006, in Martín de Agar, *I concordati dal 2000 al 2009*, op. cit., 180–182.

96 "Firma del protocollo di attuazione della convenzione doganale," 15 February 2007, accessed at: https://www.adm.gov.it/portale/documents/20182/6907210/Accordo+Italia+Vaticano.pdf/7809007b-38be-4201-85fb-43852a3e9664.

97 "Firma di Protocollo d'intesa tra il Governatorato dello Stato della Citta' del Vaticano e il ministero per i Beni e le Attivita' Culturali della Repubblica Italiana," in *L'Osservatore Romano*, 15 February 2013.

98 "Scambio di note fra la nunziatura Apostolica in Spagna e il mini-

The Vatican signed an agreement with Andorra (17 March 2008)[99] when, for the first time in history, the country adopted a constitution (1993). The text addresses the juridical status of the Church, canonical marriage, religious teaching, and economic arrangements. An agreement was also reached with Albania on certain economic and taxation policies (3 December 2007) that had not been addressed in the previous international agreement ratified in 2002.[100] A basic agreement was reached with Montenegro on 24 June 2011.[101] An accord was reached with Lithuania establishing the qualifications for teaching high school (8 June 2012).[102] A monetary convention with the European Union was inevitable, although it was officially made between Vatican City State (rather than the Holy See) and the European Union (17 December 2009).[103] This important agreement manifested the Holy See's seriousness about implementing norms to fight money laundering.

We must now turn to agreements made with African and Asian countries. An agreement was reached with the Philippines regarding the cultural goods of the Catholic Church (17 April 2007)[104] and with Azerbaijan regarding the Church's legal status (29 April 2011).[105] An

stero degli Affari esteri e della Cooperazione," 21–22 December 2006, in Martín de Agar, *I concordati dal 2000 al 2009*, op. cit., 298–300.

99 *Accordo tra la Santa Sede e il Principato di Andorra*, 17 March 2008, in *Acta Apostolicae Sedis* n. 101(2009): 330–339.

100 *Accordo fra la Santa Sede e la Repubblica di Albania*, 3 December 2007, in *Acta Apostolicae Sedis*, n. 100 (2008): 194–199.

101 *Accordo di Base tra la Santa Sede e il Montenegro*, 24 June 2011, in *Acta Apostolicae Sedis* n. 104 (2012), 587–598.

102 *Agreement Between the Holy See and the Republic of Lithuania*, 8 June 2012, in Ibid., 1062–1075.

103 *Convenzione monetaria tra l'Unione Europea e lo Stato della Città del Vaticano*, 17 December 2009, in *Acta Apostolicae Sedis* n. 102 (2010): 60–65.

104 *Agreement Between the Holy See and the Republic of the Philippines*, 17 April 2007, in *Acta Apostolicae Sedis* n. 101 (2009): 1068–1070.

105 *Agreement Between the Holy See and the Republic of Azerbaijan*, 29 April 2011, in *Acta Apostolicae Sedis*, n. 103 (2011): 528–532.

important agreement was reached between the Holy See's Congregation for Catholic Education and the Ministry for Public Education of the Republic of China that guaranteed collaboration in high school education and a recognition of the curriculum, qualifications, and diplomas of Catholic schools (2 December 2011).[106]

In Africa, an accord was signed with Mozambique (7 December 2011),[107] and an agreement was reached with Equatorial Guinea on relations between the Catholic Church and the state (13 October 2012).[108] An accord-framework of common interests was also signed with Burundi (6 November 2012).[109]

There were only two major agreements reached in Latin America. One agreement was signed with Panama regarding the establishment of an ordinariate for armed forces and other branches of state security, as well as an ordinariate for prisons (1 July 2005). This accord was signed but not ratified due to its polemical nature. An agreement was reached with Brazil regarding the juridical status of the Catholic Church (13 November 2008).[110] Focusing on religious freedom, this concordat guaranteed the protection of places of worship, reaffirmed educational freedom, specified that religious instruction (Catholic and other confessions) was an ordinary part of the school curriculum, recognized the civil effects of canonical marriages, and stipulated certain fiscal privileges for the Church. The accord did not enjoy unanimous support within the country on the issues of religious

---

106 *Agreement Between the Congregation for Catholic education of the Holy See and the ministry of education of the Republic of China*, 2 December 2011, in *Acta Apostolicae Sedis* n. 105 (2013): 93–104.

107 *Accordo su Principi e Disposizioni Giuridiche per il Rapporto tra la Santa Sede e la Repubblica di Mozambico*, 7 December 2011, in *Acta Apostolicae Sedis* n. 104 (2012): 567–586.

108 *Accordo tra la Santa Sede e la Repubblica di Guinea Equatoriale*, 13 October 2012, in *Acta Apostolicae Sedis*, n. 105 (2013): 987–1000.

109 *Accord-Cadre entre le Saint-Siège et la République du Burundi*, 6 November 2012, in *Acta Apostolicae Sedis*, n. 106 (2014): 195–207.

110 *Accordo tra la Santa Sede e la Repubblica federativa del Brasile*, 13 November 2008, in *Acta Apostolicae Sedis* n. 102 (2010): 118–129.

liberty and *laïcité*, but at least it identified religion as an essential aspect of life among the citizens and a stable factor for forming the nation's identity.[111] The national public debate surrounding the agreement also helped to distinguish between the "lay state" and the "atheistic state."

An important agreement—especially given the aftermath of the Regensburg speech—was reached in the Arab world with the *Memorandum of Understanding* between the Secretariat of State and the Secretary General of the League of Arab States (23 April 2009).[112] Beyond the content of the agreement, the very fact that the League of Arab States was willing to agree upon a text was significant.

The bulk of these agreements undoubtedly centers on Europe. This also says something significant about Benedict XVI's pontificate. At the same time, however, we must note that when it comes to these diplomatic documents we are not dealing with the pope's individual will, rather with the activity of the Roman Curia and Vatican diplomacy.

111 Cf. Emerson Giumbelli, "O acordo Brasil-Santa Sé e as relações entre estado, sociedade e religião," in *Revista Ciências Sociais e Religião*, n. 14 (2011): 119–143; Emerson Giumbelli, "A presença do religioso no espaço público: modalidades no Brasil," in *Revista Religião e Sociedade*, n. 28/2, 2008. Accessed at: http:// dx.doi.org/10.1590/S0100-85872008000200005; Lusia Ribeiro Pereira, Juscelino Silva, Márcio Eduardo Pedrosa Morais, "Acordo Brasil-Santa Sé de 13 de novembro de 2008: conflitos de hermenêutica constitucional," in *De Jure*, n. 16 (2011): 45–65; Jesús Hortal Sánchez, "Liberdade religiosa e ordenamento jurídico: do padroado ao recente Acordo Santa-Sé/Brasil," in *Direito, Estado e Sociedade*, n. 34 (2009): 232–240. The nuncio of the agreement also promoted its publications in favor of the agreement reached: See Lorenzo Baldisseri and Ives G. Martins Filho (eds.), *Acordo Brasil-Santa Sé, Comentado* (São Paulo: LTR, 2012); Lorenzo Baldisseri, *Diplomacia Pontifícia, Acordo Brasil-Santa Sé, intervenções* (São Paulo: LTR, 2012).
112 Vatican Information Service, *firma accordo con Lega Stati Arabi*, 23 April 2009. Accessed at: http://visnews-ita.blogspot.it/2009_04_23_archive.html.

Overall, these agreements point to an interesting journey for the Church. First of all, there is a clear continuity with agreements made by the Holy See in previous years. For example, there are references to the principles of Church autonomy and collaboration between Church and state. There are also references to the principle of religious freedom, even though in an agreement with Germany there are oblique references to "freedom of faith" and "freedom of religion." Another interesting case of this is found in the agreement between the Holy See and Bosnia-Herzegovina. With regard to agreements in the German-speaking world, as Romeo Astrorri notes, an idea that was present in an accord with Brandenburg (2004) is confirmed and strengthened in that it recognized "that the Christian faith, Church life, and charitable service have for human solidarity and a sense of responsibility on the part of citizens for the common good."[113] This is an explicit recognition of the positive aspect of the Church's legal status. There were further specifications of this in the accords reached during Benedict XVI's pontificate. Not only are there references to the Church's contribution to the common good and the civic responsibility of citizens, but also to the peaceful and cooperative construction of Europe (i.e., in the Hamburg accord) and the global responsibility humans have for creation (the concordat with Schleswig-Holstein). Astorri also notes that in the German accords, the Church's charitable activities, beyond being merely recognized, are granted special protection, such as the protection to worship freely.[114]

After Regensburg, not only was an agreement made with the Arab League, but conventions were ratified with predominantly Muslim countries (Bosnia-Herzergovina, Albania, and Azerbaijan) and countries with a significant Muslim population (Montenegro and Mozambique). Apparently, the aftermath of the 2006

---

113 Romeo Astorri, "La politica concordataria della Santa Sede dopo il Concilio Vaticano II," in de Leonardis (ed.), *Fede e diplomazia*, op. cit., 303–320, here 319.

114 Astorri, "La politica concordataria della Santa Sede," op. cit., 320.

Regensburg speech did not in any way impede the Holy See's diplomatic tasks. Indeed, it seems to have favored them.

The content of these agreements is also quite significant. The predominating topic is education. We see this in the agreements with France (a recognition of academic degrees), Germany (the teaching of theology, centers of formation, instruction and pedagogy), Austria (schools), Lithuania (high-school education), and Taiwan (universities and high schools). There are also references to education in the general accords (such as the one with Bosnia-Herzegovina).

The topic of cultural goods also takes center stage (Italy the Philippines), as does the Church's temporal goods (France, Italy, Spain, Albania), and the spiritual care of men and women in the military (Panama, Bosnia-Herzegovina).

One of the defining benchmarks of the Holy See's diplomatic mission during Benedict XVI's pontificate was the consistent implementation of the 1983 Code of Canon Law to new situations and new countries. And, as we have seen, the changes made to Canon Law under Benedict XVI were provoked by European concerns.

Conclusions

If the goal of pontifical diplomacy is to "find the way to suffer least," it has been difficult to achieve that goal throughout history, including during Benedict XVI's pontificate. The Holy See's objective to become a promoter of grand principles such as peace, pardon, reconciliation, freedom of conscience, religious liberty, non-negotiable values, charity, and education has not necessarily led to clear, evident results. Indeed, the goals themselves elude measurable success. They are more like general horizons than achieved facts.

Nevertheless, Vatican diplomacy intervenes at an international level, privileging the natural bond with the Republic of Italy, a relationship that has helped the Holy See in difficult international cases (such as the public display of the crucifix).

The broad international action of pontifical diplomacy is consistent with the implementation of the guiding principles of Roman diplomacy, as with all the magisterial governance of Benedict XVI, who took on the same concerns as his predecessor John Paul II, overcoming them through his own world vision that insists on the ethical requirements of human relationships. To the culture of confrontation and fear emerging in the twentieth and twenty-first centuries, Vatican diplomacy responds with dialogue, proposing a peaceful coexistence between peoples and cultures, religions, and different traditions.

If at the beginning of Benedict XVI's pontificate some feared that pontifical diplomacy would turn inward, or, giving the benefit of the doubt, expected a more spiritual and religious attitude and one decidedly less political with respect to John Paul II,[115] they were forced to revisit their expectations. Ratzinger's diplomatic approach was just as effective politically as it was religiously and culturally.

A significant feature of diplomacy under Benedict was the strategic alliance with the Orthodox—and therefore with Russia and Eastern Europe—on ethical questions in Europe and the defense of religious minorities throughout the world. These are merely first steps on a new journey, and many outcomes are possible.

The Vatican's relationship with the United States of America continued to strengthen under Benedict but became rather dependent on internal national politics and leadership. Relations have always been cordial, even though the two sides are not always in complete harmony—especially on ethical issues when the Democratic Party is in control and in the United States' political stance toward Muslim countries, especially in the Middle East.

Religious liberty has always been—and continues to be—a major theme in the Holy See's diplomatic work. Religious liberty

115 Cf. Massimo Faggioli, "La politica estera della Santa Sede," in *Il Mulino*, n. 6 (2006): 1137–1146.

thus echoes throughout many of Benedict XVI's public speeches, especially in places of intolerance or those marked by historical and juridical tradition of radical secularism, as in Mexico. (We might think of the speeches of Benedict XVI and Cardinal Bertone during their visit of March 2012). The needs of this liberal approach include appeals to the defense of the weak, the poor, and children, both unborn and born. In countries suffering under radical Islam, religious liberty and the peaceful coexistence of religions is the declared object of the Holy See's action.

The Far East is truly on the extreme. It is distant and marginal. It is a lacuna. The Western, European, Mediterranean, and Latin pontifical vision must still take note of possibilities in the East. It is true that the area is not as important because of the limited number of Catholics, but in the future it will be important to engage the region for political reasons, especially with regard to economy and finance at the beginning of the twenty-first century. One can already see the Holy See's increasing interest toward China and Vietnam. But is the Asian world just as interested in Catholicism and the pope? In fact, it is no coincidence that not only is there no ambassador representing China to the Vatican, but there is also no residential ambassador from India.[116]

The Holy See's diplomatic activity covers a wide range of international political action, but it is also unquestionably centered first on Rome, then Italy, and from there the wider Mediterranean (Europe, Maghreb, and the near East), followed by the Western world, on countries of a Catholic tradition, and then all others. This direction of diplomacy occurs not so much by choice, but because of the history of the papacy and Catholicism itself. We simply cannot prescind from this past.

116 Cf. Ueno, *Asia and the Holy See*, op. cit., 395.

CHAPTER EIGHT
RESIGNATION FROM THE PETRINE MINISTRY

It is the act for which his pontificate is most famous, the act that gained Benedict an enormous amount of respect both within and outside of the Church. It was the most unexpected event of modern and contemporary Church history—the resignation of a pope from the Petrine ministry, the resignation of Benedict XVI "from the active exercise of the ministry."[1] There were no perfect parallels at any point in Catholic history, for anytime something similar happened it has happened in very different ecclesial and canonical circumstances and with completely different consequences.

Let us first state that at the beginning of the twenty-first century, canon law allows for the possibility that a pope finish his ministry before death. The 1983 Code of Canon Law is clear on the matter without going into excessive detail: "If it happens that the Roman Pontiff resigns his office, it is required for validity that the resignation is made freely and properly manifested but not that it is accepted by anyone."[2] The possibility of a resignation was already foreseen in the 1917 Code and in prior canonical teaching.[3] The reality of someone actually choosing this, however, does not necessarily indicate its actuality. It was with Benedict XVI's resignation that canonical theory was put into concrete application. An occurrence is never without context and can never be detached from the history that paved the way for it.

---

1   Benedict XVI, "Udienza generale, non mi sono mai sentito solo," 27 February 2013, in *Insegnamenti di Benedetto XVI*, vol. IX, (Citta` del Vaticano: LEV, 2013), 268–272, here 272.
2   Code of Canon Law, 1983, can. 332, §2.
3   Code of Canon Law, 1917, can. 221.

Foreshadowing

While still cardinal, Ratzinger had occasions to speak about the possibility of a pope resigning from the Petrine office. In 1978, after the death of Pope Paul VI, and more precisely at a Mass the cardinal offered in Paul VI's memory in Munich, Ratzinger alluded to the fact that the pope "fought strenuously against the idea of resigning"[4] before his seventy-fifth birthday, and again before his eightieth. Ratzinger also said in the same homily: "And we can imagine how heavy the thought must be of not belonging to yourself anymore. To never have a moment to yourself. To be chained, as your body gives way, to a task that, day after day, calls for your full, living commitment requiring every ounce of energy." So already in 1978 Ratzinger considered the Petrine ministry something that would put a man in chains, indeed a cross from which it would be inconceivable to come down. He went on in the same homily: "More and more, the papacy meant to him (i.e., Paul VI) to put on the cloak of someone else and be nailed to the cross." Over time, however, Ratzinger's position changed. He became more realistic and less prone to spiritualize the requirements for governing the universal Church. He became more of a pragmatist. In fact, it was only after much experience in the curia that Ratzinger could say to the diocesan weekly newspaper of Munich in Bavaria regarding the long illness and slow debilitation of John Paul II: "If the pope thought he absolutely could not make it any longer, he would step down."[5] Twenty-five years had passed between Ratzinger's two judgments on the possibility of resigning from the papacy. A maturation took place. The world had changed. The Church, it seemed, was in ever greater need of a leader who could remain vigilant and strong.

4   The text was published as Joseph Ratzinger, "Trasfigurazione," Funeral Homily for Paolo VI, Munich, 10 August 1978, *L'Osservatore Romano*, 19 October 2014.
5   Marco Politi, *Joseph Ratzinger. Crisi di un papato* (Bari: Laterza, 2013²), 21.

As pope, Ratzinger again returned to the question of papal resignation, but this time he was speaking about his own. It was not a mere thought experiment or hypothetical possibility. It was something concrete and imminent. In fact, in his interview with Peter Seewald in 2010, Benedict XVI had this to say in the wake of the *annus horribilis:*

> When the danger is great one must not run away. For that reason, now is certainly not the time to resign. Precisely at a time like this one must stand fast and endure the difficult situation. That is my view. One can resign at a peaceful moment or when one simply cannot go on. But one must not run away from danger and say that someone else should do it.[6]

When asked if there was a cause or a situation that might prod the Roman Pontiff to consider the possibility of resigning, Benedict XVI responded: "If a Pope clearly realizes that he is no longer physically, psychologically, and spiritually capable of handling the duties of his office, then he has a right and, under some circumstances, an obligation to resign."[7] In the same interview, he candidly admits: "I notice my strength is running out."[8] The general public never grasped the seriousness with which Benedict made these remarks. Except for one journalist.[9]

Without getting lost in the alleged symbolism of Benedict's visit to the tomb of Pietro del Morrone (Pope Celestine V) in Aquila—a visit enshrouded in prophetic symbolism only in hindsight—we want to move directly to the facts concerning Benedict XVI's resignation.

6   Benedict XVI, *Luce del mondo,* 53. In English, see *Light of the World* (San Francisco: Ignatius Press, 2010).
7   Ibid.
8   Ibid., 29.
9   "Ratzinger is one who can resign as pope, even completely regardless of his psychophysical condition, as an act of spiritual freedom." Giuliano Ferrara, "Le dimissioni del papa," in *Il Foglio,* 10 March 2012.

The resignation

On the morning of 11 February 2013, the cardinals were meeting in an ordinary public consistory to approve some canonizations. Accompanied by Monsignor Georg Gänswein, Prefect of the Pontifical Household and private secretary; Monsignor Guido Pozzo, Pontifical Almoner; Father Leonardo Sapienza, regent of the Prefecture of the Pontifical Household; and Monsignor Alfred Xuereb, private secretary for the pope, Benedict XVI spoke these words to the cardinals present, using the official language of the Church, Latin:

Dear Brothers,

I have convoked you to this Consistory, not only for the three canonizations, but also to communicate to you a decision of great importance for the life of the Church. After having repeatedly examined my conscience before God, I have come to the certainty that my strengths, due to advanced age, are no longer suited to the adequate exercise of the Petrine ministry. I am well aware that this ministry, due to its essential spiritual nature, must be carried out not only with words and deeds, but no less with prayer and suffering. However, in today's world, subject to so many rapid changes and shaken by questions of deep relevance for the life of faith, in order to govern the barque of Saint Peter and proclaim the Gospel, both strength of mind and body are necessary, strength which in the last few months, has deteriorated in me to the extent that I have had to recognize my incapacity to adequately fulfill the ministry entrusted to me. For this reason, and well aware of the seriousness of this act, with full freedom I declare that I renounce the ministry of Bishop of Rome, Successor of Saint Peter, entrusted to me by the Cardinals on 19 April 2005, in such a way that as from 28 February

2013, at 20:00 hours, the See of Rome, the See of Saint Peter, will be vacant and a Conclave to elect the new Supreme Pontiff will have to be convoked by those whose competence it is.

Dear Brothers, I thank you most sincerely for all the love and work with which you have supported me in my ministry and I ask pardon for all my defects. And now, let us entrust the Holy Church to the care of Our Supreme Pastor, Our Lord Jesus Christ, and implore his holy Mother Mary, so that she may assist the Cardinal Fathers with her maternal solicitude, in electing a new Supreme Pontiff. With regard to myself, I wish to also devotedly serve the Holy Church of God in the future through a life dedicated to prayer.[10]

---

10 The declaration was made in Latin on 11 February, but the manuscript is dated 10 February. Benedict XVI, "Declaratio Summi Pontificis De muneris episcopi Romae, Successoris Sancti Petri abdicatione," 10 February 2013, in *Acta Apostolicae Sedis*, n. 105, 2013, 239–240. Here is the original Latin: "Fratres carissimi, Non solum propter tres canonizationes ad hoc Consistorium vos convocavi, sed etiam ut vobis decisionem magni momenti pro ecclesiae vita communicem. Conscientia mea iterum atque iterum coram Deo explorata ad cognitionem certam perveni vires meas ingravescente aetate non iam aptas esse ad munus Petrinum aeque administrandum. Bene conscius sum hoc munus secundum suam essentiam spiritualem non solum agendo et loquendo exsequi debere, sed non minus patiendo et orando. attamen in mundo nostri temporis rapidis mutationibus subiecto et quaestionibus magni ponderis pro vita fidei perturbato ad navem Sancti Petri gubernandam et ad annuntiandum evangelium etiam vigor quidam corporis et animae necessarius est, qui ultimis mensibus in me modo tali minuitur, ut incapacitatem meam ad ministerium mihi commissum bene administrandum agnoscere debeam. Quapropter bene conscius ponderis huius actus plena libertate declaro me ministerio Episcopi Romae, Successoris Sancti Petri, mihi per manus Cardinalium die 19 aprilis MMV commisso renuntiare ita ut a die 28 februarii MMXIII, hora 20, sedes Romae, sedes Sancti Petri vacet et Conclave ad eligendum novum Summum Pontificem ab his quibus

It came as a lightning bolt out of a clear sky even though the pope had in fact alluded to the possibility. In hushed tones, the question was passed from ear to ear: "Why?"

Numerous attempts were made to reconstruct the events that led to the decision. Speculation was rampant. Was it the Vatileaks scandal, the arrest and sentencing of the butler, infighting in the curia, or the pope's fragile health? Even today, we do not know much more than what Benedict XVI himself said in his resignation declaration (February 11), in his address to the entire People of God (February 27), and in the interviews given during the following years to Peter Seewald. Beyond that, we can only form hypotheses, however weak. Now that the pontificate has ended—a truly unique and historical pontificate—we can only refer back to the beginning when Ratzinger himself said he was "shocked" to have been elected, equating it with a "guillotine" that "falls and hits you" instantly. For him, the papacy was something borne and not chosen. He carried it out under the obedience of faith and with the freedom of a believer.

The text of the declaration itself is the fundamental *locus* for understanding the resignation. It was written just two weeks prior by the pontiff himself.[11] After a long period of prayer and reflection, the pope began to feel certain that "my strengths, due to an advanced age, are no longer suited to an adequate exercise of the Petrine ministry." Some say that when a pope chooses to resign out of physical weakness it is a kind of *vulnus*. In fact, "the fact that health reasons were absent make the decision even more poignant.

competit convocandum esse. Fratres carissimi, ex toto corde gratias ago vobis pro omni amore et labore, quo mecum pondus ministerii mei portastis et veniam peto pro omnibus defectibus meis. Nunc autem Sanctam Dei Ecclesiam curae Summi eius Pastoris, Domini no- stri Iesu Christi confidimus sanctamque eius Matrem Mariam imploramus, ut patribus Cardinalibus in eligendo novo Summo Pontifice materna sua bonitate assistat. Quod ad me attinet etiam in futuro vita orationi dedicata Sanctae Ecclesiae Dei toto ex corde servire velim."

11   Benedict XVI, *Last Testament*, 18.

It recapitulates the uniqueness of past history,"[12] since the resignation touches on the pope's role in the Church, or better yet, the way he exercises that role. His lack of strength due to "advanced age" (*ingravescente aetate* in Latin) was the same wording Paul VI used when deciding to exclude cardinals above the age of eighty from participating in conclaves.[13] Even more significantly the same formula is used when, according to the norms of Vatican II, bishops submit a retirement letter to the pope[14] on one's seventy-fifth birthday.[15] It now seemed the pope was applying the norms for bishops to the papacy. Could it be that the episcopal norms were now killing the life of the papacy? Not entirely, because Benedict XVI's resignation was not only due to his advanced age, but to an advanced age that "made it impossible for him to care for the universal Church."[16] The pope probably had in mind the final phase of John Paul II's life, whose health virtually incapacitated him from exercising governance over the universal Church.

Notwithstanding the example of his predecessor, or perhaps to prevent the Church from falling into a precarious situation should he fall ill, Benedict made a different decision. For the good of the life of the Church, he reflected upon the need to enjoy both elements—namely, the life of the body and the life of the soul. The former he believed had so deteriorated in the preceding months that he had to take initiative and recognize his incapacity to exercise

---

12   Massimo Franco, "*Dietro il sacrificio estremo di un intellettuale le ombre di un 'rapporto segreto,'*" in *Corriere della sera*, 12 February 2013.

13   Paul VI, Motu Proprio *Ingravescentem aetatem*, 20 November 1970, in *Acta Apostolicae Sedis*, n. 62 (1970): 810–813.

14   Paul VI, Motu Proprio *Ecclesiae Sanctae*, 6 August 1966, in *Acta Apostolicae Sedis*, n. 58 (1966): 757–758, n. 11. English translation: https://www.vatican.va/content/paul-vi/en/motu_proprio/documents/hf_p-vi_motu-proprio_19660806_ecclesiae-sanctae.html.

15   Vatican Council II, Decree on the pastoral mission of bishops in the Church *Christus Dominus*, in *Enchiridion Vaticanum*, vol. I, (Bologna, EDB, 1976), n. 21.

16   Valerio Gigliotti, *La tiara deposta. La rinuncia al papato nella storia del diritto e della Chiesa* (Firenze: Olschki, 2013), 412.

the Petrine ministry. His decision seems to have been motivated by two factors that have always had a place in the canonical tradition: physical weaknenss and the good of the Church. Hence his assertion that he was making the decision "in full liberty." We must note the difference between his terminology and that of his predecessor, Celestine V, who spoke of a resignation from the papacy (*renuntiare papatui*). He also did not use the language specified in canon law (*renuntiatio muneris*).[17] He rather announced his intention in a new way. He said he would "renounce the ministry of Bishop of Rome, Successor of Saint Peter." He renounced, in other words, only the ministry (*renuntiatio ministerii*).

It would a mistake to focus exclusively on Benedict's physical condition, advanced age, and exhaustion. His decision is not tied only—or even primarily—to himself and his physical-psychological condition as much as it is to the entire Church. This is how we need to interpret the opening section of his declaration, "in today's world, subject to so many rapid changes and shaken by questions of deep relevance for the life of faith, in order to govern the barque of Saint Peter and proclaim the Gospel, both strength of mind and body are necessary, strength which in the last few months, has deteriorated in me to the extent that I have had to recognize my incapacity to adequately fulfill the ministry entrusted to me." His resignation takes into account the Church's specific historical conditions. Jesuit priest Antonio Spadaro had this to say in those epic days: "[T]he pope is resigning from the Petrine ministry not because he is feeling weak, but because he is recognizing that there are crucial challenges that need to be met, and this requires fresh energy."[18]

In the same text in which he announces his decision to resign, the pope also specifies the date of his renunciation: 28 February

---

17   Stefano Violi, "La rinuncia di Benedetto XVI. Tra storia, diritto e coscienza," in *Rivista teologica di Lugano*, n. 18 (2003): 203–214, here 211.

18   Antonio Spadaro, *Da Benedetto a Francesco. Cronaca di una successione al pontificato* (Torino: Lindau, 2013), 36.

2013 at 8:00 p.m., after which time a conclave needed to be convened. Interestingly, the pope did not announce that he was resigning immediately. Rather, he specified a date. This was a first. It is not entirely clear why he decided to do it this way. In the seventeen days remaining in his pontificate, the pope indeed made a few more appointments. Furthermore, on 22 February 2013, Benedict XVI made a few changes to the procedures for the conclave that especially favored the participation of cardinals living far from Rome.[19]

After having thanked the cardinals present for their affection and collaboration, the pope humbly asked pardon for his mistakes and entrusted the Church to the care of the "Greatest Shepherd, Jesus Christ." He was clear about his plans for the future. He wanted to serve the Church with all his heart by dedicating himself to a life of prayer. Hence Benedict's announcement alluded not only to the work of the Petrine ministry, but also to its profound contemplative dimension.[20]

Later, he revealed his intention first to go to Castel Gandolfo, and then to the former cloister within the Vatican walls. The first move would allow the College of Cardinals to meet in conclave and elect a successor, and the second would be the first time in history that a former pope would live within the spiritual and temporal jurisdiction of his successor without in any way—even involuntarily—doing anything that would compromise the new pope's freedom or the unity of the Church.

In the interviews released in the following years, it became clear that the decision to renounce the papacy had begun to emerge in the spring of 2012, following his doctor's advice to stop making intercontinental trips. At this point, the pope's conscience

19 Benedict XVI, Motu Proprio *Normas nonnullas*, 22 February 2013, in *Acta Apostolicae Sedis*, n. 105 (2013): 253–257. Regarding conclave rules: Antonio Ciudad Albertos, "Renuncia de Benedicto XVI a la sede petrina. Aspectos canónicos," in *Estudios eclesiásticos*, n. 88 (2013): 815–832.

20 Cf. Gigliotti, *La tiara deposta*, op. cit., 411.

was unequivocal: "It was clear to me that I must step down in plenty of time for the new pope to plan for Rio."[21] It was a decision taken alone, without any consultation, or ecclesiastical, canonical or theological evaluations.[22] It was a decision that had only to be communicated. In April and August of 2012, he spoke about it to Cardinal Bertone; in September, he discussed it with Archbishop Gänswein and with Monsignor Becciu in November. In the interest of preparing for the backlash in the Roman Curia, and shortly before the resignation declaration, the pope disclosed his decision to Cardinal Ravasi, who was the preacher of the spiritual exercises of the Roman Curia for that year. For practical reasons, the pope also communicated his resolution to Monsignor Guido Marini and to an official of the Latin section of the Secretariat of State in order to have the text of the resignation revised.[23] After first desiring to depart in December, the pope finally decided, for his own reasons, to communicate the decision only on February 11, 2013, the day of Our Lady of Lourdes.[24]

What effect did Benedict's decision have on the office of the papacy up to 28 February 2013? What does it mean for Benedict XVI and the Church? Would Benedict XVI always be Benedict XVI, or Cardinal Ratzinger, or called something else? The answer to the question came quickly. After his resignation, he would be referred to as "pope emeritus." This gave birth to a new reality— an emeritus pope. There would be a need for a new canonical norm that would define in some way, even if not with complete precision, the mission a retired pope would have in the Church.

This is one of the most important events in recent papal history, and an event that some choose not to see as "an exception,"

21 Benedict XVI, *Last Testament*, 17. Cfr. Peter Seewald, *Benedict XVI: A Life* vol. II (Bloomsbury Continuum, 2021), 503. (Original text: *Benedikt XVI. Ein Leben*, 1154).
22 Cf. Peter Seewald, *Benedetto XVI. Una vita*, 1152. In English, Ibid., chapter 37.
23 Cf. Peter Seewald, *Benedetto XVI. Una vita*, 1154–1159. In English, Ibid.
24 Benedict XVI, *Last Testament*, 18.

but as a "practical norm for the future—for the very 'good of the Church,'" as Benedict XVI himself said.[25]

Reactions to the resignation

It only took a notecard for the pope to express his decision to resign. That notecard, however, resulted in an endless stream of commentaries on the pope's decision.

The first, immediate reaction emerged during the following consistory. The Dean of the Sacred College of Cardinals, Angelo Sodano, reacted with more than a notecard. It is worth considering his entire speech:

> Your Holiness, the beloved and esteemed Successor of Peter, your declaration has rung out in this hall like a thunderbolt from heaven. We have listened to it with a sense of loss, almost in a state of disbelief. We have noted the great affection you have for the Holy Church of God, for this Church that you have loved so much. Now it it is my turn to say on behalf of this apostolic *cenaculum*—the College of Cardinals—on behalf of these your dear collaborators, to say that we are closer to you than ever, just as we have been close to you in these brilliant eight years of your pontificate. On 19 April 2005, if I remember well, at the end of the conclave, I asked you with trembling voice, "Do you accept your canonical election as High Pontiff?" You did not hesitate, even with trepidation in your own voice, to say that you accepted the election, trusting in the Lord's grace and in the maternal intercession of Mary, Mother of the Church. Like Mary, you said "yes," and you began your bright pontificate with a sense of continuity; that continuity that you

25 Felix Wilfred, "Sulle dimissioni di papa Benedetto XVI" in *Concilium*, n. 49 (2013): 161.

spoke to us of in your reflections on the history of the Church; in the wake of those 265 men who preceded you on the Chair of Peter throughout two thousand years of history, from Peter the Apostle, the humble fisherman from Galilee, to the great popes of the last century, from Pius X to Blessed John Paul II. Holy Father, before 28 February 2013, as you have said, the day on which you desire to bring your pontifical service to a close—a service you have performed with so much love, so much humility; before that day, we will have a better way to express our sentiments. Just as many pastors and faithful throughout the world will do, just like so many men of goodwill will do, together with so many world leaders. But we will still have the joy of hearing your voice as pastor this month, already on Ash Wednesday, then on Thursday with the clergy of Rome, at the Angelus prayer on Sundays, in your Wednesday General Audiences. Hence there will be many occasions to still listen to your fatherly voice. But even afterward, your mission will continue. You have told us that you will always be close to us with your witness and with your prayers. Certainly, the stars in the heavens will continue to glow, and the star of your pontificate will continue to shine among us. We are near you, Holy Father. Please bless us.[26]

The reaction of the cardinals, according to *L'Osservatore Romano*, was "dismay, surprise, shock, and deeply felt emotion." The cardinals present glanced at one another and let out a "gentle rumble" of awe and unease. The newspaper remarked that those present unanimously recognized the "humility" of Benedict XVI's

---

26   *Angelo Sodano a Benedetto XVI*, 11 February 2013. Accessed at: http:// it.radiovaticana.va/ storico/2013/02/11/il_cardinale_sodano:_la_stella_del_suo_pontificato_brillera`_sempre_i/it1-663830.

decision.[27] But to recognize the pope's humility does not really get to the heart of the matter. In other words, it doesn't fully express the significance, the circumstances, and the consequences of his decision. But feelings were most important at that moment. Cardinals, bishops, and priests generally supported the pope's decision. Only Stanisław Dziwisz, once personal secretary of John Paul II, felt differently, remembering that John Paul II, Benedict's predecessor, stayed on in the papal office until the very end because he believed that it was not right for "one to come down from the cross."[28] Dziwisz seemed alone in this opinion, but he was a respected voice, nonetheless. Later, it was clear that one person in the papal entourage—someone with whom Ratzinger shared his decision to step down—actually tried to change the pope's mind: his personal secretary, Monsignor Gänswein. He could do nothing, however, because it was clearly a "definitive decision" and not simply a "hypothetical thought."[29]

There was no shortage of sadness, confusion, disorientation, and disappointment among the Christian people when they realized the pope was stepping down from the Chair of Peter. However, a different way of speaking about the resignation prevailed. Most spoke of the theologian pope's humility and love for the Church. In Catholic newspapers and magazines, his decision was interpreted as an act of strength and courage.[30] But this doesn't

27   "Nelle parole del cardinale decano Angelo Sodano la gratitudine e la vicinanza spirituale della Chiesa," in *L'Osservatore Romano*, 11–12 February 2013.

28   "Il cardinale di Cracovia e la scelta di Ratzinger," in *Corriere della Sera*, 11 February 2013. Accessed at: http://www.corriere.it/cronache/13_February_11/papa- dimissioni-Dziwisz_16e1a42e-745f-11e2-b945-c75ed2830f7b.shtml.

29   Cf. Agnese Pellegrini, "Il corpo e lo spirito," in *BenEssere*, April (2016): 34–38, here 38; Peter Seewald, *Benedetto XVI. Una vita*, 1154. In English, see Seewald, *Benedict XVI: A Life*, vol. II, 493.

30   See, for example, Marco Tarquinio, "Tutto ci è dato," in *Avvenire*, 12 February 2013; Giovanni Maria Vian, "*Il futuro di Dio*," in *L'Osservatore Romano*, 12 February 2013.

pass a superficial level. Only a few people, from the first moment, tended toward another, broader interpretation. When questioned by the press, historian Paolo Prodi underscored the sense of change the resignation entailed on the level of the exercise of the Petrine primacy.[31] The prior of the ecumenical Monastic Community of Bose, Enzo Bianchi, believed it was a "revolutionary deed" that seemed "more evangelical."[32] The journalist Gianfranco Brunelli said Benedict XVI's resignation made the pope "more worldly (and less sacred), more collegial (and less individualistic), and more functional (and less charismatic)."[33]

There were many other reactions outside the Catholic world. Politicians including Mario Monti, François Hollande, Horst Seehofer, Angela Merkel, Barack Obama, and King Juan Carlos expressed overall respect and appreciation for Benedict's eight years, highlighting also the bilateral political successes made possible by the pope's efforts (David Cameron). Still others including Joachim Gauck, Shimon Peres, and Giorgio Napolitano recognized the pope's virtues including faith, wisdom, humility, courage, intelligence, and responsibility. The Secretary General of the United Nations, Ban Ki-moon, emphasized the pope's dedication to promoting dialogue among religions and confronting global challenges (such as the battle against poverty and hunger, the promotion of human rights, and peace). The President of the European Commission, José Manual Durão Barroso, drew attention to Benedict XVI's action in his indefatigable support for ecumenical values, peace, and human rights.[34]

31 Marco Burini, "Il ministero petrino e'un tesoro della chiesa non proprieta' personale. BVXI lo restituisce per la salvezza comune," in *Il Foglio*, 14 February 2013.
32 Enzo Bianchi, "Ora piu' che mai e' il successore di Pietro," in *La Stampa*, 12 February 2013.
33 Gianfranco Brunelli, "Vox clamans in deserto," in *Il Regno-Documenti*, supplement, n. 3 (2013): 4.
34 Cf. "Minutenprotokoll: Die Stunden nach dem Papst-Rücktritt," in *Spiegel online*, 11 February 2013. Accessed at: http://www.spiegel.de/panorama/papst-benedikt-xvi-liveticker-zum-ruecktritt-des-pontifex-a-8

Reactions from other religious leaders poured in. The Orthodox Patriarch of Moscow recalled the positive contribution Benedict XVI made to ecumenical relations. Justin Welby, Archbishop of Canterbury and Primate of the Anglican Church, added words of appreciation for Benedict. The Chief Rabbi of Israel, Yona Metzger, highlighted the pope's efforts to promote interreligious dialogue, adding that Benedict's pontificate represented a highpoint in relations between the Catholic Church and the Chief Rabbi. Muslims in Germany expressed appreciation for the pope's efforts to promote interreligious dialogue.[35]

No politician or religious leader broached the topic of the pope's desire to resign since it was beyond their competence to do so. They expressed appreciation for the man and his contribution to international and interreligious dialogue. These were, in fact, standard, formal expressions of support, but they were nonetheless substantive in their assessment of political issues during Benedict's reign.

Interpretations abounded. We would expect nothing less of the media. Ernesto Galli della Loggia said Benedict's resignation was "an extremely important gesture in governance, as well as of the highest act of his spiritual teaching," with the power to trigger "an objective desacralization" of the papal office,[36] which, in turn, would change the means of exercising the office. There were those who spoke of a "humanization of the sacred office."[37] Others went further, asserting that the "pope's resignation" represented the last act in a series of crises for European

82613.html; "Dimissioni papa, le reazioni dei leader politici nel mondo," on *Sky TG24*, 11 February 2013. Accessed at: http://tg24.sky.it/tg24/mondo/2013/02/11/papa_ratzinger_reazioni_addio_pontificato.html; "Rispetto e gratitudine," in *L'Osservatore Romano*, 13 February 2013.

35 Cf. *Ibid.*
36 Ernesto Galli della Loggia, "Il seme fertile di una rinuncia," in *Corriere della Sera*, 13 February 2013.
37 Francesco Clementi, "Una scelta che 'umanizza' il Sacro Ufficio," in *Il Sole 24 Ore*, 12 February 2013.

civilization,[38] or that is was "an historical euthanasia of the papacy" signifying "the Church's retreat from the world, its fading, its surrender in Europe, its withdrawal to the more populous peripheries of Christianity."[39] Others framed it in psychological terms, claiming that Benedict XVI's resignation should be considered "a psychoanalytical act" that "forces us to change tunes, to turn the page; an act that allows things that had once been suppressed deep in the social consciousness to flourish once again."[40]

Journalists have written extensively on the topic, even while dreading the ominous nature of the resignation. Massimo Franco, an editorial columnist for the newspaper *Corriere della Sera*, wrote on the day after the announcement: "Being unable to change the curia, Benedict XVI reached a sour conclusion: he had to leave. It is he who has changed. This was the extreme, traumatic sacrifice of an intellectual pope defeated by an apparatus too encrusted with power and self-interest to be reformed." Franco could not find words to define an act "for which the adjective 'revolutionary' echoes empty: it is too small, too secular."[41]

To understand the importance of Pope Ratzinger's gesture and evaluate it properly, we must view it against the background of similar or identical cases.

Precedents

There is little doubt that Benedict XVI's resignation was a surprise, but he was not the first to resign.[42] In the first millennium,

---

38   Ida Magli, "L'ultimo colpo di grazia all'Occidente," in *Il Giornale*, 12 February 2013.

39   Marcello Veneziani, "La storica eutanasia di un mondo," in *Il Giornale*, 12 February 2013.

40   Giancarlo Ricci, *L'atto, la storia. Benedetto XVI, Papa Francesco e la fine del novecento* (San Paolo: Cinisello Balsamo, 2013), 8.

41   Massimo Franco, "Dietro il sacrificio estremo di un intellettuale le ombre di un 'rapporto segreto,'" in *Corriere della Sera*, 12 February 2013.

42   Cfr. Roberto Rusconi, *Il gran rifiuto. Perché un papa si dimette* (Brescia:

the differences between resignation, removal, deposition, and exile were fluid, confusing, and by no means stable. The most interesting case, simply because of its uniqueness, was Benedict IX, who, among depositions and resignations (encouraged by considerable sums of money), saw his pontificate commence, end, and recommence no fewer than three times. In the second millennium, Celestine V (13 December 1294) resigned just months after his election. The text announcing the act was short and sweet: "I, Celestine V, pope, considering myself incapable of this office, both because of my ignorance, and because I am old and weak, as well as for the purely contemplative life I have lived until now, declare that I want to abandon this office which I cannot handle anymore: I therefore give up the papal dignity, its duties, and honors."[43] Celestine V took off his papal garments and donned once again the monastic habit, reclaiming his former name, Pietro del Morrone. He essentially became a bishop-hermit. He died in 1296 and was canonized in 1313, not as Celestine V, but as Pietro del Morrone. After him, one recalls Gregory XII (1415), whose resignation was done for the sake of Church unity, since there were no less than three popes, each enjoying significant support at the time. Gregory died with the title of Cardinal-Bishop of Porto.

We know of three popes who considered resigning in the twentieth century: Pius XII due to the danger of deportation by the Nazis occupying Rome during World War II, as well as Paul VI and John Paul II, both for health reasons. None of these three ended up resigning.[44]

Morcelliana, 2013). Furthermore, one might consult the dossier on shortened papacies in the journal *Chiesa e Storia*, n. 4 (2014).

43 Rusconi, *Il gran rifiuto. Perché un papa si dimette*, op. cit., 74.
44 Ibid., 107–114; Valerio Gigliotti, *La tiara deposta. La rinuncia al papato nella storia del diritto e della Chiesa*, op. cit., 388–402; Fermín Labarga, *"La renuncia de Benedicto XVI a la luz de la Historia,"* in *Scripta Theologica*, n. 45 (2013): 477–488.

The uniqueness of Benedict XVI's declaration and the consequences

There was little difference between Benedict XVI's resignation and the intentions of his recent predecessors and with other popes who resigned or considered resigning. Yet the terminology Benedict used to justify his resignation—as well as the historical circumstances that prompted it and the method he used to carry it out—were unique. Above all, his resignation led to a different retirement "status." All previous resignations led the pontiff simply to return to the episcopate or to reappointment as a cardinal. This was not the case with Benedict XVI. He resigned only from the exercise of the Petrine ministry, thus becoming pope emeritus, allowing him to accept the title "His Holiness" and sign his name "Benedict" rather than "Joseph" after his retirement. This was utterly new and unprecedented. It was an original act that, in practice, may have led to a new exercise of the papacy.

Undoubtedly, such a resignation cannot be easily compared with the resignations of other Bishops of Rome since the ancient, medieval, and modern papacies are not the papacy of today. Above all, Vatican Council I, with its recognition of the universal primacy of the pope's jurisdiction and the infallibility of his *ex cathedra* teaching, was a watershed moment. The papacy and the Catholic Church are affected by a new self-awareness after 1870. "Papism" has become virtually synonymous with Catholicism. We simply need to look at the canonical codes published in the twentieth century.

Should Benedict XVI's resignation be considered an innovative exercise of the papacy?

According to the first reactions of canonists immediately after the resignation, Ratzinger should no longer be pope. Having no power of governance over the Church, he should simply retain the title "Bishop Emeritus of Rome" just like any other diocesan bishop.[45] Or perhaps, like Pietro del Morrone (Celestine V), he

---

45 Cf. Gianfranco Ghirlanda, "Cessazione dall'ufficio di Romano Pontefice," in *La Civiltà Cattolica*, n. 164 (2013): 445–462, here 447–448.

should simply be called Joseph Ratzinger, former Roman Pontiff.[46] But "Pope Emeritus" did not seem canonically viable.[47] These canonists, however, were overruled by the Holy See. As Father Lombardi, Director of the Press Office, explained, it is the Holy See that decides that Ratzinger will be considered and called "Pope Emeritus or Emeritus Roman Pontiff."[48] In short, he would continue to be called "His Holiness Benedict XVI" and would continue to wear a simple white cassock.

This, in short, is the greatest novelty of Benedict's resignation. He did not return to be being a hermit, or a cardinal, but remained a pope—"emeritus" albeit, but "pope" nonetheless. Benedict himself spoke precisely in these terms prior to *sede vacante*. During the last General Audience of his pontificate on 27 February 2013, he acknowledged not only the "novelty" but the "gravity" of his resignation. Most of all, he spoke of the future of his papal vocation:

> Here, allow me to go back once again to 19 April 2005. The real gravity of the decision was also due to the fact that from that moment on I was engaged always and forever by the Lord. Always—anyone who accepts the

In the same camp are Cardinal Francesco Coccopalmerio, the President Emeritus of the Italian Constitutional Court, Cesare Mirabelli, and the Vice-Rector of the Lateran University, Patrick Valdrini: Cfr. Carlo Fantappiè, "Riflessioni storico-giuridiche sulla rinuncia papale e le sue conseguenze," in *Chiesa e Storia*, n. 4 (2014): 91–118, here 106. The contribution has been republished in Carlo Fantappiè, *Ecclesiologia e canonistica* (Venezia: Marcianum Press, 2015), 359–398.

46 Cf. Carlo Fantappiè, "Quando Pietro depone le chiavi," in *Avvenire*, 21 February 2013.

47 Manuel Jesús Arroba Conde, "Un 'papa emerito' non può esistere," in *Zenit*, 13 February 2013: http://www.zenit.org/it/articles/un-papa-emerito-non- puo-esistere/.

48 Radio Vaticana, *Briefing, Padre Lombardi: Benedetto XVI sarà Papa emerito*, 26 February 2013: http://it.radiovaticana.va/storico/2013/02/26/briefing%2C_padre_lombardi:_Benedict_xvi_sar%C3%A0_papa_emerito/it1-668488.

Petrine ministry no longer has any privacy. He belongs always and completely to everyone, to the whole Church. In the manner of speaking, the private dimension of his life is completely eliminated. I was able to experience, and I experience it even now, that one receives one's life precisely when one gives it away.... The "always" is also a "for ever"—there can no longer be a return to the private sphere. My decision to resign the active exercise of the ministry does not revoke this. I do not return to private life, to a life of travel, meetings, receptions, conferences, and so on. I am not abandoning the cross, but remaining in a new way at the side of the crucified Lord. I no longer bear the power of office for the governance of the Church, but in the service of prayer I remain, so to speak, in the enclosure of Saint Peter.... I will continue to accompany the Church's journey with prayer and reflection.[49]

He speaks in terms of a resignation "from the active exercise of the ministry," suggesting that there is a passive exercise of that same ministry. Years later, Benedict XVI himself will declare in an interview: "If he [the pope] steps down, he remains in an inner sense within the responsibility he took on, but not in the function."[50] But what would that look like? Can the Petrine ministry be exercised in a non-active way? Is this what the status of pope emeritus means?

It is precisely here that canon law and theology come in to play. Historical canonist Carlo Fantappiè writes, "It is clear that Benedict XVI's resignation posed series problems to the make-up of the Church, the nature of papal primacy, and the extent of his powers after he ceases to exercise the office."[51] The question has

---

49 Benedict XVI, *Udienza generale, non mi sono mai sentito solo,* op. cit., 271–272.
50 Benedict XVI, *Last Testament,* 25.
51 Carlo Fantappiè, "Papato, sede vacante e 'papa emerito.' Equivoci

to do with the distinction between the person and the office that he holds, between the power of order and the power of jurisdiction.

Fantappiè considers that the "papacy is an office covered by a person and not, properly speaking, a person who assumes an office, even if it becomes merely a title."[52] In this way, if the person resigns from the *munus* (a word open to many possible translations, including "office," "function," "duty," and "ministry"), he forfeits all the prerogatives associated with the "power of governance"—namely, sacrality, infallibility, universal jurisdiction, and honor. Moreover, the history of the Church teaches us that the distinction between the office and the person holding office as functional. History itself is full of bright moments and dark shadows in the canonical and moral conduct of popes and their respective governance of the Church.[53] If such a distinction is valid, it gives birth to a new problem of what title to give to a resigned pope, especially after the theological and canonical changes introduced at Vatican II. There is no room for neutrality. As Fantappiè remarks, "The title reflects the Church's conception of papal ministry as well as a concrete theological and canonical vision."[54] The question is more complicated precisely due to the introduction of the category "bishop emeritus" into canon law after Vatican II. It certainly sets up a conceptual parallel with the papacy: just as a bishop becomes "emeritus" after retirement, so the pope becomes "emeritus" after retirement, or more precisely the "Bishop Emeritus of Rome." This possibility depends on the canonical theories that follow. If, for example, we make distinguish between the office of pope and that of bishop of Rome, then it is possible to speak of a "Bishop Emeritus of Rome." If, however, the two

da evitare," accessed at www.chiesa.espressonline.it, 9 March 2013: http://chiesa.espresso.re- pubblica.it/articolo/1350457.

52 Fantappiè, "Riflessioni storico-giuridiche sulla rinuncia papale e le sue conseguenze," op. cit., 94.

53 Cf. Ibid., 99.

54 Ibid., 105.

offices really make up one office that cannot be broken up—that is, if they are ontologically inseparable—then it is impossible to make the distinction. The Holy See excluded the first possibility (probably so as to "avoid the ambiguity of reducing the papacy to a functional office"[55]) and decided to assign the title "pope emeritus."

Other canonists, including Fantappiè, do not deem the title appropriate because, from their point of view, it introduces "anomalies and inconsistencies."[56] For example, if the papal office symbolically represents Church unity, "the simultaneity of two popes who carry the same title seems inopportune, even with the qualification 'emeritus.'"[57] According to these canonists, it is impossible to conceive of two popes in the Church at the same time, even if one has full power and the other does not.

But Ratzinger's decision and its acceptance by the Church seems to take things in a different direction. In fact, in the text of 11 February 2013, Benedict, properly speaking, gave up neither the papacy nor the office of the papacy, but only its "exercise." And during his final General Audience, he recalled that the duty he assumed at his election on 19 April 2005 was an "always" and "forever," and on the other hand spoke of a loss "only" of the "active exercise of the ministry." This clearly seems to be a novelty with respect to preceding canonical doctrine and practice.

This innovation is the consequence of a particular theological vision,[58] according to which the loss of the papal office entails the forfeiture of powers connected with it, but not the office itself. Theologians do not seem to have as big a problem with this as canonists. According to Stefano Violi,[59] a distinction between the Petrine office and the exercise of that office—that is, a distinction

---

55   Ibid., 108.
56   Ibid.
57   Ibid., 109.
58   Cf. Fantappiè, "Riflessioni storico-giuridiche sulla rinuncia papale e le sue conseguenze," op. cit., 110–111.
59   Cf. Violi, *La rinuncia di Benedetto XVI,* op. cit., 203–214.

between an "administrative-ministerial" exercise and a "spiritual" exercise—is precisely what is at stake. Violi believes Benedict XVI's resignation from the active exercise of the Petrine ministry did not entail a severance of the bond that took effect 19 April 2005, which was binding for all time. This would mean that from 28 February 2103 onward Benedict assumed a non-ministerial mission exclusively spiritual in scope (something the pope seems to have referred to specifically when he spoke of "praying" and "suffering"). In fact, according to Violi, the way that Benedict formulated the text announcing his intention to resign specified a distinction between the *munus* and the administration of the *munus*. His "strengths do not seem up to the administration of the *munus*, not the *munus* itself."[60] In the *declaratio* of 11 February 2013, the pope presents the Petrine *munus* in terms of a "spiritual essence" that allows for this distinction. In Violi's opinion, a resignation limited to the active exercise of the ministry constitutes "the absolute novelty of Benedict XVI's resignation."[61] Fantappiè does not share this opinion because it indiscriminately links the "private person" and the "public person."[62]

Another scholar, Valerio Gigliotti, speaks of a third status, "that of working continuously in the service of the Church through the contemplative life."[63] This entails a new mystic and spiritual condition. This, he says, is the way we should understand the title "pope emeritus." Gigliotti writes that it is "a dimension that shifts the institution of the *renuntiatio* from the juridical level of abandonment of the *potestas regendi et gubernandi Ecclesiae* to the mystical level of service to the Church, the People of God, in a prayerful and silent dimension of retreat from the world."[64] Gigliotti clearly speaks of a *renuntiatio mystica* that takes

60   Ibid., 212.
61   Ibid., 214.
62   Fantappiè, "Riflessioni storico-giuridiche sulla rinuncia papale," op. cit., 111.
63   Gigliotti, *La tiara deposta*, op. cit., 415.
64   Ibid., 403.

us to a meta-juridical plane, one that "established a new *status* of a pope who resigns."[65]

Some, like Alfonso Carrasco Rouco, view the form and substance of Benedict's resignation as a conception of the Petrine ministry, which from an ecclesiological point of view is clearly sacramental.[66] Another theologian, Jean-Philippe Goudot, uses categories that are not always clear, such as "passive resignation," as well as "passive Petrine ministry."[67] Furthermore, Goudot also says that the choice of the title (as well as the dress) indicates "a continuation of the Petrine ministry under a different form."[68] In reality, this approach also reflects a sacramental and mystical theological interpretation of what a "pope emeritus" is as he passes from the *plenitudo potestatis* to the perdurance of simply a universal solicitude for the Church—that is, Benedict remains "pope to a certain extent."[69] He remains pope because we can distinguish between an active, visible pontifical state and a contemplative, hidden one, just as Benedict XVI indicated both in the text announcing his resignation and in comments he made subsequently.

For Fantappiè, the problem lies in trying to figure out if the Petrine office refers to a permanent mission of a sacramental nature or one that is purely ministerial. Theologians seem to favor the former and canonists the latter in order to avoid the problem of having two popes simultaneously and the possibility that there would be conflict between them, generating divisions and consternation among the faithful.[70] The point is the origin of the

---

65   Ibid., 414.
66   Cf. Alfonso Carrasco Rouco, "La renuncia al ministerio Petrino. Nota teológica," in *Scripta Theologica*, n. 45 (2013): 467–475.
67   Cf. Jean-Philippe Goudot, "Benoît XVI: quels modèles pour une renonciation?" in *Nouvelle Revue Théologique* n. 136 (2014): 48–64, here 57.
68   "[…] une continuation, sous un mode différent, du ministère pétrinien." Ivi, 57.
69   "Benoît reste donc un peu pape," *ivi*, 58.
70   Cfr. Fantappiè, "Riflessioni storico-giuridiche sulla rinuncia papale e le sue conseguenze," op. cit., 113–116.

pope's primary power—namely, whether it depends on his episcopal consecration or on his acceptance of the election. For theologians, it comes from his consecration, and, therefore, "in the eventuality that the pope deceases from his office from some reason other than death, he never loses that power, in that it was conferred by a sacramental act with an indelible character."[71] This was also the position of Karl Rahner who, in the 1960s, affirmed the conferral of an indelible character of papal primacy, precisely in view of a sacramental conception, asserts one ought "to conceive of primacy as the highest grade of the sacrament of orders."[72]

The scenario of having two opposed popes appears highly unlikely, given that Benedict XVI, even before he vacated the see, pledged obedience to his successor. In fact, on 24 February 2013, during a farewell gathering with cardinals, Benedict XVI said, "and among you, among the College of Cardinals, there is a future pope to whom already today I promise my unconditional reverence and obedience."[73]

Pope emeritus: an ongoing evolution

All things considered, the papacy appears to be in a state of transformation, which has been accepted by the Church thus far, both by the hierarchy and by the faithful. If the resignation of Benedict XVI struck at the heart of Catholicism, it was immediately absorbed at a conceptual level, even in its novel aspects.

Neither Benedict's resignation nor its novel consequences were placed in serious doubt by those within the Church. The

---

71 Ghirlanda, *Cessazione dall'ufficio di Romano Pontefice*, op. cit., 459.
72 Karl Rahner, *Nuovi Saggi*, I (Rome: Edizioni Paoline, 1968), 513; For more on the issue, see 513–515, 557–559. (Original German: *Schriften zur Theologie*, vol. VI, *neuere Schriften*, 1965).
73 Benedict XVI, "Saluto di congedo agli Em.mi signori cardinali presenti in Roma," 28 February 2013, in *Acta Apostolicae Sedis*, n. 105 (2013): 295–296, here 296.

resignation appears as the outgrowth of natural theological-sacra-mental developments since Vatican II rather than as the result of a mystical view of the papacy or theological re-calibration of the papacy and episcopacy effected by the Council.[74]

Canon law seems to take its distance from the consequences of Benedict XVI's decision and the entire theological framework that attempts to support it. The College of Cardinals and bishops and faithful throughout the world, on the other hand, did not express doubts about the innovations involved in the exercise of the papacy as introduced by Benedict XVI. It was not a problem for them that Ratzinger, after 28 February 2013, continued to use the name "Benedict XVI" and signed letters in this way on pre-prepared stationary ("Benedictus XVI – Papa emeritus").[75] His immediate successor, Francis, follows the same approach, so much so that when he addresses Benedict XVI, he calls him "Holiness." In one of his letters addressed to Pope Ratzinger, disclosed by the Vatican press office, Francis concludes with these words: "With filial and fraternal devotion."[76] Indeed, for Francis the future may hold the possibility of many emeritus popes.[77] At

---

74   Cf. Massimo Faggioli, "Da Benedetto XVI a papa Francesco," in *Rivista di teologia*, n. 54 (201): 341–364, here 342–345.
75   One example is found in Andres Tornielli article of 18 February 2014. Another in Piergiorgio Odifreddi, 20 August 2013. Cfr. Andrea Tornielli, "Ratzinger: la mia rinuncia e valida, assurdo fare speculazioni," in *Vatican Insider*, 27 February 2014: http://www.lastampa.it/2014/02/27/vaticaninsider/ita/ vaticano/ratzinger-la-mia-rinuncia-valida-assurdo-fare-speculazioni- TqCQ4ay9Qph1uR86dvb7RJ/pagina.html; Piergiorgio Odifreddi, *Benedetto XVI: Caro papa teologo, caro matematico ateo. Dialogo tra fede e ragione, religione e scienza* (Milano: Mondadori, 2013).
76   Francis, Letter to His Holiness Benedict XVI, pope emeritus, for the death of his brother, Msgr. Georg Ratzinger, 2 July, 2020: https://www.vatican.va/content/francesco/en/letters/2020/documents/papa-francesco_20200702_lettera-benedettoxvi.html.
77   This is an extract from the pope's answers to journalists' questions on the return flight from Armenia, 27 June, 2016: https://press.vatican.va/content/salastampa/it/bollettino/pubblico/2016/06/27/0480/01111.html.

the highest levels of the Catholic Church, this novelty was digested and interpreted in light of the creation of the role of emeritus bishop, fruit of the reforms of the Second Vatican Council. Moreover, this interpretation falls within the same hermeneutic provided by Benedict XVI, who in an interview published in 2020 clarified his understanding of the role of pope emeritus: "In this formula both things are implied: no actual legal authority any longer, but a spiritual relationship which remains even if it is invisible. This legal-spiritual formula avoids any idea of there being two popes at the same time: a bishopric can only have one incumbent. But the formula also expresses a spiritual link, which cannot ever be taken away."[78] Benedict XVI reads his mandate as pope emeritus exclusively under the spiritual dimension.[79]

The role of pope emeritus was a major innovation, which if not fully understood, can easily lead to the contemporaneity of two, three, or more popes, of whom only one exercises the active ministry and the others live in a non-reversible state of retirement.

In the transitional phase of this new experiment, much depends on the persons involved. Ratzinger, humble and meek, does not pose a serious problem to eventual disagreements or even a schism. To avoid them in the future (or better, to avoid running the risk of having them), both canon law and theology will have to supply categories and concepts to structure and define the status of "pope emeritus"—a new reality for the twenty-first century. Over time, we can verify whether this new institution will be a recurring phenomenon, or if it will have happened in one, isolated case.

The resignation of Benedict XVI is thus an act of government[80]

---

78 Seewald, *Benedict XVI: A Life*, vol. II, 536–537.
79 "Esclusivamente" under the "dimensione spirituale": Benedict XVI, *Interview*, in Peter Seewald, *Benedetto XVI. Una vita*, 1208. In English, Ibid.
80 Francis, Interview, "Cariño y respeto notable a Benedicto," in *La Nacion*, 3 July 2016: https://www.lanacion.com.ar/politica/carino-y-respeto-notable-a-benedicto-nid1914942/.

and an act of renewal;[81] the initiation of a substantial process that transcends the limited attempts to restructure the curia (something widely discussed toward the end of his pontificate), to contribute precisely to an essential and fundamental reform of the head office of the Catholic Church.

81   Cf. Carlo Di Cicco, *Ratzinger, dalla paura al tempo dell'amore* (Rome: Memori, 2013), 203.

CONCLUSIONS

How should we evaluate Benedict XVI's pontificate?

On 27 February 2013, at his last General Audience, the pope offered his own, initial reflection. He did so in theological terms:

> It has been a portion of the Church's journey which has had moments of joy and light, but also moments which were not easy; I have felt like Saint Peter with the Apostles in the boat on the Sea of Galilee: the Lord has given us so many days of sun and of light winds, days when the catch was abundant; there were also moments when the waters were rough and the winds against us, as throughout Church history, and the Lord seemed to be sleeping. But I have always known that the Lord is in the boat, and I have always known that the barque of the Church is not mine but his. Nor does the Lord let it sink; it is he who guides it, surely also through those whom he has chosen, because he so wished. This has been, and is, a certainty which nothing can shake.[1]

Our task, however, has been to frame the pontificate within its broader historical context, despite the limits I discussed in the introduction, particularly the disadvantage of being so close to events we will only understand as time goes on. I have tried to identify at least some of the more salient points of his eight-year reign.

---

1   Benedict XVI, General Audience, "Non mi sono mai sentito solo," 27 February 2013, in *Insegnamenti di Benedetto XVI*, vol. IX, (Citta` del Vaticano: LEV, 2013), 268–272, here 269.

When elected in 2005, it seemed Benedict was going to be a transitional pontiff, especially because of his advanced age and the fact that it did not seem he was going to deviate from the general magisterial approach of his predecessor, John Paul II. Yet the reality of his resignation in 2013 did not conform with these initial expectations. His pontificate was much more significant due to its "cardinal moments" in the history of Catholicism.[2] In other words, there were several more cardinal moments than merely the announcement of his resignation on 11 February 2013—including a move that seemed to result in the "desacralization," or at least a demythologization, of the Petrine ministry in the eyes of the general public.

The first part of his pontificate was marked by significant reforms, reaching a climax in 2009, the year of major ecumenical, liturgical, and canonical reforms. Subsequently, his activity seemed to slow dramatically. The year 2009 was indeed important because of the release of his last encyclical (*Caritas in Veritate*, 4 December 2009). We might say his pontificate was dynamic, innovative, and forward-thinking until 2009, after which time the pace of activity slackened significantly, as if impeded or stuck in the mud. What happened?

Was the pontificate simply taken hostage? Taken hostage by Vatileaks, for instance? Or was it taken hostage by the relentless opposition of the media? Or was the claim that the media was the problem a justification or excuse offered by Benedict's staunchest supporters? The curial machine certainly began to slow down after 2010, and a certain lethargy on the part of key curial figures is undeniable. In the last four years of Benedict's pontificate, the Roman Curia did not produce any major achievements beyond a deepening of the papal magisterium.

A key figure of this pontificate, both in its achievements and failures, was undoubtedly Secretary of State Cardinal Tarcisio Bertone, who seemed increasingly isolated after 2010, earning the

2   This was the term used by Eric Frattini, *I corvi del Vaticano*, in collaboration with Valeria Moroni (Milan: Sperling & Kupfer, 2013), xii.

reputation of "merely an individual employee of the Vatican apparatus," not even having a trustworthy "support team" with which to work.[3] In the future, an accurate historical evaluation of Benedict XVI's pontificate—one that goes beyond Benedict the individual—must unravel the "Bertone question." Historians must examine closely his network of supporters and his opponents. Even if Bertone became Secretary of State directly at the will of the pope, it is equally true that there is hardly any similarity between the two personalities.

Benedict XVI's pontificate was a time of liturgical and disciplinary reforms in line with the teaching that preceded him. Ratzinger's efforts were rooted in the pontificates of John Paul II and Paul VI—that is, in the Second Vatican Council and the cultural Catholic reflection (theological, philosophical, historical, canonical, and spiritual) of the first part of the twentieth century. It was not the pontificate of "restoration" many feared—and others hoped—it would be.[4] More than anything else, it would be a pontificate of consolidation, one that also would raise the stakes and take risks. Benedict XVI knew how to confront the problem of the sexual abuse of minors by clerics with originality and determination without letting himself be overwhelmed by criticism from the media and episcopal incompetence. He knew how to direct the Church's response to these problems.

The biggest challenge for Catholicism in the last century, and more specifically for Catholicism since the French Revolution and the Age of Enlightenment, has been modernity, and she has had to confront it with her own resources. The Church has had to adapt its own doctrinal system to the challenges of today. Unlike Orthodoxy, whose system is rather fixed and rigid, and Protestantism, which, in its liberalism, tends to reduce everything to individual conscience and skims over "community," Catholicism has had to implement an adaption in a manner coherent with her doctrine, as Saint Vincent of Lerins (who reminds us we have development

3   Ibid., 257.
4   Agostino Giovagnoli, "Il teologo mite," in *Europa*, 12 February 2013.

in doctrine, but not change), Saint John Henry Newman (who wrote a book on the development of doctrine), and the Jesuit Bernard Lonergan (who wrote on the development of doctrines and their permanence) argued—that is, without caving in under a theory of "doctrinal evolution." Every development, update, or adaption in Catholicism must be explained (and thus be made intelligible), justified, and made coherent with what preceded it in the same context. This is why Catholic theology and canonical scholarship both progress primarily by making distinctions, by refining discourse and making it adhere to both the present reality and Tradition. There can be no room for incoherence or contradiction in Catholic thinking. Otherwise, the entire doctrinal system will collapse. The exception is the internal, and not the external, forum. The changes that arose from Vatican II were the fruit of highly articulated theological, historical, liturgical, and canonical thinking that distinguished the nucleus of dogma from historical contingencies. It was no accident that the important theologians at Vatican II were Yves Congar and Henri de Lubac, who always favored a historical approach to theology—in other words, a theology highly sensitive to the historicity of the Church.

This helps us to understand the pontificates from Paul VI onward as dedicated to the central and fundamental need of Catholicism to revitalize the Church, keeping the system coherent according to the classic, threefold distinction of *lex credenda, lex orandi,* and discipline. For this reason, the liturgical reforms of Vatican II could not pretend to be a complete reform of the Church without, for example, a new Code of Canon Law. Hence it is only possible to comprehend the pontificate of Benedict XVI within the view of ecclesial reform, and especially papal reform. It was no coincidence that the pope coordinated a simultaneous, systematic reform on the liturgical and theological fronts through "ecumenical" initiatives (primarily with the Lefebvrites and the Anglicans), as well as on the canonical front (changing the 1983 Code with the creation of "personal ordinariates"). But not all these reforms were brought to completion and many remained in suspense, such as the need to reform the curia and the relationship between the

Roman Curia and local church entities. Benedict's resignation in 2013, and especially his battle with the media beginning in 2010, distracted him and the Curia from continuing the reform. Hence the pontificate of Benedict XVI may also be remembered as one of incomplete reforms, or perhaps blocked reforms or reforms taken hostage. (When were reforms deemed necessary ever *not* taken hostage by a world that needed them?)

Nevertheless, Benedict did indicate a way to go about the reform. He showed that to carry out an all-inclusive—rather than a partisan—reform of Catholicism would include many different ecclesial groups and work along the entire "system" of Catholicism—that is, on the doctrinal, liturgical, and disciplinary fronts, knowing how to distinguish the core of the Catholic faith from various forms of adaptation to contemporary realities. He paved a way for revitalization and in some cases reform. Catholicism has been able to stand the test of time by distinguishing the essential from the contingent, all the while maintaining the integrity of its doctrinal nucleus. This is how it has always been able to adjust to and overcome real historical challenges, whether they emerge from Greco-Romanism or barbarism, or problems posed by the modern state and the political realities of today. The papacy today, and particularly the papacy of Benedict XVI, has focused on a reform of the Church by upholding the internal coherence of a "Catholic system." To do this, popes have availed themselves of the best minds from the Catholic intellectual world, some of whom have become popes themselves.

Ratzinger performed his role as successor of Peter along clear theological lines. Many of the best students and colleagues of his theological program became bishops and cardinals. Did he interrupt this theological program by resigning? Did his resignation mark the end of the theological current represented by Cardinals Scola, Ouellet, Koch, and Erdö, or did it rather indicate that this current finally melded with the flux of contemporary theology? We should emphasize that this theology has had an enormous effect on the life and faith of many believers. We might think, for example, of how it led to the John Paul II Institute for Marriage and Family.

How are we to evaluate the pontificate of Benedict XVI? We have a strong clue from a response Benedict gave to Peter Seewald when asked: "Are you the end of the old or the beginning of the new?" The pope responded: "Both."[5] Both the question and the answer are short and sweet. His pontificate eschews all rigid categories.

A pontificate can never be interpreted through a strictly Catholic nor through a merely religious lens. It has to be given more context. Benedict's reign followed the horrific events of 11 September 2001, which led to a very fragile Western world infused with a sense of insecurity following terrorist attacks in New York, Madrid, and elsewhere. His pontificate was underway during the great economic and financial crisis of 2008, which caused an even greater sense of insecurity, this time of a social character. The world, and particularly the West, lived in a perpetual state of precariousness that it had not experienced for decades. On the other hand, this polarizing atmosphere, in which international political tensions were taking on a religious face, Catholicism, and the Roman "headquarters," took on the task of religiously delegitimizing every armed conflict and proposing interreligious dialogue as the cultural and political way toward peace. An encyclical was even dedicated to the crisis of 2008 (*Caritas in Veritate*). This presented a Catholic social way. To international terrorism of a religious nature (be it Muslim or otherwise), Catholicism re-proposed an instrument of persuasion founded on reasonable dialogue. It might appear to be a weakness because the use of reason is rather fragile when faced with the "reason" of military arms. But Catholicism had become accustomed to this over time.

One of the characteristic elements of Benedict XVI's pontificate is that of an intellectual opening and a meeting with exponents of other cultural and religious traditions. This attitude allows for various cultural repositioning of dialogue partners that

5   Peter Seewald, "Il papa e le sue condizioni di salute," in *Il Corriere della Sera*, 18 February 2013.

up until that time were unthinkable in the context of religious violence. It remains to be seen whether this way of approaching relationships between the Church and the world will be encouraged or at least fostered over the long run, so as not to reduce them to a ray of sunshine in winter. In fact, this dialogue responded to a frequent preoccupation that "a civilization cannot survive without a great religion to sustain and animate it."[6] But the pope's motivation for dialogue is much more profound because it is primarily a pastoral concern: to make Christ known. His main preoccupation was always the "faith."

But Benedict XVI was a poor politician, and this constitutes the main weakness of his pontificate. When making decisions, he was not concerned with finding consensus before implementing his vision; he only placed the question of the just, the true, and the good in coming up with a plan. He always remained the intellectual and academic he had always been, even after his elevation to the cardinalature and the papacy. This deep, interior freedom permitted him to step away from exercising the active Petrine ministry.

Benedict XVI's reforms do not lie merely in provisions for the liturgy and new norms in the Code of Canon Law that would allow for the establishment of ordinariates. Benedict XVI's reform was really a way of thinking and feeling about the Church, and the Church in its social and cultural context. The dialogue he initiated and fostered urged Catholicism and its dialogue partners to address key questions beyond the exchange of "good sentiments" (without, of course, dispensing with these).

We will understand Benedict XVI's pontificate more fully as time goes on. He launched several new key initiatives. In this sense, his pontificate seems like an underground river: we know from where it springs, but we don't know for sure where it will go from there. We will only have a better understanding as time goes on.

6   Massimo Franco, *C'era una volta un Vaticano. Perché la Chiesa sta perdendo peso in Occidente* (Milan: Mondadori, 2010), 8–9.

But in the end, we will say that Benedict XVI's pontificate was a success or failure? I was asked this question by director Christoph Röhl while writing the last pages of this book. The question seemed premature, perhaps even a bit unfair, because we have to be clear about what we mean by it. What does "success" or "failure" mean when it comes to a pontificate? What criteria should prevail in making such an evaluation? Church affairs and politics? Pastoral, theological, or cultural impact?

I was asked this question as soon as Benedict announced his retirement on 11 February 2013. But how could such a question be addressed fairly in the midst of the media frenzy and confusion surrounding the drama? Ratzinger's decision tells us much about the beginning of his papacy. It tells us about his interior freedom. But it does not help to give us an adequate response because a free and intelligent man may also make poor decisions.

The question is undoubtedly premature, but it is inevitable. It needs to be asked. At the time, I was not able to give a short, simple answer. I still cannot, even after writing this book. As a historian, I can only go back to an event that took place over a thousand years ago. How did Gregory VII, a zealous, reforming pope who confronted major crises in the Church, conclude his pontificate? In exile in Salerno. He died outside Rome. Everything seemed a failure. And yet it was the most important pontificate of the entire second millennium of Christianity. It gave later Christianity its face and left a permanent imprint on the exercise of Church governance.

The success or failure of a pontificate cannot be measured over the short term. Only by a global, historical review can it be judged fairly. What really counts is whether the accomplishments of any specific pontificate are corroborated over time. Because Benedict XVI's pontificate was centered on key cultural and anthropological issues in the third millennium, as well as the most sensitive points of the Church's faith and its forms throughout history, everything leads us to believe that a fair, balanced evaluation will require time. Perhaps even more time will be needed than for other pontificates because the core of Benedict's political vision regarded themes that will continue to animate great debates both inside and outside the Church for years to come.

So, I ask again, was it a success or a failure? We patiently await an answer—and it will be one outside the "walls" of the Vatican, one that extends beyond the crises of the Church.

JOSEPH RATZINGER – BENEDICT XVI TIMELINE

16 April 1927
Joseph Ratzinger is born in Marktl am Inn (Bavaria).

1939
He enters the minor seminary in Traunstein.

1946-1951
He studies philosophy and theology in Freising and Munich (Bavaria).

29 June 1951
He receives priestly ordination.

11 July 1953
Doctorate in theology with the thesis *The People and House of God in Saint Augustine's Teaching on the Church.*

1956
Habilitation for teaching at the university level with the thesis *Saint Bonaventure's Theology of History.*

1959-1963
Teaches dogmatic theology at the University of Bonn.

1962-1965
Theological adviser to Cardinal Joseph Frings, Archbishop of Cologne and a *peritus* at Vatican Council II.

1963-1966
Teaches dogmatic theology of the University of Münster.

1966-1969
Teaches dogmatic theology of the University of Tubingen.

1968
Introduction to Christianity (First published in English in 1969).

1969-1977
Teaches dogmatic theology at the University of Regensburg.

1972
He launches the journal *Communio* with Hans Urs von Balthasar and Henri de Lubac.

24 March 1977
Appointed Archbishop of Munich and Freising.

27 June 1977
Created a cardinal by Paul VI.

August 1978
Participates in the conclave that elected John Paul I.

October 1978
Participates in the conclave that elected John Paul II.

25 November 1981
John Paul II appoints him Prefect of the Congregation for the Doctrine of the Faith and President of the Pontifical Biblical Commission and the International Theological Commission.

1985
Publication of *The Ratzinger Report*, an interview with Vittorio Messori

1997
Publication of *Salt of the Earth: The Church at the End of the Millennium,* an interview with Peter Seewald.

27 November 2002
He is appointed Dean of the College of Cardinals.

25 March 2005
He writes the text for the Stations of the Cross to be celebrated at the Colloseum on Good Friday.

2 April 2005
John Paul II dies.

8 April 2005
Funeral Mass for John Paul II.

18 April 2005
Ratzinger presides over the *Mass pro eligendo Romano Pontifice.*

19 April 2005
He is elected Pope Benedict XVI.

25 December 2005
Publication of the encyclical *Deus Caritas Est.*

24 March 2006
Consistory for the creation of new cardinals.

5 September 2006
Cardinal Tarcisio Bertone is appointed Secretary of State.

12 September 2006
Benedict XVI delievers the *Lectio Magistralis* at the University of Regensburg.

22 February 2007
Publication of the Post-Synodal Exhortation *Sacramentum Caritatis.*

27 May 2007
Pubblication of the *Letter to the Bishops, Priests, Consecrated Persons and Lay Faithful of the Catholic Church in the People's Republic of China.*

11 June 2007
Pubblication of the Motu Proprio *De aliquibus mutationibus in normis de electione Romani Pontificis.*

7 July 2007
Apostolic Letter Motu Proprio *Summorum Pontificum.*

7 July 2007
Letter to Bishops on the occasion of the letter *Summorum Pontificum* on the use of the Roman liturgy.

24 November 2007
Consistory for the creation of new cardinals.

30 November 2007
Encyclical *Spe Salvi.*

2007
Publication of the book *Jesus of Nazareth.*

2008-2009
Special Jubilee dedicated to Saint Paul.

21 January 2009
The Congregation for Bishops releases the Decree Remitting the Excommunication "Latae Sententiae" of the Bishops of the Society of Saint Pius X.

10 March 2009
Letter of His Holiness Pope Benedict XVI to the Bishops of the Catholic Church concerning the Remission of the Excommunication of the four Bishops Consecrated by Archbishop Lefebvre

29 June 2009
Encyclical *Caritas in Veritate.*

26 October 2009
Motu Proprio *Omnium in Mentem.*

4 November 2009
Apostolic Constitution *Anglicanorum Coetibus.*

2009–2010
Special Jubilee Year dedicated to Priests.

19 March 2010
Pastoral Letter to the Catholics in Ireland.

21 September 2010
Benedict XVI creates the Pontifical Council for the Promotion of the New Evangelization.

30 September 2010
Apostolic Exhortation *Verbum Domini.*

20 November 2010
Consistory for the creation of new cardinals.

2010
Publication of the book *Light of the World: the Pope, the Church, and the Signs of the Times.* A conversation with Peter Seewald.

19 November 2011
Apostolic Exhortation *Africae Munus.*

2011
Publication of the book *Jesus of Nazareth: From the Entrance into Jerusalem to the Resurrection.*

18 February 2012
Consistory for the creation of new cardinals.

14 September 2012
Apostolic Exhoration *Ecclesia in Medio Oriente.*

10 November 2012
Creation of the *Pontificia Academia Latinitatis.*

24 November 2012
Consistory for the creation of new cardinals.

2012
Publication of the book *Jesus of Nazareth: His Infancy and Childhood.*

2012–2013
Jubilee Year of Faith

11 February 2013
Declaratio by which the pope announced his resignation from the *munus Petrinum.*

22 February 2013
Motu Proprio *Normas Nonnullas.*

28 February 2013
The period of *Sede Vacante* begins at 8:00 p.m.